In the Polish Secret War

# In the Polish Secret War

*Memoir of a World War II Freedom Fighter*

MARIAN S. MAZGAJ

McFarland & Company, Inc., Publishers
*Jefferson, North Carolina, and London*

LIBRARY OF CONGRESS CATALOGUING-IN-PUBLICATION DATA

Mazgaj, Marian S., 1923–
　　In the Polish secret war : memoir of a World War II freedom fighter / Marian S. Mazgaj.
　　　　p.　　cm.
　　Includes bibliographical references and index.

　　ISBN 978-0-7864-3822-8
　　softcover : 50# alkaline paper ∞

　　1. Mazgaj, Marian S., 1923–.　2. World War, 1939–1945 — Underground movements — Poland.　3. World War, 1939–1945 — Personal narratives, Polish.　4. Poland — History — Occupation, 1939–1945.　5. Guerrillas — Poland — Biography.　I. Title.
D802.P6M387　　2009
940.53'438092 — dc22　　　　　　　　　　　　　　　2008041715
[B]

British Library cataloguing data are available

©2009 Marian S. Mazgaj. All rights reserved

*No part of this book may be reproduced or transmitted in any form or by any means, electronic or mechanical, including photocopying or recording, or by any information storage and retrieval system, without permission in writing from the publisher.*

On the cover: *top* Polish Warsaw Uprising, Eastern Europe 1944; *bottom* ©2008 Shutterstock

Manufactured in the United States of America

*McFarland & Company, Inc., Publishers*
　*Box 611, Jefferson, North Carolina 28640*
　*www.mcfarlandpub.com*

Ad Majorem Dei Gloriam
et Beatae Virginis Mariae

I dedicate this book to the memory of my comrades-in-arms, who died in our struggle against the inhuman forces of the Nazis, and to the families who risked their lives providing shelter and food for our military units.

# Acknowledgments

In writing my memoir and in preparing it for publication, I received substantial help and cooperation from many generous persons, to whom I owe a deep debt of gratitude. First of all, I would like to thank my first cousin Jozef Mazgaj and his brother Jan Mazgaj, both now deceased, and my younger brother, Klemens Mazgaj, for their recollections and the important materials they provided, which they mailed to me from Poland. I am also grateful to my comrades-in-arms, Colonel Witold Jozefowski ("Mis"), Lieutenant Zdzislaw Rachtan ("Halny"), Dr. Zbigniew Kabata ("Bobo"), Dr. Piotr Sierant ("Marian"), Jan Osemlak ("Straceniec"), Wlodzimierz Gruszczynski ("Jach"), Jozef Bojanowski ("Walter"), Jan Bojanowski ("Michal"), and Krystyna Bronikowska Radlinska for sharing with me their knowledge of certain aspects of our mutual struggle in fighting the Nazi forces in Poland.

In placing numerous events in time and space, I am greatly indebted to the writings of Dr. Piotr Matusak, Dr. Piotr Sierant, Eugeniusz Dabrowski ("Pliszka"), Wlodzimierz Gruszczynski, Dr. Mieczyslaw Korczak ("Dentysta"), and Capitan Henryk Kuksz ("Selim").

I owe sincere words of gratitude to my dear wife, Mildred Juanita, for letting me, at times, spread out the pages of my manuscript not only in our library but also in other rooms of our home.

I am very grateful to Dr. Kabata ("Bobo") for his constant encouragement during my work on my memoir. As a commanding officer of our machine gun platoon, he wrote to me, saying: "Marian, at your last post, as a soldier of the Home Army, you must write your recollections of our fight against Nazism in World War II."

I am also greatly indebted to Mrs. Robin Giesey for her excellent work in editing and typing the final draft of the manuscript.

# Contents

*Acknowledgments* . . . . . . . . . . . . . . . . . . . . . . . . . vii
*Preface* . . . . . . . . . . . . . . . . . . . . . . . . . . . . . . . 1

## Part One: Before World War II

*Introduction*. . . . . . . . . . . . . . . . . . . . . . . . . . . . . 5
1. The Clouds of War . . . . . . . . . . . . . . . . . . . . . . 10

## Part Two: The Time of War

2. The Beginning of World War II . . . . . . . . . . . . . . 13
3. The First Stage of the Nazi Occupation . . . . . . . . . . 24
4. The Conspiracy Begins . . . . . . . . . . . . . . . . . . . 39
5. The Deportation of the Klimontow Jews . . . . . . . . . 55
6. The Destruction of Struzki . . . . . . . . . . . . . . . . . 59
7. Life Is Stronger than Bullets . . . . . . . . . . . . . . . . 70
8. Becoming a Freedom Fighter . . . . . . . . . . . . . . . 81
9. Flying Commando in Action . . . . . . . . . . . . . . . 97
10. The Attack on Szczucin Bridge . . . . . . . . . . . . . 106
11. Disarming the Nazis in Samborzec . . . . . . . . . . . 117
12. The Visit of Cap . . . . . . . . . . . . . . . . . . . . . 122
13. Mining the Railroad . . . . . . . . . . . . . . . . . . . 126
14. Snatching Nazi Cash . . . . . . . . . . . . . . . . . . . 129
15. Attacks on Gestapo Agent von Paul . . . . . . . . . . 138
16. Military Air Drops . . . . . . . . . . . . . . . . . . . . 148

17. Sick Leave at Domoradzice Manor . . . . . . . . . . . . . . . . . 155
18. The Merger of Two Units . . . . . . . . . . . . . . . . . . . . . 161
19. The Battle of Osiek . . . . . . . . . . . . . . . . . . . . . . . . 168
20. German Raid on Our Quarters . . . . . . . . . . . . . . . . . . 173
21. Mobilization for the Operation "Storm" or "Tempest" . . . . . . 183
22. Crossing the German Front . . . . . . . . . . . . . . . . . . . 202
23. Behind Enemy Lines . . . . . . . . . . . . . . . . . . . . . . . 205
24. Demobilization . . . . . . . . . . . . . . . . . . . . . . . . . . 223
25. Our Secret Quarters . . . . . . . . . . . . . . . . . . . . . . . 239
26. Returning Home . . . . . . . . . . . . . . . . . . . . . . . . . 251
27. In School Again . . . . . . . . . . . . . . . . . . . . . . . . . 255

## Part Three: After World War II

28. Sequel . . . . . . . . . . . . . . . . . . . . . . . . . . . . . . 287
29. Epilogue . . . . . . . . . . . . . . . . . . . . . . . . . . . . . 314

*Notes* . . . . . . . . . . . . . . . . . . . . . . . . . . . . . . . . . 323
*Bibliography* . . . . . . . . . . . . . . . . . . . . . . . . . . . . . 331
*Index* . . . . . . . . . . . . . . . . . . . . . . . . . . . . . . . . 333

# Preface

The fact that I survived my experiences in fighting the Nazi aggressor in Poland during World War II was a great surprise to me and to my family. When my comrade-in-arms Kazimierz Stobinski ("Piorun") and I returned from the war in the second part of January 1945, I asked Piorun to enter my family's farmhouse a few minutes before me to gently inform my parents and younger brothers and sisters that I was alive and well. Only after such a psychological preparation did I appear in the midst of my jubilant family. At that moment, all of us shed some tears of joy.

As soon as the enemy was expelled from Poland, I continued my education. During my studies, which included high school, college, major seminary and university, I thought from time to time about writing something about my personal war experiences, which were still very vivid in my memory. However, the hostile attitude of the Polish Communist regime toward all of us who were former soldiers of the Home Army did not allow me to write anything that might incriminate me and my comrades-in-arms in the courts of Communist justice. When I left Poland in June 1957, I hoped to write and eventually publish an account of my World War II experiences in the United States. Soon after my arrival, I began classes in the graduate school of canon law at the Catholic University of America in Washington, D.C. At that time, I gave some radio and television interviews about some of the Nazi and Communist crimes in Poland and began to write a number of articles for a Polish monthly publication. As the end of my first semester was approaching, I found my graduate work more and more time consuming. I could not do anything else but attend classes and seminars, write term papers and study for exams. To improve my proficiency in English, I had to avoid speaking and writing in Polish as much as possible. Therefore, I postponed the writing of my World War II recollections until the end of the academic year.

During my summer vacation in 1958, I wrote nine chapters telling of my experiences fighting the Nazis as a member of the Sandomierz Flying Commando Unit, and I waited to publish them as a part of my memoirs.

After completing my graduate studies at Catholic University, I accepted a teaching position at St. John Vianney Seminary in Bloomingdale, Ohio. I hoped that in the academic atmosphere of the seminary, I would be able to find additional free time to continue work on my World War II recollections. Soon after I began teaching classes in canon law and theology, I discovered that preparation of my lectures and instruction took most of my time every day. On weekends I was asked to help in various parishes in the diocese of Steubenville. I found that my teaching, my writing a number of articles for publication on weekdays and my preaching on Sundays helped me to improve my English. Graduate studies in philosophy, which I began at the Catholic University and continued at Duquesne University, also greatly increased my knowledge of the English language. All I needed now was more free time to continue work on my World War II recollections. I did not get this free time until I resigned my teaching position at the seminary, after nine years of working there, and began teaching undergraduates at the McKeesport campus of Penn State University. In the spring of 1981, I completed most of the parts of the manuscript and wrote a short prologue. Then I began editing and typing various chapters, and I corrected and expanded some of the chapters and wrote some new ones. At that time, I began to realize that one of the benefits of completing my manuscript after reaching the fullness of my physical and mental powers is that one acquires certain perspective from which some things in life are better seen, evaluated and appreciated.

In the early stage of my writing, I intended to leave a written record of my life and my experiences in World War II for the benefit of my family. But now, I hope that my work will also have some historical value for all those who will study more extensively various aspects of this tragic war, after which Europe is and will never be the same. Most of the history books written about World War II by professional historians for the general public and for graduate and postgraduate students of history provide general, basic facts and narrate central events without peripheral specifics, which can clarify and illustrate these facts and events. Therefore, credible personal accounts, written by those who took part in World War II — regardless of which side they fought on — who were eyewitnesses to particular aspects, are very valuable for contemporary and future historians. As time goes on, the value of the stories left by these witnesses, who cared to write their memoirs about World War II, will grow as survivors become fewer and fewer in number until they all are gone.

In describing my prewar childhood, I attempted to capture the ethos and some distinct traditions of Polish villages and towns in the part of Poland where I was born and grew up. At the present time, this distinct ethos and these traditions are no longer noticeable. Villages are undergoing a gradual urbanization and small towns have already undergone radical changes because of the absence of Jewish people, who constituted a considerable majority of inhabitants in all of them.

In discussing my World War II teenage years, I wrote about religious and cultural life in villages. I also wrote about the inhumane treatment of Jewish people by the Nazis.

It appears to me that my generation was the last to observe and experience, somewhat, the cultural and social life of the landed gentry in the Polish country manors. This kind of life became extinct under the brutal rule of Communist dictators and most of the beautiful, historic mansions and the art objects, antiques, and libraries they contained were destroyed beyond repair.

I took an active part in or I witnessed most of the military actions that I describe in chapters 3 through 25; I consider them the core of this work and the most important from an historical point of view. The chapters dealing with my education before and after the war shed some light on the state-run and church-run educational systems in Poland during those times. My recollections of the early years of my priestly work disclose the very difficult conditions in which the Catholic Church operated under the Communist regime at a time when the church struggled for its very survival.

# Part One: Before World War II

## INTRODUCTION

During his recent visit to Poland, Pope Benedict XVI quoted Goethe in his native language: *"Wer der Dichter will verstehen, muss in Dichters Lande gehen"* (Whoever wants to understand the poet, must go to the poet's land). Strictly speaking, the "poet" in this case was Pope John Paul II and, in an extended sense, the poetic people of Poland and their tragic history. This quotation came to my mind when I was about to write an introduction to a very small fragment of World War II Polish history.

I realize that most of my readers will not be able to visit Poland. Nevertheless, as they read what I wrote they will vicariously and spiritually visit the country and thus better understand some aspects of Poland's experiences in World War II. This is my sincere intention and profound wish. In describing various essential and incidental events, which occurred before, during, and after the war, I will take my readers to various locations in Poland.

One of these locations is the small village of Gaj, where I was born, in my parents' farmhouse, on December 8, 1923. I was baptized several weeks later as Marian Stanislaus at St. Stanislaus Church in Osiek. My parents were Jozef Aleksander Mazgaj and Jozefa Soja Mazgaj. My paternal grandparents were Antoni Aleksander and Marianna Danida Bogdanski Mazgaj and my maternal grandparents Tomasz and Tekla Korzon Soja. The village of Gaj is located in the parish of Osiek and the district of Sandomierz.

In searching for my paternal roots, I discovered that one of my ancestors, Jakob Mazgajski, was born in 1772 in the part of Poland that was eventually occupied by Austria. As a young man he became a freedom fighter during an uprising against the Austrian government. The uprising failed and he was forced to leave that part of the country and seek refuge in the part of Poland occupied by Russia. At that juncture of his life, Jacob changed his original name from Mazgajski to Mazgaj, which means, in old Polish, an anointed forest.

During my early infancy, my parents and our young maid, Teofila, took care of me. At the age of three and half, I lost my dear mother. She had a miscarriage and suffered from a postpartum infection. At that time there was no penicillin. Before my father remarried, Miss Teofila took care of me for about one year. Then, my father married Miss Anna Bernacki from Osieczko, near Osiek, with whom he had four daughters and five sons. He had almost as many children as his father, who had two daughters and nine sons. So I had the privilege of growing up as the oldest son in a family of ten children. At the age of seven, I studied catechism with a parish priest and received my solemn First Holy Communion at our parish church in Osiek. At the same time, I began to attend the first grade of our elementary school in Osiek, where about 50 percent of my classmates were Jewish children. Most of my Jewish classmates studied Hebrew on Saturdays when the rest of us had regular classes in our school. The parents of my Jewish classmates were members of an Orthodox synagogue and most of them were storekeepers, shoemakers, tailors, goldsmiths, carpenters, glaziers, and bakers. As a rule, the Jewish inhabitants of Osiek did not farm.

While I attended the elementary school in Osiek, I developed a friendship with one of the Jewish boys in my class. We enjoyed building little cars out of his grandfather's spent tailor's spools. His mother was very happy about our friendship and always offered us snacks made out of her home-baked matzo. Another classmate who became my friend was named Marzec. He was from the village of Mikolajow, which was mostly inhabited by German farmers, who, I believe, were not Polish citizens. They had their own Lutheran church and elementary school. Their church services and school instructions were conducted in German. To satisfy my curiosity about the German farmers and their way of life, my friend invited me to his home and gave me a tour of their village. During one of my recent visits to Poland I visited Mikolajow and attempted to find my elementary school friend. He was no longer there, and the Germans were all gone. During the early part of World War II, the Nazi administration transferred them to larger and better farms forcefully taken from Polish farmers in Gerlachow and Mokoszyn. From there they returned to their fatherland ahead of the withdrawing Nazi armed forces in 1944. My friend's younger sister, who still lives on her parents' farm in Mikolajow, told me that some of the descendents of the German farmers came recently from Germany to visit the village and to seek a legal way of securing their ancestors' farms.

After completing three years of elementary school in Osiek, my father leased our farm in Gaj and we moved to his mother's farm in Jeziory, where he was born and grew up. Two of his older brothers and their families also lived in Jeziory. From that time on, I continued my elementary education at the grade school in Sulislawice. A number of my older cousins attended the same school. For one reason or another, the school in Sulislawice opened up new horizons in my education. It stimulated my interest in science and history and guided me to its library and the community's library and made me an avid reader of Polish, French, English and Russian classics. I read the works of Jules Verne, Victor Hugo, Alexandre Dumas (both father and son), some works of Leo Tolstoy and Fyodor Dostoevsky, Robert Louis Stevenson, James Fenimore Cooper, all of them in Polish translations, as well as works by Polish writers such as Sienkiewicz, Prus, Reymont, Zeromski, Mickiewicz, Orzeszkowa, and others. At the same time, I began collecting stamps and pictures of Polish kings and national heroes. On the practical level, the school taught me book binding, gasification of coal, and the ability to build a simple electric battery. The school's intellectual stimulation lead me to design a prototype helicopter, on which I spent many hours trying to solve the problem of controlling the torque.

Miss Julia Podolski, who was our school's principal, and Mr. Jan Pater, who followed her in this position, were outstanding educators. As such they left an indelible academic and ethical mark on their students. When I was in the seventh grade, our class, under the leadership of our teachers, went on a week-long excursion to various historic castles, churches, and other monuments. At the end of the seventh grade, I began to take some private enrichment classes in preparation for an entrance examination to high school. An unemployed teacher, Mr. Staszewski, was my instructor.

At that time, high schools were located only in larger cities. Therefore, those of us who intended to attend one of them had to live away from home and had to pay tuition and also room and board, which were rather expensive in those days. In order to earn some money for my high school education I picked cherries on about twenty trees, which belonged to two of our neighbors. I picked cherries every day and sold them to fruit sellers in Klimontow. The fruit sellers were clever businessmen who often managed to take advantage of me. Therefore, my profits were often marginal.

Before I registered for the entrance examination at the Jan Tarnowski State High School, in Tarnobrzeg, my father consulted with the principal, Mr. Smrokowski, and the parish priest, Father Jan Budzinski. I accompanied my father to the consultations but was not present at the meetings. After we returned home, my father gave a report to my stepmother about the consultations. He said that the principal encouraged him to enroll me in high school but the pastor advised my father against it. The pastor said what I needed was to learn a trade. Therefore, my father took the advice of Father Budzinski and gave up the idea of my high school education. The priest's advice was a let down for me. I liked carpentry and blacksmithing. I made my own skis and a hunting knife. I was able to fix shoes and mend clothing. I enjoyed working on the farm, but after reading so many books by Polish and foreign authors, I was hungry for a broader knowledge than a trade could provide. My thirst for formal learning was too great to be quenched by a trade. I was increasingly unhappy with rural conditions of life. The dreams and aspirations of my classmates centering on farming and marriage sounded trivial to me. I needed broader horizons and higher aspirations. I refused to speak the local dialect and spoke the language of the books, which I read day after day. I had a feeling that soon I would leave my family and friends and continue my education. In the spring of 1938 I was still taking enrichment classes, even though I was losing hope of applying for admission to high school in the fall. At the same time, the winds of war were growing stronger and stronger. On March 12, 1938, the Nazi army of Germany marched into Austria. The so-called *Anschluss* (Connection) became a painful reality. A few days later, on March 17, the Polish government of Marshall Edward Smigly-Rydz issued an ultimatum to the government of Lithuania demanding a normalization of diplomatic relations between the two countries in two weeks. Soon thereafter, the government of Czechoslovakia ordered a partial mobilization of its military forces as a response to Hitler's desire to annex the Sudetenland. The Nazi war hysteria, which was directed toward German acquisition of *Lebensraum* (living space) from neighboring countries, infected the minds of the Polish political leadership. Marshall Smigly-Rydz demanded colonies for his country and warned the colonial nations that if colonies were not given to Poland in a peaceful way, he was ready to use force. When Hitler invited the general to join him in partitioning Czechoslovakia, he responded enthusiastically. The spirit of this kind of international adventurism was promoted by nationalistic propaganda both in Germany and in Poland. In such an atmosphere, young men and even teenage boys began to talk about war every day. Whenever I joined my peers on Sundays, we always talked about our desire to fight the enemies of our country, especially Nazi Germany. We never doubted our nation's ability to win. Sometimes we wished that the Nazis would attack us so we could show them our military superiority and heroism. During the final months of 1938, Polish police agents uncovered a secret shortwave radio station, which was operated by German colonists in the tower of the Lutheran church in the village of Mikolajow.

    In the meantime, I received an application from the State Junior Air Force Academy in Krasno, which provided general and military education at the expense of the government. After submitting my application accompanied by references and numerous documents, I was acceptable to the academy. However, I could not enroll in September 1938 on account of my age — I was short three months. Therefore, I was advised by the school administration to enroll in September 1939. While waiting for the enrollment, I helped my father in his work on our farm while I kept reading books from the community's library and studying a language called Esperanto, which was supposed to become an international language. Following the harvest of 1938, I found more time to read a daily newspaper and walked to the post office in Sulislawice to get it. The more I read, the more I desired to go back to school and study. More than ever before, I lived in two worlds: the world of a small village where everything revolved around farming and the world of books, newspapers, magazines, learning, and culture. My body was in the first world but my mind was in the second. I never felt at home in our village and farm life no longer appealed to me. I could not imagine myself living the life of a farmer. My continuous reading of books and newspapers made me a displaced person of sorts, a stranger in the middle of my family and the village.

In the meantime, I tried to help my father with farm work as much as possible. I also gave him a hand in digging trenches, which were designed to improve the quality of the soil on our farm. On Sunday afternoons, I used to join a group of boys from our village and go to one of the neighboring villages to meet girls our age. A group of girls usually waited for us. We met with them for two or three hours and engaged them in lighthearted conversation. We never dated on a one-to-one basis. On the way home from such dates, we sang songs proper for the occasion. This gave us an outlet for our youthful feelings and fantasies. It was a healthy celebration of life.

The headlines of the newspapers spoke continuously about tragic political events, which were preparing the political atmosphere for a major international conflict. The dark clouds of war were gathering on the horizon of Europe.

# 1. The Clouds of War

During the fall and winter of 1938, I helped my father on our farm. Almost every evening, I read books and newspapers. From time to time, I listened to the news on our neighbor's radio. Mr. Wojciech Podsiadly was the only person in our village who had a very primitive radio. Since there was no electricity in the village, his crystal radio had to have a long antenna and earphones. Our neighbor knew of my interest in national and international news, so he invited me on Sundays to listen to his radio, which had two sets of earphones. Both the newspaper I read daily and the radio I listened to on Sundays spoke about Hitler's preparations for war and his desire to expand the territory of Germany at the expense of Poland. In the final months of 1938 the government's police agents uncovered a secret shortwave radio station, which was operated in the tower of the Lutheran church in the village of Mikolajow. The village was 99 percent inhabited by German colonists, some of whom obviously became spies for Nazi Germany. The radio station was seized by police and the Nazi agents were arrested. This local news item increased suspicion and vigilance toward all German villages in our area The attitude of the local farmers began to change not only toward the German minority but also toward all ethnic minorities, including Jews. Rumors began to spread that in case of Hitler's attack on Poland, the German ethnic groups were not only to spy for the Nazis but also to perform acts of sabotage in mills, factories, and so forth. One of the acts of sabotage was supposed to be poisoning of wells near the roads by which army units were to pass.

At the end of 1938 our area witnessed an unusual activity. Stone, sand, and other materials were accumulated for building a highway, which appeared to have a strategic purpose in case of war. At the same time preparations were made for construction of a bridge across the Vistula River near the city of Baranow. These two activities were a part of the same project, which was sponsored by the central government.

# 1. The Clouds of War

As soon as the early spring of 1939 came, frantic construction of the highway and the bridge began. Local farmers were requested to report with their horses and wagons to various construction sites, where they were engaged in hauling stones, sand, and lumber. This hurried construction confirmed people's thinking about the nearness of war.

When the construction of the highway and the bridge were nearing completion, the people of the area could not believe their own eyes when they saw that the wooden guard rails on each side of the highway and the bridge itself were painted white. Soon the local government issued an order to paint all bridges and guard rails white. Even the farmers were encouraged to use white paint in painting their barns and fences. People began to laugh at the stupidity or naïveté of their government. They were convinced that the Nazis infiltrated the government and issued orders to paint things white so that, in case of war, the Nazi pilots could easily spot them. This policy and others indicated more and more to the local people that the Polish government was slowly losing control over its own destiny. Nevertheless, its propaganda repeated, like a broken record, the same slogans on readiness to fight the Nazis in defense of the fatherland.

When we seeded our fields in the spring of 1939, my father prayed, as he always did, that we may enjoy a successful harvest. Sometimes as the war hysteria reached its peak, my father and I wondered if we would be the ones to celebrate this year's harvest. As the spring ended, the crops reached an abundant growth promising an exceptionally good harvest. At the same time rumors of a general mobilization began to circulate. Many young farmers in our area, who were subject to mobilization, were anxious to finish their harvest before they were called. I regretted the fact that I was not old enough to join the army. For one reason or another, I did not hear anything from the Air Force Academy. I suppose military preparations took a precedence over academic concerns of the air force.

Soon harvest time came and mobilization was not called. Our family and other farm families in our area worked very hard to finish the harvest as soon as possible. One could not have asked for better weather. It was warm and dry. Therefore, in the beginning of August, the grain was stored in barns and thrashing began. At the same time the first mobilization letters reached our village. At first, only a few men received them but then more men were called day after day. The first mobilization letters were issued on August 24, 1939.

I will never forget the departure of the first group of men from our village. They received their mobilization letters in the afternoon of that day and departed for their units in the early evening. Farmers with the best horses and wagons in the village were assigned to transport them to the railroad station in Sandomierz or to the army base, also in Sandomierz. As they were leaving, they did not indulge in long good-byes. They did not want their mothers and wives to cry in their presence. They just hugged and kissed their dear ones, jumped in the wagons, and were gone. I had tears in my eyes not because they went to war but because I could not go with them to fight the Nazis.

From the day the first contingent of men from our village responded to the general mobilization, the local stores became crowded with customers who were buying large quantities of salt, sugar, kerosene, among other necessities. Soon there were shortages of these things in every store. In the second part of August, the outbreak of war was anticipated from day to day. Our parish church was crowded on Sundays more than ever before. Older people who remembered the evils of World War I, and women and children prayed for peace. Most of the young men, excited by the government's propaganda, welcomed war as a chance to prove to the world that, unlike Czechoslovakia and Austria, Poland was determined to fight Nazi Germany and win.

In spite of the ongoing mobilization, the war hysteria in the newspapers and on the radio decreased for some reason in late August and one could experience a certain calmness, a calmness that in nature precedes a storm.

# Part Two: The Time of War

## 2. THE BEGINNING OF WORLD WAR II

*Call to Arms*

I will never forget the early morning of September 1, 1939. One of the men from our village, who was assigned that week as a night watchman, came to our house, pounded on the door, and told us that the Germans had attacked Poland. He also told us that a man and a woman came to our village during the night and, shouting on the top of their voices, encouraged people to flee east from the German army. They gave him the impression that the German troops were approaching the city of Staszow, which was about twenty miles west of our village. They were unknown to him, perfect strangers, and did not give their names. Later we discovered that they were Nazi agents, fifth columnists, planted to create confusion and disorder among the people, who would clog the roads so the Polish army would be impeded in its movements.

When the night watchman woke us up, it must have been about four o'clock in the morning. It was still dark. My father, who had fought the Germans in World War I, made an instant decision to secure some emergency provisions for our family. He asked me to follow him to the tool shed, where we picked up our shovels, and then he told me of his plan, which called for digging a deep hole in our backyard in which we were to hide some grain and other nonperishable provisions. Before sunrise, we buried the emergency provisions, winter clothes, some shoes, and family valuables. After we completed the work, my mother served us an early breakfast.

In the meantime, my first cousin, Jan Mazgaj, who was three years my senior, and I talked the situation over and decided to volunteer for the army. When Jan's friend, Waclaw Kos, came to see us, we talked him into joining us in our venture. Then each of us went home to get some blankets, extra clothing, and food. After Jan and I were ready to go, we walked to Waclaw's home. He waited for us. One of his brothers was a military policeman on active duty and the other one was just mobilized; therefore, Waclaw's father was not happy to see him go.

From Waclaw's home we walked to the city of Sandomierz, where a part of the Second Regiment of Infantry had its permanent base.[1] After reporting there we were told that the regiment was on its way to the front. It left Sandomierz on August 29, 1939, under the command of Colonel Ludwik Czyzewski and was deployed near the possible front. The military personnel left at the base advised us to join one of the regiments stationed across the Vistula River in the eastern part of the country. At the Sandomierz regimental base, we met a group of young men, about ten in number, from Osiek who also attempted to join the regiment. They included Stanislaw Ostrowski, Stefan Kitlinski, and Edmund Kopciowski. They too were advised to go east across the river. Since Jan and I knew some of them, we decided to join their group in search of a military unit, which would accept us and issue us uniforms and rifles.

As soon as we crossed the Vistula River, we discovered that hundreds and hundreds of young men like us had walked east with the same burning desire to join a military unit and fight the Nazis. In addition, we discovered thousands of men, women, and children of all ages who had left their homes carrying the most valuable of their possessions and heading east for fear of the Germans. Most of them walked, some rode bicycles, and a very few used motorcycles or cars as a mode of transportation. These two motorized types of vehicles were often abandoned on the road, broken down or without gas.

From time to time, German bombers flew over us to drop their loads on bridges, railroads, mills, factories, cities, and towns. They also bombed military columns as they moved toward the front. We could hear distant explosions. Here and there columns of smoke appeared on the horizon.

If I am not mistaken, we spent our first night in the pine forest near the city of Stalowa Wola, a newly developed industrial city, which was bombed in the morning. We slept on the ground using pine needles as our mattresses. We were awakened in the middle of the night by rifle fire and shouts "Infiltrators! Spies! Apprehend them!" There was a commotion among the people in the forest. People ran in all directions in an attempt to catch the alleged infiltrators. Due to the excitement, no one could sleep to the end of the night. In the morning we were told that a small detachment of soldiers who guarded an ammunition depot fired at the German fifth-column agents dressed in Polish military uniforms who attempted to blow it up.

In the morning we continued walking east toward the city of Janow Lubelski. The number of refugees increased tremendously. Army vehicles rode in the middle of the road and refugees marched on its sides. As we passed through towns and villages we replenished our water supply. In some cases there was no more water in wells. Food also became scarce. From time to time Nazi pilots bombed and machine-gunned people on the road. This created a considerable panic. As soon as we heard the sound of airplanes, we looked for cover under trees and bushes. At first we did not see anybody killed. We saw military convoys destroyed and horses killed. Toward the end of the day, we noticed both military and civilian casualties. The tragic reality of war began to come over us. Nevertheless, each time we met a group of soldiers we asked whether we could join them. The answer was always the same, "We have no authority to recruit anybody, we hardly have enough weapons for ourselves." Some soldiers had no military uniforms, just army hats. Others had uniforms but no hats. Only a few wore helmets. Something was terribly wrong with the general mobilization. Somebody had failed our patriotic young men who offered their lives to defend the fatherland.

In a small town where we stopped to stay for the night, to wash dust from our bodies and to replenish our water supply, I noticed a group of about one hundred infantry men. They stood in line to get their dinner, which was just cooked in a field kitchen. I watched the servicemen approach the cook and receive their portions. I spotted the officer and went to ask him about the possibility of joining the unit. The answer was, "No." He gave me the same explanation I heard from the other officers before. He was very sympathetic toward me but he could not do a thing. By the time I finished my conversation with the officer, the line of soldiers waiting for the dinner became very short so I went to the end of the line and waited my turn. I carried a large tin cup on me and held it out to receive a portion of food from the cook. He noticed that I was a civilian, hesitated for a moment, and then gave it to me. When I looked closer at the food I realized it was mashed potatoes. Poor provisions I thought. How in the world can our army fight a war against Nazi Germany on mashed potatoes?

In the morning we kept marching east. As we were coming closer to Janow Lubelski, we saw more and more military equipment abandoned on the road. Some equipment was destroyed by the Nazi bombs and some was still usable but the horses that pulled it were killed. For the first time in my life, I saw a Polish tank. It had run out of gas and was left on the side of the road. It was rather small, probably of World War I vintage. It was unlike the tanks pictured in the newspapers.

After about one week of marching east, we came close to the city of Janow Lubelski. For the first time since we left home, we could hear sounds of the German and Polish artillery behind us. It meant that the front line followed us. Soon we heard rumors that enemy tanks were spotted not far behind us. The Luftwaffe increased its activities from day to day. Fires appeared on the entire horizon. We saw more and more panic among the refugees and the inhabitants of towns and villages we were passing through. Some of the local people joined us in a mass exodus. Others took food and their most valuable possessions and hid in the forests, which were plentiful in the area. The refugees also began to avoid streaming through towns as happened in the beginning. They looked for country roads.

As we approached Janow Lubelski, our group decided to separate itself from the main body of refugees and go through the city. We were running out of food and hoped to buy it there. As we reached the suburbs, we were struck by an absence of people on the streets. Anticipating the imminent arrival of Nazi tanks, most of them left for the forest. Some were hiding in the basements of their houses and dugouts. By the time we came to the first houses of the city proper, we had the feeling of being in a ghost town. Everything was so quiet and so still that we began to be disturbed by the sound of our shoes striking the stone pavement. All of a sudden a group of men appeared from behind a brick house. There were about six men in the group. They wore long black topcoats and black hats. One of them carried a loaf of bread on a tray and another a dish of salt, symbols of hospitality. They were representatives of the Jewish community in the city who waited to welcome the first soldiers of the Nazi army entering the city. When they heard our footsteps on the street they thought we were the German soldiers. After discovering their mistake, they were embarrassed and returned behind the building to wait for the Germans. We proceeded through the abandoned streets of the city and soon gave up hope of buying food. All the stores were closed. After crossing Janow Lubelski, we rejoined the mass of refugees, which went around the city and walked east. Soon we came to a crossroads. One road led east toward the city of Zamosc and the other went north to the city of Krasnik. Some of the refugees kept walking straight toward Zamosc. Others, after being informed by the refugees from Janow Lubelski about a German panzer unit racing up from Przemyśl, decided to go toward Krasnik and Lublin. Our group joined the refugees going in the direction of Lublin. We still hoped to join an army unit and did not want to be overrun by the Germans.

It must have taken us two days to arrive near Krasnik. Instead of going through Krasnik, Jan, Waclaw, and I decided to split from our friends from Osiek and go into the countryside in search of food. We walked a few miles away from the road that led to Lublin and came to a village. The farmhouses in it were large and prosperous. When we entered one of the houses to buy a loaf of bread and cheese, the farmer and his wife asked us to sit at their kitchen table and offered us a free meal. They knew that we were hungry, thirsty, and tired and watched with joy how their good food disappeared from the table consumed by three growing men. After we finished our meal and bought some food, we intended to continue our walk toward Lublin. But the farmer, who knew more than we did about the most recent movements of the German forces, advised us to stay put until the military activities passed by the area. He was very convincing and his arguments made sense. We took his advice. Even though the farmer and his wife offered us free meals during our stay with them, we offered to help them in the farm work. They were pleased with our offer and showed us the hay section of the barn where we could fix our bedding. Sleeping on fresh hay reminded us so much of our homes.

The following day we helped the farmer to thrash his rye. We were familiar with this type of work and the farmer was pleased with our exertions. The farmer's wife cooked good meals and we enjoyed her cooking very much. We were happy with our decision to stay put for the time being. But after two days of our pleasant life on the farm things began to change. The news came to the village that the front line was approaching and that a number of Polish infantry and artillery units were dug in on the hills near Krasnik. The people in the village speculated that in case of battle, the village would be caught in the crossfire. Therefore, they began to pack their most important belongings, load them on farm wagons, and seek refuge in the nearby forest. We helped the family we stayed with pack their possessions and carried them to the wagon. Grain, food, bedding, clothes, and some furniture were stored away from the buildings in the dugout. The farmer and his wife encouraged us to leave the village with them and hide in the forest. We were grateful for the offer but since we were on the go for some time, we chose to stay in the village to thrash rye and guard the remaining property. The farmer told us that we were free to use the house. He also showed us where the food was and encouraged us to eat anything we wanted. Knowing that we were the sons of farmers, he trusted us with everything.

By about nine o'clock in the morning, all the farmers and their families left the village. The three of us thrashed rye and could not quite figure out why the farmers left the village so hurriedly. Did they know something that we did not? Perhaps they knew for sure that the Polish units that occupied the positions on the hills near Krasnik would not pull out without a fierce battle. Perhaps the village was burned during World War I when the Russians and Austrians fought each other in the very same area and the memory of it still lived in the minds of the older people.

It was very quiet in the village after the villagers left. The sound of our thrashing was the only noise there. We had very little fear. At noon we took a break for lunch. There was still no sign of the approaching Germans. After lunch we went back to the barn to continue our work. Only then did we hear artillery fire and the whizzing of shells over the village. The Polish artillery fired first. After a while the Germans responded and then an artillery duel followed. Some shells fell short of their targets and exploded in the village. None of them exploded near the barn in which we worked. However, the artillery battle continued and more shells exploded in the village, setting fires. Several shells fell in the neighbor's yard. At that point we began to fear that we might get hit by shrapnel. We left the barn and hid in the dugout. After staying there for a short while, we became convinced that the shells that fell on the village were no longer those that missed the target but they were purposely aimed there. The frequency of explosions in the village confirmed the correctness of our conviction. No doubt we found ourselves in a very dangerous place. We quickly decided to leave the village and seek safety in the fields.

After leaving the dugout, we dashed into the orchard and then opened a small gate near the barn and ran into the field. We kept running to distance ourselves from the village as much as possible. Artillery shells continued to explode in the village one after another. We noticed that about a mile and a half from the village there was a grove of trees in the midst of barren fields, which appeared safe. Instinctively we rushed in the direction of the grove. We were halfway between the village and the grove when a number of the enemy's bombers swept over the tops of the trees and opened up with machine-gun fire. Fortunately, we were in a potato field with deep furrows made by a cultivator between the rows of plants. As the bombers flew over Krasnik and the surrounding hills where the units of Polish artillery were, they dropped bombs and machine-gunned the soldiers. The artillery commenced firing at the bombers but since its pieces were placed on the hills and the airplanes flew very low, its fire was both ineffective and disastrous to the Polish infantry dug in the lower terrain. Refugees scattered along the main road. Soon more and more bombers appeared above us and silenced our artillery altogether. They became masters of the sky. Where was the Polish air force? Not even one airplane took off to fight the Nazi intruders!

After the bombers dropped their loads on Krasnik, which by this time was in flames, they flew around and around mowing down everybody in sight. There were about fifteen Nazi bombers above us. Their machine-gun fire was the most terrifying. Each time the airplanes flew over us, the bullets whizzed by our ears and the dust of the dry ground indicated the spots they hit. They flew in a pattern of a merry-go-round and were coming over us with their blazing machine guns in short intervals. I prayed to God for letting me survive this terrible danger and pushed my body in the furrow as deeply as I could. I never realized until then that a farmer's cultivator, which made furrows between the rows of potato plants in the spring, might be so helpful in saving human life.

The air raid lasted about one hour. When the bombers flew away, we remained in the potato field for a while not knowing what to expect next. We thought that another group of bombers might come and continue the work of terror, destruction, and death. As we waited in uncertainty and lifted our heads up, we discovered that half of the horizon was on fire. The city of Krasnik and neighboring towns and villages were being gutted by the conflagration. What a waste, I thought, as I looked around. The war began to show me its various faces — terrible faces.

Since the air raid did not resume, we left the potato field and walked toward the grove. After reaching it we decided to stay there for the night. It was quiet during the night but we could not sleep. The air raid was too fresh in our memory and tomorrow too precarious. In the morning some local people came to the woods and told us that Nazi panzer units had already occupied the whole area of Krasnik and controlled the main roads. There was no use for us to go any farther east. The Nazis were already ahead of us. It was time to return home. We felt disappointed and hurt for not being able to join the Polish army and fight the enemy. The realization that our armed forces were not adequately prepared to defend the country from the Nazi aggression increased our pain and disappointment. We felt victimized not only by the Nazi invaders but also by our own government.

## *Returning Home*

During the early hours of the day, we remained in the safety of the grove. We did not see any military activities in the surrounding fields but the sound of rolling tanks was coming continuously from the direction of the highway. Around noon we decided to start on the way home. As we began walking west, we did everything possible to avoid highways. It took us about three days to reach the Vistula River near the town of Zawichost. Those three days were rather uneventful. I don't remember much about those days except the fact that we were hungry and raided farmers' orchards for apples and plums. Our feet were full of blisters. We were tired and apathetic.

Near Zawichost we joined others who, like us, were returning home. We crossed the Vistula River. On the bridge we met German soldiers for the first time. They did not bother us at all. They ignored us. That is why from Zawichost on we chose to follow the main highway west. We were only one day's walking distance from our village.

As soon as we left Zawichost on our way to Sandomierz, we saw the first German tanks. In comparison with the Polish tank we saw broken on the road near Janow Lubelski, they were huge and moved fast. It did not take me long to realize that the small and antiquated Polish tanks were no match for them.

Once in Sandomierz, we rested for a while and replenished our water supply and then continued our march toward Koprzywnica. This part of the highway was also busy with rolling tanks and heavy trucks. Some of the trucks carried soldiers in full combat gear. As we walked along the side of the highway, we observed with a great curiosity the well-ordered might of the enemy on the way to pursue and destroy the remnants of our army in the east.

After reaching Koprzywnica we inquired about our village. We feared that it might be burned. The people we met assured us that our village was spared destruction although some artillery shells had exploded in the fields near it. Osiek, however, was burned to the ground. From Koprzywnica we proceeded toward our village by the back roads on which there were no German troops. The closer to home we came the more energy we gained. We missed our families and the comforts of our homes.

It must have been about 8:00 P.M. when I entered the kitchen of our home. The family dinner was just over. Empty plates were still on the table. My father and stepmother rushed to me with tears in their eyes. They hugged me and kissed me and were happy to see me return home alive. My brothers and sisters looked up to me as if I were a hero of sorts. Before I finished washing the dust from my body, there was steaming food on the table. My stepmother knew that I was famished and she cautioned me not to eat too much at first so I would not get sick. Our farm food and homemade bread tasted so good and I could not help but eat until I was not hungry anymore.

The following day, I went into our fields to examine the craters made by the artillery shells. They were made by Polish artillery, which fired at the approaching enemy. My parents and our neighbors told me about many fearful hours they spent in the dugouts during the shelling. Fortunately there was no damage to either the village, farm buildings, or life. However, some horses used by the Polish military units were killed and wounded. Some wounded horses dispersed into the fields and wooded areas around our village and grazed there. My Uncle Franek caught one of these horses and kept him in his orchard. The horse was wounded by fragments of bombs or artillery shells, which lodged themselves deep into its body. He was a huge Belgian horse used, most probably, by the artillery or transport unit. At first he seemed to recover well but then infection set in and the horse died.

Within several days after my return, I returned to work on our farm. In the evenings or on rainy days, I read books as ever before. Also, I borrowed from our neighbor's son, Wacek Podsiadly, a basic German textbook and began to study the German language. I continued borrowing books from the library operated by the Savings and Loan Cooperative in Sulislawice. Each Sunday before mass, I returned the books I had read and after mass I selected new books. One Sunday as I went to the library to borrow some books, I was told by the librarian that the Nazis intended to confiscate the books in the library and, therefore, he asked the readers to take as many books as possible for the duration of the war. In two or three trips to the library, I brought home more than fifty books I had never read before. If I am not mistaken, most of the best books were taken to the readers' homes. When I finished reading all the books I had taken home, I began exchanging books with other readers who, like me, stored a portion of the library books in their homes. Later on, my first cousin, Jan, Uncle Franek's son, stored some books from a library in Starachowice and let me use them as much as I wanted. The books he stored included complete works of the best Polish novelists and poets. No wonder I spent every free moment of time reading and studying.

## Salvaging Arms at Baranow Bridge

One Sunday afternoon at the end of September or in the beginning of October 1939, I joined a group of boys from our village in an excursion to the site of the strategic bridge near the city of Baranow. The bridge, which Polish authorities built in a hurry just before the Nazi aggression, spanned the Vistula River. In order to stop Polish troops from moving east, Nazi bombers attempted to destroy the bridge, but their bombs missed the target over and over again. The bridge survived until the morning of September 9. On that day Polish troops, which guarded the bridge, noticed a number of German tanks enter the village of Swiniary so they blew up a section of it.[2] Then they discovered that many of the Polish units still remained on the western side of the Vistula River. The critical situation of these units forced them not only to repair the bridge but also to build a new temporary bridge.

On September 11 and 12 most of the Polish units under the leadership of General Sadowski, which were trapped by the Germans in that area, crossed the Vistula River. However, some of the units under the same command were unable to make it to the bridge. These units were forced to cross the river at its shallow points, leaving behind wagons of provisions, weapons, and ammunition. The boys in the group I joined that Sunday were driven by a patriotic desire to salvage some of the abandoned weapons and ammunition, hide them, and eventually use them against the Nazis.

It took us about two hours to reach the area of the bridge. On the way we examined a Polish cannon abandoned on the side of the road. It was in excellent condition, but its essential part, the breech, was missing. When we came to the bridge area we were very disappointed. Rifles and machine guns, which we hoped to find there in abundance, were all gone. Even broken ones were already salvaged.[3] What we found were countless boxes of rifle ammunition, explosives, artillery shells, and fuses. We loaded our pockets with rifle ammunition and took some fuses. On our way home, we went across the fields to avoid the Nazis patrolling the area.

On my return home, I concealed the ammunition and fuses in our barn. My father did not know anything about it. From time to time, I examined my military "treasure" and put it away again. I took apart some of the rifle cartridges and studied their content. They differed somewhat from one another. Some were simple projectiles. Others were tracers with short-tempered steel cores to be fired at heavier armor. The artillery fuses, which were to arm projectiles, were of two types, long and short. They puzzled me, but I did not know how to take them apart without risking their exploding in my hands. So I waited for somebody who could explain their functioning to me. As it happened, I did not have to wait too long for a specialist in these types of fuses. My first cousin, Jozef Mazgaj, who, before the war began, was drafted into the Polish navy, had just returned home from the war. Before the war, as a trained specialist, he worked in a military ammunition plant in Rembertow near Warsaw. When I mentioned to him something about the fuses, he wanted to see them right away. I brought him only two of them. He recognized them and told me that they were produced in his plant. In explaining them to me, he cautioned me about the danger they presented to a person who handled them. Then he told me that the long fuses were meant for projectiles to be fired at airplanes and the short ones for the ground targets. After these preliminary explanations, he took me to his father's shop, took the fuses apart, and showed me how they worked step by step. I was grateful to him for sharing his professional knowledge with me. He was a fine teacher. From that moment on, he was my teacher of applied physics. I watched him work in the shop for hours and helped him build a muzzle-loader shotgun from scratch.

Besides my first cousin, Jozef, a number of my other relatives returned to their parents' homes on account of the war. Since they had some influence on my life, in one way or another, I must say a few words about each of them.

Jozef's wife, Maria, came with him from Rembertow, where they lived for a number of years before the war began. Jozef and Maria had no children. Since Jozef worked in the government's ammunition plant, with the arrival of the Nazis in Poland there was nothing for him to do in Rembertow. The comfortable life and bright future he and his wife enjoyed collapsed. If I am not mistaken, Maria was employed by some company, possibly PPG, in Warsaw. A very intelligent, beautiful, and kind person, she was a great asset to the Mazgaj family. Jozef and Maria lived with Uncle Franek for about one year. Later on, they rented an apartment of their own.

Jan Mazgaj-Marglewski, son of my Uncle Wladyslaw, worked as a teacher in a grade school in the western part of Poland. As an army officer, he was mobilized shortly before the outbreak of the war and took part in the war from its very inception. Then he fought the Nazis during the siege of Warsaw to the very end. After the capitulation of Warsaw, he managed to avoid being taken by the enemy as a POW and safely returned to his parents' farm. He was still single and lived with his parents until his arrest by the SS in the spring of 1943. During many lonely evenings, Jan played the violin to entertain his parents and visitors.

Antoni Mazgaj-Marglewski, Jan's younger brother, was also mobilized before the war. He was a college-educated person and worked as an official of some government agency in Katowice. Like his brother, Jan, he was a reserve officer and fought the invaders during the month of September 1939. After the German and Russian armies overran Poland, Antoni returned to Jeziory and stayed with his parents until he joined an underground unit of the Home Army. He also played the violin and enjoyed reading.

Stanislaw Mazgaj-Marglewski, my Uncle Wladyslaw's youngest son, returned home from college at the end of June 1939 for his summer vacation and also stayed home with his parents. His older brothers financed his education but he experienced considerable difficulties in his studies. Stanislaw resided with his parents until the end of the war.

The return to Jeziory of Jozef and my other cousins gave me a chance to learn not only military things but also explore some subjects taught on the college level. In my conversations with them, I was exposed to some Greek and Roman literature and German literature but, most of all, to an academic analysis of Polish writers whose works I had read during my grade school years. I attribute my initial acquaintance with Latin and German to the association with them. They also helped me to develop an idea of what life in large cities was all about.

# 3. The First Stage of the Nazi Occupation

## *The New Order*

In spite of the Nazi occupation, life in our village was almost normal at first. But as soon as the potatoes were harvested, the Nazi government issued an order commanding each farmer to deliver so much grain, potatoes, milk, eggs, pork, and beef to its warehouses. In order to prevent the farmers from butchering cattle and hogs, the government sent its agents to tag and register every single farm animal. The tags, made of metal, were attached to the animals' ears. A village head was responsible for the farmers' compliance with the government's order. In our county, the government's agents enlisted the help of SS men in persuading the heads of the villages to be dutiful in exercising their authority. During a meeting of the county's village heads, a number of SS-men were present to threaten and terrorize them.[4] To my knowledge all farmers in our village meticulously complied with the order and delivered all they were ordered. In our area, the grain was stored in an old Cistercian monastery in Koprzywnica. I helped my father to take our grain there.

If I am not mistaken, the Nazi government issued another order at the end of October 1939. According to this order, all men and women above the age of fourteen had to appear in the county office to have pictures and fingerprints taken for official identification cards. As I have learned later, these ID cards classified the people according to the potential danger they presented to the Nazi government. Each ID was rubber-stamped with a seal. The emblem on the seal consisted of the Nazi eagle, which held in his talons a wreath. Under the wreath a swastica was suspended. In the middle of the wreath there was a number, hardly noticeable, which indicated a class of people to which an individual belonged. Highly educated persons such as university professors, scientists, and writers were given number one. College professors, priests, ministers, former military officers, and social activists were assigned number two. High school and grade school teachers, lawyers, engineers, and technicians obtained number three and so on. Landless and illiterate individuals received the highest number.

The methodical extermination of the Polish people, which was about to begin, was designed according to the numerical classification. The Nazi timetable provided for a certain time period during which a given class of people was to be eliminated. Of course, the class designated number one was the first one to go.[5]

From time to time the SS and Gestapo units staged a roundup during which ID's were checked and persons belonging to a certain class arrested and taken to death camps. The campus of the famous Jagiellonian University in Cracow provided the stage for a roundup of the faculty. The Nazis used deception in gathering the members of the faculty on the campus. The professors were made to believe that the Nazis were to meet with them to discuss the reopening of the university. Those who believed the Nazis and came to the meeting were arrested and sent to extermination camps. Most of the faculty members went to that fatal meeting.

Since our village was about ten miles away from a highway, the Nazis were seldom seen there. An SS unit was stationed in Koprzywnica, about sixteen miles from us and in Loniow, which was about ten miles from Jeziory. These two units were there from the very beginning of the occupation. Several months later another SS unit was placed only two and a half miles from our village in Ruszcza manor. This unit was too close to us for comfort. Especially when rumors began to circulate about a torture table the SS men were using there in the interrogation of their prisoners.

One day in the late fall, a small group of SS men from Ruszcza came to our village. They searched for pine timber, which some farmers allegedly cut without authorization from the neighboring state forest. When they arrived in the village no one knew what they were after. My father and Uncle Franek thought that they were taking young boys and girls for forced labor in Germany; therefore, they hid my first cousin, Maria, and me in the attic of our stable. When the Nazis came to our yard my father waited for them there. There was some pine timber in our yard, which my father and I had cut. My father was concerned about it. When the SS men noticed the timber, they began questioning my father about it. Fortunately, my father spoke some German and managed to explain to them the fact that the timber they saw came from his own forest. They were gratified to hear him speak German and accepted his explanation. This was the first time I had ever heard my father speak German.

As soon as they left our yard and went to our neighbors' farm, Maria

The palace of Count Moszynski in Loniow was occupied by the SS unit that terrorized the whole area from the very beginning of World War II. Author's photograph.

and I came out from hiding. We managed to peek at the Nazis as they searched for timber in the Podsiadlys' yard. Not finding any suspicious timber, they left Jeziory for the village of Bukowa. There, as we learned by the end of the day, they found some government timber and arrested a number of men.

The SS men stationed in Ruszcza also enforced delivery of grain by the local farmers. An elderly farmer by the name of Strzesniak from the neighboring village of Wojcieszyce failed to deliver the required amount of grain to the Nazi warehouse. It most probably happened by some bureaucratic error. Soon he received a summons from the SS men in Ruszcza to appear in person at their post. Knowing about the beating other farmers suffered at the hands of the Nazis under similar circumstances, he was very much concerned and frightened. Being, however, a clever man, he decided to play a fool with the SS men. The people who knew him well told me that he was quite an actor. The day before he was to appear at the SS station, he put an old worn-out topcoat below the roosts in his chicken coop. The following day, in the morning, he put on the coat spotted with the birds' droppings, soiled his shoes in stable manure, and walked to Ruszcza for his appointment with the SS men. Holding in his hand the paper that summoned him, he walked into the office at the appointed hour. A terrible stench of manure filled the office. As an SS man looked at the visitor, he realized immediately the source of the repugnant odor. He grabbed the paper out of the farmer's hand and shouted, "*Raus! Raus!*" pointing toward the door. Szczesniak left the office as fast as he could, gratified with the desired effect of his act. Then he discarded the topcoat, washed his boots, and walked home laughing all the way. This was not his first clever act. He was known in the whole area for playing humorous tricks on many well-placed and educated people.

Some of the people in our county underestimated the Nazis' ability to subdue and control the people they conquered. Two large villages in our county paid a terrible price for their misconception of the Nazi invaders. One of these villages was Swiniary, a village situated on the western side of the Vistula River near where the strategic highway and bridge were constructed before the war.

As I mentioned before, after the unit of Polish soldiers destroyed the bridge, the retreating Polish army, in order to cross the shallow parts of the river, left a great amount of weapons, ammunition, and other valuable things near the bridge. The men of Swiniary were the first ones to salvage as much of the weapons and ammunition as they could. Older and more experienced men hid their weapons, hoping to use them at the proper time against the invaders. Younger men began to fire their firearms at night and even used light machine guns for hunting deer. The SS men stationed at Loniow manor soon became aware of what was going on in Swiniary. They took their time in making a list of those possessing weapons. After the list was completed, the Nazis surrounded the village early in the morning and arrested scores of men, who never returned to their village. They were all shot.

Another village that lost most of its men was Beszyce. This village belonged to our parish and was only about five miles from Jeziory. For a long time before the war, Beszyce had a very bad reputation. Thefts and robberies in the surrounding area were traceable to the village. Most of the men in the village had police records and were incarcerated at one time or another.

After the Nazi invasion, many men of Beszyce returned from prisons and replenished their weapons and ammunition at the Vistula River near Swiniary. They also underestimated German vigilance. As soon as the military activities ceased in the area and the Nazis rarely appeared in remote villages, the men of Beszyce became active as thieves and robbers. As a rule they avoided the area of our parish and went to distant villages and towns to commit their criminal acts. The Nazi authorities, having in their possession Polish prewar criminal records, kept an eye on the village of Beszyce. After an investigation of robberies was completed, it was obvious that traces led, in a number of cases, to the village; therefore, the SS men administered a radical solution.

They rounded up most of the grown men in the village and sent them to death camps. To my knowledge none of these men returned. Needless to say, there was very little sympathy toward them on the part of the area's population.

## *The Fate of Osiek*

For a long time after my return, I heard my parents and neighbors talk about the battle of Osiek and its disastrous effect. To satisfy my curiosity, I walked about ten miles to Osiek or, more correctly, to what was left of it. After arriving there, I discovered that, with the exception of some buildings in the downtown area and the church, the whole town and its suburbs were in ruins. Everything was burned to the ground. How did it happen?

During the German attack on Osiek on September 11, 1939, the Polish units, which were dug in on the hills west of Osiek, were ordered to halt the progress of the Germans coming by the highway from the city of Staszow. They were ordered to do so to enable the majority of the other Polish units to cross the Vistula River on their way east. In spite of the shortage of tanks and heavy artillery, the Polish units, under the leadership of Colonel Wladyslaw Adamczyk, performed acts of supreme heroism to halt the invaders. They made good use of the hills overlooking the highway and other approaches to Osiek and of their heavy machine guns. Colonel Adamczyk commanded the 201st Regiment of Infantry. He posted the Second Battalion northwest of Osiek near Suchowola and Grabowiec and his First Battalion southwest of the town toward the villages of Pliskowola and Niekrasow. The Third Battery of the 65th Regiment of Light Artillery was to deter an imminent attack of the German infantry and tanks. Other light artillery units were to provide a general support of the front line.[6]

In order to prevent the Polish troops from crossing the Vistula River, the Germans pushed ferociously. Between 8:00 A.M. and 9:00 A.M., a good number of the Luftwaffe bombers began a concentrated attack on the Polish units crossing the Vistula near Baranow. At the same time, a German panzer unit began to roll toward Osiek from the village of Niekrasow to the south and a battery of artillery appeared on the horizon near Pliskowola. Soon the enemy began to move forward from the west and its units grew in numbers. Then, the enemy appeared also from the north, from the direction of Grabowiec. The attacking Germans belonged to battalions of the 27th and 68th Divisions of Infantry and the panzer units were a part of the Fifth Panzer Division. The Polish units opened fire at the approaching enemy around 9:00 A.M. and its units halted for a while, but soon the attack continued at a slow pace. After a while, the enemy's artillery set Osiek on fire. The Poles withdrew east of Osiek.[7]

## 3. The First Stage of the Nazi Occupation 29

At about 1:00 P.M. the Poles not only halted the enemy but also began a counterattack during which they took Osiek from the Germans and pushed them back to their original positions. At the same time, they captured more than 160 German POWs. Unfortunately, the lack of ammunition forced the Poles by evening to withdraw under the cover of darkness and retreat toward the Vistula. The Germans took Osiek again on September 12, 1939, but they paid a very dear price. Hundreds of their dead soldiers littered the fields near the town. The battle of Osiek was also costly for the Polish side: 98 killed and 180 wounded.[8]

Most of the residents of Osiek left their burned town and found shelter in the neighboring villages. In most instances they constructed temporary shanties. Some of them lived in dugouts. My stepmother's parents lived in a suburb of Osiek called Osieczko. Their house, stable, and barn were burned to the ground. Together with most of the other people, they decided to stay in one of the villages near Osiek. After their son, Jan Bernacki, returned from the war (his unit guarded the Polish border with the Soviet Union) and their daughter, Janka, married a young man named Leon Piekniak, they began construction of a shanty to serve them as a shelter. All five of them were to live in it. Since the Bernackis' farmland was adjacent to a lake whose shoreline was covered with growing reeds, my stepmother's brother and his brother-in-law decided to use reeds for the roof on the shanty. The November weather was cold and the lake's surface was frozen. Jan Bernacki and his brother-in-law, Leon Piekniak, hitched their horse to a farm wagon and went to the lake to cut reeds. After loading the wagon with reeds they decided to load also a number of artillery projectiles, which were in abundance near the lake. I never learned the reason they put the projectiles on the wagon. When they brought the load to the construction site, Jan's mother came out of the friends' house to see what they had brought. Jan was on the top of the wagon and his brother-in-law on the ground. My stepmother's father and sister were inside the house. Jan picked up one of the projectiles and threw it on the frozen ground. His mother shouted, "Janek, for God's sake what are you doing?" He smiled, picked up another projectile, and threw it down against the first one. An explosion shook the whole area. Windows blew out in the neighborhood. Both Jan and his brother-in-law were blown to bits. Fragments struck the mother but she lived for about a week.

I will never forget the day the tragic news was brought to our home. My stepmother's cousin, Stanislaw Niekurzak, was the bearer of the bad news. He came to our home early in the morning as we were just getting up. My stepmother was cooking our breakfast when she heard knocking on the door. She opened the door and when she saw the bewildered face of her cousin, Stanislaw Niekurzak, she knew that something was wrong. In the meantime, my father and I had come into the kitchen, greeted him, and were puzzled by his unexpected early visit. He was silent for a short while, looked at us with eyes full of pain, and began describing the terrible drama. My stepmother wept, my father and I were shocked by the news and looked at Niekurzak with disbelief. As we all sat down for a while, he shared some details of the tragedy with us.

As soon as our painful breakfast was over, my father hitched a horse to a wagon and helped my stepmother into it. Niekurzak and my father got into the wagon too. All three of them sped to the scene of the tragedy as fast as the horse could run. As soon as they arrived there my father took charge of things. First of all, he saw to it that his mother-in-law got some medical attention. Then, using side boards from the farm wagon, he constructed a primitive coffin to bury the fragmented bodies of the two men. After their simple funeral at the parish cemetery, my father brought his in-laws and sister-in-law to our home in Jeziory.

In spite of the physician's recommendation, my stepmother's mother refused to go to the hospital. Numerous fragments of the two artillery shells had lodged themselves deep in various parts of her body, especially in the areas of her chest and abdomen. An infection developed, and she died. My parents buried her in the Osiek cemetery next to the bodies of her son and son-in-law. My stepmother's father and sister stayed with us until the spring of 1940 and then returned to Osieczko to take care of their farm. Out of the half-burned pieces of wood left from their house and farm buildings, they managed to construct a shanty and lived there for a number of years.

The winter of 1939-40 was rather quiet in our area. The Germans did not disturb us too much. Once in a while a group of SS men came to take Waclaw Podsiadly to serve them as an interpreter. Waclaw, the son of our next door neighbor, was a college student. His studies were interrupted by the war. Since both in high school and in college the German language was a part of his curriculum, Waclaw knew the language fairly well. The SS men needed him for their raids on villages and towns during which they arrested and interrogated people.

At first, Waclaw went with the Nazis on a number of occasions but as soon as he realized that he was cooperating with them in the persecution and even death of his own countrymen, he used to hide each time they were spotted entering our village. Most of the time he hid in the farm buildings. One time I saw him run away from the SS men into the reeds, which grew on the shore of our small lake.

If the Nazi troopers could not get hold of Waclaw, they usually went to the village of Bukowa to pick up another interpreter whose name was David Stawiarz. He spent a part of his life in Germany, where he learned German.

## 3. THE FIRST STAGE OF THE NAZI OCCUPATION

I was told that he was more cooperative with the Nazis than Waclaw. I met him only once later in the war and by that time the young man was already a member of the Polish Home Army.

From time to time, I saw small units of Nazi troopers skiing by our village. They never stopped in the village. At that time no one in Jeziory was involved in underground activities. The Nazis felt quite secure in our rural area.

## *The Winter Story Time*

As a heavy snow covered the earth during the early wintertime, we seldom left the village, with the exception of walking to the church on Sundays. In the evenings our neighbors used to come to our home to visit. I always enjoyed when men gathered together and talked about their experiences in World War I in light of which they attempted to understand the reality of the German occupation of Poland. Since the Nazi government prohibited publication of Polish newspapers and all radio sets were confiscated, such meetings were one of the main ways in which news items were disseminated. During these neighborly meetings, I always put my books away and listened to the men's conversation and stories. I will never forget those wonderful moments, which were both instructive and pleasant.

Some of the men who visited with us did not take part in World War I. They had spent those years in the United States or Canada working in mills, factories, and mines. They would recollect their experiences abroad. My uncle Wladyslaw Mazgaj, in particular, had many interesting and colorful stories to tell about his life in Lackawanna, New York, and his friendships with the blacks he met at work.

Uncle Wladyslaw also told stories about District Judge Basili (Wasyl) Pietrow, who lived with his wife and children in a beautiful palace in Dzieki but worked in the district court house in Sandomierz.

The judge came from a very interesting, fascinating Russian family that had gradually become culturally Polish. The progenitor of the family, General Basili (Wasili Wasilewicz) Pogodin, came to Warsaw, Poland, in 1831, shortly after the Russian army crushed the Polish Revolution of 1830. At first, he was in charge of the supplies for the Russian army and then he supervised the settlements of the claims for damages inflicted on the civilian population by the military activities of the Russian Imperial Army during the revolution. Later on, the emperor appointed him a senator. In all the positions to which he was appointed General Basili Pogodin performed very well.

For the faithful and exemplary services that General Pogodin rendered to the crown, Emperor Nicholas I granted him 125,000 rubles and a large estate

Legendary district judge Basili (Wasyl) Pietrow lived at this castle-palace during pre–World War I times and worked in the district court in Sandomierz. The progenitor of his family was Russian general Basili (Wasili Wasilewicz) Pogodin, who came to Warsaw in 1831. He had this palace constructed as his summer residence some time thereafter. Author's photograph.

consisting of about fifteen thousand acres. Near the ancient village of Wiazownica, General Pogodin built a beautiful summer residence, which the people of the area called a castle. As a practicing Orthodox Christian, the general also was instrumental in building a new Roman Catholic church for the people of the Wiazownica parish. General Pogodin died on January 21, 1863, and his body was buried at the old cemetery in Wiazownica. His daughter, Aleksandra, inherited her father's estate. Her husband, Judge Aleksander Pietrow, was, in his time, the greatest chess player in the world. During the couple's residence in Warsaw, Aleksandra Pietrow was very active in religious, social, educational, and charitable organizations. She identified herself more with Polish people than with her own nationality.

Seven years after he was ennobled by the Russian emperor, Aleksandra's husband, Judge Pietrow, died in 1867. Aleksandra Pogodin Pietrow died in 1883. Their son, District Judge Basili (Wasyl) Pietrow inherited the parents' estate. He married Aleksandra Lisiecka, a daughter of Baron Lisiecki. The couple made their home at the palace in Dzieki. The judge commuted from the ancestral residence to the district court in Sandomierz. He inherited not only the Pogodins' and the Pietrow's wealth, privileges, and honors but also their intelligence. At the same time, he was a very colorful and imaginative person. From time to time his personality exhibited a slight tendency toward eccentricity. However, as it often happens in such cases, the people of Dzieki, Wiazownica, Bukowa, Osiek, and many other villages that encompassed Judge Pietrow's jurisdiction do not remember him as a very intelligent and capable district judge but rather as a very wealthy, colorful, and, at times, eccentric, high-ranking Russian official. In the stories told about him, he was never called Judge Basili Pietrow or Basili Pietrow but rather Bazili. When I listened to my Uncle Wladyslaw's stories about Judge Pietrow, I was convinced that Bazili was his last name.[9]

According to my grandmother Mazgaj, Judge Basili Pietrow was a great lover of hunting. She also told me that even though the judge was the richest man in the whole area and kept a small unit of cavalry at his own expense, he and his family lived in their residence very modestly. She was convinced that Judge Pietrow was a very honest and honorable person.

Uncle Wladyslaw told me that Judge Pietrow was a very generous person whose generosity bordered on prodigiality. Many a time while riding through villages, he gave money to women who wore nice dresses or had beautiful hair. He also spent a great amount of money on some ill-conceived projects. For example, when there was a scarcity of jack rabbits in his forests, he bought thousands of domesticated rabbits and turned them loose with the hope that they would become wild and provide abundant game. A few months later most of the rabbits were lost to dogs, foxes and poachers.

According to Uncle Wladyslaw, Judge Pietrow was a great lover of horses. He considered himself an expert in discovering valuable and promising horses. On a number of occasions, he selected and bought from local farmers young horses and spent a great deal of money on them to be trained for racing. After they were trained, his horses competed in various places, including foreign countries, but they seldom won any prizes. Nevertheless, he tried over and over again.

Uncle Wladyslaw said that one time, as Basili rode a horse, he noticed that a farmer was plowing a field. The horse he was using for the work had an extremely bent back. There was no doubt the line of the animal's back was rather unusual. The farmer considered it a freak of nature but not Judge Pietrow. He judged the horse to be an unusual specimen of strength. Against the best advice of his cavalrymen, he bought the horse and put him on an accelerated diet. Several months later, when the animal put on more weight, Judge Pietrow ordered a few of his cavalrymen to hitch the horse to a wagon loaded with stones to test its strength. The horse failed to pull the wagon.

The judge, convinced that his men did not know how to handle the horse, took the reins and the whip and tried to make the horse pull. The horse refused to do so and, when Basili whipped it again and again, the animal became furious and began kicking at the master. At that point Basili lost his temper, pulled out a revolver, and shot the horse.

As a district judge, Basili adjudicated cases in the court house in Sandomierz. He traveled from Dzieki to Sandomierz by his private coach. According to my uncle's story, when Basili traveled to the court house in Sandomierz or to some other destination and noticed a funeral procession on the road, he ordered his driver to turn around and go back to Dzieki. He did not attempt to go again to the court house on that day.

It appears to me now that since all the stories about Judge Basili Pietrow were told to entertain the audience the tellers exaggerated to a degree. Therefore, they should be taken with a grain of salt. It is a well-known fact that the manners of speech, clothing, and behavior of educated people tend to appear funny and unusual to country people. The country people were drawn to considering the judge's behavior as unusual, funny, and eccentric because he was a high-ranking official of the foreign government of Russia, which, at that time, was the number one enemy of Poland as one of its rulers. It is quite natural for people who are conquered militarily not to accept defeat but to carry on a psychological warfare against the enemy by ridiculing its officials.

Uncle Wladyslaw had a gift for storytelling. Besides Polish and Russian, he spoke some English. In telling stories, he used his knowledge of foreign languages very effectively. This way of storytelling enhanced their authenticity. Most of the other men who spent evenings in our home used foreign languages while talking about their experiences in Russia, the United States of America, or Germany.

In addition to his stories about Judge Pietrow and the ones that reflected his experiences in the United States, Uncle Wladyslaw enjoyed giving summaries of his favorite sermons, which were preached in our church by various priests. In doing this, his oratorical gifts came to the fore. I am sure he would have made a wonderful preacher.

During this first winter of the Nazi occupation, my first cousin, Jozef, his brother, Jan, and I began preparing weapons to use against the enemy. First of all, we discovered several World War I bayonets hidden in the attic of our house. Then we built from scratch a muzzle-loaded shotgun and finally we made a number of daggers. All of these weapons were hidden in our barn. We intended to use them at an opportune moment but when the time came to fight the Nazis, we did not use these antiquated weapons; rather, we secured better ones.

## The Jewish Question

As we were enjoying a rather cozy life in our village during the winter, the Jewish people of Sandomierz, Koprzywnica, Klimontow, and Osiek were given the first taste of the Nazi attitude toward them. They were ordered to wear the Star of David on their arm. Since the winter was very snowy, the Nazis organized Jewish work brigades, which were charged with the removal of snow from streets and highways. As soon as a new snow fell, Jewish brigades, under the watchful eyes of the Nazi troopers, marched with shovels on their arms to remove the snow. It is a known fact that very few Jews were used to physical work. A great majority of Jews in Poland were involved in commerce and other trades, which did not demand strong muscles. Therefore, the work on the roads was extremely taxing to them. The Nazis made fun of Jewish inexperience in physical work and forced the road brigades to sing a song in Polish, which had the following refrain:

> "That Smigly-Rydz
> Taught us nothing about work
> But this Golden Hitler,
> Teachers us how to work."[10]

Many Jewish men froze to death removing snow on highways.

In organizing Jewish work brigades in Sandomierz, the Nazis requested that Father Jan Stepien serve as an intermediary between themselves and the Jewish community. As a professor of biblical studies in the diocesan seminary of Sandomierz, Father Stepien knew the Hebrew language and spoke German. He did all in his power to persuade the Nazis to exclude from the work brigades Jews who were old and disabled. At times, he was successful in his persuasions. The Jews of Sandomierz loved and respected him.

One time, Father Stepien went to a watchmaker in the city who happened to be an elderly Jewish man and asked him to repair his watch. The watchmaker took the watch and asked the priest to pick it up the following day. When the priest came back the next day, the watch was repaired. The priest asked the watchmaker how much he owed him. "One single zloty," was the answer. The priest looked at the Jewish man with disbelief because one zloty represented very little monetary value. The watchmaker noticed his customer's surprise and said, in a way of explanation, something to this effect.

> A long time ago there was a very famous monarch. One of his ministers was a Jew. On the occasion of the king's birthday, he invited his friends to his palace for a banquet. A Jewish minister was one of the invited friends. When the dinner was over, the king went around the tables and offered each guest a cigar. Men lit their cigars and began to smoke but the Jew did not. He held his cigar respectfully in his hand and waited. The king noticed this and asked as to why

he did not smoke the cigar. The minister replied, "This cigar, which came from your majesty, is too valuable for me to smoke. When I return home, I will frame this cigar and inscribe underneath, *This cigar was given to me by His Majesty, the King*. My children and grandchildren will read it with a great respect and admiration." You understand what I am trying to tell you, Father? I will not spend this single zloty I asked of you. I will frame it and write under it that it came from a great priest who knows our sacred language and who saved me and many other Jews from the Nazi forced labor and possible death. My children and grandchildren will view it with a great reverence.

I was told that the Jewish road brigades from the town of Klimontow were sent by their Nazi bosses to remove snow even during snowstorms. As they removed the snow from the road, the wind blew it back — an endless and hopeless work similar to that of the mythical Sisyphus. The Nazis in charge of the Jewish work groups in Klimontow subjected them to every possible humiliation.

Each Thursday there was a very popular farm market in Klimontow to which thousands of farmers came to sell their products and buy goods from the local merchants. Most of the farmers, at that time, used horses and wagons for transportation. At the end of the day when the farmers left town, the town's market and the streets were covered with horse manure. The Nazis used Jewish work crews to remove the manure.

In the Jewish section of Klimontow, the Nazis discovered some outhouses used by the public, which were overflowing with human excrement. Instead of requesting that the town's administration take care of these outhouses, the Nazis forced at gunpoint Jewish road crews and community leaders to clean them up. I was told by one of our neighbors, who was an eyewitness, that the troopers brought most of the leaders of the Jewish community to perform this work by dragging them by their beards. He also told me that those Jews who did not have buckets to carry out the excrement had to use their hats.

In the city of Tarnobrzeg, the Nazis forced Jewish workers to destroy their own cemetery. Its tombstones were used for paving the ground for the farmers' market. From the time the Nazi administration in Poland forced Jews to wear an armband with the Star of David, Jewish peddlers ceased to come to our village. They were afraid to be killed by the police. At the end of April 1940, the leadership of Nazi Germany took initial steps in building the infamous concentration camp in Oswiecim (Auschwitz).

Shortly after Easter 1940, news spread all over the area that a group of robbers broke into our parish church in Sulistawice, desecrated the miraculous image of Our Lady, and took with them votive offerings and precious crowns that adorned the sacred image.

Several months later, the Nazi police tracked down the perpetrators of this crime, surrounded the house in which they were found, and set fire to it. They were all killed. Most of the people in our area considered this to be an act of divine retribution.[11]

## The Arrests in Jeziory

Just before the beginning of the sowing season in the early spring of 1940, a group of policemen, who served the Nazis, invaded our home and arrested my father. Three other men were arrested in our village during the same night. My father and the other men were arrested because they opposed the government-sponsored land consolidation in our village.

When my paternal grandfather, Antoni Aleksander Mazgaj, his brother, Jan Mazgaj, and three others originally bought the land of the manor of Jeziory, they divided it into three sections: the northern fields, the southern fields, and the forest. Then each of these sections was subdivided into five equal parts. The northern fields were much more fertile than the southern ones. In addition to these three basic sections of the land, the original settlers left a small and sandy section for their common use. Later this section, too, was subdivided into individual plots of land. Hence, each farmer in our village had his farm in four different places. The purpose of the land consolidation was to redivide the land in such a way so that each farmer would have all his land in two sections: the fields and the forest.

My father and three other farmers in the village were not opposed to such consolidation. But when they discovered that the land surveyor, who had the authority to determine as to where the fields of each farmer were to be located, was taking bribes from a couple of farmers, they voiced their opposition. When their vocal opposition did not accomplish anything, they removed the surveyor's stakes from their land. Without a warning, the surveyor reported this action to the German authorities. The reaction of the authorities was swift — arrests of the four opponents.

After the arrests, my father and his three fellow farmers were taken by the police to the area's concentration camp in Gerlachow near Sandomierz. It was not a death camp but rather a labor camp in which people were detained for various minor offenses against the Nazi new order.

Since my father's detention lasted about four months, all the work on the farm fell on my shoulders. I was sixteen years old and did not mind the challenge of operating a farm on my own. So I cultivated the fields, sowed barley and oats, spread manure, plowed, and planted potatoes. My mother and younger brothers and sisters began to treat me with a kind of respect I never experienced before. This meant so much to me. It was a token of their gratitude for my challenging work. They all did what they could to help me both at home and in the fields. They were especially helpful in planting potato seeds and during the first haymaking.

On Sundays, I walked to Gerlachow to visit with my father. My stepmother always prepared a food package for him. During my visits, I gave my father a report about my work on the farm and sought his guidance.

My father was released from the concentration camp just in time for the harvest. I will never forget the day he returned home. We all cried out of joy. Soon he wanted to see the fields. He and I walked through the fields of grain and potatoes. Everywhere we went the harvest looked very promising. My father was pleased with my work and he told me so. This made me feel very happy and grown up.

In the summer of 1940, I helped my father, as usual, in the farm work. We harvested rye, wheat, barley, and oats and stored them in our barn. Also, we threshed some rye to make more space in the barn. From time to time when my father did not need my help, I helped our neighbor, Wojciech Podsiadly, who had a much larger farm than ours. Our neighbor's son, Waclaw, and I worked together in the fields and soon became good friends. He was about five years older than I. As I have mentioned, the war interrupted his college studies in Sandomierz and forced him to return to Jeziory. Many times he asked me to take his place in the work on the farm so he could take off for a day or two. In such instances, he remunerated me from his own resources. His father obviously approved of these arrangements. I never asked Waclaw the reason for his absence. I considered it his private affair. However, as time went by, he needed to be away from home more and more.

# 4. The Conspiracy Begins

One day in the summer of 1940, I was picking cherries behind our barn when Waclaw Podsiadly came to see me. At first, I was convinced that he needed me to substitute for him as usual but soon I noticed that he was uptight and very serious. Something of importance was on his mind. After a few minutes of small talk, he asked me whether he could confide in me. When I said yes, he asked me to repeat after him an oath of secrecy. I did so. Then he revealed to me the fact that he was an active member of a secret patriotic organization. All of a sudden his frequent absence from work on his father's farm became clear to me. After describing the main goals of the organization and the scope of his activities, he encouraged me to join. How could I refuse him? I always looked up to him as my senior and a college-educated man and felt privileged to be asked to join the organization. Having given my consent, I took another oath, an oath of allegiance to the secret organization. Waclaw was very happy. He congratulated me and wished me good luck in the new adventure.

## *The Underground Newspaper,* Odwet

Soon after being sworn in, Waclaw assigned me to the task of delivering, once a week, a package of underground newspapers from Jeziory to the village of Wnorow. A boy of my age in Wnorow was my contact and the recipient of the package. From time to time I also delivered packages of secret papers to a man in Wnorow. He must have been in his thirties and lived with his parents. His name was Wladyslaw Zwirek ("Mirecki"). I was told that he taught high school in the north of Poland before the war. He was a soft-spoken man but there was a lot of strength in his voice. Our first contacts were rather brief and limited to general conversations. But as we became more and more acquainted with each other, he began to tell me about his vision of

**We used bicycles to distribute freshly printed issues of the secret newspaper *Odwet* (Revenge). However, from time to time we ran into spring or fall mud. Courtesy of Dr. Piotr Sierant.**

Poland that would emerge from World War II. It was to be Poland for the Poles. Minorities were to be resettled to the countries of their origin. Jews, who had always had a detrimental influence on the nation, should be resettled to some uninhabited island. In presenting his vision of Poland, the name Dmowski came up again and again.[12] Zwirek's vision of a new Poland appealed to me very much. My grade school education was rather nationalistically oriented. Waclaw Podsiadly, while on his summer vacations, indoctrinated me in anti-Semitism and asked me at times to distribute anti-Semitic literature and posters. As time progressed, Zwirek's conversations with me became longer and longer. My part in these conversations was mostly that of a student while he was a lecturer and a teacher. It did not take me long to become his follower. His knowledge of literature, especially political literature, was far greater than any educated person I had met up to that time in my life. Under his influence I began to study Dmowski's writings. What I read I shared with my more intellectually inclined friends. Of course, I did not reveal anything to anybody about my relationship with Wladyslaw Zwirek.

Soon I discovered that Zwirek was a regional head of a nationalist organization that was supported by local landed gentry, priests, and many well-educated people. The underground newspaper, which brought me in contact with him, was one of the peripheral activities of the organization. Its main activity was recruitment, motivation, and training of combat units that were to fight for a nationalistic and Christian Poland. At the time I became an admirer and follower of Zwirek, recruitment and motivation of members were the most important activities of the organization. Military training was to take place in the future. I was ready for action — military action against the Nazis. From time to time, Waclaw Podsiadly let me use his small automatic pistol and his bicycle when I delivered stencils of the underground press to the areas that were infested by Nazi agents. Carrying a pistol gave me a thrilling feeling of importance.

The underground newspaper, which I helped to distribute, was called in Polish *Odwet*, meaning retaliation. It was established by a young lawyer, Wladyslaw Jasinski, and a group of patriotic people who responded to his leadership in opposing the Nazi occupation of Poland. The group developed into a secret organization and assumed the name of the Polish Insurrectionist Organization. Its initial goal was to salvage, preserve, and store weapons and ammunition left on various battlefields near Tarnobrzeg during the German attack on Poland in September 1939. The weapons and ammunition salvaged by the organization were to be used to fight the Germans.

Soon, Jasinski and his followers realized that a successful fight against the Nazi aggressor could not be limited to the accumulation of weapons and ammunition. The people who lived through the tragedy of September needed encouragement and hope in the final victory. Besides physical weapons, there was a need for psychological weapons. Jasinski and his organization responded to this need in the region around the city of Tarnobrzeg by typing British Broadcasting Company radio bulletins and distributing them to the members of the organization and other trustworthy persons. These bulletins always carried some encouraging news.[13]

As the demand for the BBC bulletins increased, Jasinski decided to seize a typewriter and a mimeograph from the city hall of Tarnobrzeg and use them to produce a more detailed edition of the underground press. This new equipment enabled him to increase the circulation and expand the network of distribution to the towns around Tarnobrzeg. Wladyslaw Jasinski's brother, Stanislaw, Karol Wojteczko, and Zdzislaw DeVille helped him in mimeographing the bulletins.

From the Tarnobrzeg area the production and distribution of *Odwet* spread on both sides of the Vistula River. In the summer of 1940, the underground newspaper was produced in the village of Ruszcza, near Sulislawice. Ludwik Gutkowski, an administrator of Ruszcza manor, cooperated in its production and granted the use of the grain warehouse for this purpose. Waclaw Podsiadly, Marcin Kozlowski, the Szczesniak brothers, and a number of others helped in mimeographing and distributing *Odwet*. My work for *Odwet* was limited to carrying typed stencils from one center of production to another and distributing mimeographed copies of the newspaper to the villages of Wnorow, Kolonia Wojcieszyce, Sosniczany, Osala, Trzcianka, and Ruszcza, and the city of Klimontow. In Sosniczany, my contact was a young high school student, Edward Sliwinski; in Klimontow, Kazimierz Rutkowski; in Osala, a young man named Sowa; in Trzcianka, the Wiacek brothers; in Ruszcza, Ludwik Gutkowski; and in Wnorow, Wladyslaw Zwirek and a young man whose father was a forester in the Loniow Forest.

Wladyslaw Jasinski, chief of the organization, came to our home in Jeziory twice. The first time he came was to ask me to deliver some secret papers to a remote place. Since the winter of 1940-41 was approaching and he saw my light coat on me, he said that soon we would be getting from the organization winter shoes and clothes. He was quite concerned for everybody who worked under him. He came to our home for the second time when I failed to return on time from one of my missions. He expressed his anxiety to my stepmother and asked her to notify him if I did not return by the evening. Shortly after he left, I returned home and regretted missing his visit.

My underground activities brought me in contact with a number of people I would have never otherwise met. In addition to Mr. Zwirek of Wnorow, I met Jozef Wiacek and his younger brother, Stanislaw, from Trzcianka, a small village near the Vistula River. They were somehow related to our next door neighbors, the Podsiadly family and the Kasprzycki family in Gaj. The two Wiacek brothers operated a large farm and were involved in patriotic work against the Nazis. I delivered typed stencils to them once a week. They always treated me very nicely and, one time, fixed my bicycle with their farm tools.

My route from Jeziory to Trzcianka led through Osiek. One time, as I rode my bicycle by the edge of the town square, a group of SS men were all over the town. It was a miracle that they did not halt me. I rode through smiling at them. If I had lost my cool, I would have been apprehended or shot. I carried on me a small pistol and stencils of the underground newspaper. Some of the people of Osiek who saw me go through the SS men could not believe their own eyes as was reported to me later. I was the talk of the town on that day. When I returned from Trzcianka, I rode through Osiek very cautiously. The Nazis were gone.

Klimontow was another town where I delivered stencils of *Odwet*. There was a machine shop in the western end of the town where I made my deliveries. The son of the machine shop owner, Kazimierz Rutkowski, was a member of our organization. He worked with his father in the shop day after day so I had no trouble getting in touch with him. Unlike his father, he was very friendly and easygoing. During one of my visits to the shop, he gave me a hand in manufacturing a part for a carbide lamp of my own making.

My most dangerous delivery of the underground press materials was to the village of Sosniczany. A high school student, Edward Sliwinski, was my contact there. He was the son of a farmer and many times I found him working in the barn. Since Sosniczany was near the highway, I had to travel by country roads to avoid the Germans, who used the highway extensively.

My shortest route was to the wooded area behind the village of Kolonia Wojcieszyce, called Piachy. There, under a bush, an artillery casing was placed in the ground at a certain angle into which I dropped secret papers. Sometimes these papers consisted of newspapers, stencils, coded orders, or intelligence data. At times, I removed secret papers from there and delivered

*Top:* Lt. Jozef Wiacek ("Sowa"), who became the second commanding officer of the Odwet-Jedrus Group. Courtesy of Dr. Piotr Sierant. *Bottom:* Marcin Kozlowski ("Lysy") from Sulislawice, an early member of the Odwet-Jedrus Group. Nazis murdered his wife Bromislawa Kozlowski ("Ksiezna") on August 22, 1943. He became my contact in Odwet after the death of Waclaw Podsiadly ("Wacek") at the hands of the Nazis. Courtesy of Dr. Piotr Sierant.

them to my immediate superior, Waclaw Podsiadly. I never knew the other person who had access to our clandestine depository.

When our farm work was over in September 1940, I decided to start a business venture. While visiting my Aunt Machnicki in Polaniec, I learned that farmers west of there grew tobacco. Even though the Nazi government required that they sell all the tobacco they harvested to the cigarette factories, the farmers kept some of their crops for their own use and to sell privately at a higher price.

Since tobacco and cigarettes were very scarce in the stores in our area, I figured that buying tobacco wholesale and selling it in small quantities might be profitable. Therefore, after borrowing some money from my father, I walked to Polaniec, stayed overnight with my relatives there, and the following day walked to the village of the tobacco growers. It seems to me it was the village of Beszowa. Once in the village, I found a farmer who was willing to sell me some of his raw tobacco at a reasonable price per kilogram. After packing my knapsack to the brim, I returned to Polaniec for another night and on the following day walked home. At home, I divided large bundles of tobacco leaves into small portions to be sold, at a certain price, to individual buyers. The buyers, in turn, rolled the tobacco leaves and cut them into thin bits out of which cigarettes were made.

Karolina Stawiarz ("Lalka"), a secretary at the center of the underground newspaper *Odwet* in Wisniowka, died in a hail of bullets at the hands of the Nazis with Jan Sobieraj ("Zdzich II") and Longin Zajaczkowski ("Yolek") on March 17, 1942. Courtesy of Dr. Piotr Sierant.

At first, I began selling my tobacco to men in our village and the neighboring villages. This method of retailing entailed a great deal of walking from home to home and from one village to another. In order to avoid so much walking, I decided to try selling tobacco at the farmer's market in Klimontow, which was held on Tuesdays. My first sale at the farmer's market met with great success. After three or four hours I had sold my whole load. I could not believe that there was such a demand for tobacco. I returned home encouraged by my success and the reasonably good profit I had made.

After several trips to the tobacco grower, I was able to return the money I had borrowed from my father, and I operated my business with my own capital. Soon I discovered a more direct way to travel to the tobacco grower so the round trip took me only two days instead of three. The farmer invited me to stay overnight in his home so I no longer had to go through Polaniec. Instead, I walked through Borzymow, Wilkowa, Sichow, the Rytwiany Forest, Wiazownica, and Bukowa. Since the new route led through wooded areas, it was much safer to travel with the illegal merchandise.

When my business venture proved to be a success, my first cousin, Jan Mazgaj-Marglewski, decided to follow my example. He joined me in my trips to the tobacco growers' village and to Kilmontow to market the tobacco. He found another farmer who supplied him with tobacco but it was of a slightly lower quality than the tobacco I purchased. At the farmers' market he sold smaller bundles of tobacco than mine for a higher price. I was amazed that many times people would rather buy his tobacco than mine. They thought his tobacco leaves were of a finer quality.

(Left to right) Stanislaw Wiacek ("Inspektor"), Kazimierz Rutkowski ("Puszkarz"), and Zygmunt Stylski ("Zygmunt") in Warsaw during their automobile training in March 1942. Courtesy of Dr. Piotr Sierant.

Jan Mazgaj-Marglewski made a number of trips with me to the tobacco growers. I enjoyed his company and felt more secure with him. But from time to time he had something else to do on the days I had to go there; therefore, I walked alone. Then after a time he lost interest in our tobacco enterprise altogether and again, I made the long trips alone. My interest lasted until the fall of 1940 when I became a member of the secret organization that was known in Poland as ZWZ (Confederation for Armed Struggle).

## *The Home Army*

The underground organization, which later became known as the Home Army, was organized and governed by the Polish government-in-exile in London, England. In some areas of Poland under Nazi occupation, the core of the Home Army units were groups of Polish soldiers and officers who at the end of September 1939 did not give up their fight against the enemy. They found hiding places in deep forests from which they conducted guerrilla warfare.[14] In most areas of the country, the Home Army was organized by former

The author stands at the monument that commemorates the patriotic struggle and death of Wladyslaw Jasinski, the founder and the first chief of the underground newspaper *Odwet*, and of the military Jedrus Group. He died from Gestapo bullets on January 9, 1943. Author's photograph.

## 4. The Conspiracy Begins

Polish officers and soldiers. In our area, my cousin, Antoni Mazgaj-Marglewski, was an army officer in charge of the regional Home Army.

When I joined the Home Army, I severed my relationship with the nationalist organization called NSZ (Narodow Sily Zbrojne), the National Armed Forces. Mr. Zwirek of Wnorow, who attempted to indoctrinate me in the basic philosophy of his party, was very unhappy with this development. I am sure he realized that military training, which the Home Army provided for its members, attracted me more than his political indoctrination.

As soon as I became a member of the Home Army unit, I was trained for guerrilla warfare with the limited weapons accessible to it at that time. Our troops met for training in the Bukowa Forest, which was about three miles south of our village. I will never forget our first meeting in the forest, which almost ended tragically. This is what happened. The first point on our agenda at that meeting was instruction in the component parts and usage of hand grenades. My cousin, Antoni Mazgaj-Marglewski, handed a hand grenade to the instructor, who used to be a drill sergeant in the Polish army, and asked him to begin the instruction and then he walked away from the group to talk to another instructor. Obviously, the sergeant took for granted that the hand grenade given to him was a training hand grenade without a real fuse and explosives. That is what he must have used in training recruits during peacetime.

There were about fifteen of us trainees who stood in a circle around our instructor. After explaining various parts of the hand grenade, he removed the fuse from it and let us examine the fuse and the main body of the hand grenade and then he assembled it. Once it was assembled, he held it in his right hand and, holding the trigger down with his left hand's index finger, he began to remove the safety pin. When the pin was removed, he let the trigger spring up on the palm of his hand. A small explosion similar to one that accompanies the striking of a match took place in the fuse and a bit of smoke issued. We looked at our instructor with disbelief and seeing confusion in his face, we ran for cover. The hand grenade fell down on the ground from the instructor's hand and he too took cover. I ran about ten yards away and hit the ground behind a large pine tree. A powerful explosion shook the air. Fortunately, no one was hurt. Only trees were lacerated by the fragments. Our military instruction from that moment on proceeded with utmost caution. We learned quite well not to take anything for granted when dealing with deadly weapons. Stanislaw Cieniek of Antoniowka, a former Polish army corporal, was in charge of our troop. He was a professional soldier who served in the Polish army in the area of Przemysl. After the Germans and Russians occupied Poland, he and his wife came to Antoniowka, where his parents lived. Even though he stuttered, Cieniek had a very outgoing and friendly personality. No wonder then that the Home Army commander of our region entrusted him with the leadership of our troop. He was responsible not only for training us in the military art but also for purchasing arms and ammunition. In those days individuals who managed to keep their weapons hidden were willing, because of patriotism or because they needed money, to give or to sell them to the underground army.

From time to time Cieniek sent reports about the acquisition of weapons to his superiors in the district and requested more and more money for pending purchases. The superiors were impressed by his reports and promoted him to the rank of sergeant. All of us who were members of his troop received promotions too. I was promoted to the rank of corporal. After a few months of training and working under Sergeant Cieniek, we discovered that he liked parties at which both whiskey and women were abundant. Truthfulness was not his favorite virtue. At times he led our troop at night to private homes in search of hidden weapons. If the weapons were found, he confiscated them in the name of the Home Army. Soon he began seizing food, bicycles and other things for his troop from wealthy farmers. We who served under him were sometimes apprehensive about these things but were able to justify them. But as soon as he ordered us to seize people's property, which had no

Zdzislaw DeVille ("Zdzich"), who died with his girlfriend, Wanda Szczesniak, in a hail of gunfire in Sulislawice on Sunday, August 22, 1943. He could have saved himself, but returned to aid Wanda after she was hit. He himself was wounded, and he fought the approaching Nazis to the last bullet. Courtesy of Dr. Piotr Sierant.

immediate military use in fighting the enemy, we began to grumble and resent it.

One night as we raided several homes in a village near Staszow, a man named Wrona from the village of Gieraszowice and I stood guard on the road during the raid. He was twice my age and I trusted his judgment. Therefore, I told him that I did not feel right about the raid and expressed a wish to disassociate myself from the troop. His feelings were similar to mine. He did not like what we were doing. From that moment on I avoided the sergeant and, when it was impossible, I began to fabricate excuses to avoid night excursions with the troop. I hated myself for not discerning our sergeant's loose ethics much sooner. I went to Easter confession and sought guidance from the priest. The confessor confirmed my feelings and advised me to avoid the man as much as possible. I did my best.

Soon, there was an investigation of Sergeant Cieniek by his superiors. It happened in one of the houses in the village of Gieraszowice. The investigation covered two areas. The sergeant's reports about the weapons he purchased and the money he paid for them came under scrutiny. The investigation revealed a very painful truth. The reports were phony. The sergeant spent the money designated for weapons on parties and other things. All he was able to produce at the investigation were a few rusty rifles and a pistol. I do not know where he got the rifles. Most probably, they were seized by force from farmers. I know that the pistol was seized by the sergeant from a

Marcin Kozlowski ("Lysy") (left) and Josef Wiacek ("Sowa") at the graves of comrades-in-arms at the cemetery in Sulislawice. After the founder and first commanding officer Wladyslaw Jasinski ("Jedrus") died from Nazi bullets, Sowa took over the command of the Jedrus Group. Courtesy of Dr. Piotr Sierant.

farmer in the village of Ruszcza named Swierk. By accident, the sergeant almost shot me with this pistol. That is why I remember it so well. Investigators also examined the sergeant's raids on private homes in search of weapons, food, bicycles, and so forth. It was discovered that these raids were not authorized and thus illegal.

As the result of the investigation, the sergeant and all the members of the troop were demoted one rank. In addition to that, he was deprived of command of the troop. After being removed from his position of leadership, Cieniek organized a band, which simply robbed well-to-do people. His companions were corrupt members of various underground organizations.

If I am not mistaken, Cieniek kept in touch with a disreputable nationalist group of NSZ in Pliskowola or Suchowola near Osiek that was composed of former Polish soldiers who were more interested in dishonest enrichment than in fighting the enemy. They became a threat to many wealthy farmers and Jews in the whole area. The Jedrus Group under the leadership of Jozef Wiacek came to the conclusion that eliminating the dishonest band was the only way to stop their criminal activities. Jozef Wiacek, through his emissary, contacted the leader of the group and asked him to mobilize all the members for a joint action on a given night. When the band arrived at the meeting place, the members were disarmed and most of them were shot. To my knowledge only two were spared.

Sergeant Cieniek's post was given to a middle-aged man who led the local Home Army organization wisely and in accordance with the orders of his superiors. Our activities were limited only to practical and theoretical training in the art of guerrilla warfare. From time to time, we took part in destroying Nazi property. For instance, one night we destroyed all the German road signs on a given section of the main highway. These activities were rather rare. Therefore, I spent more time at home than when I served during Sergeant Cieniek's time of leadership. However, I kept myself busy helping my father and preparing my weapons of war.

One of my friends gave me an old Polish rifle and a German automatic pistol. Both of them must have been buried in the ground because their wooden parts were rotten. The steel was relatively well preserved. I decided to rebuild the rifle's stock and the handle for the pistol. I spent long evenings doing this work. At the end, I was proud of my accomplishment. I kept my weapons hidden in a stock of fence posts stored away from our yard. It was the safest place on the farm. When the Nazis were expected in our village, I used to take the weapons and go into the farm fields to hide.

One time a messenger arrived from the village of Bukowa with news that a group of SS men made a number of arrests there and were about to come to Jeziory. As usual, I grabbed the weapons, jumped on my bicycle, and rode away from the village. This time, however, instead of riding into the fields behind our barn, I decided to ride toward the Bukowa Forest. My riding toward the forest necessitated crossing the road that led from the village of Bukowa to Jeziory. Crossing this road on that day almost cost me my life. As I rode across the road, I stood on the bicycle's pedals and looked toward Bukowa. I could not believe my eyes. The SS men were about two hundred yards away from me. Their helmets shone in the bright sun. Their horses, which pulled the wagons, were in a full gallop. They wanted to surprise the people of Jeziory. I bent my body as much as possible and sped up the hill on the dirt road. After riding about three hundred yards, I turned my bicycle into the forest of young pines, which I was well acquainted with. I left the bicycle under a bushy pine tree and, with weapons in my hands, I ran deeper into the forest and then stopped and listened. No one followed me. The SS men rode into the village.

After the Nazis left, I returned home to learn that they intended to capture my first cousin, Antoni Mazgaj-Marglewski, who was an active officer in the Home Army. Fortunately, he was not home that day. The parents of Antoni and his sister were terrorized by the SS men who searched the house and the farm buildings. In asking where Antoni was, they referred to him as a "Polish bandit." This is the way they always called the members of the resistance movement. Following the SS attempt to apprehend him, Antoni seldom visited his parents. From that moment on, he stayed in various safe houses in the area under his command.

## *The Spring of Hope*

The spring of 1941 began hopefully. Somebody coined an encouraging expression: "The sun rises higher and Sikorski comes nearer." General Sikorski was then the prime minister of the Polish government-in-exile in London. He was also the commander in chief of the Polish forces that fought against the Nazis on the side of Britain and France. As the new spring progressed, the farmers of our area repeated the slogan in every political conversation. There was a ray of hope in the midst of the gloomy reality of the Nazi occupation. To hope in a seemingly hopeless situation is a mark of people possessed of a great and invincible spirit.

The hope in the eventual defeat of the Nazi power was supported that spring by the massive movements of German troops toward the new border with the Soviet Union.[15] It did not take the people too long to figure out that the German forces were getting ready to attack the Russians. The people were convinced that the more enemies the Germans made for themselves the better the chance for their defeat. Since both Nazi Germany and Communist

Russia were the mortal enemies of Poland, no one in Poland felt sorry for either of them. There was a possibility that both sides would spend themselves in the war and this would enable Poland and other enslaved countries to be free again.

The German army units, which traveled eastward through our area, followed main highways. For obvious reasons they traveled under the cover of darkness and rested during the days in forests. As a rule, the troops did not disturb the local population in any way. They moved with the traditional Germanic orderliness and with a solicitude for orchards and farm fields.

On June 22, 1941, Nazi Germany attacked her ally, the Soviet Union. The people of our area, after watching the German troops move eastward for several months, were not surprised when they learned about this attack.[16] The German troops kept moving toward Russia but now they did not attempt to conceal their movement. They traveled in trucks singing and rejoicing as if they were going to a great celebration. They bragged to civilians about their destination and about a future victory over communism.

The war with the Soviet Union diminished considerably the labor force in Germany. The Nazis in Poland did everything they could to entice young people to volunteer to work in Germany. Since this enticement did not produce desirable effects, the SS units and even the Wehrmacht's detachments were directed to arrest young people and send them to Germany.[17] In our village of Jeziory only two young ladies, Henryka and Maria Nawrocki, were arrested and sent to Germany. Their arrest, which took place after midnight on November 1, 1942, was a cause of great tragedy.

By this time the Nazi police had not only lists of persons who were fit to be sent to Germany for forced labor but also lists of people who were to be arrested and placed in the death camps. Waclaw Podsiadly, who was my immediate superior in the *Odwet* organization, was convinced that his name appeared on the list of those to be exterminated. Therefore, he no longer slept at home. The night the Nazis came to arrest the Nawrocki sisters, he happened to sleep in their home. When the police pounded on the door of the Nawrocki farmhouse, everybody in the house believed that they were after Waclaw. So when the Nazi policemen entered the house, Waclaw opened fire on them with his small caliber automatic, which jammed after the first shot. They returned fire and wounded him. After receiving a wound, Waclaw ran out of the house but was seized by the policemen. His older brother, Stefan, witnessed this.

When the Nazis left our village, they took with them not only Waclaw and the Nawrocki sisters, but also Mr. and Mrs. Nawrocki and their son, Zygmunt. They imprisoned all of them in the old Sandomierz Castle that had been converted into a prison. Several weeks later Waclaw Podsiadly was taken

## 4. The Conspiracy Begins

The Sandomierz Castle, constructed during the reign of Casimir the Great (1309–1370), was used by the Nazis as a prison in which many Polish patriots were imprisoned and murdered. Waclaw Podsiadly ("Wacek"), who was my supervisor in the underground newspaper *Odwet*, was imprisoned here and executed in the prison yard in the early part of the war. Author's photograph.

outside of the prison and shot.[18] No one knows where his body was buried. The Nawrocki sisters were sent to Germany, their parents and a brother were released and permitted to return home.[19] I will never forget the tragic night in the Nawrocki home. It must have been shortly after midnight when the Nazis surrounded the farm buildings and entered the house. When the shooting began, everybody in the village was awakened. I slept that night on hay in our barn. When my father awakened me, I put on my clothes and shoes in a hurry and was ready for the worst. Soon I learned that the Nazis surrounded only the Nawrocki's farm buildings and they were not seen in the other parts of the village. My cousins and I went toward the lake which was behind our barn and hid there in the bushes. We stayed there until the Nazis left and then walked cautiously toward the east end of the village where the Nawrockis lived. There we found a group of neighbors, including Stefan Podsiadly, who told us the bad news. We were all shocked. After a short while, few men joined our group. We knew them. They were members of the Jedrus Group. One of them, Walenty Ponikowski ("Walek") from Koprzywnica, with a large pistol (broom-handle Mauser) in his hand, encouraged us excitedly to

The old church in Sulislawice. Its major part was constructed of stone in the Romanesque style in the twelfth century. During the early part of World War II, the underground newspaper *Odwet* was printed in the basement of this church. Father Jan Budzinski, pastor of the parish and a great Polish patriot, jeopardized his life in cooperating with the underground. Following the war, the sacristy of the church was converted into a museum of the Odwet-Jedrus Group. Author's photograph.

follow the Nazis and rescue Waclaw. I could not figure how we were to attack the Nazis without weapons. His colleague who came with him had a pistol and I had a rifle and a pistol but of what use were two pistols and a rifle for the whole group of about six or seven of us? After a while he cooled off and began to realize that a rescue was impossible.

After the death of Waclaw Podsiadly, I continued my work for *Odwet*. Marcin Kozlowski ("Lysy") from the village of Sulislawice, became my new superior. He gave me orders and secret papers to deliver to various places and contacts described above.

The news, which reached us at the outset of the German campaign in Russia, was not good at all. The Russian resistance was minimal and many divisions of the Communist Army surrendered to the Nazis. We heard rumors that the Russian people greeted the Germans with bread, salt, and flowers as their liberators from the slavery of communism and invited them to their towns and villages.[20]

# 5. The Deportation of the Klimontow Jews

Klimontow was a typical Polish town in our area. Its population was predominantly Jewish. Businesses and trades were the main source of income of the town's inhabitants. Most of the clothing stores, shoe stores, groceries, bakeries, and jewelry stores were owned by Jews. They also conducted the grain, cattle, and poultry trade. Farmers from the villages around Klimontow seemed to live with local Jews in a wonderful symbiosis. They needed each other economically.

Each time I went to Klimontow I felt that the town was overcrowded. After the Nazis occupied Poland, two hundred foreign Jews arrived in Klimontow.[21] They were mostly from Vienna, Austria. The Nazis expelled them from Vienna and forced them to settle in Klimontow. The town became markedly overcrowded. The Jews from Vienna differed greatly from the local Jews. They were immaculately dressed, spoke German rather than Yiddish, and appeared to be very civilized. The Jewish community of Klimontow did everything possible to help the exiles from Vienna. They shared their homes with them and incorporated them into the life of the community.

As soon as the Viennese Jews came to Klimontow, rumors began to circulate that the Nazis intended to deport all Jews from Klimontow to concentration camps.[22] On hearing these rumors, the Jews were deeply concerned about their future. The Nazis took advantage of the fearful rumors and began demanding, from the Jewish community, ransom in cash, precious metals and precious stones. The Jews of Klimontow were made to understand that after the ransom was paid, they would be exempted from deportation. It seems to me that the Jewish community of Klimontow paid three ransoms to the Nazi authorities. Each ransom bought the Jews some time but did not exempt them from deportation. When the Nazis discovered that the Jews had exhausted all of their resources, they decided to deport them to a death camp. Several weeks before the deportation, I happened to be at the farmers' market in Klimontow. The atmosphere at the market was very tense because of an expected visit to Klimontow by the SS officials from the city of Sandomierz.

Before the officers arrived, a Jewish community delegation waited for them for a long time. The members of the delegation were dressed in their best suits. A number of young Jewish men, who were appointed by the Nazis to keep order in the Jewish community (Jewish policemen), were also a part of the delegation. The policemen were tall and energetic. Many people at the farmers' market, including myself, stood on the southern side of the town square to see the arrival of the Nazis instead of shopping.

When the SS officers arrived in Mercedes-Benz cars, there was an excitement in the delegation. The young, order-keeping Jews (policemen) were the most excited of all. They quickly approached the officers' cars, as they were coming to a stop and attempted to open the doors. The Nazis did not allow them to do so. That made them even more nervous and excited. After the Nazis came out of their vehicles and gathered together, they were ushered toward the delegation. One of the young Jewish policemen stood at attention and seemed to give a report to the highest ranking officer. Then, one of the delegates appeared to give a short speech. To my best recollection there were no handshakes at all. The Germans were crusty and condescending, the Jews accommodating and subservient. It appears to me that the meeting dealt with the final ransom, because soon thereafter the deportation of the Klimontow Jews took place. Again, I was an eyewitness of this terrible and tragic event.

On Thursday, November 29, 1942, the Nazi barbarians deported the Jews of Klimontow. It seems to me that an SS unit from Sandomierz was responsible for the deportation. Early in the morning on that day, my father sent me to Klimontow to buy some hardware items that he needed. On the way to the town, I joined a few boys of my age who also were walking in the same direction. When we passed the village of Wolka Gieraszowska and entered the Klimontow Forest, we were able to hear rifle and submachine gun fire coming from the direction of Klimontow. We wondered what was happening there but kept walking. After a while, we noticed something unusual at that time of the day. People were already returning from the town. They seemed agitated when they talked to a group of men and women who were walking toward Klimontow ahead of us. When we joined the group, we learned that the Nazis had surrounded Klimontow and were rounding up Jews.

Against the advice of the people in the group, the three of us boys decided to approach Klimontow as closely as possible to see for ourselves what was actually happening there. After coming to the northern edge of the forest, we managed to reach the top of the hill overlooking the town in the immediate proximity of the Jewish graveyard. From there we were able to see the southern and eastern part of the town. As I looked to the right and to the left, I noticed about a dozen bodies of Jewish men who attempted to escape from the town. (I did not see women's bodies.) The bodies were in the fields. Most of them were in the fields between the town and the forest through which we walked. Obviously, those killed in these fields were trying to seek safety in the forest. As I looked toward the outskirts of the town, I could see SS men herding groups of people toward the town's market. They were shouting and urging men, women, and children to hurry up. Most of the people, even children, carried bundles of clothing, bags of food, or suitcases.

As we watched the tragedy unfold step by step, my friends and I were determined to see it to the end. Therefore, we remained on the hilltop even though we could not see anything which was taking place at the market. However, we heard rifle and pistol shots in various parts of the town. We knew that people were being killed and we could not do anything about it except to wait to the end of this horrible tragedy. After waiting for about two hours, we noticed the head of the Jewish marching column emerge from the town into the open road, which led toward Sandomierz where there was the closest railroad station. The column grew longer and longer as time passed. On each side of the walking captives' column walked SS men with weapons ready to shoot. Soon after the column left the town, the Nazis began to shoot elderly or physically weak persons who, on account of their health or the bundles they carried, could not walk as fast as was expected of them. The road was marked by human bodies and blood. With every mile of the road, the number of killings increased.

In the column of Jewish captives there was a very popular physician, Dr. Kaplan. He was a fine professional and a humanitarian. He was instrumental in healing many hopeless patients. He treated the rich and the poor equally. However, his heart always went to the poor. He never took money from them. Many times he paid for their medicine. Sometimes before the fatal deportation, a number of his Polish patients approached him and offered him and his family a shelter for the duration of the war.[23] He was very grateful for their generosity but refused to accept it saying, "When the Nazis decide to take my people to the concentration camp, I will go with them because they will need me more than ever." He went with them on that tragic day, offered them his professional skills, and perished with them.

After the SS men and their victims disappeared from our view, we began to descend the hilltop and cautiously approached the town. As we came closer to it, we noticed that some shady characters, both men and women, began taking off shoes and valuables from the bodies of the Jews shot by the Nazis. At the same time we discovered that a group of Polish policemen who served under the Nazi jurisdiction patrolled the streets. There were very few people in town. As we walked down the street toward the market square, a volley of rifle shots sounded behind us. We took cover. After a while the shooting stopped. Then somebody who came from the direction of the shooting told us that the policemen fired as some scavengers began to enter Jewish homes to steal valuables. A few men involved in this managed to escape, but a woman scavenger was shot and killed. Her body was left on the street as a warning to other potential thieves.

Several weeks after the deportation of the Jews of Klimontow, the Nazis held an auction of the property left in the Jewish homes. As an eyewitness of the auction, I know for sure that no one in our village of Jeziory or in the neighboring villages bought anything at that auction. Our good people were saying, "Why should we buy Jewish property from the Nazi criminals? As soon as they liquidate the Jews, they will begin liquidating us."

After witnessing what the Nazis did to the Jewish people in Klimontow and the annihilation of the village of Struzki, I was determined more than ever to learn in the art of war so I could protect myself, my family, and others from extermination by the criminal SS men. I was convinced that if all the young people and middle-aged Jews of Klimontow would have had weapons and some military training, most of them could have saved their own lives and the lives of many others. Passive resistance was useless in dealing with Nazi barbarian criminals. Therefore, toward the end of 1942 and in the beginning of 1943, I faithfully attended all the meetings and activities of our underground military unit called the Loniow Outpost. The Loniow Outpost was in turn a part of the Sandomierz District, which belonged to a larger entity called the Sandomierz Inspectorate.

During our military training against the Nazi government in our area, I met a number of outstanding men. The commanding officer of our outpost was Second Lieutenant Adam Hamerski, whose pseudonym was "Babinicz." Sergeant Stefan Franaszczuk, "Tarzan," was a leader of a section of the outpost that specialized in diverting the enemy in its war effort. After so many years I still remember some of the names of the men with whom I served in the Loniow Outpost, such as Julian Franaszczuk, "Kmicic," who was a younger brother of Stefan Franaszczuk; Jozef Jaworski, "Jawor"; Jan Osemlak, "Straceniec"; two of his older brothers, Stanislaw and Jozef, Kazimierz Stobinski, "Piorun"; and Henry Dudek, "Smigly."

# 6. THE DESTRUCTION OF STRUZKI

In the southern part of the district of Sandomierz and not too far from the town of Polaniec, which was made famous by Kosciuszko's Manifesto (May 7, 1794), lies the small village of Struzki. On its north side it borders with the large and well-established village of Osala, and on its southeast side lies the historical village of Tursko. The village of Struzki belongs to the parish of Niekrasow, which boasts of its ancient and beautiful wooden church.[24]

During World War II, the residents of Struzki were rather poor and earned their livelihood by tilling small and sandy farms and working as loggers in the nearby forest. Their homes and farm buildings were small and covered with straw roofs. The central point of the village was the community building, which housed not only community offices but also a local grade school. The road that linked the village with the outside world ran on its western side from the north to the south. The northern part of the road connected Struzki with Osiek and the southern part with Polaniec.

Shortly before the outbreak of World War II, the government began constructing a highway from Osiek to Polaniec and many residents of Struzki found employment close to home. Even though the highway was not completed before September 1, 1939, the village of Struzki nevertheless gained some recognition in being situated in the middle between these two towns.

The war activities of 1939 did not greatly disturb the life of this peaceful village. The Polish as well as the German armies bypassed the area of Struzki due to the lack of good roads. The people of the village were happy about this, and after three years of Nazi occupation, they hoped and prayed they would remain safe until the end of hostilities. Unfortunately, they underestimated the barbarism of Hitler's evil empire.

For some time already, a unit of the Nazi Gendarmerie, which was stationed in the town of Rytwiany, terrorized the population of the whole area. Under the guise of requisition (foraging) of food, pigs, and poultry, they beat farmers and shot those who attempted to run away from them. They engaged in plain robbery and murder of innocent people.

The underlying purpose of this criminal activity on the part of the Nazi government was to demoralize and inhibit the organization and development of the Polish underground resistance movement. The rationale was conceived in 1942 by Karl Eberhard Schongarth, an SS intelligence officer, who at that time was one of the higher leaders of the SS and Gendarmerie in that part of Poland called by the Germans, the Generalgouvernement. The Nazis were afraid that well-organized and active Polish organizations would slow down their exploitation of Polish agriculture and discourage young people from volunteering to work in agriculture and industry in the Reich. In 1943, Schongarth's idea was developed and perfected by augmentation of so-called small bases (*Stutzpunkte*) in which sizable units of SS and Gendarmerie were stationed. These small bases functioned not only to carry out confiscation of Polish agriculture and supervise the orderly shipment of forced labor from the Generalgouvernement, but also to destroy Polish underground military units and those towns and villages suspected of cooperating with such military units.[25]

The Nazi administrative district of Radom was divided into five areas of security (*Schutzgebiete*), which in turn were subdivided into small bases. Tursko Wielkie County, in which the village of Struzki was located, was situated in the security zone that consisted of two districts: Opatow and Busko (*Schutzgebiet* Opatow-Busko). The small base in Rytwiany was in charge of this security area. The distance between Rytwiany and the village of Struzki was about eight miles The small distance between Rytwiany and Tursko Wielkie County made it easy for the Gendarmerie stationed at the Rytwiany base to raid the villages in the county and terrorize their inhabitants. For example, in March 1943, a group of members of the Gendarmerie from Rytwiany confiscated the cattle in every farm in the county and then sold the cattle to its previous owners for exorbitant prices.

In the first part of May 1943, the Jedrus Group, a very well-organized and well-trained military underground unit, moved into the forest near the village of Struzki. At that time, Lieutenant Jozef Wiacek ("Sowa") was in charge of the group. He was a well-known and highly respected person not only in Tursko Wielkie County but in the whole region as well. His brother Stanislaw Wiacek ("Inspector") was a member of the group and one of its leaders.

In the middle of May 1943, Sowa met with the chief of the Committee for Civil Struggle, Stefan Korbonski, who ordered him to sabotage the work of the Nazis in confiscating farm crops and recruiting forced labor for Germany. During the night of May 22-23, 1943, Sowa divided the Jedrus Group into four units and ordered his men to destroy in 22 counties all the records that the Nazi administration used in exacting from the farmers grain, cattle, milk, pigs, poultry, and other farm products. They also destroyed numerous centers in which the Nazi administration used forced labor to prefabricate some of the farm products. This sabotage took place in the regions of Sandomierz, Opatow, and Stobnica and met with great popular approval. At the same time it stopped, for the time being, the brutal exploitation of the farmers. The Nazi administration became furious and immediately ordered its small bases to intimidate and terrorize the farmers and the entire population of the regions.[26]

In order to curb such criminal behavior, six members of the Jedrus commando unit decided to eliminate without a trace the Nazi "foraging expedition." With this purpose in mind, they hurriedly prepared an ambush on the road that led from Struzki to Rytwiany on Wednesday, June 2, 1943. Under the leadership of Stanislaw Wiacek, the members of the commando unit took up their positions on the edge of the forest with a view of the road. Soon they discovered that their firing positions were not good enough. But they had no time to change; the Germans were coming. They were riding in two farm wagons. Unfortunately, the wagons were at a considerable distance from each other. There was a great need for more men and weapons to take care of both wagons at the same time.

Soon the first wagon with three Germans and a Polish driver (Kalina) arrived on the scene. Inspektor shouted, "Fire!" The machine gun fire killed the driver and the German officer in charge and wounded two German gendarmes. The wounded gendarmes managed to escape into the forest. The horses, frightened by the gunfire, carried the corpses away. In the meantime, the second wagon came to a halt and the Germans jumped down from it, took firing positions, and began to fire. During the exchange of violent gunfire, one German was killed, another (Von Tutze) surrendered, and the third managed to escape. Those who escaped returned to their post in Rytwiany and reported the attack.

The day after the attack, Thursday, June 3, 1943, which was the feast of the Ascension of Our Lord, the people of Struzki were getting up and dressing for early mass when somebody reported the sound of many motor vehicles. Soon 23 black trucks appeared on the road.[27] They carried SS men and Gendarmerie.[28] Besides the SS men and Gendarmerie, who came in military trucks, there were also members of the Wehrmacht who were on furlough in the area of Sandomierz and Hitlerjugend from the German settlements of Luszyca, Mikolajow, Przeczow, Mokoszyn, Gerlachow, and Chwalki. The trucks halted on the road in front of the community building. The Germans came out of the trucks armed with machine guns, submachine guns, rifles, and hand grenades. They also brought with them several smaller-caliber cannons.

As soon as the Germans surrounded the village, they opened fire at about 6:00 A.M. At first there was one pistol or rifle shot. Then they began to fire the small-caliber artillery from the vicinity of the community building.[29] The shells of the artillery started fires in the farmhouses and other farm buildings because they were incendiary shells. When fire began to gut the buildings, the people attempted to save their property as much as they could. The Germans did not allow them to do so and shot them as soon as they came out of their houses. Those who were not shot in front of their houses were forced to go inside to burn alive. Children who ran outside of their homes were caught by the Nazi "supermen" and thrown into the flames.

The SS men did not spare even a woman who had just given birth to a child; they burned both of them. The elderly and sick persons were given the same treatment. In the Nowicki house, there was the body of Ignacy Nowicki in a casket ready to be buried on Friday, June 4. The Nazi barbarians did not respect the sacredness of the human body; they opened the casket, threw the body out, and burned the house with the widow in it. The perverted Hitlerites tortured the children of Wincenty and Wladyslawa Bobek: Natalia, 4; Wieslaw, 3; and Teresa, 6 months. Then they threw them into the flames of their house, where they burned alive together with their parents.

One of the Nazi criminals pierced with his bayonet the six-year-old daughter of Ludwik and Stanislawa Drozdz and threw her into the flames. When she was being consumed by the fire, he also pushed her bewildered parents into the flames. As the Nazi came to the farmhouse of the Strzelecki family, they found fifty-year-old Jan Strzelecki holding in his arms two of his one-year-old grandchildren, Leon Tworek and Anna Wieruszewski. In the house were two of Jan Strzelecki's daughters, Eleonora Tworek, the mother of one of the children, and her sister, Helena Strzelecki. The murderers first wounded Helena, then set fire to the house and threw both sisters into the fire. Then they took Jan Strzelecki away from his burning house and killed him while he was still holding his grandchildren in his arms. After he fell to the ground, the Nazi beasts smashed the heads of the infants with the butts of their rifles.

On the road nearby, the Nazis apprehended twenty-year-old Wladyslawa Kurgan from Luszyca, who was on the way to visit her relatives in Struzki. They tortured her first and then shot her in the chest. On the edge of the forest, the vicious criminals found four women: Waleria Salat, 40; Maria Sztucinska, 47; Helena Sztucinska, 16; and Jozefa Wnuk, 17. They brought them to

# 6. The Destruction of Struzki

Early in the morning on Thursday, June 3, 1943, the Nazi troops arrived in 23 military trucks, surrounded the village of Struzki, and began the demonic work of destruction, which resulted in the killing of 74 men, women, and children and the burning to the ground of their homes and farm buildings. Some of the victims were thrown into the flames. The core of the Nazi force was the 3rd Company of the First Battalion of the Seventeenth Regiment of the SS. Courtesy of Dr. Piotr Sierant.

the front of the community building and killed them in front of about 30 officers.[30]

Some of the younger residents attempted to save themselves by running away, but almost every one of them was killed by the bullets of the Germans, who maintained a cordon around the village. Only a very few persons managed to escape into the forest or into the already tall rye, which grew abundantly in the fields along the edge of the village.

Eight members of the Jedrus Commando Unit, under the leadership of Jozef Wiacek ("Sowa"), attempted to save the village of Struzki from total annihilation. They attacked the Germans with a heavy machine gun, two light machine guns, and rifles, killing about forty of them. Although they had to withdraw because of the overwhelming numerical strength of the enemy and the superiority of the enemy's weapons, their attack nevertheless created considerable disorder in the ranks of the Germans and thus facilitated the escape of some of the villagers. By the time the Jedrus men were forced to withdraw, most of the buildings in the village were in flames.

At the same time, the Nazi arsonists and murderers approached the fence of the Izbinski farm buildings, where an unusual occurrence took place that led to saving the lives of the entire family.

The heroine of the occurrence was seventeen-year-old Maria Izbinski, who was at home at the time. Both of her parents and three of her sisters were also at home. Her fourth sister, nine-year-old Zofia, was able to escape from the village before the Germans surrounded it.

When Maria saw the SS men approaching, she started to look for a hiding place. At first, she ran into the house but there she was overcome with a greater fear since she realized what had happened to the other houses in the village. Then she thought about hiding in the dugout built in the garden for storing potatoes in the winter and milk in the summer. As she was leaving the house, her eyes rested on the picture of Our Lady of Czestochowa that was hanging on the wall, which her mother had bought in Warsaw about one month before this fateful day. The moment Maria's eyes rested on the picture of Our Lady, she was immediately struck with the thought: "I shall take the picture and I shall be saved." She went to the wall and with trembling hands took hold of the picture. Then, holding the picture before her like a shield, she went out to meet the approaching SS men, reciting in a loud voice the words of the popular antiphon: "We fly unto Thy protection oh Holy Mother of God...."

Photograph of the original picture which 17-year-old Maria Izbinski carried in front of her as she went to meet the Nazis who were coming to murder her and her father, mother, and three of her sisters. Another sister, Zofia, escaped before the Nazis surrounded the village. Author's photograph.

When Maria stepped out into the garden, the SS men, with weapons ready to fire, had begun to approach the fences of the farmyard. Some were coming through the gate; others were breaking the fences in order to get close to the farm buildings to set them afire. Those who were entering through the gate were bringing back Maria's father who had attempted to escape on his horse. Kicking him and beating him with the butts of their rifles, the Germans were forcing him back into the house. Among the Germans who were entering the Izbinskis' farmyard was the commanding officer.

After they noticed Maria walking toward them with the picture of Our Lady, the Germans began to shout in Polish: "Throw the picture to the ground!" It appeared to Maria that the murderers were afraid of Our Lady's picture.

When the commanding officer saw Maria with Our Lady's picture and heard the words of her prayer, he stopped, lowered his submachine gun, and stood at attention as if rooted to the spot. When his subordinates wanted to shoot Maria's father, he did not allow it; when they attempted to set fire to the house, he forbade them. He ordered Maria's father and her sisters to climb onto the roofs of the house and the farm buildings to protect them from catching fire from the fragments of burning roofs of the houses and barns in the immediate area. He, himself, went about the farmyard putting out fires

Mr. and Mrs. Izbinski, the parents of the 17-year-old Maria and her sisters. Author's photograph.

in the straw that was lying around. Then he ordered his subordinates to search the Izbinski house and the farm buildings. The SS men made a thorough search but did not find anything incriminating, even though there were some weapons and ammunition hidden in one of the buildings.

When the search was completed, the commanding officer ordered his men to leave the Izbinskis' farmyard and go to the neighboring farmyard, which belonged to the Wnuk family. Being the last to leave, the commanding officer turned to Maria and her family and said: "You were very fortunate." Then he walked out through the gate, closed it, and followed his men who were already engaged in murdering the Wnuks and burning their farm buildings.

Maria went back into the house and put the picture of Our Lady back on the wall. She gathered some flowers in the garden and placed them before the picture. Deep in her heart, she knew that the Mother of Christ had not disregarded her petitions.

By noon, the SS men had completed their bloody work of annihilating Struzki. Upon leaving, they took with them the mayor of the village, Jan Salat, whom they killed later at the prison in Sandomierz. At the scene of the mass murder and destruction there remained the ashes of 60 persons who

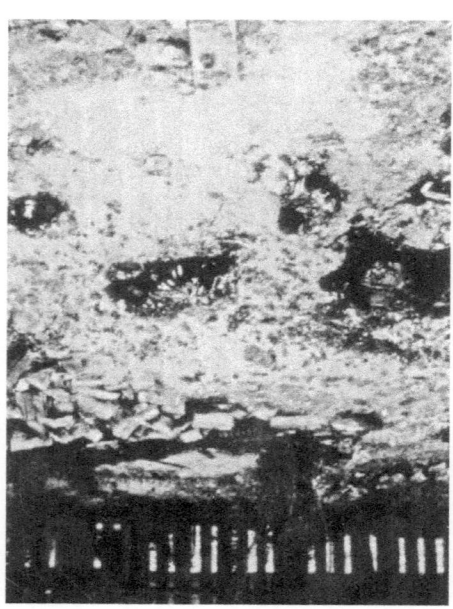

These pictures were taken of what was left of the village of Struzki after the Nazis burned it. Courtesy of Dr. Piotr Sierant.

were burned alive, the bodies of seventeen persons who were shot and killed, and the ashes of most of the houses and farm buildings in the village.[31]

I witnessed the tragedy of Struzki from a distance of about two miles. My friends, with whom I was staying in Niekrasow, and I were awakened by the fire of the small-caliber German cannons and machine guns. We dressed in a hurry and walked through the fields toward the village of Struzki. From a safe distance, I could hear the shouting of the Nazi murderers and the voices of the victims. Our hearts were full of pain for the people of Struzki and frustration because of our impotence to help them in any way. We had only a few small-caliber pistols and a very limited amount of ammunition. After the SS men completed their demonic work and left the village, we hesitated to go there for fear of their unexpected return. We spent most of the day in the fields and returned to Niekrasow for the night.

The following morning, I arrived on the scene of this horrible and inhuman tragedy. Smoke was still coming from the burned ruins and the air was filled with the odor of burned human bodies. I walked from one ruin to another in order to see as much as possible. I saw the scorched bodies of men and women with arms and legs burned away. I saw the bodies of little children shrunken to the size of a man's arm. Among the embers there were bodies of mothers surrounded by the charred bodies of their children. The villagers who succeeded in saving their lives were moving about in a trance among the smoldering ruins. They were alive but they could just as well have been dead, seeing the murdered and burned members of their families. Some of them, in fact, went mad and attempted to throw themselves into the still-burning ruins.

After a few days, there was a mass funeral, which was attended by thousands of people, not only from the parish of Niekrasow but also from other parishes in the area. The local pastor, Father Jan Smigielski, and Father Jan Sroczynski conducted the funeral services. The funeral procession extended about 500 yards in length. It was an overwhelming manifestation of patriotism. The coffins were draped with red and white flags and seventeen huge wreaths made by the girls in the parish were carried in the procession to the cemetery.

When the remains of the murdered victims were lowered into the common grave, there was a deadly silence except for the sound of sobbing throughout the crowd. As soon as the gravediggers began to cover the coffins with the fresh soil, there was much weeping and lamenting, not only for those whose bodies were being buried but also for those who were still alive and yet subject to a similar fate at the hands of Nazi barbarians.

During my summer vacation in 1952, Father Jan Smigielski, who was still a pastor of the parish of Niekrasow, did me a great favor. He helped me

Memorial plaque with the names of the victims murdered by the Nazis in the destruction of Struzki. It was placed on the cemetery monument near the mass grave at the parochial cemetery of Niekrasow. Author's photograph.

find the heroine of this story, Maria Izbinski, who was married to a young man named Wawrzkiewicz. Maria and her husband lived, at that time, in the village of Pliskowola, which was in the parish of Osiek. Father Smigielski and I met Maria in the fields where she was tending her cows. She willingly told us the details of her unusual experiences on that tragic day in Struzki. She spoke slowly to give me a chance to take notes. From time to time she paused momentarily because her emotions and tears prevented her from talking. At times her body trembled and she cried like a child.

She ended the recounting of her experience with these words: "We are all convinced that the intercession of Our Lady of Czestochowa miraculously saved us from death. In gratitude for her intercession and protection, my father promised to build in our village a chapel in honor of the Blessed Mother of Christ so that each year on the anniversary of the burning of Struzki, Mass may be offered for the repose of the souls of the murdered villagers. My father died before he could fulfill his promise. He managed, however, to buy enough stones for the chapel. Now we, his children, have a sacred duty to complete his unfinished work."

Today the village of Struzki has been rebuilt. On the ruins of the burned buildings and on the ground soaked with the blood of innocent victims stand new houses and farm buildings, and fruit trees and fields of wheat are growing. In the walls of many houses one can find some partially burned beams, the remains of the former buildings, reminding the present residents of the tragic events of bygone years.

# 7. Life Is Stronger Than Bullets

My first cousin, Jozef Mazgaj, served in the Polish navy during the Nazi invasion of Poland that began on September 1, 1939. Shortly after the beginning of the war, his ship was damaged by superior firepower from a German ship and Jozef was captured by the enemy and placed in a POW camp. After spending a few days in the camp, he managed to escape and return to his apartment in Rembertow near Warsaw. His wife, Maria, waited for him there. Since the ammunition factory in which he worked as a production supervisor was now in German hands, Jozef decided not to work for the enemy and returned with his wife to his parents home in the village of Jeziory. Because his two brothers and a sister still lived with their parents, the living space at home was rather limited. Therefore after five or six months of living at home, Jozef and Maria rented an apartment from the Stawiarz family in the village of Antoniowka. After living in this apartment for about one year, they found a larger apartment at the Adamczaks' farmhouse in Jeziory. The farmhouse was on the edge of the forest that belonged to my father and to two of his brothers, Wladyslaw and Franciszek Mazgaj. Franciszek was Jozef's father. The proximity of the farmhouse to the forest seemed to provide some security during the Nazi occupation. Therefore the young couple were convinced that they found a very comfortable and safe dwelling where there was a reasonable chance of surviving the war. The Franek Adamczaks' farmyard was surrounded by a six-foot high picket fence. There were two gates made of boards: the main gate opened toward the country road and the other, which was very seldom used, opened toward the path. In the middle of the yard there was a deep well full of good water. Adjacent to the barn was a firewood shed with plenty of wood for cooking and for heating the house in the winter. Mr. Adamczak was a good, well-organized farmer. As were all other farmers' families in the village, the Adamczaks were accustomed to rising early every morning. They had to feed and water their farm animals, groom horses, and milk cows. In addition to that, Mrs. Adamczak had to cook breakfast for her family. Soon, the young couple became accustomed to their landlords' daily routine and they too were getting up early in the morning day after day.

In the beginning of 1943, the Germans suffered many setbacks both in the Soviet Union and in North Africa as well. Therefore, some of the people in Jeziory who read the underground newspaper, *Odwet* (Revenge), and managed to listen to the BBC on the radio began to talk about the end of the war.

Jozef and Maria and other persons who, like them, had left their jobs in various cities and came home due to the war were already discussing their plans to return to city life and work. Jozef and Maria planned to return to Rembertow as soon as the war ended.

I visited Jozef and Maria in their new apartment on a number of occasions and heard them talk about their future. Other relatives and friends visited them as well. Maria always served homemade cookies and tea during such visits. One of their most frequent visitors was Jan Mazgaj-Marglewski, who was also Jozef's first cousin. Jan was a teacher who was employed before the war in the Katowice area school district. He was also a Polish army officer who took an active part in defending Warsaw against the Germans in September 1939. Jan too was eager to return to his professional work in the city of Katowice. Their hope and that of many other people that the war would soon end grew in intensity from day to day, but a terrible tragedy unfolded at the Adamczaks' farmhouse and its yard on February 7, 1943.

On that tragic day both the Adamczaks and the young couple were, as usual, on their feet early in the morning. Mr. Adamczak was working in the farmyard when Jozef went to the shed to bring some firewood so Maria could cook their breakfast. It was still dark and very quiet outside. Shortly after breakfast, somebody knocked on the door of the apartment. Jozef answered the door and was rather surprised to see his first cousin, Jan Mazgaj-Marglewski, so early in the morning. Jan noticed surprise on Jozef's face and apologized for coming at such an unusual time. Jozef's wife also came to the door and both of them invited the guest in. As soon as the men sat at the kitchen table, Maria offered them hot tea and cookies and joined them at the table. In their conversation they recollected the good days before the war and talked about future hopes. The time was spent in a pleasant conversation. It was already ten o'clock when the violent barking of the Adamczaks' dogs interrupted their conversation. Maria went into the hallway to see what was happening outside. She returned soon to the kitchen and whispered, "Germans. They are trying to open the gate." As he approached the door to the hallway,

Jan said, "We must run." Then he went to the hallway and from the hallway into the yard. Since the gate that the Germans were trying to open was on his left side, Jan turned to the right and walked slowly toward the firewood shed. As he entered the shed, he noticed that Franek Adamczak was already there. Jan removed his pistol from under his belt and hid it in the pile of firewood. As soon as he finished hiding the pistol, several Germans entered the shed. They arrested both men and ordered them at gunpoint to walk to the front of the barn. There the Germans forced them to kneel down and raise their hands. After the Nazis searched the men, they began questioning them about their identity.

In the meantime, Jozef opened a window on the eastern side of the apartment, crawled through the opening into the orchard, and began to run toward a deep trench that was on the northern side of the farmhouse. The Germans noticed him and shouted, "Halt! Halt!" Jozef ignored their order and kept running toward the fence that was his last hurdle on the way to the deep trench. The Germans opened fire but missed him. They kept firing at him as he was scaling the fence and missed him again. There was a small field between the fence and the trench. As Jozef was dashing across that field to take cover in the trench, one of the Germans fired his submachine gun at him. At that time Jozef hit the ground and pretended to be dead. The German with the submachine gun was convinced that his bullets hit the mark. He and one of his companions began to approach Jozef very cautiously. They came very close to Jozef and looked him over and one of them said, "*Das ist richtig*" (This is all right). Then they left him on the ground and went to the farmyard to search the premises.

At the time the Germans opened fire at Jozef, Mrs. Adamczak took Maria into the larder and hid her under the floor. Soon thereafter, the Germans entered the house and began to search it from the bottom to the top. As they were approaching the area of the house where the larder was, Maria could hear their shouts and conversations louder and louder. Moments later, the Germans were in the larder. Maria was full of fear and anxiety. Her heart pounded loud, so loud that she was afraid that the Germans could hear it. She was terrified by the stomping sound of the Germans' boots on the floor over her. But fortunately they did not notice the trap door under their feet. Cursing in frustration, the Germans left the larder and closed its door behind them. Maria began to feel safer; however, she would not dare leave her hiding place.

After the Germans completed a meticulous search of the farmhouse, the yard, and the other farm buildings and having interrogated Jan, Franek Adamczak, and his wife, they took Jan under guard to one of their wagons and were getting ready to leave. In the meantime, Jozef, whom the two Germans considered dead and had left on the ground in the little field, was convinced that the time had come for him to complete his final dash for the trench. Obviously, not knowing that the Germans were about to leave, he viewed the area from his limited perspective and seeing no Germans anywhere, he began to run again. Unfortunately, one of the Germans noticed what was happening and fired a rifle shot at him. The bullet hit Jozef in one of his legs but he kept running. The same German fired again and the bullet pierced Jozef's second leg. He could run no more but managed to roll to the bottom of the trench. The German who wounded Jozef in both legs followed him to the trench. The wounded man was motionless in the trench with his face down. This time, the German knew that his victim was still alive; therefore, he aimed his rifle from a considerable distance and fired again. The bullet went between Jozef's legs and ripped his abdominal muscle and peritoneum. The German came close to his victim to examine him. Jozef pretended with sounds and motions of his body that he was expiring. The German was obviously pleased with his marksmanship and left Jozef in the trench to die but his life was stronger than the Nazi bullets. Jozef refused to die. Cold water from the melting snow on the bottom of the trench kept him conscious even though he fainted from time to time. During one of his moments of consciousness, Jozef had a feeling that he was in the trench for a long time and that the Germans must have left. Therefore he decided to crawl out of the trench and seek some help. Jozef was soon on his knees. He held his abdomen with one hand and used his knees and the other hand to crawl out onto the slope of the trench. When he reached the top of the slope and looked toward the Adamczaks' farmhouse, Jozef noticed, to his horror, that the Germans were still on the road near the gate. All of them were in their wagons ready to depart in the direction of the village of Ruszcza but they were still there. What was worse, some of them were looking at him. It was too late for Jozef to roll again to the bottom of the trench. One German came down from his wagon and began to walk toward Jozef. He was the same one who already wounded him three times. As he came close to the wounded man, he reached out with his right hand for his pistol and, with his left hand, he tried to help Jozef stand up. At the same time, the German said, "Do not be afraid, I will help you." As Jozef attempted to stand up, the German aimed his pistol at the back of his victim's head. Before he fired, Jozef began to turn his head in order to see what the German was about to do. When the executioner squeezed the trigger, his victim fell down on the slope of the trench. The killer returned to his wagon and the Germans in both wagons rode toward the village of Ruszcza. They took with them Jan Mazgaj-Marglewski and lodged him in the Sandomierz prison.[32]

When the Germans in their wagons disappeared behind a slight elevation in the terrain, Mrs. Adamczak brought Maria out of her hiding place and explained what happened to her husband. Maria ran out to the trench as fast as she could to see her husband living or dead. As she descended into the wide trench, Jozef was lying motionless in a pool of water and blood. She put her hand on his chest. His heart was still beating. He is alive, she thought. There is still hope. "Perhaps the Merciful Lord, through the intercession of Our Lady of Sulislawice, will save him," whispered Maria, shedding tears and trembling from her terrible experience. Crying, she began to call out, "Please, someone, come and help me! Please help me to carry him out of this trench! He is still alive! Please come!"

Several frightened people who came out of their homes to see what had happened at the Adamczaks' farm responded to Maria's cries for help. They helped her pick Jozef up by his arms and legs and carry him into the apartment. As they were carrying him, his blood was dripping along the way. Inside the apartment, they put him on the bed, gently removed his clothing, and washed away the mud and blood from his body. In order to stop the bleeding, Maria bound his wounds. In the meantime, one of the local farmers hitched his horses to the farm wagon and drove to Sulislawice to bring Father Jan Budzinski so he could give the last rites to Jozef. At the same time, Stefan Padsiadly drove his wagon to Koprzywnica to bring a physician, Dr. George Ejmont.

Jozef felt a little better after his wounds were dressed. The bleeding stopped and he remained conscious so he was able to answer his wife's questions. The people in Jeziory and Antonowka overcame their fear of the Germans and began to come to the Adamczaks' house to see what had happened. The first ones to arrive were Jozef's parents, Franciszek and Julia Mazgaj, and his sister, Maria. His younger brother, Jan, happened to be in Polaniec at that time. His parents notified him of Jozef's fate and he returned home two hours after the shooting. Soon the crowd of people increased considerably. The women who were present made necessary preparations for the coming of the priest with the Holy Viaticum.

Soon, Father Jan Budzinski, pastor of the parish of Sulislawice, arrived in a carriage drawn by hard-driven and exhausted horses. When the people heard the tinkling of a small bell, they fell on their knees. The women, kneeling in two rows at the entrance of the house, began the popular Eucharistic hymn: "At Thy Door I Stand, O Lord."

The priest descended from the carriage and immediately proceeded to the bed of the wounded man. The family left the bedroom. The door was closed. The confession began. After the confession was over, the priest opened the door so that the family and friends could enter the room and be present during the further ceremonies. After a short prayer, the priest took the Sacred

Host, elevated it slightly, and said to the wounded man: "Receive, brother, the Holy Viaticum of the Body of Our Lord Jesus Christ," and placed it on his tongue. Then Father Budzinski administered to Jozef the sacrament of Extreme Unction.

When the pastor concluded his priestly functions, he returned to the people and asked them to pray to God through the intercession of Our Lady of Sulislawice. He assured them that God would hear their prayers. As the priest was returning to the carriage, Jozef's younger brother, Jan, returned from Polaniec and rushed to the wounded man's side. Jozef was conscious and recognized Jan. When Jan asked him, "How are you feeling?" Jozef responded: "The bone in my ankle hurts me so much." Jan checked his brother's ankle and noticed that it was slightly wounded by one of the German bullets.

After Father Budzinski left, everyone was filled with a new spirit. Almost everyone was convinced that Jozef would survive. Maria was especially convinced of this. The words of the priest brought her peace, comfort, and confidence. "The Germans tried to kill him four times and he is still alive; there is something mysterious about it. Perhaps God does will that he should die yet ... we must get him to the hospital as soon as possible," thought Maria.

Soon Stefan Padsiadly brought Dr. George Ejmont from Koprzywnica. The doctor rushed to Jozef's bedroom, where he professionally dressed the wounded man's wounds and examined him. Then he asked Jan to follow him to the farmyard. "Your brother does not need more medical care," he said. "One hour from now he will be unable to speak any more and then the end will come unless there is a miracle through the intercession of Our Lady of Sulislawice." While concluding this statement, Dr. Ejmont pointed with his right hand toward Sulislawice.

The day came on and Jozef was still alive and able to speak. Dr. Ejmont's prognosis did not materialize. Jan spent all night with his brother and Jozef rested as well as possible under the conditions.

When morning came, Maria, Jan, and his friend, Waclaw Kos, decided to take Jozef to the hospital in Tarnobrzeg. Soon the farm wagon was ready. Maria made a comfortable bed for her husband in the back of the wagon. She sat at Jozef's feet and Jan and Waclaw sat in the driver's seat. The road to Tarnobrzeg was difficult and in some places very rough. The horses were driven at a slow pace to reduce Jozef's pain to a minimum. Maria's parched lips whispered sincere prayers asking God that Jozef would arrive at the hospital alive. Her prayers were answered. Jozef was still alive when they arrived in front of the hospital in Tarnobrzeg.

While Maria and Waclaw Kos remained in the wagon, Jan entered the hospital and began to look for the chief surgeon. Soon he found Dr. Ferdynand Rusinowski and asked him to examine Jozef and admit him to the hospital. Dr. Rusinowski decided to examine the patient in the wagon. After he removed the dressing placed on the wounds by Dr. Ejmont, he looked at Maria, Jan, and Waclaw and said, "Why did you bring this corpse to me? Neither I nor anybody else can save his life." What a statement to make in front of a patient! What kind of bedside manner was this for a physician who had taken the Hippocratic Oath to save human lives? Needless to say, all of them were shocked. Nevertheless, Jan began to plead with Dr. Rusinowski. He said, "Sir, my brother is alive and conscious; please admit him to the hospital and operate on him." "I have no place for him in the hospital," replied Dr. Rusinowski with arrogance. "If you cannot admit him to the hospital, won't you dress his wounds, Doctor?" asked Jan. "I have no bandages to dress his wounds!" replied the angry surgeon. "My brother's wounds were dressed when we brought him to you. You took his bandages off during the examination. Please replace them. You must do it; this is your duty!" argued Jan. The surgeon gave in and dressed Jozef's wounds. He then walked away without a word.

In spite of the scandalous behavior of Dr. Rusinowski, which was very painful and discouraging to Maria, Jan, and Waclaw, they did not give up hope of saving Jozef's life. They decided to travel to the Holy Ghost Hospital in Sandomierz. The road from Tarnobrzeg to Sandomierz was rather good and easy to travel so they reached Sandomierz in the afternoon. As soon as they arrived at the hospital, Maria met one of the Sisters of Charity who worked there and asked her whether she could speak to Dr. Aleksander Dobkiewicz. The sister found Dr. Dobkiewicz and brought him to Maria, who explained her husband's condition to the surgeon. Dr. Dobkiewicz ordered them to bring Jozef to the examination room. After examining Jozef, he said to Maria and Jan, "I will do my best which is humanly possible and I will leave the rest to the Almighty God."

Soon Jozef was in the surgery room. Dr. Dobkiewicz, an excellent surgeon who valued human life very highly, began the surgery. First, he sutured the large abdominal wound. Then he treated both wounds on Jozef's legs. Finally, he undertook the most difficult part of the operation; that is, the removal of the pistol bullet that had entered the back of the head below the brain and lodged itself under the left eye. Dr. Dobkiewicz made the incision near Jozef's left eye and removed the bullet. "Thank God!" exclaimed the surgeon. The operation was a success. However, Jozef had to remain in the hospital for a long time.

His wife, happy with the successful outcome of the operation, rented a room in town in order to visit Jozef every day and cater to his needs. A few days after the operation there was a marked improvement in the health of the patient, even though the pistol bullet destroyed Jozef's optic nerve, thus depriving him of sight in the left eye. The gloomy days full of pain and anxiety were replaced with the bright rays of life, which inevitably would still at times be darkened by some stormy clouds.

During his extended hospitalization, Jozef had many visitors, who came to cheer him up and to assure him of their prayers. Maria was by his side day in and day out. His parents and relatives visited him as much as possible. Jan, his brother, visited rather frequently.

After a few weeks of hospitalization, Jozef was recovering well and gaining strength. He was looking forward to the day he would be discharged from the hospital and would be able to return to a normal life.

On March 19, the day the church celebrates the feast of St. Joseph and the day on which Jozef always celebrated his Name's Day, his younger brother, Jan, came to visit him and wish him Happy Name's Day.[33] He spent several hours with Jozef and left the hospital shortly before noon. At about noontime, a few uninvited visitors, members of the Nazi Gendarmerie, entered the hospital room in which Jozef and a number of other patients were. They were looking for a Polish policeman who, while in the service of the Germans, was attacked and wounded by somebody and brought to the hospital for treatment. The wounded policeman happened to be in the room with Jozef.

Jozef recognized one of the uninvited visitors as the killer "Bloody Eddy" and began to pray that the Nazi killer would not recognize him. Soon, the gendarmes found the wounded policeman and interrogated him about the circumstances under which he was attacked and wounded. They wanted to find out who the attacker was.

When they completed the questioning of the wounded policeman and were on their way out, Bloody Eddy seemed to recognize Jozef. As both of the Nazis approached Jozef's bed, he became aware that they were intoxicated. They transfixed Jozef with their drunken eyes, eager to find out who he was. Bloody Eddy appeared to be pensive, trying to recollect something. He peered into the patient's face with a great intensity and seemed to think, "Where have I seen this man before?" He pondered for a while and all of a sudden he recognized Jozef. Extremely surprised, he asked, "Is that you? Are you still alive?" Turning to his companion, he said, "I shot him four times and he is still alive! That's impossible and incredible! Now I'll finish him for sure." As he was saying this, Bloody Eddy began to pull out his pistol. But his companion grabbed the killer's hand and said, "*Du hast viele zeit*" ("You have a lot of time"), pulling him away toward the door.

As soon as the gendarmes left the hospital, there was a great degree of commotion there. The hospital sisters notified Dr. Dobkiewicz about Jozef's predicament and he, in turn, notified the local post of the Home Army. The members of the post came immediately and removed Jozef from the hospital room to a bathroom, helped him to put on his street clothing, and took him to a horse-drawn cab, which waited in front of the hospital. By 2:00 P.M., Jozef had left and no one in the hospital knew where he had gone.

At about 6:00 P.M., Bloody Eddy came to the hospital to kill Jozef but did not find him in his bed. He was extremely disappointed and angry. He asked Dr. Dobkiewicz what had happened to his patient. The surgeon explained that, according to the report he received from the nurses on the floor, Jozef had left the hospital. He added that he, as a physician, treated equally all the patients who came to him and did not inquire into their background. Bloody Eddy accepted the surgeon's explanation as valid and did not cause him any problems.

The members of the Home Army placed Jozef in one of their safe houses and then took him to another place and then still another, where he recuperated under the watchful supervision of a capable physician and his wife. When Jozef was well enough to travel by farm wagon, the post of the Home Army in Sandomierz sent a messenger to Jan so he could come with a farm wagon and take his brother away. On that same day, Jan went to Sandomierz and picked up Jozef and Maria, who were staying with a family in a secluded home. From Sandomierz, the three of them rode the farm wagon through the countryside to the village of Wiazownica, where their aunt Stepien and her family lived. There, Jozef was to spend the time of his convalescence.

The village of Wiazownica was situated in the immediate vicinity of a large forest known to the local population as the Staszow Forest. Although Wiazownica was located away from heavily traveled roads, it was nevertheless necessary to take all precautions so the Nazis would not discover Jozef was there. No strangers were allowed to enter his bedroom. Jozef and Maria had to give up their correspondence with relatives and friends. With the exception of his parents, his brother Jan, and his sister Maria, relatives were discouraged from visiting Jozef. The neighbors who knew about Jozef's presence in the home were warned to be confidential. The aunt's children, Bogdan and Frank, were asked not to talk about Jozef to anybody.

Now Jozef was spending his entire days talking with his wife, his aunt, and his nephews. When Maria was preparing meals and he was alone, Jozef thought about his past life.

He recalled the years of his childhood: he thought about his playmates and the tender love of his mother and grandmother. Then he remembered the years of his boyhood grade school in Sulislawice. There were so many moments of joy and happiness. His friends always respected him because he was a good student and because of his physical strength, which he developed by helping his father in the blacksmith shop.

## 7. Life Is Stronger than Bullets

Then Jozef's thoughts turned to the technical school in Wloclawek. His classmates and his sweethearts — what had happened to them? Were they still alive or dead? Then he began to recollect his experiences in the Polish navy in Pinsk and later in Gdynia. His new friends and his new life in the navy brought him much joy. Everything in his new life had been so interesting. At that time, he was full of energy and life. And today, what? Lying confined to his bed, weak and exhausted. When his service in the navy ended, then came the Military Pyrotechnical School in Warsaw. Constant assignments and studies did not leave much time for other activities. Time was passing very quickly. It was during that busy period of his life that he met Maria. Her charm attracted and delighted him. She was always so good and pleasant.

One day, Jozef's parents arrived for a visit and they brought some stupendous news. They said that Bloody Eddy had been seized and hanged by the partisans. It happened in the village of Konary. Eddy, as usual, was making excursions into the area, always leaving behind him a trail covered with corpses. His last trip into the area ended tragically for him. A group of partisans from the Peasants' Battalion (B. Ch.), learning that Eddy was intending to come to Konary, set up an ambush by the road leading from Kilmontow to Konary. Eddy, riding in the company of other gendarmes, was not even aware of what was happening when all of a sudden he was surrounded by a well-armed group of partisans. There was a short period of shooting, during which his companions were killed.

Eddy himself was taken alive by the partisans. On his person, he had many photographs taken of himself against the background of victims whom he had shot or hanged. He was pleading for his life because he feared death. The partisans interrogated him. He admitted all of his crimes, explained the photographs, and enumerated the various places where he had murdered innocent people.[34] When all possible information was obtained from him, he was ordered to prepare for death. Then the partisans led him to a bent tree on which was hanging a halter. The one who had brought terror to the inhabitants of the entire Sandomierz District now walked to the place of his demise, trembling like a leaf in the wind. After a short pause, the death decree was read and the criminal was executed. The justice of this world was satisfied, and there remained only the satisfaction of divine justice.

The news about the death of Bloody Eddy was received favorably by Jozef because it brought with it the opportunity for his return to his own home and to his beloved Jeziory. Until now, he never thought about returning for fear of again meeting the murderer, who surely would not spare him. Now, however, the situation had changed.

Several weeks later, Jozef returned to his home. He was completely well and able to get down from the wagon all by himself. The Adamczaks welcomed Jozef and Maria with great joy and invited them to continue living in their home. Jozef, however, decided to live elsewhere because he was afraid of encountering the Nazi police again. He and Maria took up their new residence in the village of Ruszcza. Both of them remained there to witness the end of World War II and the total destruction of Hitlerism.

Shortly after the capitulation of Nazi Germany, Jozef and Maria moved to Kowary, a lovely town in the Sudeten Mountains. Jozef worked there in a factory as an inspector of quality production and was very popular with the factory workers. From Kowary, Jozef and Maria went to Blonie, near Warsaw, where Jozef obtained a supervisory position in the ammunition factory. A few years after his retirement, Maria passed away. The lonely life of a widower was not to Josef's liking so he remarried and the newly married couple remained in Blonie near Warsaw. More powerful than Bloody Eddy's bullets, old age overcame Jozef, who died in his early nineties.

# 8. Becoming a Freedom Fighter

In the early part of July 1943, I joined a guerrilla group that was just being formed. My first cousin, Antoni Mazgaj-Marglewski, was the first commander of the group.[35] When he was given another responsibility in the underground organization of the local Home Army district, Sergeant Stefan Franaszczuk became our new commander. As his pseudonym, Franaszczuk assumed, at first, the name "Tarzan" and then "Orlicz." Therefore, in the beginning our group was called the Tarzan Group and, later on, it was referred to as the Orlicz Group. Its official name was the Sandomierz Flying Commando.

The early members of the group included: Jan Osemlak ("Straceniec") from Loniow, Henryk Dudek ("Smigly") from Koprzywnica, Kazimierz Stobinski ("Piorun") from Loniow, and myself, Marian Mazgaj ("Kozak") from Jeziory. During our stay at Faliszowice manor on July 14, 1943, Wlodzimierz Gruszczynski ("Jach") and Arkadiusz Swiercz ("Iskra"), both from Kielce, joined the group.[36]

In order to get weapons for our small group we disarmed eight Polish policemen who served the Nazis and thus gained eight rifles and one pistol.[37] I had my own rifle and a small-caliber pistol, which I had reconditioned before joining the group. At the age of seventeen, I was very proud to be a member of the groups and ready to fight the Nazis who invaded our land.

Our early quarters were in a number of manors, including the small and impoverished Skwirzowa manor near Sulislawice. The owners of the manors accommodated us with exemplary hospitality. By doing so they jeopardized their own lives and the lives of their entire families. At Skwirzowa manor, the owners, Mr. and Mrs. Mieczyslaw and Michalina Kosterski, had very limited material means. Nevertheless, they gave us fine quarters and good meals. The lady of the house, Mrs. Kosterski, was my former grade school teacher in Sulislawice and was very happy to see me as a freedom fighter. She was convinced that her lessons in patriotism were bearing fruit.

During our stay at Skwirzowa manor, we developed a simple daily routine. We got up early in the morning, took care of our bedding, washed, and had breakfast. After breakfast we had classes in topography, leadership, weapons and explosives, guerrilla tactics, and even in etiquette. After lunch we received more instruction. After dinner we had free time to socialize with each other or the host family. We took turns guarding our quarters twenty-four hours a day.

Since most of the gentry in our area were members or sympathizers of the Home Army, various families invited our group to stay in their homes for a week or two at a time. There was always enough space, food, and good company in the manors. We experienced great hospitality and love from the gentry in those days. They always gave us an impression of sympathy and solidarity with us in fighting the Nazis. They felt honored to have us in their homes. We were always invited to their dining rooms for every meal and encouraged to spend evenings in their drawing rooms. Such encounters called for a basic savoir vivre. That is why we had classes in etiquette.

As we soon discovered, the manors of the gentry were the safest places for us to hide. For some reason the Nazis did not expect guerrillas to hide among the gentry. Most of the time, the workers employed by the owners of manors and the people of adjacent villages did not always know who we were because the social life in Polish manors was always active. Relatives and friends frequently came and went. Some stayed for weeks at a time. Also, in many manors, young people gathered together for high school classes conducted by private tutors.

In order to appear as members of the region's gentry, we wore their type of apparel, namely, riding boots, breeches, and sports jackets. Some of us rode horses and visited neighboring manors with our hosts. For the first time in my life, I began to discover the life of the manor. It was a life that had always attracted and interested me in the past. For such a long time, I had wanted to have access to manors as an equal to those who inhabited them. What a pity that it took the Nazi occupation of Poland and my membership in the guerrilla group and, consequently, my putting my life on the line for Poland to open the door of the manor to me. It seems to me that patriotism aroused by the war established a kind of equality among the classes.

After a few months of socializing with the gentry in various manors in our area, we began to feel comfortable both in their drawing rooms and in their dining rooms. In the evenings we sang songs and danced. On a number of occasions some curious ladies asked me in which manor I had grown

## 8. Becoming a Freedom Fighter

Sergeant Stefan Franaszczuk ("Tarzan" vel "Orlicz") in uniform as a cadet and as an army man with his brother Henryk before 1939. Courtesy of Dr. Piotr Franaszczuk.

up. Since we were not permitted to reveal our real names and places of our origin, I had no trouble in declining to answer such questions. I was happy to have an excuse because, to be honest, I was not proud of my village background at that time in my life. One's village background carried with it a certain stigma of inferiority in those days. At the same time, I was not mature enough to appreciate and love my life on the farm, even with all of its shortages and limitations.

From Skwirzowa manor we moved to the neighboring manor of Beszyce Dolne. It was a small estate, perhaps the size of Skwirzowa. We never met the owner of the manor, who, being a Jew, was deprived of his property by the Nazi authorities. The manor was administered by Stanislaw Zarzycki, who lived in the manor house with his wife, Zofia, a daughter, Barbara, a son, Stanislaw, and a cousin, Domicela. The administrator and his family treated us very well. I will never forget the well-prepared dinners and long-lasting conversations we enjoyed at the table.

The administrator's son and daughter attended private classes at the neighboring Niedzwice manor. They introduced us to the young ladies from that manor. Their father, a Polish officer, was in a POW camp in Germany. In his absence, his wife managed the manor. Once or twice we were invited by the lady of the house for dinner and socializing. The young ladies played the piano, which provided a background for our entertainment.

The young lady from Beszyce Dolne manor, Barbara Zarzycka, was very refined and lovely. No wonder that a number of the younger members of our group competed for her attention. One of our men who grew up in a city was, in the estimation of our chief, the most prominent in the competition. I counted myself out because I was the youngest and also very shy in the presence of young ladies. However, one time when Barbara wanted to visit her girlfriends at Niedzwice manor, she requested from her parents and the chief of our group that I accompany her in her walk and visit. It was an extremely pleasant excursion. We enjoyed each other's company very much. For the first time, we were able to talk to each other away from the presence of others. She was very open in expressing her feelings about her parents, the classes she was taking, and her appreciation for my company. In this private conversation, I discovered how more mature she was than she appeared to me until then. I liked her youthful openness and honesty. However, I was too timid and shy to be as open and honest as she was in expressing my feelings. As we were returning home from the visit, I discovered that she was attracted to me from the very beginning of our stay at the manor, and I grew more and more attracted to her as time went by.

After returning to the manor, I was congratulated by the chief, because of my friendship with the beautiful young lady, to the consternation of my older friend who was supposed to be the "first runner." The members of the group never stopped teasing him about losing his girlfriend.

A few days after our walk to and from Niedzwice, the young lady asked me to go for a walk with her into the fields beyond the village of Beszyce Gorne. A heavy snow had covered the ground the night before. The sun was shining during the day and the deep snow melted on the surface and then froze. After obtaining proper permission, we took a walk on the top of the snow for most of the afternoon. We had so much fun walking on the surface of the snow and trying to avoid breaking it. At times, it broke under her and then under me. While helping one another to get on the surface again, both

## 8. Becoming a Freedom Fighter 85

Sergeant Stefan Franaszczuk ("Tarzan" vel "Orlicz"), chief of the Sandomierz Flying Commando Unit, and his wife, Wladyslawa Stawiarz Franaszczuk, who was an active member of Polish underground. Her sister-in-law was Karolina Lukasiewicz Stawiarz ("Lalka"), who died from the Nazi bullets on March 17, 1942. Mrs. Franaszczuk's photograph is taken from the World War II ID document issued by the Nazi regime in 1943. Courtesy of Dr. Piotr Franaszczuk.

of us found ourselves in the snow up to our knees. Our laughter vibrated through the pure winter air and the whiteness of the snow gave a serenity to the pure and innocent youthful experience of our mutual attraction. No words can fully describe what we experienced that afternoon. It was an innocent, pure, beautiful, and deep experience, which remains in my mind even after the passing of many decades.

During our stay at Beszyce Dolne manor, a number of new men joined our group. They included Stanislaw Podolecki ("Rys") from Sandomierz, Leon Siatrak ("Orzel"), Corporal Zarzycki ("Czarny") from Sandomierz, Janusz Szczerbatko ("Zygfrid") from Sandomierz, Stanislaw Duma ("Topola") from Sandomierz, Kazimierz Krobath ("Niedzwiedz") from Sandomierz, Feliks Wryk from Sandomierz, Romuald Nowakowski ("Msciciel"), Henryk Zarzycki ("Grab"), Tadeusz Zulinski ("Goral"), and Jerzy Staszewski ("Murzyn") from Sulislawice. Then, in Janowice a group of four young men joined us.

They were Boleslaw Szelong ("Blyskawica") from Wielogora, Jan Szpakiewicz ("Pikolo"), Edward Stawiarz ("Sep") from Komorna, and "Zbik" from Wilczyce.

From Beszyce Dolne we moved to Janowice and then to Skotniki manor, where we began intensive military training. The curriculum was designed to prepare us, as younger officers, to be capable of leading units in battle. In addition to our chief, "Orlicz" (Stefan Franaszczuk), who was our only instructor thus far, a number of new instructors appeared on the scene. The most prominent of them was Captain Tadeusz Strus ("Kaktus") whom we admired from the first encounter and called him *Dziadek* (grandfather) among ourselves. He was about thirty-five years old at that time and was a fine instructor and a great leader. We did not know his real name or his background.[38]

Another officer who instructed us was Lieutenant Witold Jozefowski ("Mis"). He must have been about twenty-five years old at that time and appeared to have a very close relationship with the family who owned the manor of Skotniki. At this point in the history of our group, he was appointed the commanding officer of the group and "Orlicz" became his assistant. He was a very good instructor, always kind and polite, sensitive for our needs. He recognized my knowledge of guns and whenever he was away from our group, he entrusted me with his two excellent pistols: a German Lugar and a Polish made Vis. Neither Captain Kaktus nor Lieutenant Mis stayed with us all the time. They came periodically to instruct us, lead us in our attacks on the Nazis, and spend some leisure time with us.

Day after day we studied various topics of military science. In our studies there was a great emphasis on guerrilla warfare. In the evenings we trained in open terrain. After the completion of our training, we were subjected to very rigorous examinations, which consisted of two parts: theoretical and practical. The first part of the examination took place at Skotniki manor and the second part in the fields nearby. I do not remember the questions I had been asked in my theoretical examination but I do remember very well the practical part of my examination. I was ordered to lead our group at night to a given village and to disarm an imaginary unit of the enemy's soldiers stationed there. I performed well both in my theoretical and in my practical exams. My instructors and fellow students were proud of me and congratulated me.

After the exams, all of us who passed were promoted to the rank of younger officer. Our promotion was crowned with a special dinner party. Even though most of us were very young, our instructors began to treat us as their younger colleagues, rather than as subordinates. This was quite a gratifying experience.

It seems to me that after leaving the manor of Skotniki, we moved to

## 8. Becoming a Freedom Fighter

Ostroleka manor and then to Zajeziorze manor. In spite of the presence of SS men unites in Sandomierz and nearby Samborzec, we felt secure in this area. At Ostroleka manor, Marian Mieczyslaw Gaj ("Cap") joined our group. Cap brought with him a fine German rifle and an account of his dramatic experiences with the Nazi police and of disarming one of them. I will describe these experiences in one of the following chapters.

From Zajeziorze we moved to a very secluded area of Wiazownica. We did not stay in the village proper but in Mrs. Bak's farmhouse, which was located on the verge of the forest. Mrs. Bak and her family treated us very well and soon we became an extension of her family. The forest provided an excellent place for our training. We spent many exciting weeks in this area. During that time I had a heartbreaking experience.

Since my home was not too far from where we were stationed, I obtained permission to visit my parents for a few hours. I used a bicycle as a means of transportation. It took me about one hour to reach my home. My parents and my brothers and sisters were happy to see me after many months of absence. Our watchdog received me with great joy. He was jumping around me and licking my hands and face. We had raised him from a little puppy and had given him a Latin name, Ars, which means "art." He was the finest watchdog we ever had.

I stayed with my family for dinner and then extended my visit until the sunset. When I left home it was already dark. Upon arriving at our secret quarters, I discovered that Ars had followed me all the way. I reported this to the chief and asked him whether I should take the dog home right away or wait for a day or two. Since it was a dark night, he advised me to wait for a few days before taking Ars home. The following day I was assigned for a few hours to watch a section of the road that linked Osiek with the Village of Wiazownica, and Ars went with me. Most of the time, he stayed near me but from time to time he investigated the immediate wooded area. When one of my friends took over the guard duty, I returned to quarters and Ars followed me. When I entered the farmhouse to which I was assigned, Ars remained outside. After a few hours, it was "Piorun's" turn to be on guard duty. He asked me for permission to take Ars with him. I consented and the dog followed Piorun.

When Piorun returned from guard duty, Ars did not return with him. I asked Piorun whether the dog remained in the forest with the man who followed Piorun on guard duty but he gave me a very ambiguous answer. His answer made me wonder what actually happened to Ars. I kept asking probing questions and Piorun attempted to avoid answering them directly. I became angry and challenged him to tell me the truth as a good soldier should. With a cynical smile, he kept avoiding my questions. At that point I decided to ask the chief to intervene but, at the last moment, I changed my mind and waited for the guard who followed Piorun to return to quarters. When he returned I asked him whether he knew anything about the disappearance of Ars. Before he answered my question, he looked at Piorun and exchanged a small smile with him. I believed, then, that both of them were covering up something. His shifty answer confirmed my belief and I went to see the chief. The chief listened to my complaint and then asked Piorun and the guard who followed him on guard duty to join us. Soon the truth came to the fore. Piorun killed Ars with a rifle shot in the presence of the other guard. In order to lessen his responsibility, he claimed that the shot which killed Ars was fired accidentally. Piorun claimed that he was practicing aiming his rifle using Ars as a target. He alleged that he forgot that the rifle was loaded when he pulled the trigger. The chief did not accept this explanation and, as a penalty, assigned him to an extra guard duty at night for a week. I buried Ars and mourned his death for a long time but hesitated to communicate the bad news to my family.

In the early summer of 1943, we left the village of Wiazownica and moved to the small and hospitable Bystrojowice manor, which belonged to Mr. and Mrs. Bielawski. The owners of the manor were not wealthy but very generous. They shared the manor house and food with us. The Bielawskis had two adult daughters, who helped their parents to entertain us. Several of my older friends fell in love with the beautiful young ladies. "Blyskawica" fell in love with the younger daughter. He was tall and handsome and many young ladies were attracted to him. This time, again, a very beautiful girl was attracted to him. Cadet Stanislaw Podolski ("Rys") fell in love with the older daughter, who was also very beautiful. Due to our group's moving from place to place and the uncertainty of our lives, the romance of both of the couples did not last beyond a few months.

After our stay at Bystrojowice manor and several other places, we moved on to Byszow manor, which belonged to Mr. and Mrs. Ropelewski. It was an old manor with a very beautiful park. Four members of the family resided in the manor: Mr. and Mrs. Ropelewski, their young daughter, Wanda Ropelewski, and an adult brother of the lady of the house, Andrzej Lukasiewicz, who looked to me like a cavalry officer. All of them were very friendly and hospitable.

I will never forget our first dinner at Byszow manor. When we arrived it must have been about 8:00 P.M. The family must have had their dinner earlier. The dining room was very spacious and it had a long table. There was enough table space for all of us. The maids served the dinner but the lady of the house and her daughter supervised and helped them. It was a wonderful dinner with all the trimmings. Toward the end of the dinner, the lady of the

## 8. Becoming a Freedom Fighter

house and the beautiful daughter stood near the chief's chair and talked to him in subdued voices. From time to time, they looked at this or that end of the table. After the ladies left the dining room, the chief looked toward me and said, "Kozak, our hostesses like you." Everybody at the table looked at me. I felt uneasy. After we got up from the table, the chief elaborated on his remark and told me that the young lady liked me and expressed an interest in getting acquainted with me.

From the dining room, we all moved to the drawing room. There the family entertained us for a while and the daughter played piano. As soon as the music was over, the young lady and I were introduced to each other.

The following day Wanda and I made plans for our first date. We were to go to the park after dinner and take a long walk. Unfortunately, the schedule of our guard duty changed and I had to be on duty after dinner. We were both disappointed and postponed our date until the next evening. I looked forward to our date and felt that the day was extremely long and that evening would never come. But it finally came and after dinner we had our date.

After we left the manor house, we walked to the park. It was beautiful there. Our walk was refreshing. I felt great in her company. I realized she was wealthy and educated but at the same time Wanda had the honesty and innocence of a child. She talked about herself very openly and made me feel at ease. I admired her openness and honesty and wished to be like her. For some reason, I tended to conceal my real feelings and thoughts. We grew up and lived in different economic, social, and educational environments. Perhaps this made a great difference in the way we related to others.

In speaking about each other's background, I did not reveal to her the fact that I had never attended high school and grew up as a farmer's son in a small village. The pseudonym which I had to assume was a very convenient veil for my background.

During our walk along the paths of the park, we sat on one of the benches placed near the paths and talked until we felt like walking again. After sunset, even though it was getting dark, we kept walking close to the manor house. I did not want the evening to end. It was too beautiful to come to a close. We returned to the manor shortly after sunset. We did not want to jeopardize Wanda's parents' permission for our future dates. Her parents were happy about our timely return and seemed delighted on account of our successful date. They were very loving and gentle parents.

After we left Byszow manor, I never lost an opportunity to visit the family and have a chance to spend some precious moments with beautiful Wanda. Since our group stayed in the area for several years, there were many opportunities to visit the charming manor and the hospitable Ropelwski family.

From Byszow we moved to a number of farmhouses in the village of

Postronna. It happened that I was assigned to stay in a farmhouse that belonged to the parents of Marcin Mazgaj's wife, the Zwierzyks. Marcin was my first cousin. The families with whom we stayed were very supportive of the Home Army and did everything possible to make us comfortable.

When we left Postronna, after several weeks' stay there, we went back to the Bak farmhouse near Wiazownica. It was like a homecoming. We were familiar with the area and its people who provided quarters for us. There was a great deal of sympathy, support, and love for us on the part of our hosts. On our part we felt a growing appreciation for their sacrifices for the cause of free Poland. Our hosts were becoming more and more our extended family.

It seems to me that when we returned to the Wiazownica area it must have been in the fall of 1943. During this extended stay there, we secured some shotguns, ammunition, and German foresters' uniforms. This is how it happened. Our chief, Orlicz, received a report that the German authorities supplied the Center of Forest District Administration with shotguns, which were to be distributed to a number of foresters in the district. The center was

This picture was taken with Mr. and Mrs. Jan Osemlak on September 26, 1999, in Loniow, Poland, Jan's home town. Jan Osemlak ("Straceniec") and I did considerable mischief to the Nazis in the area of Sandomierz; we were lucky to survive the war. Author's photograph.

located in the castle that was formally owned by the Pogodins and the Pietrovs. The chief forester and his family also lived there. Under the leadership of Orlicz, we surrounded the castle after sunset and began knocking on a heavy oak door. When the chief forester came to the door to ask who we were, Orlicz explained to him that we were an armed group of the Home Army. After the forester asked about the reason for our visit to the castle, Orlicz replied that he would explain the reason not through the door but in a face-to-face conversation. After a short hesitation, the chief forester opened the door and let us in. Once inside of the castle, our chief assured the chief forester and his nervous wife that we did not intend to harm them. All we wanted were shotguns, ammunition, and uniforms. Without any delay they led us to the storeroom. There we found about ten shotguns, some ammunition, and a few dark green uniforms and belts. We took all these things. Our chief gave the chief forester a written receipt in which he itemized the things seized. It was meant to protect the chief forester from the Nazi authorities investigating such seizures.

After returning to our quarters, we discovered that one of the shotguns we acquired was one of the finest weapons made in Belgium.[39] Orlicz claimed use of it.

Several weeks after our seizure of the Nazi goods at the castle of Dzieki, we seized some shotguns from a number of foresters. All the shotguns were old but in excellent condition. One of these shotguns was assigned for my use. It was a beautiful weapon. Both the steelwork and woodwork were richly decorated with very fine engraving. I speculated that the Nazi authorities confiscated this shotgun from one of the local manors.

During our stay in the farmhouse near Wiazownica this time, Orlicz needed a motorcycle to travel fast from place to place in a case of necessity. He knew that a certain Nazi road official from Sandomierz used a motorcycle to inspect a section of the state highway, near Gaj, which was being resurfaced. Therefore, he selected "Straceniec" and myself and ordered us to confiscate the motorcycle for the use of our group.

Straceniec and I dressed in foresters' uniforms and rode our bicycles from Wiazownica to Gaj. After hiding the bicycles in the forest, we walked through the woods to the highway. The Loniow Forest stood on each side of the highway. I knew the forest well because our farm on which I was born bordered the forest. After a while we located the part of the highway that was being repaired. Men worked on one side of the highway while the other side was in use. The traffic was rather light. From behind dense trees, we observed the workers without being noticed. The time of day made us believe that the highway official was about to arrive. As the time passed, our excitement increased. After about an hour of waiting, we heard the sound of a motorcycle coming from the direction of Zawidza. We got ready for action. Since Straceniec knew the highway official personally, he was to remain on the edge of the forest while I was to seize the official and his motorcycle. We both were armed with semi-automatic pistols and hand grenades. The sound of the motorcycle was louder and louder, and finally we noticed the rider as he was slowing down to stop where the road crew worked. When the motorcycle came to a stop and the official began talking to the crew supervisor, pistol in hand, I started to run toward the highway. Unfortunately, before I emerged from the forest, the official resumed his ride toward the village of Gaj. I was terribly disappointed. Luckily, neither the motorcycle rider nor any of the workers noticed me as I ran through the trees.

After I shared my disappointment with Straceniec, he advised me to take my position as before and wait for the highway official's return to the work crew. It was sound advice, and I followed it. After a while a passenger car came from the direction of Zawidza and stopped near where the road crew worked. Two men came out of the car and began inspecting the work and talking to the supervisor. I suspected they carried side weapons on them. After consulting with Straceniec, I decided to surprise them. Since they walked somewhat away from their vehicle, I approached them in a normal pace. My forester's uniform did not arouse any suspicion. When I came very close to the men, I produced my pistol and asked them to raise their hands. They followed my order without hesitation. They were both Germans and spoke limited Polish. After searching them and their car, I found no weapons. I was friendly in my treatment of them and shook hands with them and explained to them as much as I could that I was a member of the Polish Home Army and had no intention of harming them or taking away their car. They smiled and thanked me for my kindness. Both of them were older men and appeared very cultured. At the end of our encounter, I asked them to proceed on their way toward Gaj and Osiek without mentioning the incident to anybody until their return to Sandomierz. They promised to honor my request. We shook hands again and they drove away. Needless to say, I did not trust their promise. Before returning to the woods, I stood on the side of the road and watched their car disappear on the curve of the highway. Then I said a few words to the road crew and started to walk toward a high bank on the western side of the highway when all of a sudden a military or a police Mercedes-Benz appeared on the highway. There were at least four uniformed Nazi officers in it. They all looked at me in surprise. I held a pistol in my hand—barrel down—and had a couple of hand grenades hanging at my belt. As the car was passing me, the Nazis fixed their eyes on me and I looked straight into their eyes smiling. They did not know what to make of me. Only after the car passed me and kept climbing the hill, I accelerated my walk toward the woods. Straceniec saw what had happened and could not believe his eyes. He was afraid that the Nazis might open up with submachine gun fire at me.

Before I had a chance to cool off after the close encounter with the Nazis, we heard the sound of a motorcycle coming from the direction of Gaj. It was the highway official we had waited for since early in the morning. He stopped again to see the work of the crew but remained seated on the motorcycle, his legs on each of its sides and the motor running. Obviously, he asked the workers to come close to him for some instructions because they stood in a semicircle in front of him. My pistol in hand, I began to run toward the group. The official's back was toward me so he could not see me. As I approached within one hundred feet of him, several workers, seeing my pistol ready to fire at the official, took to their feet. They were closest to him and were afraid that in case he decided to defend himself, a bullet coming from my pistol might miss him and hit one of them. The highway official was so engaged in giving instructions to the crew that he did not pay much attention to the two workers who were all of a sudden running away.

After I came within fifteen feet of the official and his back was still turned toward me, I shouted, "Hey!" After finishing his sentence, he began to turn slowly toward me, unhappy that somebody had disturbed him in his work. As soon as his eyes caught the sight of my pistol and he heard my command "Hands up!" his face and the rest of his body became electrified. He raised his hands very fast and the expression on his face changed rapidly from one of self-assurance to fright. With his hands up, I searched him for a weapon. He had none. When I asked him where his pistol was, he replied that he had left it at home. He was a Polish German who spoke very good Polish. Without any explanation, I ordered him to turn the motor off and steer his motorcycle into a forest road while several road workers pushed it. Once we were within a safe distance from the highway, I dismissed the workers, asking them not to talk to anybody about what they saw. After the workers left, I asked the official to sit down on a log. I also sat down while Straceniec walked noisily nearby to give the official the impression that I was not alone. With the pistol in my hand, I lectured him for a while. I told him that I knew about his cruel treatment of road crews and beating of workers. He began to sweat and fear for his life. To relieve him of further fear, I assured him that his life was not in danger. I asked him to start treating his workers well and bring me his pistol. I pointed out a place where he was to drop his pistol. I told him also that his official motorcycle was being confiscated for the Polish army. He promised to bring me his gun, and he did not object to the loss of the motorcycle. He began to engage in conversation with me, relaxed, and even smiled. He told me about his wife and children and expressed a wish for an end to the war. At one point in our conversation, he told me that I looked

All these men in uniform (with the exception of the two young soldiers) are my comrades-in-arms. These pictures were taken during the blessing and dedication of the commemorative plaque in Loniow on September 26, 1999. Author's photograph.

## 8. BECOMING A FREEDOM FIGHTER

Between her daughter-in-law and her son is Mrs. Michalina Kosterski, who became the spiritual mother of the Sandomierz Flying Commando Unit. The photograph was taken during the unveiling and dedication of the plaque commemorating the creation of the unit at St. Nicolaus Church in Loniow on September 26, 1999. The Skwirzowa Manor House, which belonged to her and her husband Mieczyslaw Kosterski, opened its hospitable doors to the newly formed unit for long periods of time. Author's photograph.

familiar to him. Toward the end of our encounter, I asked him to delay his report to the Nazi authorities for a few hours. When we parted, I apologized for causing him an inconvenience in having to walk to the telephone in Zawidza. He was rather a big man and walking was not easy for him.

Once the highway official walked away, Straceniec came to give me a hand in taking the motorcycle to a hiding place in the forest. We took it about a half-mile away from the highway and hid it in very dense bushes. It was a perfect hiding place. Even though we did not seize any firearms, we were delighted with the acquisition of a fine German motorcycle.

After several days, the chief, a motorcycle expert, Straceniec, and I transported the motorcycle in a farm wagon from the forest near Gaj to our quarters. Straceniec and I walked to the place where the highway official was to drop off his gun. We found nothing. A week later I returned to the same place and there was no gun. Soon we learned that the official was transferred to another post in a different part of the country. He refused to work on the road, which reminded him of a very fearful experience he had encoutered in the Loniow Forest.

From the postmaster in Loniow, we learned that the Nazi officers whom I encountered on the highway used his office telephone to report to their headquarters in Sandomierz that they had met a Polish partisan near the village of Gaj. In their report they expressed a belief that he must have been one of many in the forest because he was not afraid of them. Shortly after this report, a group of SS men was dispatched to scout the forest. They must not have scouted the forest too far from the highway. Otherwise, they would have found the motorcycle.

Chief Orlicz learned how to operate the motorcycle and used it from time to time in his work, especially in emergency cases. Later, during the war, when the Nazis became more aware of our activities, we could not take the motorcycle with us while moving from place to place under the cover of night. Therefore, we left it in the basement of Beszyce Dolne manor.

# 9. Flying Commando in Action

After a number of smaller actions by our group against the Nazis stationed in our area, the superiors of the Home Army in the district of Sandomierz decided that the time had come for larger attacks on the enemy. Most of the members of our group had already some theoretical and practical training, sufficient weapons, and a modicum of experience. These things had to be put to use in our struggle against the evil Nazi empire. I recall that our superiors decided to attack and disarm a group of German military men when we were still at our quarters in Wiazownica during the early fall of 1943. With the exception of Captain Kaktus, Lieutenant Mis, and Chief Orlicz, no one in the group knew anything about the forthcoming action.[40] When we left our quarters in Wiazownica, we were told to leave our belongings there, with the exception of weapons and ammunition. I do not remember how we moved from Wiazownica to the proximity of Sandomierz. What I remember well is that the night before the action we walked through the fields in the general direction of Sandomierz. The city of Sandomierz was south of us.

The night was dark on Thursday, November 11, 1943. An autumn rain had been falling for several days. We were walking like ducks in a row behind Captain Kaktus (Tadeusz Strus), wading practically up to our ankles through drenched fields. No one except our leader knew where we were going. Along the way, we passed many villages, which dotted the darkness of the night with dim light from their oil lamps.

After several hours of wearisome marching, our group, consisting at that time of twelve persons, reached the village of Kamien Plebanski, which was located in the general area of hilly country known as Pieprzowki. There we stopped to rest in two houses standing apart from the village. The captain assigned the hours of watch and ordered the rest of us to go to sleep as soon as possible. Tired and weary, we fell into a deep sleep on the straw spread out on the floor.

Following our morning awakening and breakfast, the captain called in a few of us at a time for a conference. Plans of a rather large building and various notes lay on the table in the captain's room. The captain, as usual at such times, immediately came to the point. We were to take control of a building that served as the quarters for approximately fifty Germans. Most of them were railroad police (Bahnschutzpolizei) and Air Force (Luftwaffe) men. The purpose of our action was to disarm the Germans and thus secure for ourselves badly needed weapons. The captain, therefore, acquainted each of us with the layout of the building and gave us our assignments. The time of this action was set for the evening. Despite the discomfort of the previous day, our faces beamed with joy and enthusiasm in anticipation of the coming action.

The rest of the day we spent cleaning our weapons and checking and rechecking their proper functioning. Finally, evening came. We hurriedly put on our long topcoats, hiding underneath them our pistols and hand grenades. One of our men who was assigned to operate a light machine gun found the task of hiding his weapon under his topcoat a little more difficult, but he finally succeeded in doing so.

It was dusky outside when we started on our way to Sandomierz. We had to be at our destination at 18 Mickiewicza Street at 7:00 P.M., when the majority of the Germans would be sitting down to supper in the large dining hall. We marched through fields, thereby avoiding Sandomierz to the south. On one of the side roads, we accidentally captured a policeman who happened to be in the German service. The unfortunate man kept justifying himself and pleading for forgiveness. He promised to cease all work with the German police. After searching him, we released him with the admonition not to mention to anyone that he had met us.

Coming into the section of the town bustling with activity and people, we split up into pairs in order not to attract the attention of the German police patrolling the streets. Thus, mingling with passersby, we finally arrived at our destination. Before our eyes stood a large three-story building. A concrete sidewalk connected the city sidewalk to the building. At its main entrance there was a dim electric light. The door to the building was closed and a uniformed guard stood in front of it. On the western side of the building there was a side door, also with a light above it, but it was not guarded.

The action began when "Iskra" (Arkadinsz Swiercz), wearing the uniform of the German railroad police, appeared in front of the building, briskly walked toward the guard and saluted him with, "Heil Hitler." As soon as he passed the guard, he pulled out his pistol, put it to the guard's back, and softly said to him, "*Still! Hände hoch!*"[41] Without uttering a word, the guard raised his hands and let Iskra take his pistol. At that point, two of our machine gun men took their positions on the porch of the neighboring building and the rest of us, under the leadership of Captain Kaktus, began to enter the building by the side door. As soon as we entered, all of us, mostly in pairs, went to our assigned positions.

Captain Kaktus led Jach and Smigly to the dining hall, where over thirty Germans, totally oblivious to what was happening around them, were sitting at the dinner tables. Only the captain's order, "*Hände hoch!*" and the barrels of three pistols made them aware of their situation. A deathly silence fell. The Germans stood up in their places and raised their hands. Three German women who were in the dining hall were also asked to raise their hands. Both Captain Kaktus and Jach, who spoke German, ordered the Germans to approach, with their hands raised, the main wall in the dining room, face it, and put their palms against it. They obediently executed the order. This enabled our men to search each person individually and disarm them one by one. Before all the Germans were disarmed in the dining hall, Iskra brought in the guard whom he had disarmed in front of the building. The captain

The building at 18 Mickiewicz Street in Sandomierz in which the Flying Commando Unit, under the leadership of Captain Tadeusz Strus ("Kaktus"), disarmed German air force (Luftwaffe) men and railroad police (Bahnschutzpolizei) on November 12, 1943. Author's photograph.

ordered the guard to stand against the wall with the others. Then Iskra returned to keep guard in front of the building. During the disarming in the dining hall, the three women were disarmed as well. From one of the women Smigly took a small pistol, with which he accidentally shot himself in the hand.

After the disarmament of the Germans in the dining hall was completed, Captain Kaktus and Smigly went to the second floor to help the others while Jach remained in the dining hall to guard the Germans. As Jach stood in the middle of the dining hall and watched the backs of the uniformed Germans, he became aware that one of the Germans was his size and wore a very well-cut uniform. He decided to trade his old and worn out high school uniform for it. The German officer who wore the pretty uniform was not happy at all to trade clothes with Jach, but Jach's order gave him no alternative. He undressed at the wall and threw the uniform toward Jach. Jach also asked for the officer's boots. Jach then undressed and put on the uniform and the boots. Both of them were a perfect fit. After a short while, Jach forced the unlucky German to wear his wet clothes and muddy shoes. Jach realized then how poorly his high school suit looked on the new owner.

In the meantime, a number of us rushed to the second and third floors of the building. As we climbed the stairs between the first and the second floor, we noticed that there was a sort of extended stairway landing where the Germans placed their telephone switchboard. Straceniec, who had previous experience with telephone switchboards, quickly disabled it.

When we reached the second floor, Captain Kaktus, Cap, and a number of others burst into the rooms on the left side of the hallway and began to disarm the Germans. In one of the rooms that Cap entered, all the Germans raised their hands with the exception of one, who began to reach for his pistol. Cap shouted, "*Hände hoch!*" for the second time and when the German did not raise his hands, Cap aimed at him and squeezed the trigger of his Stayer. Fortunately, for the German, there was a misfire. Now realizing that Cap was not joking, the German raised his hands in a hurry. Cap reloaded and disarmed the Germans. In order to punish the German who reached for his gun, Cap ordered him to lie down on the hallway floor.

In another room, Captain Kaktus was disarming a group of Germans. One of them asked the captain to let him keep his World War I artillery Luger (long barrel), which was a memento given to him by his father. The captain was sympathetic but unbending. The German had to give up his beautiful and valuable pistol. Our captain could not afford sentimentality. He was a leader of a group of young men who fought for their own lives and for the life of the nation. When the German kept pleading for his pistol, the captain ordered him to prostrate himself on the floor in the hallway.

## 9. Flying Commando in Action

Blyskawica and I were assigned to disarm the German pilots who occupied the third floor. Straceniec was to join us a few moments later. In the meantime, the two of us rushed quietly to the third floor where the pilots from two adjoining rooms (dormitories) were gathered together for a small celebration, which appeared to be a birthday party. Most of them were sitting around a table full of food, which appeared to have come from their families in Germany. The pilots were totally relaxed; their tunics and belts with pistols were hanging on chairs and on a hallway stand. They were eating, drinking, and talking.

When Blyskawica and I entered the room, the pilots interrupted their conversation and, their faces full of surprise, turned toward us. We pointed our pistols at them and I said, half smiling, "*Guten Abend Herren.*"[42] Before they could respond, I ordered, "*Hände hoch!*" Their hands went up and they trembled with fear. One of the pilots, who thought we were going to shoot them, began to cry. We took their pistols and belts and put them on our hips. In the closet we found some rifles and more pistols. After we collected all the weapons in the adjoining rooms, we told the pilots to put their hands down and enjoy their food. At that point, one of the pilots picked up a tray of cookies from the table and asked us to take some. We did and thanked him for the treats. After we tasted the cookies, the pilots relaxed and began to smile. I understood their smile as a smile of gratitude to us for treating them in a humane manner.

As we were enjoying the pilots' cookies, I looked into the hallway to see what was going on there. A number of our men walked this way and that way and one of them smoked two cigarettes at the same time. When I saw it, I could not contain my laughter.

Soon Straceniec joined us and brought with him a woman who, oblivious to what was happening around her, carried a tray of food for several pilots who were kept locked up in one of the rooms on the third floor. When Straceniec inquired why the pilots were locked in, the woman replied that they operated a Luftwaffe radio station through which sensitive military information was being received and transmitted. Having learned this, Straceniec ordered the woman to carry on her duties as if nothing had happened. So she kept walking to the third floor and Straceniec followed her until they came to the door of the radio station room. There the woman knocked on the door and told the pilots that she brought their supper. One of the pilots opened the door and Straceniec forced his way into the room and pointed his pistol at the Germans. Both of them were relaxed and wore tee-shirts. When they saw Straceniec with his gun, they were dumbfounded. When he ordered, "*Hände hoch!*" one of them raised his hands quickly but the other one looked like a zombie with his mouth wide open and his arms hanging helplessly. Only when Straceniec fired his pistol near the pilot's ear did he revive and raise his hands. At that time, Blyskawica joined Straceniec and together they disarmed the pilots. After the pilots were deprived of their pistols, Straceniec disconnected the radio station. Then they searched the room and found more weapons. All told, they gained three pistols, two submachine guns, and three pairs of military boots.

After the Germans were disarmed on every floor, some of our men watched them while the rest of us were ordered to break into the rooms that were locked because their occupants were in town or on furlough in Germany. The hatchets that we carried on our belts proved to be quite useful for this task. We chopped the doors above the locks and then two of us together leaned into them with our shoulders until the doors gave in. Chopping doors and breaking locks caused a considerable commotion. During this noisy activity, a German railroad police officer happened to walk by on the sidewalk in front of the building and heard the pounding. He came up to Iskra, who kept guard in front of the building and asked him, "*Was ist los?*" (What's the matter?) "*Ach, Scheisserei!*" (obscene expression), replied Iskra. The officer scornfully waved his hand and said, "Yes, indeed." As soon as he turned around to resume his walk, Iskra put the barrel of his pistol to the officer's back and disarmed him. Then Iskra took him to the dining room where Jach was guarding the other Germans. Since the officer's uniform was of a better quality than the uniform that Iskra was wearing, Jach advised him to trade with the officer. When Iskra accepted the suggestion, Jach took the guard duty in front of the building while Iskra changed uniforms and boots.

Our breaking into the unoccupied rooms yielded five rifles, a great deal of ammunition, a number of uniforms, boots, sweaters, blankets, and thirty knapsacks. By the time we finished our work, every one of us was loaded with pistols, rifles, and other military supplies, which came in very useful in our struggle with the enemy.

Cap, who carried his share of the German weapons, managed also to deprive the Germans of their medals, crosses, and other Nazi insignia. He enjoyed collecting such things.

After the door to the last unoccupied room gave in under the pressure of our shoulders and the weapons were taken, the captain ordered us to get ready to leave. As we began to leave the third floor, Captain Kaktus walked from room to room and told the Germans not to leave their rooms or start an alarm until one hour after our departure. He added that if any of them should try to leave the room before one hour, he would be shot — neither the captain nor any of us trusted the Germans

On the second floor, we found two or three Germans prostrated on the hallway floor. As we walked by, we avoided stepping on them. As we descended to the first floor, we saw more Germans on the corridor's floor. Jach told us that the ones who were on the floor had stayed in town too long and were late for dinner. Iskra disarmed them outside and Jach kept an eye on them inside the building.

As all of us, who were inside, gathered together on the corridor of the first floor, Captain Kaktus counted us and led us two by two across Opatowska Street toward the sidewalk on the edge of the city park. The machine gun crew and Iskra followed us. As soon as we reached the park, we felt secure in the darkness of the night. The captain led us toward a vacant area full of small valleys behind the park, which was known as Piszczele. Before we managed to cross the city park, the Germans fired a flare. The sky became bright and we could hear the shouts of German soldiers who were stationed in various parts of the city. Then we heard the rumbling of motor vehicles and machine gun fire. The alarm was in full swing. The disarmed Germans did not keep their promise.

It appeared to me that in disarming the Germans we had overlooked a flare gun or one of our men who found it did not think it was worth taking since we had seized so many valuable weapons. After the first flare started the alarm, many other flares burst in the sky in various sections of the city. The Germans sounded a general alarm. Fortunately, we were now out of their reach.

Quickening our pace, we entered the hollows of Piszczele to quickly lose ourselves in the darkness. From Piszczele, we headed through the fields in the direction of the village of Kobierniki. When we were in the midst of the fields, we noticed ahead of us a small light, as though from an oil lantern, which was moving away from us. At first, we paid no attention to this light but when we heard the sound of a moving wagon from the direction of the light, we started to surmise that perhaps it could be a German army wagon riding into the area.

We were enthusiastic as a result of our successful action, and we did not want to pass up the opportunity to seize at least one more rifle or pistol. We all begged our captain to permit us to overtake the Germans and disarm them. The captain agreed and gave the order to quicken our march. Despite our exhaustion and the heavy load that each of us was carrying, we all got some new strength — a second wind — for the chase. After several minutes, we were not too far away from the wagon. Our guess was correct. This was a German military wagon. In a few more minutes, we would be beside the wagon, which we had already planned to use to transport our booty.

While we were taking a shortcut across the field in order to get ahead of the Germans, we heard German voices all around us and here and there flashlights were blinking out signals. Immediately, we recognized that we were in the midst of German soldiers engaged in military night training. We decided to abort the mission. Fortunately, we were near a row of willow trees growing along the side of the road. The branches of these trees were hanging to the ground, providing a perfect curtain. There we found a good hiding place. We hoped to avoid unnecessary shooting and perhaps even bloodshed; nevertheless, we were ready and prepared to fight if we should be discovered.

As soon as the nearest German flank passed us, ignoring the willows, we immediately started to withdraw from the area. The hilly terrain was our ally. After several minutes marching quickly and cautiously, we slipped away successfully from the Germans. We stopped finally beside a windmill in the neighboring village of Zurawica. There we obtained a wagon, which carried our booty the rest of the way. After an hour's ride, we arrived at one of our secret quarters near Samborzec. After washing ourselves and taking some nourishment, we took a count of the German weapons. We found ourselves in possession of many of the latest model rifles, pistols, ammunition, and uniforms. Since there was a unit of SS men in Samborzec, we decided to proceed to Jachimowice manor.

It was already morning when we arrived at our secret quarters at Jachimowice manor, owned by Mr. and Mrs. Bronislaw Bronikowski. There we found a heartfelt welcome and rest, as well as pleasant companionship. From Jachimowice manor, we went to our quarters in Granicznik near Wiazownica. Our quarters there consisted of two adjacent farms, which were on the end of a large forest.

As soon as we arrived in Granicznik, we kept examining our newly acquired weapons. Smigly, who had shot himself in the hand with a small-caliber lady's pistol, kept playing with the pistol from time to time. He was loading and unloading it over the dining room table. Some of us, including a ten-year-old farmer's son, were sitting about the table when Smigly introduced a round into the chamber and the pistol fired. The bullet hit the top of the heavy table under 45°, bounced off, and lodged itself in the boy's arm. All of us at the table got up with a great degree of anger at Smigly and his childish behavior that could have resulted in a death. One of our men, who was near Smigly, gently took the pistol from his trembling hand because there was a new round in its chamber. Our immediate superior, Orlicz, scolded Smigly and assigned him extra guard duty.

Then Orlicz asked for two volunteers to take the wounded boy to the physician's home in Osiek. Straceniec and I volunteered. Soon the farm wagon and horses were ready to go. We rode to Osiek as fast as the horses could go. It was late in the evening when we reached the physician's residence. He dutifully opened the door of his office and let us in. After examining the boy's arm, he told us that the bullet did not damage the bone nor any important blood vessel. It pierced the muscle and remained under the skin on the opposite side of its entry. The physician gave his patient a local anesthetic, disinfected the skin of his arm, cut the skin open over the bullet, and removed it with great ease and skill. He gave the bullet to the boy as a memento. We offered to pay for the surgery but the physician refused to take anything. The boy's wound, inflicted by a stray bullet, healed very fast and painlessly.

Upon further examination of the small-caliber pistol, we discovered that its trigger mechanism was defective. This fact alleviated Smigly's guilt feelings. After a few days of rest and military lectures, we went out for our next action in Szczucin, where we expected to seize a tremendous quantity of arms and ammunition. This action, however, ended differently from that in Sandomierz.

# 10. The Attack on Szczucin Bridge

After disarming the Germans at 18 Mickiewicza Street in Sandomierz on November 12, 1943, our Flying Commando Unit began preparations for another attack on the enemy. This time, our leaders decided to attack a post of the Wehrmacht (Army) soldiers who guarded the Szczucin Bridge on the Vistula River.[43] According to the intelligence that Captain Kaktus received several days before the attack, twenty-four German soldiers were stationed in the guardhouse near the bridge on the right (eastern) side of the river. Their guardhouse was fortified by an earth rampart, which had a small gate. The windows of the guardhouse were covered with an anti-hand grenade screen. The soldiers stationed in the guardhouse were armed with pistols, rifles, hand grenades, a few submachine guns, and a couple of machine guns. Four soldiers were always on guard duty. One pair guarded the bridge on the eastern side of the Vistula and the other on the western side. The soldiers on guard duty were armed with rifles and pistols.

The purpose of our attack was to disarm the Wehrmacht soldiers on the bridge and in the guardhouse and thus secure weapons and ammunition to be used in our struggle against the enemy.

A few days before our attack on the Wehrmacht post, a devout Catholic woman gave each of us in our unit a picture of Our Lady of Exiles and assured us that we would find it comforting in moments of danger. I put the picture of Our Lady in my wallet and carried it with me wherever I went.[44]

The preparations for the attack were nearing completion, and we were waiting impatiently for zero hour. Finally, the moment arrived. Our hearts beat faster and more excitedly. After our last successful venture, everyone was full of optimism. Captain Kaktus assigned eighteen of us to take part in the attack, and each of us was given a specific function to perform. The captain

## 10. The Attack on Szczucin Bridge

also selected Ruszcza manor as our assembly point in case we should be dispersed during the attack.

On Friday, November 19, 1943, exactly one week after our attack on Sandomierz, we left our quarters in Beszyce manor in two large farm wagons and headed toward the Szczucin Bridge. For safety's sake, Captain Kaktus rode on horseback ahead of our wagons. As we rode, the autumn mud splattered about us under the pressure of the horses' hooves and wagon wheels and the cool November air penetrated our bodies to the bone. When we arrived near the town of Rytwiany, we deviated from the main road to avoid it because there was a post of German police there. After we passed by Rytwiany, we proceeded toward Lubnice. When we reached the vicinity of Lubnice, we left our wagons and horses there under the watchful eyes of Iskra (Arkadiusz Swiercz) and Mat (Jerzy Kurczyk).

According to the captain's plan, we were to return to our wagons and horses by train after disarming the German post at the bridge. Having instructed Iskra and Mat to keep the horses and wagons in readiness for our return with the German arms, the captain led us to the railroad station in Lubnice. There, in accordance with our plan, we were to catch a train for Szczucin. After reaching the railroad station and waiting for a while, we discovered that the schedule of arrivals and departures had been changed. Instead of waiting for the train without having the slightest idea when it would arrive, we decided to walk the railroad track toward Szczucin.

After walking for a few miles, we heard the familiar sound of the locomotive behind us. We stopped and waited. Most of us had had enough of walking on the track. As the train came closer, we took our positions on the track and one of our men, who had a red flashlight, attempted to stop it. The engineer ignored the red light and kept going. At that moment, Jach (Wlodzimierz Gruszczynski) ran into the middle of the track and raised his rifle horizontally above his head. This time the engineer understood the signal and stopped the train.

As soon as the train stopped, the passengers, curious and frightened, opened the windows of the cars to see what had caused the train to stop. At the same time Orzel (Leon Siatrak) and Pikolo (Jan Szpakiewicz), with a light machine gun, entered the locomotive cab. The rest of us, dressed as German air force men and railroad policemen, entered the cars. As soon as we boarded the train, it continued on toward Szczucin. The passengers with whom we shared the cars soon discovered that we were not Germans but their own "boys from the forest." They were very friendly and well disposed toward us.

Soon the train began to slow down. The Szczucin railroad bridge was near. As the locomotive approached the bridge, the engineer slowed the train even more. As our car approached the entrance to the bridge, Jach (Wlodzimierz Gruszczynski) and Straceniec (Jan Osemlak) jumped out from the car to disarm the first pair of guards. Ahead of them, near the bridge, they saw in the dim light two German guards who were standing near the tracks and watching the train. Jach and Straceniec approached the guards very briskly in military fashion. The guards stood at attention, expecting to be greeted by fellow Germans. Instead of the customary greeting, however, Jach and Straceniec pointed their pistols at them and ordered "*Hände hoch!*" The guards had no trouble raising their hands because their rifles were hanging on their shoulders. They were caught totally by surprise. The soldier whom Straceniec ordered to raise his hands gave his rifle without any resistance. But the one whom Jach approached raised his hands tardily and refused to give Jach his rifle. Jach became angry. He pushed the barrel of his pistol into the guard's abdomen and said to him in German, "*Was wollen Sie: Leben oder Tot?*" (Do you want to live or die?) This worked very effectively. The guard became panicky and let Jach take his rifle without any trouble.

As our car was passing the entrance to the bridge, I saw the guards with their hands up and was encouraged by the successful disarming. Now one of our men and I were ready to jump out of our car and disarm two guards on the other end of the bridge. As the train approached the other bank of the Vistula River, my companion and I noticed that the guards were not together as usual; instead, each of them stood on opposite sides of the tracks. At the last moment, we had to change our plan of acton. We quickly decided that my companion would disarm the guard on the left side of the train and I would take care of the guard on the right side. Soon we jumped from the car at the same time. In a moment, the train stopped and its cars separated us. I could not see what happened on the left side of the train. It appeared to me that my companion disarmed the guard without any problem.

The guard on my side of the train was tall and appeared to be about forty years old. He wore a long winter coat with its collar up and military earmuffs that covered not only his ears but also a part of his face. As I walked toward him, he observed me very intently. His rifle was hanging from his left shoulder and his right hand was on the level of his chest, hidden under the winter coat. When I pointed the barrel of my rifle at him and shouted, "*Hände hoch,*" he began to raise his left hand, but at the same time, with his right hand, he pulled out, with the speed of lightning, a pistol from behind his coat and began to fire at me. I squeezed the trigger of my rifle and fired at him. He stopped firing, stood on his feet for a short time, and then fell to the ground and rolled down the slope of the ramp. I tried to reload my rifle but the casing of my first round was stuck in the chamber and the extractor stripped the rim of the casing. My Mauser rifle was reconditioned and there was a little pit caused by rust in its chamber. I had no cleaning rod in my

## 10. The Attack on Szczucin Bridge

rifle so there was no way to remove the empty casing. Now my small-caliber pistol and two hand grenades were my only weapons.

As a result of the guard's pistol shots and my rifle fire, pandemonium broke out. Our men began to fire at the guardhouse and the Germans who were in it opened fire with everything they had: machine guns, submachine guns, rifles, hand grenades, and flares. When some German soldiers came out of their fortified guardhouse to fire at Captain Kaktus (Tadeusz Strus), Blyskawica (Boleslaw Szelong) and Cap (Marian Gaj), who began to move toward the gate of the guardhouse, Orzel (Leon Siatrak) and Pikolo (Jan Szpakiewicz), who were with the light machine gun on the locomotive, opened fire at the Germans. When the Germans returned their fire toward the locomotive, the machine gun crew left the locomotive and took up a position on the ground. The clever engineer took advantage of this and pulled the train out of the battle zone.

The fire from our light machine gun and from a small group of our men under the leadership of Captain Kaktus near the gate of the rampart made the Germans barricade the door to the guardhouse. The German soldiers who remained outside fell victim to our machine gun and submachine gun bullets. Then Captain Kaktus, Blyskawica, and Cap went through the gate of the rampart and came close to the guardhouse. In order to subdue the fire from within the guardhouse, the captain kept firing his German submachine gun (*Machinenpistole*) at the windows. At the same time, Blyskawica used his rifle to remove the screen in the windows, which protected the Germans from hand grenades. He was convinced that only our hand grenades could smoke out the soldiers from the guardhouse. Cap was aiding Blyskawica in his task and Piorum (Kazimierz Stobinski) who happened to be near the gate began to shout, in German, the summons to surrender: "*Soldaten ergeben Sie sich!*"

After disarming the guards on the left side of the Vistula River, Jach and Straceniec walked over the bridge to the right side where our attack was about to commence. They were in the middle of the bridge when the first shots were fired. At that moment, they shot the guards, pushed their bodies into the river, and ran toward the battle. After they arrived there, they took firing positions and began to fire into the windows of the guardhouse. In the meantime, the submachine gun, with which the captain fired so effectively at the windows of the guardhouse, jammed. As he was attempting to fix it, a German hand grenade, which we called a "potato masher," landed near him and exploded. As a result of the explosion, the captain sustained a wound on his forehead and Cap lost his eye. Blood covered their eyes and faces. They could not see. With the help of others, the two men began to withdraw toward the bridge.

There was still a chance of taking the guardhouse, but the German units, which were stationed in Szczucin and in the neighboring towns, were already alerted and getting ready to help their comrades near the bridge. As a matter of fact, we could hear the sound of their sirens. The key to our success was the element of surprise by which we had hoped to quietly disarm the guards at the bridge and in the guardhouse. We had lost the element of surprise, and so we did not have enough time to take by force the fortified guardhouse. Therefore, after a short consultation with Orlicz (Stefan Franaszczuk), who was next in command, Captain Kaktus said, "Boys, let us retreat." As a result of the captain's decision, all our men near the guardhouse began to withdraw toward the entrance of the bridge. Those who were not wounded helped the captain and Cap.

When our men under the leadership of Captain Kaktus began to withdraw from the area around the guardhouse, Orzel and Pikolo, with their machine gun, remained at their firing position at the railroad tracks. Their position was the farthest from the bridge. My position was somewhere between their position and the entrance to the bridge. There I was, lying on the railroad ramp, pinned to the ground by German tracer bullets that were coming from the guardhouse. For all practical purposes, my jammed rifle was useless and the small-caliber pistol that I carried was insufficient against the powerful weapons of the Germans. Since the body of the guard whom I shot had rolled down the slope of the ramp under a complicated network of barbed wire, it did not occur to me to retrieve the guard's rifle whenever the enemy's flares illuminated the area.

When our men began to withdraw from the guardhouse area, the German fire intensified toward the ramp. A number of times, I crawled toward the top of the ramp and near the railroad tracks to see what was happening. But each time, the enemy's machine gun fire forced me to take cover behind the steel of the tracks and the dirt of the ramp. As I crawled the ramp for the last time, all of our men were already on the bridge and the Germans began to come out of the guardhouse to fire at them. Soon the Germans came near the entrance to the bridge and kept firing at our men, who were already close to its western end. Enemy bullets wounded Sep (Edward Stawiarz) and Zbik, who walked close to each other. Both of them were hit in one of their arms. Then Blyskawica was seriously wounded. The bullet pierced his rib cage and penetrated his chest cavity on the right side. Immediately, he began to lose strength and experienced a choking sensation and an oppressive feeling in his chest. He could no longer walk. In order not to slow the retreat, he pulled out his pistol and attempted to shoot himself. Two of our men took the pistol from his hand.

It was too late for me to follow my companions. My chance of crossing the bridge was gone. Therefore, I decided to swim across the Vistula River under the bridge. All of a sudden, my left ear began to burn. When I touched it, I felt sticky blood on my fingers. Obviously, during my efforts to disarm the guard, one of his bullets had come close to my head. In order to reach the bank of the river, I had to crawl under a network of barbed wire, which the Germans had installed. After doing this, I entered the water and began to cross the river. At first, the water was rather shallow and I managed to reach the first pier of the bridge. Encouraged by my initial success, I continued walking toward the second pier. The water was getting deeper and deeper but I still felt ground under my feet as I came to the second pier.

As I walked between the second and the third pier, I lost the bottom of the river and began to swim. The weight of the jammed rifle became an obstacle in swimming so I let it go to the bottom. In my knapsack, I carried five kilograms of explosives. I could not use my hands for anything but swimming; therefore, I did not make any attempt to remove it. My winter coat and military boots interfered more and more with the free movement of my arms and legs. The river's current, which became stronger now, began to carry me away from the bridge. The bright light from German flares illuminated the river and the bridge. Some of the Germans were already on the bridge. They must have noticed me because a series of bullets splashed near me. When the Germans fired their next flare, I attempted to swim under the water. With each new flare, I did the same thing a number of times.

I was losing my strength and taking in water. The Germans kept firing at me. I began to lose hope of saving my life. I became terrified. At the same time, death appeared to me as a liberating factor. I began sinking deeper and deeper. I was drowning. A thought came to my mind that my life was rapidly coming to an end. From all appearances, there was no hope. I regretted that fact that I would die at such an early age. The most important events of my life flashed in my mind as if projected on a movie screen. Fear of death left me and, in fact, I experienced a blissful feeling. In what might have been the last moment of my life, I remembered the pious woman who gave me a picture of Our Lady of Exiles and assured me of her prayers. In fact, I had the picture on me in my pocketbook. My heart started to beat rapidly and the words of prayer came to my mind, "Mary, Mother of God, pray for me ... help me...," I prayed.

Suddenly, something happened to me. Some force, as it were, lifted me from the bottom of the Vistula. A new strength entered my body. With all my might, I began to swim again. As I moved my legs with a new energy, my military boots came off. Relieved of them, I continued swimming with the current, farther and farther from the bridge and the Germans, who upon seeing my struggles in the water must have assumed that I had drowned. Since swimming on my back was easy for me, I turned on my back and let the current carry me. After a while, I tested the depth of the river and was surprised when my feet touched bottom.

I walked toward something that looked to me like a small island and reached its shore. It was wonderful to be on land again. I thought of resting there for a moment and then making an attempt to swim to the opposite shore of the Vistula. But as I walked farther, I discovered a path that fishermen must have made. I followed the path and suddenly realized that I was not on an island. It was a piece of land in the shape of a peninsula. I was pleasantly surprised and kept walking away from the river.

Momentarily, I deviated from the path and walked into a place where basket makers had cut, near the ground, young willow twigs. I wounded my feet on the sharp stubs. In order to examine my feet, I removed my socks and then threw them away; they were wet and muddy. From that point on, I walked in my bare feet. Since the ground was freezing, my feet became numb and soon I felt no pain in them.

The frosty air and my wet clothing made me accelerate my walk to stay warm. Soon I reached a system of dikes, which were built along the river to prevent floods. I began to proceed in the direction of Polaniec.

The shooting stopped for a moment, only to resume again away from the bridge. I wondered whether the Germans had caught up with our men, resulting in the exchange of fire. Actually, a detachment of Germans, which was rushing to aid the unit at the bridge, opened fire on the Germans who pursued our group. In the darkness of the night, it took the Germans some time to discover their mistake. In the meantime, our men gained a safe distance from the enemy.

After an hour's walk along the dike, I noticed a distant light, which looked like that of a naphtha lamp placed near the window in somebody's home. Since I was in need of dry clothes and shoes, I decided to walk toward the light hoping to find some help from the people who possibly lived there. When I came close to the light, it became clear to me that it was indeed coming from the window of a house that stood somewhat distant from the other houses in the village. As I cautiously approached the house, the light in the window went out. I went to the window and tapped on it lightly. No one responded. In a hushed voice, I said, "Please let me in. I am a partisan, a Polish soldier. I need your help." Again, no one answered. I tapped on the window again, this time more loudly and with greater perseverance. A woman answered and said, "Sir, I am afraid to let you in. Please go somewhere else." I intended to plead further with the woman, but a window opened in another part of the house and an older man appeared in it and said, "I will let you in, sir; please come to my door. I am an old legionnaire and I understand." Immediately, he opened the door to his part of the house and let me come in. His wife was also on her feet and ready to help. Both of them were extremely hospitable and helpful. They helped me take off my wet clothing, took care of my minor wounds, and told me to warm up in their bed.

My wounds were superficial. The bullet from the pistol of the German whom I had attempted to disarm had nipped my right ear. Fragments of hand grenades or bullets had lacerated my left buttock in two places and barbed wire had cut the skin on both of my hands.

While I was getting warmed in the couple's bed, the legionnaire went to his wardrobe to procure some clothing and shoes for me. At the same time, his wife boiled a pot of milk to warm my insides. After drinking a few cups of hot milk, I felt well enough to be on my way. I dressed, put my pistol and hand grenades on my belt, strapped my knapsack with explosives on my back, and was ready to go to Polaniec, where my relatives lived. My hosts felt that I should not walk to Polaniec because the Germans were alerted and probably watched the roads. The legionnaire offered to take me to his relative's secluded farmhouse, where I could stay for several days. He told me that his cousin was a member of a local post of the Home Army and could easily get me in touch with my group. I accepted his offer and soon we were riding in his farm wagon to the secluded farm. It was almost morning when we reached the farm.

The farmhouse was indeed secluded and far away from any road. The farmer, his wife, and their red-haired teenage daughter were as hospitable as the legionnaire and his wife. After a short conversation, they offered me the warmest bedroom and advised me to take a rest. They stayed up and did their morning chores. In spite of the dramatic experiences at the Szczucin Bridge, I fell asleep and did not wake until noon. As I woke up, an aroma of chicken soup filled the farmhouse. The lady of the house and her daughter were preparing a fine chicken dinner, which farmer's wives usually serve only on Sundays.

During the meal, the farmer told me that he had reported my presence to the commandant of the local Home Army post and the commandant was expected to arrive at any moment to see me. The commandant arrived in the afternoon bringing with him a farm wagon, which took me to his subordinates in Polaniec. I was very grateful to both farm families and the local commandant for the wonderful help they offered me in my moments of extreme need. By helping me to save my life, they endangered their own lives and the lives of their dear ones.

When I was swimming across the Vistula River and walking to the farmhouse for help, the majority of our men under the leadership of Captain Kaktus, having crossed the bridge, walked into the fields near the railroad tracks. The fields were full of thorns and briers. Fortunately, the thorns and briers grew only in the vicinity of the railroad tracks. As they went farther, they entered cultivated fields that made both walking and carrying the wounded much easier. Soon they came to a meadow, where Captain Kaktus ordered a short stop and asked for a bandage for his wounded forehead. Jach offered his bandage to the captain and dressed his wound.

After his wound was properly dressed, the captain reorganized the group. He assigned some men to take care of those who were seriously wounded, appointed several scouts, and pointed out the direction in which the group was to proceed. At the same time, he sent one of the men to the drivers of the farm wagons, which we had left in the forest near the railroad station of Lubnice. They were ordered to drive the wagons to Ruszcza manor near Polaniec, which, according to our original plan, was to be the gathering point of the group in case of dispersion.

After walking a while through the farmland, the group came to a farm. The captain hoped to get a team of horses there and a farm wagon to carry the wounded. When the farmer was bringing his horses out of the barn to hitch them to the wagon, several German military personnel carriers appeared on the road near the farmhouse and stopped there. When the soldiers came out of the trucks, Captain Kaktus ordered his men to withdraw from the farmyard into the adjacent field. As they were pulling out into the field, the scaling of the fence proved to be somewhat difficult and noisy. The Germans on the road must have heard the noise because they fired a few flares to illuminate the field. However, a heavy fog protected our men from the eyes of the soldiers. At the same time, the fog, which covered the whole area, hindered orientation in the terrain.

After getting away from the farm, the captain became disoriented and asked his men for suggestions on which direction to proceed. Jach was the first one to speak. He said, "Captain, the Germans are behind us, to the right of us and to the left we can hear the barking of the dogs; only in the front of us seems to be quiet and safe."[45] Since no one in the group had better advice, the captain asked Jach to lead. Jach stepped in front of the group and asked everybody to follow him.

As the group walked behind Jach, German flares illuminated the area from time to time. Each time a flare appeared in the sky, they all hit the ground and then walked again. After marching for a while, Jach discovered that he had lost the group that followed him. He obviously overestimated the speed with which the group could proceed with the wounded and got so far ahead of the group that he lost contact with it. He went back in search of the group but did not find it. So he resumed his walk in the previous direction.

The wet soil of the farm fields made his walk very difficult. On his boots he carried loads of heavy mud. He was getting tired and needed rest. After

## 10. THE ATTACK ON SZCZUCIN BRIDGE

dragging his feet for a while, Jach could hear the barking of dogs. This indicated that there was a village nearby. He decided to go in the direction from which came the sound of the dogs' barking. After he had been walking for a while, farm buildings emerged from the havy fog. Jach cautiously entered the farmyard and noticed that there was a pile of logs. The logs were somewhat elevated from the ground. Since the dogs in the neighborhood kept up their agitated barking, Jach crawled under the logs. Soon a group of German soldiers entered the farmyard. With their flashlights, they explored the area. Jach buried his wallet, in which he kept his identification card, driver's license, and so forth in the mud. He removed his pistol from the holster to end his life if the Germans discovered him.

After a while, the soldiers left the yard. They went to search the neighboring farm buildings. As soon as they left, Jach rushed to the barn and buried himself in the straw. Soon he fell asleep and he remained asleep until several farmers came to the barn and began the work of thrashing. When he came out of the pile of straw, the farmers were greatly astonished. After Jach explained to them who he was and why he was in the barn, the owner of the farm invited him to the farmhouse. There, the farmer's wife gave him water to wash with and a warm breakfast. Then she asked him to stay in the house and rest for a few hours. Having rested, Jach took the shortest and safest road to Polaniec.

When Jach was walking toward Polaniec, I was already in Polaniec, where I met several other members of the Home Army. They invited me to their favorite restaurant, where we celebrated our newfound acquaintance with some cold cuts and whiskey. They were very interested to hear of my exciting experiences at the bridge and asked me to tell and retell some of the highlights. They told me that the men of my group took horses and wagons in Ruszcza near Polaniec to carry their wounded in the direction of Osiek. Soon Jach and Piorun also arrived in Polaniec.

The local Home Army men transferred us by means of horse and buggy to our quarters in Ruszcza manor near Sulislawice. I did not realize until we arrived on the grounds of Ruszcza manor that I was supposed to be dead. A man who was on guard duty expressed great surprise at the sight of me. Reflecting the belief of others, he told me that everybody took for granted that I was killed by the Germans at the bridge. Some men in the group were convinced that they saw me on the ground dead or mortally wounded. So when we entered the manor house, there were more expressions of surprise, shouts of joy, and fraternal hugs. Soon I was struck by the absence of Cap, Blyskawica, Zbik, and Sep. All four of them were wounded and hospitalized at the Holy Ghost Hospital in Sandomierz. Captain Kaktus, with a bandage on his forehead, was on his feet to greet us. He was already planning a new attack on the enemy.

During my conversation with my comrades-in-arms, I learned that Orzel and Pikolo, who manned the machine gun, were also unable to withdraw over the bridge. However, they did not attempt to swim across the Vistula River. They walked along its right bank until they found a boatman who took them to the other side of the river. They returned to the unit unharmed.

As is true with any failure, our lack of success at the Szczucin Bridge had a cause: our failure to coordinate our group's activities with other partisan groups in the Szczucin area. We learned that a few hours before our attack on the Germans at the bridge, another guerrilla group, not knowing of our plans, engaged the Germans, who then, instead of sleeping in barracks as usual, waited for an attack in full military readiness.

# 11. Disarming the Nazis in Samborzec

Shortly after Jach, Piorun, and I rejoined the group in Ruszcza manor near Sulislawice, Capitain Kaktus and Orlicz decided to change our quarters. It seems to me that there were two reasons for the move. The first was due to safety concerns. After our battle with the Wehrmacht unit at the Szczucin Bridge, the SS-men were on the alert and they were trying to find us. The second reason was because the owner of Ruszcza manor did not reside there. He lived in another manor, which was more comfortable. One of the relatives, a middle-aged lady, lived there and operated the manor with the assistance of a professional administrator. She treated all of us as unwelcome guests and offered us very poor meals. I sensed a diplomatic coolness in the relationship between her and our leaders.

I recall that from Ruszcza we moved to the small but hospitable Bystrojowice manor. Ad soon as we arrived, the younger Miss Bielawska, who was in love with Blyskawica, wanted to know about the seriousness of his wounds sustained at the Szczucin Bridge. We assured her that he was recovering well under the supervision of an excellent surgeon.[46] His chest wound was healing very well and he was expected to return to the group soon.

While the members of our group enjoyed the comforts of Bystrojowice manor, Capitain Kaktus was staying in Samborzec, where he had his private apartment.[47] On December 19, 1943, Captain Kaktus entertained two visitors in his apartment: Lieutenant Witold Jozefowski ("Mis") and Jozef Bojanowski ("Walter").[48] Before the visitors left, a miller's boy from the Misiuda Mill came to see the captain with a very important message: a small group of Nazis had arrived at the Misiuda residence and demanded food and schnapps. Captain Kaktus and his visitors went to the window through which they were able to see a black car parked in front of the Misiudas' residence.

Soon, Lieutenant Mis asked Walter to go to Bystrojowice manor and, in his name, instruct Orlicz to choose a small group of men who could disarm the Nazis at the Misiudas' residence without shedding blood, if possible.[49] As soon as Walter reached our quarters, Orlicz selected five of us to do the disarming quietly and bloodlessly. The five of us were Jan Osemlak ("Straceniec"), Wlodzimierz Gruszczynski ("Jach"), Edward Stawiarz ("Sep"), Arkadiusz Swiercz ("Iskra"), and I.

Josef Bojanowski, who knew the area very well, led us through the frozen fields and meadows. After walking, or rather running, for about three miles, we approached the Misiuda's mill and residence, which was near it, from the northern side. The last few hundred yards we walked across the meadow and along the bed of a small stream and used a building there for cover. When we reached the building, Walter remained there and the five of us went toward the Misiudas' residence. The entrance to the residence was from the southern side, which stood along a busy highway. Soon we were in the yard and began to walk toward the entrance of the residence. Since the black car was still parked in the yard, we knew that the Nazis were indoors. Straceniec was the first one to approach the door of the house. Jach and I were a few steps behind him. Iskra and Sep, who followed us at a certain distance, were to remain outside to secure our action in the residence.

As Straceniec entered the door, Mrs. Misiuda met him there with her arms stretched out in an attempt to prevent him from entering the dining room where the Nazis were. Unceremoniously Straceniec pushed Mrs. Misiuda to the side of the hallway and rushed toward the dining room. Mrs. Misiuda attempted to follow him and to plead with him but Jach and I followed Straceniec and she became preoccupied with us. We, as quietly as possible, forced our way around her and rushed toward the dining room. When we entered the dining room, Straceniec was already there standing near the door, aiming his pistol at the Nazis and shouting *"Hände hoch!"* When one of the Nazis did not raise his left hand, Straceniec fired and wounded him in the left arm. The Nazi grabbed his wounded hand with his right hand and began to scream at the top of his voice. He fell to the floor, kicked the air with his feet, and became totally hysterical.

Needless to say, I was extremely surprised at the Nazi "superman's" behavior. I began to understand that the Nazi claim that Germans were racially superior was nothing more that a stupid myth. I felt pity for the wounded man so I went to him and tried to calm him by assuring him that we did not intend to kill him or his companions and by helping him to sit down. When this gentle approach did not work at all and he kept kicking and screaming like a child in a tantrum, I decided to use a more basic method. I kicked him in his rear end. He responded to my primitive method instantly. He regained his self-control and became quiet and docile. I asked him to get up and after he did so I searched him and took away his pistol, which he kept in his left pocket. Having done this, Jach and I disarmed the other two men and a woman. All of them had high-quality pistols. What remained was to find the most modern submachine gun, which we knew they had with them. Jach, who spoke German well, questioned the Nazis about the weapon. One of them pointed at the sofa, which was near the wounded "superman." I went to the sofa and, indeed, under the winter coats of the "guests" there was a brand-new model of a submachine gun designed by Bergmann along with a 22-caliber rifle. The magazine with 9mm ammunition was inserted in the submachine gun. Since I could not find extra magazines for the submachine gun, I asked the Nazis where they were. One of them told me that they were in the car. So I went to the car and found a few of them filled up with 9mm ammunition.

Before we left the Misiudas' home, Straceniec disabled the telephone and Jach ordered the Nazis and the Misiudas to prostrate themselves on the floor and to remain in that position for a half-hour. As we were leaving the premises and were walking by the Germans' car, we were tempted to take it with us but at the same time we realized the difficulties of doing this. So we just took the key from the ignition so that the Misiudas' uninvited guests would be unable to operate it for some time.

Soon, we disappeared into the woods and valleys north of Samborzec and returned to our quarters in Bystrojowice. There we examined the weapons that we had taken from the Nazi "supermen." The three pistols that they carried proved very useful for the new members of the group. The small pistol, a 6mm automatic, which the woman carried in her purse, was beautifully made but it was too small for our needs. Besides, its trigger mechanism was very sensitive and Smigly, who played with it, accidentally fired it and the bullet passed near Iskra's head and hit the wall. Our chief Orlicz was furious because this was Smigly's second accident with a lady's small pistol.

After a while, Captain Kaktus and Lieutenant Mis came to our quarters to learn about the details of our attack and to see the weapons that we had taken from the Nazis. Needless to say, they regretted wounding one of the Nazis. Nevertheless, they were impressed with the weapons, especially with the submachine gun, which proved very valuable in our future attacks on the enemy.

Since I took a great interest in the mechanical aspects of guns, both Kaktus and Mis asked me to figure out how the submachine gun worked. After examining the submachine gun and figuring out how it operated, I explained to them and others in the group how to load and how to fire it. The gun was constructed in such a way that it could fire semi-automatically like any modern pistol or could be switched to fire automatically a series of shots like a machine gun. The Captain liked the submachine gun and claimed use of it for a few days. Then he went away and left the gun with our chief, Orlicz. One evening, as we rode on a farm wagon through the Bukowa Forest, Orlicz decided to test the submachine gun. First, he fired a couple of individual shots and then switched to firing a series of shots. The gun failed to fire automatically. Obviously, there was something defective about the switch. I asked the chief to let me look at the gun. He refused and attempted to locate the problem himself. After examining the weapon for a while, he became discouraged and said that it was made to fire only single shots. I knew that he was wrong. So I asked him again if I could check the gun. He was reluctant but, persuaded by other men in the wagon, he handed me the weapon. It did not take me long to figure out how to fire a series of shots with a single squeeze of the trigger.

Several days after we disarmed the Germans at the Misiuda's Mill in Samborzec, we learned that the Nazi who was wounded by Straceniec was recovering well. Nevertheless, the Nazi authorities took ten prisoners from the Sandomierz prison and executed them publicly near the church in Koprzywnica. We were very disturbed by this terrible news and felt somewhat responsible for the death of the people whom we never knew. At the same time, we realized that our fighting the Nazis entailed sacrifices that we could not avoid in the struggle for Poland's freedom. We also learned the identity of the three Nazis whom we disarmed. The one who pointed out the places where we found the submachine gun and the extra magazines was Otto Schultz, who at that time served as an assistant to Captain Donath, commandant of SD in Opatow.[50] After Donath was liquidated by Szaszka on September 22, 1943, Otto Schultz became the commandant of SD in Opatow. Eventually, Schultz too was shot by Zdzislaw Dus ("Sierpien") on June 29, 1944. At the time when we disarmed him at the Samborzec Mill, he was already sentenced to die by the regional court of the Home Army. The Nazi whom Straceneic wounded was Richard Hospodar, a member of the SD unit in Ostrowiec. When we disarmed him, he acted as Otto Schultz's driver and bodyguard. The third Nazi was a member of the Gestapo[51] unit in Sandomierz who acted under the assumed name of Szymanski. His real name was Flohr. We never learned the identity of the woman. Most probably she was a girlfriend of one of the men.

As the war went on, the grain quota imposed on the farmers increased. The German attack on the Soviet Union and the devastation of farming there created a greater need for grain. Therefore, even the smallest obstacle in the shipment of grain, from countryside warehouses to mills, was harmful to the Nazi war efforts.

## 11. Disarming the Nazis in Samborzec

Our plan of seizing a grain warehouse in the vicinity of Sandomierz called for disarming of a few policemen working in the German service, transporting the grain to numerous locations, and destruction of the records in the office. The first and the third tasks were rather easy. The transportation of grain presented some problems. In doing this we had to depend on dozens of farm wagons and drivers. We had very little fear of being surprised by the Germans. During the winter of 1943-44, they did not dare to leave at night the security of their city bases. Only larger military units moved in the countryside in case of necessity.

The night during which we seized the German grain was very favorable for our action. The country dirt roads were frozen and the starry sky slightly illuminated the darkness of the night. We had no trouble traveling on wagons from our quarters in Samborzec to the grain warehouse. After disarming the guards, we found the warehouse manager, Stanislaw Klusek ("Fugas"), who unlocked the facility. He was a former sergeant of the Polish Corps of Engineers and a member of the Home Army. As soon as the warehouse was opened, dozens of wagons began to arrive to be loaded with grain sacks. The loading operation went very smoothly. By about four o'clock in the morning the warehouse was empty and the records destroyed. Before we left, at the conclusion of the operation, Orlicz left a receipt for the Germans in which he spelled out the amount of grain we had seized. The manager of the warehouse was afraid of retribution from his German bosses and, therefore, decided to join our group. He was received with open arms. From that moment on, he became our sergeant, who trained us in the art of using explosives against the enemy. Soon he became one of our favorite instructors. In addition to his in-depth knowledge of engineering, he had a tremendous physical stamina and a sense of humor. His lectures were always full of real-life stories, which beautifully illustrated the topics under discussion.

# 12. The Visit of Cap

In the middle of December 1943, we moved from Bystrojowice to Byszow manor, which was one of our favorite quarters. After a few days staying there, Chief Orlicz sent Sep to Suliszow manor to visit with Cap and to Jachimowice manor to see Blyskawica. Both of them were recovering from wounds received at the Szczucin Bridge. They eagerly welcomed Sep and were anxious to hear the most recent news from our commando unit. Under the solicitous care of Dr. Dobkiewicz, their wounds were healing very well. Since Cap was almost ready to return to the unit, he felt that a short visit to our quarters at Byszow manor would be beneficial to his health. The local post of the Home Army provided him with a bicycle so he could accompany Sep to Byszow.

Shortly after lunch, Cap and Sep started on their way. The weather was nice so the bicycle trip was pleasant and invigorating. In the early afternoon, they were approaching the village of Byszow. When the houses of the village appeared on the horizon, they accelerated their ride. But as they came closer to the village, they noticed, on the road ahead of them, four Russian Cossacks who were in the German service. The Cossacks were armed with rifles and appeared to be waiting for someone. It was too late for the cyclists to attempt a successful escape. When Sep became anxious, Cap said to him, "Don't worry! If they stop us, I will take care of them." The two continued riding toward the village. As soon as they came near to the place where the Cossacks stood, the Cossacks pointed their rifles at them and ordered them to stop. They obeyed the order. Then the leader of the Cossacks approached them and asked for their German identification cards. At that point, Cap put his bicycle on the side of the road, faced the leader, and, instead of producing his identification, turned back the lapel of his winter coat on which a number of German military medals were pinned. This had an electrifying effect on the leader and his subordinates. They snapped at attention and saluted him. Cap cursed in German and slapped the leader across the face. The leader tried to explain his "mistake," and he asked for forgiveness. Cap began to lose his temper and ordered the Cossacks to leave immediately. They left as fast as their feet could carry them. Sep was astonished by Cap's resourcefulness. He never realized that the mild and tender-hearted Cap could play so well the role of a Gestapo agent. Sep now saw clearly why his companion always collected German military medals.

When the Cossacks fled, the cyclists continued their ride to Byszow manor. We were very glad to see Cap among us again and sympathized with him on account of the loss of his eye. He seemed to be unconcerned about his handicap. The time of his visit passed very quickly. We recollected our mutual experiences and talked about an imminent collapse of Hitler's empire. Cap's dealing with the Cossacks was a great source of amusement for all of us. We asked him and Sep to repeat the details of the episode over and over again. He obliged in order to make us happy. He liked to see us laugh and he laughed with us.

Once we got him in a mood for talking, which did not happen too often with Cap, he told us of one of his previous adventures, which was much more dangerous than the one with the Cossacks. It happened in the early spring of 1943, shortly before he joined our group. The dawn was already breaking when Cap drove a horse-drawn farm wagon from the village of Struzki to the village of Niekurza on the Vistula River. He was heading for the ferry that was to take him across the river. In just a few more minutes, he thought, he would be on the other side of the river. The horses were tired after having been driven during the night by the partisans and they walked slowly. The driver was sleepy and at times had trouble keeping his eyes open.

As Cap arrived in Niekurza, the village was asleep. He drove through the village quietly. The road on the western side of the Vistula led straight to the ferry. The cold and humid air coming from the river refreshed the driver. His sleepiness left him. Even the horses quickened their pace as they smelled the nearness of the water. In a moment Cap could see the Vistula and the ferryboat moored to its bank, but there were no ferrymen. He watered his horses and started to look for the ferrymen. As he walked in the direction he thought the ferrymen might be, German policemen appeared and pointed guns at him. "Hands up!" they shouted. Cap raised his hands. He had no alternative. A few policemen searched him and found no weapon or papers. After the search was over, the chief of the police interrogated him about his name, address, occupation and the reason for his travel. Cap answered all the questions truthfully. In explaining why he was away from his home in Padew, which was on the other side of the Vistula, Cap admitted that he had transported partisans, who forced him into their service. The chief did not believe him and accused him of being one of the partisans. Therefore he ordered his subordinates to bind Cap hands and feet with a string and put him in the back of his own wagon. Then the chief demanded that Cap disclose the name of the village to which he took the partisans. Cap lied and gave the name of some remote village. The policemen found the name of the village on their map and decided to go there. In the village of Niekurza they forced several farmers to transport them to the village Cap named. Cap's wagon was also taken and driven by one of the policemen. When they reached the outskirts of the village, they left the wagons on the road and began to search houses and farm buildings. They left the prisoner under the watchful eyes of one of their men, who sat on the wagon and kept his loaded rifle pointed at Cap.

Lying on his back and keeping his hands under his body, the prisoner did everything he could to untie his hands without attracting the attention of the policeman. After a while, he succeeded. Now he waited to catch the policeman off guard. But the policeman was very vigilant and did not take his eyes off the prisoner. Therefore Cap decided to use some means to distract the policeman. He asked the guard for a cigarette. The guard refused. While pleading with the guard, he lifted his head and purposely loosened the scarf wrapped around his neck. Then after a while pretending to feel cold, Cap asked the policeman to pull the scarf closely to his neck. This time the guard decided to comply with the request. He put his rifle aside and with both hands attempted to adjust the scarf around the prisoner's neck. The prisoner, of course, waited for such an opportunity. As soon as the guard leaned over him, Cap grabbed the policeman's arms with the speed of lightning. Shocked, the policeman became immobilized for a moment. Cap had no problem subduing and disarming him. Now the roles were reversed. The prisoner became a guard and the guard a prisoner. As soon as the policeman regained his wits, he begged for his life and said that he had a wife and children.

After freeing himself, Cap did not intend to kill his enemy. All he wanted was to get away safely. Before leaving, he asked the policeman not to go after his friends in the village but wait until they returned. The policeman made a promise and Cap disappeared with his horses and wagon into the wooded countryside he knew so well.

About an hour after Cap's escape, the Nazi policemen returned from their futile search for the partisans. They were angry and intended to beat up the prisoner for sending them on a wild goose chase. But fortunately, he was not there when they returned. The frightened policeman, who guarded the prisoner, must have fabricated a story as to how he was surprised and disarmed by a large group of partisans.

In the meantime Cap arranged for his horses and wagon to be returned

## 12. The Visit of Cap

to his parents' farm in Padew. He, with his newly acquired rifle and ammunition, began to search for our group, which at that time was just being organized. With the help of some of his friends, he managed to locate the group before the day was over.

After Cap finished telling us this interesting and true story, we realized for the first time why and how he became a member of the Orlicz Group. At the same time, we regretted that he had to return so soon to Suliszow manor to continue his convalescence.

The following day Cap returned to Suliszow. One of our men accompanied him all the way. Under the lapel of his winter coat were German military medals attached just in case Cossacks, police, or others who served the Nazis might stop them on their way. Fortunately their ride to Suliszow was uneventful. A week or so later Cap returned to the group for good. He stayed with us and what happened to him later on, I will write in one of the following chapters.

# 13. Mining the Railroad

Shortly after our successful seizure of the grain warehouse near Sandomierz, Captain Kaktus gave us a new assignment: mining the railroad between Zawichost and Ostrowiec. This railway was used by the Germans to transport troops and war materiel between Germany and the eastern front and vice versa. The Home Army intelligence service provided Captain Kaktus with exact schedules of military trains. The train we were to blow up was to carry ammunition and enough troops to protect it.

A new member of the group, Sergeant Stanislaw Klusek ("Jastrzab" vel "Fugas"), who joined us after our raid on the grain warehouse, prepared our explosives, wires, electric primers, and a detonator. For explosives, we decided to use plastic which was easy to carry and easy to apply to the rails. The captain selected Sergeant Fugas, Straceniec, Pikolo, and myself to undertake the operation. The five of us left the group in the evening and arrived in the vicinity of the railroad. In order to reach our safe house, we had to cross the railway. It was a secluded house near a wooded area. There we rested for the rest of the night on the straw spread on the floor in the living room. After our late breakfast, the captain took a long walk near the railroad to select the best spot to mine and to find the best way to get away after the explosion. Having done this, he returned to the safe house and explained to us, over and over again, all the phases of our operation.

As soon as evening came, we left the safe house, crossed the rails, and walked to the closest manor to procure five riding horses. The owner of the manor let us have his best horses and wished us good luck. He had no idea what we were about to do. After mounting the horses, we rode toward the spot on the railroad that the captain had chosen for the mining. As we approached it, we discovered that there was a small grove nearby. The captain explained that the grove was a good place to hide our horses and led us there. After dismounting we let Pikolo take care of the horses and walked down the slope to inspect the section of railroad under which we were to place the explosives. Since we did not have much time before the arrival of the train, we began to work right away. While the sergeant and Straceniec placed the explosives under the rails, the captain and I unwound the electric wire in the direction of the grove. Since we anticipated the explosion of the German ammunition, we had a long enough electric wire to keep the man who was to press the handle of the detonator at a safe distance. Soon the explosives were placed under the rails, primers inserted, and electric wires connected to them and to the detonator. All we had to do was to wait for the train. As the time for the arrival of the train was approaching and we did not hear it, we feared that its schedule had been changed. One of our men volunteered to return to the railroad and listen to the sound of the rails. In a moment he ran back saying that the train was on its way. We were all excited. Even though the captain suggested that we should go back to horses so as to be ready to withdraw quickly when he pressed the detonator's arm, we decided to stay with him and see the spectacle of explosion. The headlights of the locomotive were shortly within our sight. Our hearts pounded with excitement. As the locomotive passed the point where the first explosives were placed, the captain pushed down the handle of the detonator! We stopped breathing for a short moment to hear the explosion. But no explosion took place. The captain released the handle and pushed it again. Nothing happened. Terrible disappointment. The captain's face became icy with anger. The train loaded with heavy ammunition was still moving over our explosives but we had no way to ignite them. It kept speeding and soon disappeared from our sight.

After we recovered from the initial shock of failure, the sergeant examined the wiring and discovered that one of the wires was faulty. However, he could not find which section of the wire did not conduct electricity so he discarded the entire section, cut the good wire in half, and reconnected the wiring to the explosives and the detonator. By doing so he shortened by half the distance between the mines under the rails and the detonator. In the excitement caused by the failure and the rewiring, no one paid attention to the fact that whoever would push down the handle of the detonator to blow up the next military train might lose his life as a result of the explosion.

As we waited for the next train, which was to come within an hour or so, we became aware of how close we were to the railroad. If the next train, like the previous one, carried ammunition, especially artillery ammunition, the explosion might be very powerful. Captain Kaktus, who at first did not think that the detonator was too close to the rails, began to have second thoughts. Even though a number of men, including myself, volunteered to detonate the explosives, the chance of losing one of us began to dawn on him.

The sergeant also began to be apprehensive about our immediate proximity to the contemplated explosion, but he did not want to appear timid in the face of his first dangerous action with the group. I sensed this and expressed my doubts about the prudence of our dangerous action. My doubts had an obvious effect on the captain's thinking and he seemed to agree with my comments. Nevertheless he refused, at that time, to call off the action. He hesitated and wanted to have more time to think the whole thing over. He had a hard time making up his mind. He waited until the very last moment. Even when the train began to approach the mines, he was still struggling to come to a decision. Finally, he asked us to go to the horses. He himself wanted to detonate the explosives. I pleaded with him to change his mind. As the train's locomotive came into full view, the captain agreed to my reasoning. As the train was going by, we noticed that there were more passenger cars on it than in the previous one. It was quite possible that German troops were in these cars but it was also possible there were Polish passengers traveling in them.

We were all relieved that the captain decided against blowing up the train. He, too, was happy with his decision, but he shook his fist at the Germans on the train and promised to return to the same spot with better and longer electric wires. As soon as the train passed by, the sergeant and Straceniec removed the explosives and I removed the wiring. Then we mounted the horses and rode to the manor from which we took them. At the manor, we procured a farm wagon, which transported us to our quarters in Bystrojowice.

# 14. Snatching Nazi Cash

In the early spring of 1944, some members of the Home Army in Sandomierz notified our leaders that a German bank official, accompanied by three well-armed bank security men, transported large sums of money each week from the state-owned bank in Sandomierz to the city of Stalowa Wola. They walked from Sandomierz to the railroad station in Nadbrzezie and then took a train for the rest of the way. Our leaders, who needed both weapons and money to support the activities of the Orlicz group (Sandomierz Flying Commando Unit), received the notification with gratitude. After studying various locations at which to intercept the bank employees, they concluded that the best place to hold them up was a stretch of road between the bridge and the railroad station. Straceniec and I were given the job to hold up the Natzi bank employees. It was a very dangerous assignment because each employee carried a pistol; and in addition to that, one of them was armed with a submachine gun, which we called an MP (*Maschinenpistole*). Furthermore, the road on which we were to carry out our assignment was busy with German vehicles and pedestrians. Escape routes in the vicinity were also very limited.

After establishing contacts with our people in Sandomierz and Nadbrzezie ("Zygfryd" and "Topola") and determining the day and the hour of the attack, Straceniec, Jach, and I left our quarters in Wiazownica for the city of Sandomierz. As usual we traveled in farm wagon. Once in the city, we proceeded to the vicinity of St. Paul's Church, where we met our contact. We knew him from our previous encounters. His name was Janusz Szczerbatko ("Zygfryd"). He provided for us a horsedrawn cab, which was to take us to Nadbrzezie. The cabman was a member of the local Home Army and knew what we were about to do.

Since the time for our action was approaching, we were soon in the cab and on our way to the other side of the Vistula. Each of us carried several hand grenades and loaded pistols. While hand grenades were attached to our belts, our right hands were on the pistols, which rested on our knees concealed by the lap cover. Our main concern lay with the guards on the Vistula River bridge. As we were entering the bridge, one of the guards looked us over without stopping the cab.

When we arrived at the place on the road where we were supposed to intercept the state bank employees, we discovered that they already had passed that place and were approaching the railroad station. We got out of the cab and, walking fast, attempted to catch up with them. Unfortunately it was too late. As we came closer to the station, there were uniformed Germans everywhere. Our chance of success diminished greatly. Therefore, we decided to postpone our action until the following week. Fortunately our cabman had waited for us and was able to take us back to the wagon, which we had left near St. Paul's Church in Sandomierz.

In spite of heavy German traffic on the road, we returned safely to Sandomierz. Late in the afternoon, we reached our quarters in Wiazownica. Our chief was somewhat disappointed because we had returned without money. He approved, however, of our plan to seize the German money the following week.

Our unsuccessful attempt at intercepting the bank employees helped us to improve our plan of action. Since going from Sandomierz to the railroad station in Nadbrzezie via the bridge was risky to us and the cabman, we decided to cross the Vistula south of Sandomierz by a small boat. Rather than using a farm wagon as a mode of transportation from Wiazownica to the Vistula, we agreed to take bicycles. In case of an emergency, it was easy to hide bicycles or dispose of them. Our men in Nadbrzezie promised to provide a boat for us and to fire a flare at a certain spot on the bank of the river. We were to acknowledge their signal with a pistol shot. After we responded to their signal with a shot, they were to send us a boat. After crossing the river, we were to go to our friends' quarters and wait for a few days for the German bank employees to walk their customary route. Once the money was seized, we intended to escape into the willow shrubs that grew abundantly along the Vistula near the village of Wielowies.

As the new week began, Straceniec and I rode our bicycles from Wiazownica toward the Vistula River. The weather was poor. An abundant spring rain made the country road rather muddy. The closer we came to the river the more mud we encountered. Our bicycles became useless and we had to walk and push our bicycles the rest of the way. This unforeseen obstacle in our travel made us late for our rendezvous with our friends across the river. We kept walking as fast as possible and pushed our bicycles beside us. As soon as we reached the river's dike, Straceniec fired his pistol. There was no response from the other side of the river. We waited for a while and I fired another shot. No sign of life on the opposite back. We were angry and terribly disappointed; we did not know what to do. Our clothing and shoes were wet and the wheels of our bicycles clogged with black mud. We had a problem.

After discussing various options, we decided to spend the night in the village of Michalowskie Doly. On account of muddy roads and darkness, our bicycles became not only useless but a burden to us. Therefore we were inclined to leave them behind and walk to Michalowskie Doly. We knew a farm family there who had offered us shelter and food on a previous occasion. In order to protect our bicycles from thievery, we put them in the river and tied them to its bank with willow twigs. We thought it was a clever way of hiding them. Once the bicycles were secured, we started our grueling walk in the darkness to Michalowskie Doly. Even though the distance between the Vistula and the village was not very great, it took us half of the night to traverse it. By the time we arrived at our supporters' farm, it was already early morning. The farmer and his wife were busy doing their morning chores. They were surprised to see us disheveled and wet. After we explained our predicament in general terms, the farmer's wife invited us to the house, prepared beds for us, and promised to treat us to a good dinner. Then she went outside to continue her chores.

As soon as we took our wet clothing off and were about to rest, the farmer's wife returned to the house in a hurry saying, "Germans are in the village." We grabbed our pistols and waited near the bedroom window to see what was happening. A few moments later the farmer came in and informed us that it was not Germans but rather Cossacks who had entered the village. After hearing this, we were somewhat relieved because we considered the Cossacks less dangerous than the Germans. Before the farmer returned to his work in the yard, four Cossacks, armed with rifles, left their horses and wagon on the road and attempted to open the gate to the farmyard. The farmer went out to see what they wanted. As soon as he approached the gate, the Cossacks ordered him to open it. He complied and they entered the yard. To keep them away from the house, he offered them hay and oats for their horses but they kept coming closer and closer to the house. When the Cossacks approached the porch, the farmer's wife went out to meet them so as to prevent them from entering her home. The Cossacks persisted and kept walking toward the kitchen door. At this point, Straceniec and I could hear them say in Russian, "Give us whiskey and bacon." The farmer's wife replied, "I am sorry, gentlemen, but we have no whiskey in the house." The Cossacks did not trust her and entered the kitchen. At that point, Straceniec and I took positions on each side of the door that led from the kitchen to our bedroom. Our pistols were loaded and ready to fire. We felt that if they entered our bedroom, we would have to kill them. The farmer's wife opened her kitchen cabinet and showed the intruders that there was no whiskey there. Now the Cossacks believed her and asked whether she had some bacon. She admitted that she had bacon in the pantry. "Where is the pantry?" the Cossacks asked. The lady felt greatly relieved and said, "It's not here, please follow me." She led them outside and to the granary in which her pantry was located. The farmer followed her. The lady's persuasiveness worked. The Cossacks were out of her kitchen. Straceniec and I began to breathe freely. We admired our hostess's gift of persuasion. Obviously the Cossacks were well pleased with the bacon and other food the lady gave them because they left the pantry, went to their wagon, and drove to the next house in the village. After a while they went to the village of Zolta near Sandomierz.

After the Cossacks left, Straceniec and I could not fall asleep for a long time. Nevertheless we rested and our clothes dried. Around noon our hostess called us to her kitchen for a good farm meal. We celebrated our mutual delivery from the danger of losing our lives. We all thanked God for His protection. Straceniec and I expressed also our deep gratitude to the farmer and his wife for endangering their lives for us.

Shortly after the meal, Straceniec and I started on our way to the Vistula. We set out early to give ourselves enough time to travel. It stopped raining and the weather was nice. We reached the bank of the river before the sun set. We had an agreement with our friends in Nadbrzezie that, if for one reason or another, we could not establish contact the first evening we should try the following. Therefore, we hoped that this time we would succeed in crossing the Vistula. As soon as it became dark, a flare burst in the air on the opposite bank. Straceniec responded to the signal by firing his pistol. A few moments later, we heard splashing in the water and then a small boat approached our bank. One of our men from Nadbrzezie was in the boat with the owner. We got into the boat with them and crossed the Vistula. Another of our men from Nadbrzezie waited for us on the other side of the river.

After we left the boatman, the four of us proceeded along the river toward the Nadbrzezie railroad station. In order to reach our two friends' quarters, we had to cross railroad tracks and ramps that were guarded by German soldiers. Both of our friends, Janusz Szczerbatko ("Zygfryd") and Stas Duma ("Topola"), were well acquainted with the railroad station area and led us around the guards with great skill. In one instance, hidden behind a stack of crates, we had to wait for a guard to walk by on his beat before we could go on.

Once we managed to cross the prohibited area of the railroad station, we found ourselves on the street that led from the station to the bridge on the Vistula. Walking on that street even at night was relatively safe. Military personnel as well as civilians walked to and from the station most of the time.

## 14. Snatching Nazi Cash

We mixed with the passengers who walked from the railroad station and traveled in the direction of the bridge. Soon we arrived at a small trailer that stood below the street level and about two hundred yards away from the bridge. In that trailer Janusz and Stas lived. The trailer was so close to the street and the military traffic that the Nazis did not suspect it to be a safe house for Home Army guerrillas.

Before retiring for the night, we reviewed our plan of action for the following day and decided to be on the road much sooner than the last time so that, this time, we would not fail to intercept the bank employees who carried the money.

As we got up in the morning, we reviewed once again our planned action and the escape route. Before leaving the trailer, we loaded our pistols, put them behind our belts, and attached hand grenades to the belts. When we walked up to the road, we noticed that the traffic on it was as busy as usual. We joined the people who walked toward the railroad station and looked for the German bank employees. Even though we had a good view of a long stretch of the road, we did not see them either ahead of us or behind us. After walking toward the station for a while, we turned back and walked toward the bridge. According to our timing, they should have been on the road, but they were not. We walked back and forth for about half an hour and they did not show up. By that time we felt that something was wrong. Greatly disappointed, we returned to the trailer. Our friends sympathized with us and tried to cheer us up. One of them suggested that the bank administration changed the day and the hour for delivering the money to Stalowa Wola. Around noon our friends received confidential information, which confirmed his suggestion. Since the information did not spell out the new time for transferring the money, there was no need for us to stay in Nadbrzezie for another day. Straceniec and I decided to cross the river in the evening and return to our quarters in Wiazownica. In the early afternoon, however, one of the members of the Home Army, who worked at the railroad station, notified us that the German authorities were about to ship, via freight train, a large sum of the government's money, which we could seize the following day. The money was already delivered and deposited in the safe at the railroad station office. Our informer told us also that the best time to seize the money was in the early morning. After a short discussion, we decided to take the German money. We did not want to return to our quarters empty-handed for the second time. We stayed in the trailer for another night. During the evening hours our friends provided us with a layout of the railroad station offices and pinpointed the office in which the safe was located. They also helped us choose the escape route. All of us realized that seizing the money was much easier than getting away with it. Groups of uniformed Germans appeared to be omnipresent at the station, around it, and on the roads leading to it. As a safety measure, Straceniec and I decided to walk at a normal pace to the railroad station and act there as quickly as possible while seizing the money, and then to get away as calmly as possible. Our getting away in a hurry would have been disastrous to us. The Germans would have halted us before we could have made a few steps.

In the early morning of April 29, 1944, Straceniec and I were ready for action. After checking and rechecking our pistols and hand grenades, we left our friends' barrack at 9:00 A.M. Each of us carried an empty briefcase that might have made us look like officeworkers going to work, but our wind and sunburned faces tended to contradict that. On the way between the barrack and the railroad station, we met many uniformed Germans who walked and rode to and from the station. They paid no attention to us. As we approached the station, we noticed about two hundred Cossacks commanded by German officers who waited for their train near the military ramp. As usual, at the railroad station, German soldiers were walking this way and that way. A German police vehicle was parked near the main entrance to the station. Policemen were searching passengers' suitcases for contraband. Straceniec and I entered the building through the side door, which led to the offices of the railroad station. On each side of a rather narrow hallway there were various railroad offices. The office with the safe was the first one to our left. As we were about to enter this office, a uniformed German appeared in the hallway and walked briskly in our direction. We thought that he intended to enter the office where the money was but, fortunately, he went to another office. As soon as he closed the door behind him, we approached the door of "our" office. Straceniec energetically pressed the door handle and stepped in first. I followed him. While I was closing the door, Straceniec said, "Good morning," and produced his pistol. I did not bother to pull out my pistol but unbuttoned my coat and displayed it stuck behind my belt. Then Straceniec explained the purpose of our "visit" and asked the officeworkers to raise their hands. As they all stood up with their raised hands, I searched them for handguns. They had no weapons. Then I disconnected the telephone. Straceniec commanded all the men to lie down on the floor with the exception of the office manager, who knew how to open the safe, and a beautiful young lady. After the manager opened the safe, Straceniec loaded his briefcase full of money. I kept an eye on the men on the floor. Then, while Straceniec watched the officeworkers, I packed my briefcase with money. As soon as I finished packing the money, Straceniec left the office and began walking away from the station toward the village of Wielowies. I waited in the office for a minute or two. Then I ordered the man to lie down on the floor for another fifteen minutes and left. As I left the grounds of the railroad station, I noticed Straceniec walk, in an accelerated pace, on the road that led to Wielowies. He was about one hundred and fifty yards ahead of me. From time to time he looked back to see whether I was walking behind him. After noticing me, he began to walk faster and gave me signs with his hand to increase my speed. I was still in the area where many Germans were and refused to rush. I knew that Straceniec was loosing his cool. His behavior could have endangered the success of our operation. Fortunately the Germans did not notice his nervous behavior.

After walking for a few minutes, I caught up with Straceniec. At that point we left the road and began walking through wooded area toward the willow bushes that grew along the Vistula. Before we reached the safety of the bushes, we heard a shrill siren at the railroad station, a series of submachine gun shots and shouts of the German officers in charge of the Cossacks. We knew that the Germans had discovered our seizure of the money. They were sounding an alarm, blocking the roads, and searching for us. Straceniec and I considered ourselves lucky to be out of their reach even though the danger of being apprehended still hovered over us. In order to reach the security of the bushes on the banks of the Vistula, we began to run toward them as fast as we could. Soon we were in the bushes and, after resting for a moment, we walked through them in a southwesterly direction. As we kept walking we bypassed the village of Wielowies, which was to our left. The village was built on each side of the road that led from Nadbrzezie to the city of Tarnobrzeg. After coming close to the village of Sielec, we found the spot where, several days before, we had crossed the Vistula. There we were to wait until late afternoon for the arrival of Janusz and Stas. They were supposed to bring us something to eat and arrange for our crossing the river.

As we waited for the afternoon to come, we were bored so we counted the money. Most of the bills were in new, crisp one hundred zlotys denominations. If I am not mistaken, in both of our brief cases, we had close to fifty thousand zlotys. It was a substantial sum of money in those days. After counting the money, we walked to the bank of the Vistula, sat down and watched the water go by. Soon we heard the sound of a motorboat. Before we saw it, Straceniec and I got up and walked into the bushes again. There we lay down and watched the river. After a moment a military motorboat appeared. The Germans were patrolling the river. We thought that they expected us to cross it during the day. Later, as we watched the opposite bank, we discovered that a group of uniformed Germans were walking along the river. At one point they came across a fisherman whom they obviously questioned about something. After seeing what was happening there, we were convinced that the Germans were also searching the bushes on our side of the river. Therefore we hid our brief cases under a bunch of old willow branches and prepared ourselves to fight to the last bullet. As we took the best defensive positions available and listened attentively to the possible sounds of the Germans' steps, we could not hear anything in our immediate proximity. All we could hear was the sound of German motorized vehicles on the road between Nadbrzezie and Tarnobrzeg, and the motorboat patrolling the river.

About five o'clock in the afternoon, our friend, Janusz, arrived on a bicycle. He brought some food and he told us about the Germans' reaction to our seizure of the money. According to him, a number of events took place at the railroad station after our seizure of the cash. The sequence of events began when the station's manager attempted to make a routine telephone call to the office that Straceniec and I raided just a moment before. Unable to get a connection, he decided to walk to the office. Upon entering it, the manager found the office workers prostrated on the floor. From them he found out what had happened and immediately notified the German police, who were searching passengers' suitcases at the station. The police sounded an alarm, which initially resulted in great confusion. Most of the uniformed Germans and the Cossacks at the railroad station who waited for their trains were convinced that the sound of the siren announced an imminent air raid so they took cover wherever they could. Only submachine gun shots fired by the police made them realize that the sound of the sirens meant something else. So they began to rally around the Nazi police to learn what actually happened and to offer their help. The Cossacks, led by their German officers, appeared very comical. Since the train they waited for on the military ramp was not due for hours, some of them fell asleep and others were mending their shoes and clothing. When the alarm sounded they were in a total disarray. On the way to the railroad station building some of them walked without shoes and some without trousers or coats. All of them shouted excitedly and some even fired their guns.

After surrounding the railroad station and searching for us, the Germans learned from somebody that we had left in the direction of Wielowies. Therefore they pursued us in that direction. Then they surrounded the village and searched for us there. After failing to find us in the village, they requested the river police to patrol the Vistula and its western bank.

Janusz told us that, according to reports from his friends at the railroad station, the chief of the German police was extremely angry after his return from his search for us in Wielowies. He was heard to say that he saw us walking to the railroad station in the morning but we did not appear suspicious to him. He was angry with himself for not being perceptive enough. Perhaps Straceniec and I looked too young to appear suspicious.

When evening came Janusz arranged for our crossing of the river. He asked the boatman to go by himself to the other bank and check whether it was safe for us to cross. He did so. Moments later he returned, then we said goodbye to Janusz and boarded the boat.

After crossing the Vistula River, Straceniec and I found our bicycles without any trouble, walked to the river's dike, and began to ride on its top toward the village of Bogoria. In spite of the darkness, we managed to ride well on the dike's hard and level path. While approaching Bogoria we discovered that a large group of Cossacks was stationed there. According to the report we received from a farm boy, the Cossacks posted their guards on every road that led to the village, including the path on the top of the dike. Therefore we were forced to go into the bushes on the bank of the river and under their cover walk by the village. It was a strenuous walk but we made it safely and returned to the dike to continue our ride in a southerly direction. We were convinced that the further we went from Bogoria the safer we were from the Cossacks. But when we arrived in the vicinity of the steam mill in the village of Speranda, we were terribly surprised to see, in the light of the outdoor electric lights, about ten Cossacks who were loading sacks of flour on their wagons. They were shouting to each other and laughing at the top of their voices. Since the outdoor light of the mill illuminated the dike we were riding on, Straceniec and I had a very slim chance to pass unnoticed by the Cossacks. We were apprehensive to take this chance. We could, of course, walk through willow brush near the river but we had very little energy left to do that. Therefore we decided to frighten the Cossacks by firing a flare. When the flare went across the sky and burst above the mill, the Cossacks became panicky, jumped on their wagons as fast as they could, and rode away. They obviously thought that a group of partisans was about to attack them. When we saw the Cossacks' fright and a very quick withdrawal, we were roaring with laughter. We could not believe our eyes. Our path on the dike was now opened to us. So we continued our journey that night until we came to the village of Chodkow. In that village Straceniec knew a hospitable and dependable family who gave us shelter, warm beds, and food. After a day's rest, we proceeded through the villages of Gagolin and Dlugoleka to the town of Osiek. From Osiek, we pedaled to our quarters in Wiazownica.

Needless to say, our chief Orlicz was extremely pleased with our performance and the money we brought. He needed the money to pay for our food, shoes, clothing, and ammunition.

# 15. Attacks on Gestapo Agent von Paul

Von Paul was a member of the National Socialist German Workers' Party (NSDAP) and also a Gestapo agent who, during World War II, resided in Skrzypaczowice manor in the district of Sandomierz. As an administrator of the manor, he organized a small convalescence center for groups of Wehrmacht and SS officers, especially for those who were wounded at the Russian front. In addition to the convalescent officers, there was a group of 15 to 20 SS men who guarded the manor and its inhabitants.

The Polish underground intelligence service became aware that von Paul's activities were directed at the destruction of Polish secret organizations in the district of Sandomierz. Through his network of informers, whom he recruited by means of terror, blackmail, and money, von Paul was responsible for the imprisonment and death of many Polish patriots. In the village of Skrzypaczowice itself, he was responsible for the deaths of fifteen young men.[52] In order to stop his destructive intelligence-gathering activities, the district court of the Home Army condemned von Paul to death. Captain Stanislaw Glowinski ("Mirski" vel "Czarski") signed the death sentence and ordered the Sandomierz Flying Commando Group to execute the sentence. Lieutenant Witold Jozefowski ("Mis"), who was at that time a commanding officer of our group, organized the attack on the Gestapo agent. In planning this action Mis was aware that in the past the Nazis always retaliated by killing ten Polish prisoners for the death of one of their own, so he chose the place for the attack away from inhabited areas. The place that Lieutenant Jozefowski chose was located on the edge of the Skrzypaczowice Forest and in the immediate proximity of the main road that went from Staszow through Osiek, Loniow, Skrzypaczowice, Koprzywnica, and Sosniczany to Sandomierz.[53] The lieutenant knew that every Friday von Paul went to Opatow or Sandomierz. Usually, he

## 15. ATTACKS ON GESTAPO AGENT VON PAUL

left Skrzypaczowice manor between 10:00 A.M. and 11:00 A.M. and returned to the manor about 5:00 P.M.

In his recollections of our attack on von Paul, Lieutenant Jozefowski described it in the following words,

> I have been summoned by the commandant of the district, Mirski, who ordered me to abduct von Paul. On the basis of the intelligence that he had, Mirski determined the day and the time when von Paul was to return by carriage from Opatow via Koprzywnica to the manor of Skrzypaczowice. In giving me his order, Mirski stated very firmly that during the abduction, I should see to it that neither von Paul nor any of his military escort should be killed. The reason for this firm statement was the fact that a few weeks before two German soldiers were killed at the farmer's market in Koprzywnica and the Nazi authorities retaliated by killing forty Poles. Therefore, his order was single minded: to abduct von Paul alive and if his military escort would open up fire, to withdraw without killing any Germans.
>
> According to our plan, I was to dress in such a way as to appear like a begging musician. On my head I was to wear a large hat, my body was to be covered with a long dustcoat and in a violin case I was to hide my submachine gun. According to our plan, upon reaching the edge of the Skrzypaczowice Forest, we were to notice a lady who was to take a position near the sharp bend of the road

On the right is Colonel Witold Jozefowski ("Mis"), who was in charge of the attack on Von Paul on the highway near Skrzypaczowice Forest on March 13, 1944. On the left is Captain Henryk Kuksz ("Selim"). Author's photograph.

in the direction of Koprzywnica. She was supposed to drop her white handkerchief to the ground as a signal that von Paul's britzka (carriage) was coming. At that moment I was to appear on the road and walk toward Koprzywnica to halt the britzka when it reached a certain distance from me. When the britzka would have come to a stop, the six of you were to jump from the trenches to the road, disarm the escort, and take the escort to the forest and keep it there for one hour during which time I, von Paul, and one of you (I do not remember which one of you) would travel to a certain safehouse. In case the britzka would not stop, "Sep" (or "Sokol") was supposed to drop the horses with his light machine gun and thus would have stopped the britzka without killing any of the Germans. This is how it was supposed to be.[54]

In the middle of March 1944, our Flying Commando Unit took up quarters in Jachimowice manor, which belonged to Mr. and Mrs. Bronislaw Bronikowski, and in the Adamczyk's farmhouse in the village of Jachimowice. It was early in the afternoon when a messenger from the intelligence service arrived in our quarters and notified Lieutenant Jozefowski that von Paul was in Opatow and would be returning home late in the afternoon. As usual, he would be riding in a britzka accompanied by three SS-men. As soon as the lieutenant learned about this, he called six or seven of us and ordered us to get ready for an ambush on the Gestapo agent and his bodyguards.[55] Moments later, we were on the way to the edge of the Skrzypaczowice Forest near the road by which von Paul was to return from Opatow via Koprzywnica. We walked toward our destination through the fields to avoid meeting anybody on the country roads. According to my best recollection, Jozef Osemlak from Loniow, an older brother of John Osemlak ("Straceniec"), took his bicycle and rode to Koprzywnica to intercept von Paul's britzka there and to ride about two hundred yards ahead of it in order to alert us about his imminent coming because the road near the ambush area had a sharp bend and we could not see much of it in the direction of Koprzywnica.[56]

After we arrived to our destination, Lieutenant Jozefowski assigned each of us his part in the attack and his firing position. He himself decided to start the attack by appearing on the road with his submachine gun (MP) to stop the von Paul britzka. Soon Jozef Osemlak appeared on the road riding his bicycle from Koprzywnica toward Loniow, looked at us in our firing positions, flashed us his usual big smile, and accelerated his speed. We knew exactly what he meant and our hearts began to beat faster as we checked and rechecked our weapons. Since Mis ordered us to take von Paul alive and if possible spare the horses, our task was not very easy.

Soon the britzka with the Nazis appeared on the road. Mis with his submachine gun ready to shoot rushed to the road to halt it. He raised his submachine gun to the firing position and shouted, "*Halt und hände hoch!*" The britzka slowed down its speed and began to come to a stop. At that moment, Mis, holding his submachine gun with one hand, caught the bridle of the horse with the other hand. The britzka came to a complete stop. The rest of us jumped up from our positions and, with our weapons ready to fire, moved quickly toward the Nazis to terrorize them. Instead of raising their hands, the SS bodyguards stood up and opened fire at us. We returned our fire at them. Both the bodyguards' fire and our fire spooked the highly jittery horses, who jerked the britzka and plunged ahead with great speed. One of the SS-men fell out of the britzka and began to run away.[57] Lieutenant Mis opened fire at the britzka with his MP, but Sep's light machine gun, which was so much needed now, failed to fire. According to Lieutenant Jozefowski's orders, Sep was to kill the horses in case the britzka would not stop. Now we lost our main fire power. At the same time the britzka, with von Paul and his two bodyguards, was speeding on the road toward the manor Skrzypaczowice. Soon, it disappeared on the curve of the road and we concentrated our efforts on catching the SS-man, who remained within our reach. He was armed with a German artillery Luger, which has a rather long barrel, and fired at us as we tried to encircle him in the field adjacent to the road. We carried rifles and could have killed him without any problem but we wanted to take him alive. As we were coming closer and closer to him, he kept shooting and moving near the road on which the farm wagons were coming down the hill from Koprzywnica toward Loniow. He obviously sensed that we would not shoot at him near the road for the fear of killing innocent people. Finally, he managed to come close to the road and found protection behind a pile of sand. Protected now by the sand pile, he resumed shooting at us as we were approaching him. But after shooting a few times, some sand got into the mechanism of his pistol and disabled it. So he left his Luger on the sand pile and pulled out of his pocket a small caliber pistol and ran into the middle of the road, halted a farm wagon that was coming down the road, and ordered the farmer to turn around and take him to Koprzywnica. The farmer had no choice and obeyed the SS-man. We had no choice either. We could not fire at the wagon without endangering the lives of our own people.

Since von Paul and two of his body guards were speeding toward Skrzypaczowice manor and the third bodyguard was on the way to Koprzywnica, we could not remain near the road any longer for fear German rescue units would be coming to attack us. So we walked through the fields on the edge of the forest in a northwesterly direction. After walking for about one mile, we noticed a group of German troopers, who arrived at the ambush area and were looking for us. They also noticed us and watched us through binoculars. We were too far from them for effective machine gun and rifle fire. Nevertheless, the Germans fired at us with their machine gun and we returned fire with our rifles.[58] Soon, we disappeared in the wooded area and went to Beszyce Dolne, where in the manor there we took up our quarters.[59]

After we reached our quarters, we began to evaluate our attack on von Paul and his three bodyguards and we came to a number of conclusions.

First of all, we agreed that the place that Lieutenant Mis had chosen for the ambush was very suitable. It was far enough from Skrzypaczowice manor, where von Paul kept a unit of SS-men and also far enough from Koprzywnica where SD troopers were stationed in the school building near the historic church. It was also close to the forest in which we could disappear with our prisoner and his bodyguards and move away safely to another area. Second, the number of our men who took part in the attack was quite sufficient to cope with the four Germans. It would have been more difficult to disappear in the countryside with a larger group.

Third, all of us were convinced that our light machine gun should have been test-fired in a basement or a dugout at our quarters before it was used in the attack. I believe that the gun had not been fired since our attack on the Wehrmacht unit at the Szczucin Bridge on November 12, 1943.

Fourth, we tended to believe that since the place of the ambush was on the bend of the road, we should have placed some light obstacle on the road so the German britzka would have been forced to stop for a moment. Such a momentary stop would have given us a better chance for a successful attack.

Finally, we admitted that all of us underestimated the training and combat experience that the SS-men had. They totally ignored the order, *"Hände hoch!"* and instead opened fire at us. We were forced to admit their courage and combat skill and decided to be more careful in dealing with SS men in the future. We also underestimated the unpredictable behavior of gun-shy horses. After hearing gunfire, they become erratic, uncontrollable, and capable of running a considerable distance with bullets in their bodies.[60] We should have never attempted to save the horses from the very beginning of our attack. Needless to say, all of us were deeply embarrassed at our failure to seize von Paul and hoped to have another chance of catching him alive.[61] Unfortunately, the superiors of our district's Home Army did not give us another opportunity to abduct von Paul. This opportunity went to a relatively small group of young men led by Jozef Bojanowski ("Walter"), who was born and grew up in Niechlodow manor, near the German border in the district of Leszno, province of Poznań.

Jozef Bojanowski was one of six children. When World War II began on September 1, 1939, Jozef was sixteen years old. After the Nazi authorities deprived the Bojanowskis of their possessions and exiled them to the district of Sandomierz, their relatives invited them to Uzarzow manor near Klimontow. While there, Jozef and his younger brother, Jan, joined the Polish underground resistance movement. As a member of the resistance, Jozef made himself known as a brave and a daring young man, who in most instances, with the help of his younger brother, Jan Bojanowski ("Michael"), and Zbigniew Piatek ("Grabina")[62] — both of them as brave and daring as himself— managed in a spectacular way to attack and eliminate some of the most dangerous Gestapo men and their agents. They included Lescher, a notoriously cruel commandant of the German police in Klimontow, and Ploczynski, Trzmiel, and Hichlaszko, all three very dangerous Gestapo agents in Sandomierz.

Following our failure to apprehend von Paul, the inspector general of the Home Army in the district of Sandomierz, Colonel Antoni Zolkiewski ("Lin") gave an order to Captain Leon Torlinski ("Kret") who was in charge of the district's intelligence service, to apprehend von Paul and to interrogate him about his network of agents. The order also stated that if taking von Paul alive became impossible, he should be killed in the attack. Captain Torlinski, in turn, asked Jozef Bojanowski and his men to execute the order. Recollecting these events, Jozef Bojanowski writes as follows: "Speaking again about von Paul.... Kret (Captain Leon Torlinski) asked me to take charge of the attack on von Paul. He never ordered me to do any jobs (execution of death sentences) but always proposed, suggested, so I could have a chance to refuse if I would not like to do it.... Kret stated that von Paul does not have any bodyguards because there were no military men anymore at the manor of Skrzypaczowice. In this case he made a mistake. This was not the first time that our intelligence service made a mistake ... but that is a different subject."[63]

As usual, Jozef Bojanowski asked his brother Jan Bojanowski, Zbigniew Piatek, and Tadeusz Chmiel ("Alfred") to take part in the attack on von Paul. For the location for the attack Walter chose the village of Sosniczany, which is situated on the main road from Koprzywnica to Sandomierz. The attack was scheduled for Friday, July 14, 1944. Walter and his men came to Sosniczany by a britzka at 5:00 A.M. so the local people would not notice them. At first, they stayed in the house that belonged to a member of the Home Army. The house was near the road and had a window through which a certain section of the road could be observed. However, due to the curve in the road, the visibility was rather limited. Therefore, after observing the road through the window for some time, Walter and his men decided to leave the house and wait for von Paul in the orchard adjacent to the road. The Gestapo agent was expected to ride through Sosniczany between 10:00 A.M. and 11:00 A.M. Waiting long hours was a nerve-racking experience for the attackers. They had nothing to do except to watch the road and check their weapons, which though not very good were sufficient for the attack. Walter and Grabina had submachine guns; Michael and Alfred were armed with large caliber pistols and hand grenades. Of course, they kept their weapons concealed.

As the time approached at which von Paul was expected to ride through Sosniczany, the attackers left the orchard and came closer to the road. Now, they did not have to wait long for action to begin. This is what Jan Bojanowski wrote:

> Soon, there appeared on the road a farm wagonette with three passengers and behind it a britzka which was pulled by two large and well fed horses going with an accelerated trot. We recognized in the britzka German uniforms. The time of the day agreed with the information which we have received from our intelligence service. Now, we had no doubt that von Paul was coming. In a moment, the road near us will become a stage and we will become actors just like in a good western movie. We began our accelerated walk on both sides of the village road, which led to the main road on which the Germans were riding. Walter and Zbigniew walked ahead with the submachine guns under their topcoats. Alfred and I followed them. We approached the main road from its left side.[64] From our perspective, we were able to see quite well the britzka and the passengers. On the left side of the front seat sat an SS man holding his rifle between his knees; the driver sat on his right side. In the back seat there was another German in uniform holding his rifle on his knees and the barrel of the rifle was turned toward us. On his right side sat von Paul, who was only slightly visible. As soon as we came to the crossing of the roads, the farm wagonette arrived there and in it Walter recognized Kret, chief of our intelligence service but he had no time to warn us.[65] Soon, we were 15 paces from the main road and the britzka with von Paul and his bodyguards reached the crossroads. At this very moment, we pulled our weapons from under our topcoats and shouted, "*Halt!*" Stop! The driver disappeared from his seat. The German in the back seat lifted up his rifle from his knees to a firing position but at the same time fell to the bottom of the britzka because we were firing all our weapons. Simultaneously, the SS man, who sat in the front seat, fell backward and his foot made a semicircle in the air. He joined his comrade on the bottom of this britzka. Our first shots spooked the horses and made them go into a gallop. The britzka began to run away from us. We could no longer see neither the bodyguards nor von Paul, because the high back of the seat obscured everything. At that time, we directed all our fire at the left horse whose left side was still visible and at the heads of the horses that were also somewhat visible above the britzka. Nothing worked. As in a bad dream, the britzka took off farther and farther and disappeared from the range of our effective fire. It appeared to us that von Paul, living or dead, whose horses seemed to be bulletproof, would escape capture for the third time. At that moment, a helpful accident occurred. The galloping horses (without the driver) caused a collision of the britzka with the farm wagonette, which fell apart. At the same time, the britzka tilted decisively to its left side and almost turned upside down. At that moment, von Paul jumped out of it and dashed into the field of ripened grain. Then, the britzka regained its balance and disappeared behind the curve of the road. One of the wheels of the disintegrated farm wagonette rolled down the road. On the other side (the right side) of the road emerged the driver of the German britzka. He was pale and without his cap but otherwise quite well. Now was the highest time to catch von Paul. Zbyszek (Zbigniew Piatek) was the first

one to pursue him and catch up with him. In a moment, von Paul was disarmed and led to our own britzka. On the way to the britzka, Walter stopped to see the passengers of the broken farm wagonette. Fortunately, all three of them were alive.[66]

We left Sosniczany in a hurry and rode to Wisniowa where the Jedrus Group was supposed to have its headquarters. Von Paul had three bullet holes in his left arm but the bone was intact.[67] Bandages were put on his arm. We had a relatively long way before us. In one of the villages through which we were going, some people told us that a number of German patrols were conducting a manhunt in the area.[68] It was not very difficult to figure out that they were looking for von Paul.[69] Nevertheless, while riding by the village of Jachimowice, Walter displayed a reckless bravado. This is how Krystyna Bronikowska Radlinska remembers it: "It was an early afternoon in June 1944. My father with Roman Ciesielski vel Milewski, who was a displaced person, supervised weeding of our sugar beets. Suddenly, they noticed a britzka speeding from the direction of Koprzywnica. Jozef Bojanowski was driving it. When the britzka reached the area where the workers on our farm were located, Jozef, a daredevil, removed a light dustcoat with which a stout German had been covered. He was a Gestapo man, von Paul from the *Liegenschaft* of Skrzypaczowice."[70]

According to Zbigniew Piatek who was riding in the britzka with von Paul, Bojanowski stopped the vehicle when he came close to the farm workers and engaged in a brief conversation with Bronislaw Bronikowski and his assistant, Roman Ciesielski.[71] Jan Bojanowski goes on to describe the outcome of these dramatic events in the following manner:

The Jedrus Group was not in the place where we expected it to be and no member had left a message as to where we could get in touch with them. Since the reports of the German patrols came to our attention over and over again, Walter concluded that our riding in the countryside could end up very badly for us. Therefore, the life of von Paul had to be terminated as soon as possible. One has to admit that he broke down only at the very end and revealed the names of only two informers who, as we learned later on, were already dead. Since there were no volunteers, Walter carried out the death sentence.[72] While writing the second part of this chapter, I had a telephone conversation with Zbigniew Piatek, who told me that von Paul was briefly interrogated by Walter in a forest at a certain distance from a road that was seldom used. There he was killed and buried. In order to conceal the grave, Walter and his associates covered it with some dead tree branches.

Following the execution of von Paul, the Germans kept searching for him in the whole area. They must have had some leads as to the direction in which Walter and his men abducted the Gestapo agent because, several days after the abduction, the Nazi police descended on Jachimowice manor, by which Walter drove the britzka with von Paul on the way to Wisnowa. The manor belonged to Mr. and Mrs. Bronislaw Bronikowski, great Polish patriots, who were very active in the resistance movement. Their young daughter, Krystyna, described what happened:

> ...it was Sunday and there was a rather large social gathering in our home. The lovers of bridge sat at the tables and others took advantage of the beautiful weather and walked in the park. In the dining room the table was being prepared for dinner. "Kruk" (Antoni Jozef Wiktorowski) and "Tarnina" (Tadeusz Pytlakowski) were among the guests. Around noontime, we heard the sound of a motor. The German police came in a large truck. They shouted, "Give us back von Paul whether he is alive or dead!" They searched our entire home. In the attic, they stripped the boards from the floor. They opened all the wardrobes calling continuously, "Paul! Paul!" and shouting, "He must be here!" They checked all the covers on the hangers. They found a light dustcoat similar to the one that von Paul used to wear. There were blood stains on it. The members of the family and the guests ignored the Germans. The bridge game continued. "Tarnina" ordered me to destroy the mail which I flushed down in the bathroom. He himself burned the sensitive papers that he had on him.
>
> As the search of our home was progressing, we noticed that a britzka was coming in the direction of our home. It was the same britzka in which Jozef (Bojanowski) abducted von Paul. Jozef was riding in it. However, he did not come in front of the house but went the side way along the park and to the barnyard. I went to see him immediately. He was unhitching the horses and taking them to the barn. I said to him, "Mr. Jozef, the Germans are here. Do you have anything incriminating?" "Yes, von Paul's notebook. It has to be hidden." I took from him a thick black notebook and put it under my arm. Jozef threw his pistol on the floor of the barn and with his boot covered it with the manure. At the same time a German policeman was on the way to the barn to take a look at Walter and to examine his ID. I went to the orchard and buried the notebook under the currant bush. In the meantime, the Germans brought a group of people from the village and from the homes of our farm workers. They asked the people if they saw anything connected with the abduction of von Paul. They were shouting on the top of their voices. "He must be here! His trail ends here!" The people responded that they did not see anything and do not know anything. It was very edifying to see such solidarity and such a common front of various classes of people against the Germans. Even one careless word or gesture would have brought grave consequences.
>
> The search of our home did not produce any results. However, they took my father's bloodstained dustcoat to analyze the blood. After they left, we sat down at the table for dinner and had a drink. Shortly after the dinner, our guests began to leave one by one. The first ones to leave were Kruk, Tarnina, and Walter.[73]
>
> Toward the evening, I noticed, all of sudden, a covered truck full of uniformed Germans returning from Byszow and I became frightened. So, together with Jerzy and Roman, we escaped into the field of rye. I listened, trying to hear

any gun shots. The wait seemed to stretch into centuries because I remembered how the Nazis had murdered some people in Zbydniow.[74] Finally, I heard the sound of the truck going away. Obviously, our house had been watched. The Germans knew that one of our guests fell out from the boat into the water. As I learned later on, they returned to inquire as to who were our guests. At that time, my father was able to give them any names which came to his mind. The Germans asked my father to appear in their headquarters the following day in the morning. Mr. Luczek represented my father with the Germans. He was expelled by the Nazis from Poznań and was a very capable accountant. As such, he worked for a number of manors in the area. At the same time, he gathered intelligence on the German police. Due to his excellent knowledge of the German language, social talents, incredible audacity, and ability to use vodka ... he felt very comfortable in the midst of the German police. Through his influence among the Germans he rendered great services to the Home Army by freeing many persons from the hands of the police. After a number of hours of hard bargaining with the police, he returned from Koprzywnica and reported that even though the police discovered that the blood stain on the topcoat came from a butchered calf, nevertheless, the policemen insisted that von Paul's trail ended in Jachimowice and they viewed the place with great suspicion.[75]

Shortly after the abduction and execution of von Paul, the Germans closed down their Gestapo stronghold in Skrzypaczowice manor. The SS-men who were stationed there as von Paul's bodyguards abandoned their post in such a hurry that they left behind one rifle and a case of hand grenades.[76] They never returned to Skrzypaczowice.

While visiting Poland in April 1997, I went to see the two places where von Paul had been attacked: the edge of the Skrzypaczowice Forest and the village of Sosniczany. I also went to Skrzypaczowice manor to see what was left of it. Like most of the manors in the whole area, it was destroyed beyond recognition during the Communist administration in the country. The older people in the village still remembered von Paul and his criminal activities as a Gestapo agent but they also remembered him as an excellent administrator of the manor.

# 16. Military Air Drops

As Soviet military might began to overpower the Nazi divisions and armies in Russia and push them west toward the Polish border, the leadership of the Polish Home Army realized that these developments portended the beginning of the end of Hitler's criminal empire. At the same time, various units of the underground Home Army began to swell with hundreds of new and patriotic volunteers who were ready to take an active part in the liberation of their country from the Nazi barbarians. All these volunteers had an urgent need of weapons such as rifles, pistols, submachine guns, machine guns, hand grenades, explosives, ammunition, and so forth. Almost all of the weapons in our underground units were taken by force from the German police or from members of the German army. Some of the weapons were brought to our units by defectors from the enemy's military establishment. When Benito Mussolini sent a few of his divisions to help his friend, Adolf Hitler, in his Russian adventure, many of the Italian soldiers sold their weapons and ammunition to the agents of the Home Army. They hated the Germans and despised the Russians and needed money to have a good time before they were sent to the front. Unlike the Nazi military men, the Italian soldiers and officers were very human and fun-loving men. Our college-educated agents did not have much trouble in communicating with them because in Polish colleges and high schools before the war Latin was one of the obligatory languages. It is a well-known fact that anybody who knows Latin will have very little trouble in understanding Italian. Due to such favorable relationships between the Polish population and the Italian soldiers, many good Italian rifles, pistols, submachine guns, and a great deal of ammunition were acquired by the Polish underground army. However, in spite of all the acquisitions, there were still not enough weapons and other military hardware for the masses of the new volunteers. There was an obvious need for airdrops of military hardware from the Western allies. The United States and Britain responded promptly to the urgent need of military supplies for the Polish Home Army.

Most of the military drops made in Poland under the German occupation came from either Britain or the airports near Bari and Brindisi in southeastern Italy, which were already under the control of the American and British forces. Each of these airdrops called for a very thorough preparation on both sides. On the one side, the commanding officers in Britain or Italy who were in charge of the airdrops had to send coded messages by way of popular songs broadcast by BBC Radio, which indicated the date, the time, and the location of the drop. On the other side, the commanding officers of the Home Army in Poland had to prepare proper and save locations for the airdrops (in most instances alternative locations). At the same time, they had to have a sufficient number of armed men to secure the roads leading to the airdrop areas. They also had to have enough men to light fires and to form a light arrow using powerful flashlights to indicate to the pilot the area of the drop, called a basket *(kosz)* and the direction in which he should fly while dropping the military supplies. They had to have enough strong men to unhook the parachutes from the containers and to carry the containers to the farm wagons, and, finally, they had to have enough farm wagons and drivers to transport the military supplies to a safe place.

Our Flying Commando Unit received the first airdrop in the fields near the village of Sadlowice during the night of April 29-30, 1944. We came to the area two or three days earlier before the expected airdrop and had very comfortable quarters in a large farmhouse surrounded by many trees. As usual, one of our men stood guard at the gate of the park from which the road was quite visible. As our guard watched the road, he noticed an innocent looking young man who seemed to be passing by. All of a sudden, the young man turned toward the guard, pulled out his pistol, and fired at him two shots, which missed the target. In self-defense, our guard, Niedzwiedz, aimed his pistol at the attacker and squeezed the trigger, but the pistol misfired. The attacker lost his cool and began to run away as fast as he could. The sound of the attacker's fire alarmed us in the farmhouse. Straceniec, Sokol — with a light machinegun — and I ran outside to see what was happening. Niedzwiedz pointed to us the direction in which the attacker ran and we began to pursue him. We also fired several shots at him, which made him leave the road and run through the fields on the right side of the road. Sokol tried to fire his machine gun but the unevenness of the terrain prevented him from taking a good aim. If I am not mistaken, Straceniec took a shortcut through the field and was the first one to catch up with the young man. He terrorized the attacker with his gun and disarmed him without any problems. Soon, Sokol and I joined Straceniec and we began to question the attacker who was trembling with fear. When we asked him as to why he attempted to kill our guard, he responded: "They ordered me to kill him." Soon we discovered that he was a member of the Polish Communist Party and his superiors ordered him to kill our man on guard duty. When our commanding officer, Mis, arrived on the scene, he took the young attacker to the side and questioned him again. The young man cried during the interrogation and begged for his life. Mis admonished the offender, let him go, and said to us: "He is just a stupid young man — he will never do it again." We were impressed and edified by the wisdom of our officer's decision. Unlike the Communist superiors of the attacker, he did not want to spill fraternal blood.

Several days after the above incident, we made preparations for the first airdrop in the fields, which were not too far away from our quarters. I remember that somebody leaked the information about the imminent airdrop to the members of the underground organization called the Peasant Battalions, who at that time were not a part of the Home Army. They knew that the airdrop was destined exclusively for the Home Army; nevertheless, they hoped that the wind might carry some of the containers away from the basket and into their hands. With this in mind, they observed our movements and preparations and when we went into the fields on the night of the airdrop a small group of their men sneaked into the fields also. They had an advantage over us because they knew the area much better than we did so they could hide in the darkness of the night and wait for the proper moment. Their proper moment came when the aircraft began to drop its load and the containers hit the ground. At that time, they cautiously emerged from the darkness and attempted to drag three containers not to our wagons but away from them. I happened to guard that section of the basket where they appeared and I saw quite well what they intended to do. At that time, I asked some of our men to help me to expel the intruders from the basket area. They left in a great anger and promised to return with a larger force. As I learned later on, they did not return to the airdrop area but went to our unguarded quarters and took four of our best bicycles, which were at the barn near our quarters.

After all the containers, crates, and parachutes were collected and loaded on the farm wagons, they were transported to the village of Naslawice and stored in the farm buildings of Mrs. Zareba. Following the departure of all wagons and men from the basket, my friend Jan Szpakiewicz ("Pikolo") and I remained longer in the field to see to it that nothing of the airdrop was left there. As we wandered around the basket area crisscrossing it this way and that way, we found a broken crate full of 45-caliber semi-automatic Colt pistols and ammunition. Needless to say, we were delighted with such a find and decided to report it to our commanding officer. However, as a reward for discovering the lost crate of Colt pistols and ammunition, we decided to keep four pistols for our own use. Therefore, he took two pistols and some ammunition and I did the same. Of course, we did not realize that each airdrop was accompanied by a detailed list of all the items that were supposed to be received by us. In order to protect the crate with the Colts and ammunition, one of us guarded the weapons and the other went to our quarters to get some help in transporting them to a safe place. After the transportation was arranged, we escorted a farm wagon to our quarters and then decided to rest for a few hours before sunrise. During our sleep we put our newly acquired pistols in our boots and when we got up in time for a late breakfast we hid them behind our belts.

Shortly after our breakfast, Pikolo and I discovered that the tire prints of our stolen bicycles were quite visible on the ground; so, with the permission of our commanding officer, we decided to follow the tire prints that led to the country road west of our quarters. After we followed the prints for about four miles, we saw that they turned from the main road to the small farm road. We followed that road and came to a secluded farm. At first, we went to the farmhouse and knocked on the door and, when no one answered, we went to the barn. No one seemed to be in the barn either, but nevertheless we opened the large door of the barn and saw all four bicycles that were stolen from our quarters. Then, we took our bicycles outside of the barn, closed the door, and went again to the farmhouse to knock on the door. This time, a man answered the door. He must have been about thirty-five years old and was visibly upset. We introduced ourselves to him as members of the Sandomierz Flying Commando Unit and asked him whether he was aware that stolen bicycles were in his barn. He replied that the bicycles in the barn belonged to his underground organization and we had no right to take them out of the barn. I told him that the four bicycles were stolen from our Commando Unit the night before and that we followed the tire prints from our quarters to his barn. He refused to accept my statement and said, with a great deal of agitation, that he would not let us take the bicycles from his yard. At that moment, both of us pulled from behind our belts four new 45-caliber Colts. He looked at the barrels of the guns and changed his tune; he decided to become very cooperative. Therefore, we took our bicycles and returned to our quarters.

After returning to our quarters, we were very jubilant on account of our successful encounter with, what appeared to us, a leader of a Communist underground organization. We were also happy because we recovered our stolen bicycles. We spent most of the afternoon telling and retelling everyone about our experiences with some members of the Peasants Battalions who wanted to snatch a few of the containers from the airdrop area and about the broken crate full of pistols and ammunition that we found in the field. Of course, we did not advertise the fact that both of us carried two Colt pistols and quite a bit of ammunition. We shared this secret with only a few trusted friends. Toward the evening of the same joyful day, our happiness was marred by a large crowd of armed men gathering on the road near our quarters. Soon, we became aware that they were members of the Peasants Battalions. They came under the leadership of their officers to our quarters in order to take by force their share of the airdrop which we prevented them from taking from the basket, and to complain about the manner in which we recovered our stolen bicycles from one of their officers. Lieutenant Witold Jozefowski ("Mis") went out to speak to their commanding officer. He explained to him and his associates that the airdrop was made for the exclusive benefit of the Home Army and they had no right to interfere in the operation. At the same time, Mis complained to them about some of their undisciplined men who stole our bicycles when we were engaged in receiving the airdrop. Obviously, the commanding officer did not realize that my friend and I did not seize their bicycles but recovered our own bicycles from the barn of one of their officers. At the end of the meeting between our commanding officer and the officer of the Peasants Battalions who was in charge of the group, the two men had a meeting of minds and they parted as friends. There was a feeling of relief on both sides. Personally, on the one hand, I too felt relieved on account of the peaceful solution of the misunderstanding but, on the other hand, I felt uneasy because I carried two new Colt pistols that were not officially given to me. My conscience bothered me until I decided to talk to my friend Pikolo and convince him that we should disclose our secret and return the pistols to our commanding officer.

The following day, I persuaded my friend to reveal our secret to Lieutenant Witold Jozefowski ("Mis"). I was very happy with our decision because as I learned after the fact, our superiors counted all the items that came from the airdrop and checked them against the list that also came from the drop and became aware that four Colt pistols were missing. Their suspicion fell on some innocent men in our unit. When we learned about that, we rushed to see Mis in order to confess our dishonesty to him and thus free the innocent men from an unjust suspicion. When we went to see Mis to confess, to return the Colts, and to express our heartfelt apologies, he was very kind and understanding toward us. When we left, we had no doubt that we were very fortunate to have such a great man as our superior officer.

The second airdrop to our unit took place on the night of May 4-5, 1944, in the fields of Polanow. For one reason or another, I do not remember much about this airdrop. According to my comrade-in-arms, Wlodzimierz Gruszczynski ("Jach"), everything that came from the airdrop was stored at the manor of Mr. and Mrs. Swierzynski in Zurawica.[77]

## 16. Military Air Drops

We received the third airdrop in the fields near the village of Wiazownica during the night of May 18-19, 1944. The airdrop area was very close to our quarters in Granicznik where we stayed at Mrs. Bak's farmhouse and the neighboring farm. As soon as it grew dark, some of us in our unit were ordered to secure the roads coming from Staszow, Osiek, and Bukowa. It was possible that the Germans might come along these routes to endanger the drop area. In all honesty, the possibility of a German intervention during the drop was very remote because, in 1944, the German units stationed in our section of Poland were very hesitant to travel at night outside of their well-fortified and well-guarded military bases. I was assigned to the group of men who secured the road that came from Staszow to Wiazownica. This assignment gave me a very fine perspective from which to observe not only the road from the direction of Staszow but also to see quite well the area of the airdrop.

After all the preparations for receiving the airdrop were completed by our unit on time, there was nothing else to do but to watch the roads and the starry sky. In spite of its being spring, the night was rather cold and we had to move in our positions to keep warm. Around one o'clock in the morning, we began to hear the remote sound of an airplane, which was coming from a southwesterly direction. At the same time we could see a number of German searchlights scanning the sky. The sight of the searchlights made us feel apprehensive about the safety of the pilots, and we began to pray for their safe and successful flight. Obviously the pilots avoided the searchlights because we did not hear any fire from the German antiaircraft artillery. After a while, the sound of the heavy aircraft became louder and louder, especially when it began to lower its altitude. As soon as the airplane became visible against the background of the starry sky, our commanding officer, who was in charge of the reception, fired a flare, which illuminated the sky over the large field where we were. At the same time, a number of our men, using powerful flashlights, formed an arrow that pointed to the southwest. Soon, the aircraft flew over us toward the north and then turned around and, when flying over the arrow formed of flashlights, the crew began to open the bomb bay with a rather loud noise. Shortly thereafter one parachute after another began to open with a cracking sound and slowly descend toward the ground. A group of our men, who were assigned to pick up the drop, rushed toward the places where the parachutes and their precious cargo landed. They unhooked the parachutes from the containers and the crates and immediately carried them to the farm wagons. Most of the containers were round and made of metal — they were about 12 feet long. In order to make them more visible at night, small pieces of metal treated with phosphorus were attached to them. After the first discharge, the pilot flew over and over again back over the basket area until the last drop of containers and crates was floating on parachutes in the air above us. Then the pilot flew over the field again just to say good-bye by blinking the lights on the wings of his aircraft. Now we could see him gain altitude as his engines were roaring full-throttle and we prayed for his safe return to his base.

As soon as the airplane disappeared in the sky, some of our men continued loading the containers, crates, and parachutes on the wagons while others were searching the field to make sure that nothing would be left behind. In order to achieve a greater degree of certainty in this respect a couple of our men were left in the basket to search it again in the morning. After the farm wagons were loaded with the heavy containers and crates, the wagon train began to move slowly and cautiously on country roads toward the Loniow Forest. The home of the resident forester, Borycki, contained secret storage space for all the weapons, ammunition, hand grenades, medical supplies, British military uniforms, shoes, radios, and field telephones. From Borycki's storage, weapons and other military supplies were distributed to various underground units of the Home Army.

# 17. Sick Leave at Domoradzice Manor

A few days after we received the airdrop near the village of Wiazownica, I did not feel good. Soon, I developed a high temperature and had to see a physician. The physician diagnosed pneumonia, prescribed some medicine, and advised a sick leave under a physician's supervision. I do not remember who made the arrangements for the place where I was to spend my sick leave. In any case, I was sent in a farm wagon to Domoradzice manor, where an excellent physician from Bogoria, Dr. Jan Aleksandrowicz, was to supervise my recovery. Mr. and Mrs. Jan Kozlowski were the owners of the manor. The couple and their older son, Zbigniew, were active members of the Home Army. They always supported a number of Home Army military units in the area and provided a hospitable shelter both for groups and for individuals.

When I arrived at Domoradzice manor, the Kozlowski family received me with open arms. Soon, I became acquainted with all the members of the family. Besides Mr. and Mrs. Jan and Antonina Kozlowski (née Gliszczynski) and their son, Zbigniew, who was about twenty-two years old, there was also a younger son, Janusz, who must have been about seventeen. Since Janusz Kozlowski was of high school age, he had a tutor, Mr. Tadeusz Kolodziej, who also resided at the manor. In addition to the Kozlowski family and the tutor, there were in residence two or three maids who, under the supervision of the lady of the house, took care of cooking, cleaning, and doing the laundry. The workers, who cultivated the land that belonged to the manor and also kept the grounds and took care of the animals, lived with their families in the housing units provided by the manor owners. Life at the manor was very well organized. Mrs. Kozlowski supervised the work at the manor house and in the garden, and Mr. Kozlowski and the older son, Zbigniew, superintended the work in the fields and in the barns. Tadeusz Kolodziej began classes with Janusz at eight o'clock in the morning. The nature of the work called for getting up early and putting in a long day.

As a member of the Flying Commando Unit, I was used to an organized, regimented way of life and work. Therefore, I had no trouble in blending in with the way of life at the manor. Since Zbigniew shared his room with me, when he was getting up in the morning, I got up with him and followed him to the dining room where the whole family gathered together for an early breakfast.

After a few days of rest at the hospitable manor house, Mr. Kozlowski took me to Dr. Aleksandrowicz's office in Bogoria. The doctor examined me, prescribed some medicine, and declared that I was recovering very well. Since his office was in one section of his residence, Dr. Aleksandrowicz invited Mr. Kozlowski and me to have tea with him and his wife. So we went to the residential part of the house and enjoyed tea and cookies, which Mrs. Aleksandrowicz offered us. She was a very beautiful lady and very hospitable. Needless to say, I was very grateful to the doctor for treating me and to his wife for her gracious hospitality. When the time came for my second visit to the doctor's office, I took some flowers with me for his wife. She liked the flowers and thanked me for them. Mr. and Mrs. Kozlowski thought that I acted properly by giving flowers to Mrs. Aleksandrowicz, but the young men at the manor house never stopped teasing me about my secret love for her. I was very shy at that time in my life and very unskilled in defending myself in such a situation, so I let them have fun at my expense.

Following my second visit to Dr. Aleksandrowicz, my health improved considerably and I began to enjoy life at the manor. From time to time, I went with Zbigniew to supervise the farm work in the fields and enjoyed fresh air and the beauty of nature. On other occasions, I visited the neighboring manors in Jurkowice and Julianow or accompanied Mr. Kozlowski on his business trips to Klimontow. On Sundays, all of us from the manor house rode in a britzka to the parish church in Szczeglice for the High Mass. After mass, we always paid a short visit to the rectory to see the pastor. Then we went quite often to have lunch with Mr. and Mrs. Stefan Krajewski and their teenaged daughter Barbara Rytel. Barbara was Mrs. Krajewski's daughter from her first marriage with Mr. Kazimierz Rytel, who lived during the war in the small Szczeglice manor. Their main manor was in Mydlow near Opatow. They were very good friends of the Kozlowskis and had several great swings attached to the trees in their park. When the elders enjoyed bridge following lunch, we younger folks walked in the park and entertained ourselves on the swings. The Krajewskis were also frequent visitors at Domoradzice manor. It was obvious to me that Zbigniew Kozlowski and Barbara Rytel liked each other. (They eventually completed their university studies, married after the war, and made their home in Poznań. They have two daughters: Ania and Marysia. Both are married.) Besides Mr. and Mrs. Krajewski and their daughter Barbara, Mr. and Mrs. Czeslaw and Alicja Rozycki of Witowice manor and their daughter Janeczka used to visit Domoradzice manor from time to time. During my stay at Domoradzice manor, they visited the Kozlowskis for about a week. They were a very sociable and friendly family. I enjoyed their company, especially the company of Miss Janeczka who had a very beautiful and noble personality. Janeczka and I spent many hours walking in the park and in the orchard and talking about experiences in our young lives. She told me about her life at Witowice manor, where she grew up, and then about her high school experiences and her present life in the city of Ostrowiec, where the Rozyckis resided during the war. I was impressed by her honest and authentic manner of speech. She was very interested in my life and experiences in the Flying Commando Unit and liked to listen to my description of our daring attacks on the Nazis in different places of the Sandomierz-Ostrowiec region. I enjoyed her company very much and had a feeling that she enjoyed my company as well. Unfortunately the Rozyckis' visit came to an end and they returned home. Life at the manor returned to its normal routine, which was interrupted from time to time by Zbigniew's production of homemade candies and by Tadek Kolodziej's photography sessions but most of all by Sunday picnics.

Zbigniew Kozlowski learned to make candies from his mother or from the cooks in the kitchen. Since the homemade candies were produced at the Kozlowskis' manor only for some great occasions, Zbigniew, who liked candies and preferred homemade ones to the candies produced commercially, began to moonlight the production of such candies in his bedroom, which was equipped with a small stove. Being his roommate, I assisted him in the production. I do not remember all the ingredients he used in making candies but I remember the basic ones: sugar, butter, and flavors. After the ingredients were mixed and cooked on the stove, the liquid candy was poured into baking pans to cool off and coagulate. After its coagulation, Zbigniew used a knife to cut the content of the baking pan into small pieces. Then, he sent me to invite his younger brother, Janusz, and Tadeusz Kolodziej for a small, private party. I will never forget these youthful parties and the fantastic taste of Zbigniew's homemade candies.

Tadeusz Kolodziej, the teacher in residence, had a great interest in photography. He carried his camera with him wherever he went and he took some good pictures. During my short residence at the manor, I saw him taking pictures of everybody who came to the manor. Sometimes, he took pictures of us young folks at the most unexpected moments and places. Since he developed the pictures himself, we did not mind him doing this to us and, with his help, we learned to laugh at ourselves.

Our Sunday picnics were usually held away from home and in secluded places such as in forests and meadows. Mr. and Mrs. Kozlowski with the assistance of their son, Zbigniew, organized them and saw to it that there was enough food and drinks for all in attendance. They usually invited Mr. and Mrs. Antoni and Wanda Targowski and their daughter, Irena, and son, Roman, from Dmosice manor, the Krajewskis from Szczeglice, and Father Stefan Gliszczynski, a first cousin of Mrs. Kozlowski, who served as pastor of the church in Gozlice near Klimontow. One of the main attractions of the Sunday picnic was homemade ice cream, which Zbigniew produced at the picnic out of sweet cream, sugar, and vanilla flavor. I believe that Zbigniew's ice cream was the best ice cream I ever ate in my whole life. He had a great talent for making sweet things. Following the meal topped with the delicious ice cream, the men engaged in sports and the ladies stayed in a group and enjoyed catching up on the society news. From time to time one could hear an explosion of laughter from their group. They must have always talked about something that was very funny. The men also had a lot of fun. They chased the soccer ball all over the field, shouted at the top of their voices, and roared with laughter at each other's inability to kick the ball in the right direction. There was a critical need for humor in order to keep a mental sanity and to survive the tragedy of war and the brutality of the Nazi occupation.

Toward the end of my sick leave at Domoradzice manor, I did something very imprudent, which made the Kozlowskis worry about my safety. This is what happened. Mr. and Mrs. Kozlowski invited a young lady, who was a public school teacher, to have dinner with the family. After the dinner, all of us went to the living room for a while and then we walked and talked in the park until sunset. When the time came for the lady to return, I was asked to walk her to her residence, which was in one of the neighboring villages. I felt honored to be asked and gladly walked with her to the village. Since the distance to her home was much longer than I anticipated and since we walked rather slowly, it took us quite a bit of time to reach it. Although I accelerated my walk on the way back to Domoradzice, nevertheless, when I reached the manor, its lights were turned off and the door was locked. I was too embarrassed to knock on the door and wake up the whole family; therefore, I walked around the manor house to see whether some windows were opened. I discovered that all the windows were closed with the exception of the windows of the bedroom that Zbigniew shared with me. All I had to do now was to find a ladder. I looked around and found one near the basement door. It was long enough to reach the second floor window. Soon, the ladder was against the wall and I reached one of the windows. I looked into the bedroom and had the impression that Zbigniew was soundly asleep. There-

## 17. Sick Leave at Domoradzice Manor

fore, I entered the bedroom as quietly as possible, took off my shoes and clothing, and crawled into my bed. When Zbigniew got up early in the morning, he was surprised to see me in my bed but was convinced that his father opened the door for me. Soon, I got up and narrated to him my experiences of the previous night. He was disappointed with himself because he did not hear me enter the bedroom. When Zbigniew and I went to the dining room for breakfast, Mr. and Mrs. Kozlowski were happy to see me because they spent a sleepless night worrying about my safety. They thought that I fell into the Germans' hands. I thanked them for their concern, explained what happened, and apologized for coming home so late, and I promised not to do it again. They accepted my apology and told me that they were happy to see me safe and sound. They were very understanding and forgiving of my youthful mistakes.

When my sick leave at Domoradzice manor was coming to an end and I was about to return soon to the Flying Commando Unit, Mr. and Mrs. Kozlowski had a serious talk with me. During this conversation they asked me whether I would consider staying with them on a more permanent basis and supervising their farm workers so their son, Zbigniew, could undertake a formal study of agriculture away from home. It was a very tempting offer on their part and I appreciated their kindness; nevertheless, I felt at that time in my life that fighting Nazi Germany was more urgent than supervising manor workers. Therefore, I expressed my sincere gratitude for their offer and said that I was committed to stay with the unit and fight the Nazi forces until the end of the war. They were great Polish patriots and understood my determination to serve our country. They were not only great patriots but also great Christians and humanitarians. As I learned later on, when SS troopers were about to round up the Jewish population of Klimontow and transport them to Auschwitz, Mr. and Mrs. Kozlowski offered shelter to a very popular Jewish physician, his wife, and their children. The physician's name was Dr. Kaplan, about whom I wrote in the chapter on the deportation of the Klimontow Jews. From the perspective of time, I believe the Kozlowskis had outfitted Zbigniew's large bedroom with a cooking stove in preparation for the possible arrival of Dr. Kaplan and his family.

When I went see Dr. Aleksandrowicz for the last time, he told me that I was totally recuperated and therefore could return to my regular duties in the Flying Commando Unit. The following day, after expressing my gratitude to the Kozlowskis for their kindness and hospitality, I left the lovely manor of Domoradzice and returned to the unit. Leaving the manor was not easy for me because I left behind the Kozlowski family and their friends, whom I learned to love and respect.

When the Russian front approached the Vistula River between Sandomierz and Baranow, Russian artillery shells ignited some of the buildings at Domoradzice manor. This situation made the Kozlowskis look for shelter in Klimontow. They then left Klimontow and moved to the house that they owned in Kielce. I attempted to visit them in Kielce in 1953 but no one was home. Jan Kozlowski died in Kielce in 1952 and is buried there. After the death of her husband, Antonina Kozlowski moved from Kielce to Poznań to be with her sons. She died in Poznań 1962 and is buried there. Both Zbigniew and Janusz Kozlowski completed their university studies and worked in their respected professions. According to the letter, dated March 20, 2000, which came to me from Zbigniew, Janusz Kozlowski still works as a university professor. His field is medicinal plants. He suffered a great tragedy. In a car accident he lost his son Hubert, his wife, and a granddaughter.

# 18. The Merger of Two Units

When I came back to the Flying Commando Unit, I learned that it had merged with the Jedrus Group a few days before my return. The merger took place in the village of Lesisko on June 12, 1944. Captain Kaktus, who was a good friend and a supervisor of both fighting units, was instrumental in the consolidation. He and his military superiors in the Polish Home Army believed that the time had come to combine smaller units and groups into more formidable forces.

At the time of the merger, there were forty active members of the Flying Commando Unit who became an integral part of the Jedrus Group. Their names are as follows: Boleslaw Szelag ("Blyskawica"), Czeslaw Czapow ("Boleslaw"), Zbigniew Rolski ("Boruta"), Marian Mieczyslaw Gaj ("Cap"), Kazimierz Zarzycki ("Czarny"), Feliks Wryk ("Dab"), Mieczyslaw Pawlikowski ("Ghandi"), Henryk Zarzycki ("Grab"), Unknown Name ("Grabina"), Wlodzimierz Gransztof ("Wicher"), Unknown Name ("Grom"), Unknown Name ("Grot"), Mieczyslaw Bokwa ("Huragan"), Arkadiusz Swierszcz ("Iskra"), Wlodzimierz Gruszczynski ("Jach"), Mieczyslaw Jajkiewicz ("Jajos"), Stanislaw Klusek ("Jastrzab" vel "Fugas"), Zbigniew Smolinski ("Korsarz"), Marian S. Mazgaj ("Kozak"), Romuald Nowakowski ("Msciciel"), Jerzy Staszewski ("Murzyn"), Henryk Nowakowski ("Nalecz" vel "Doktorek"), Pawel Jodlowski ("Okon"), Wlodzimierz Milbert ("Pat"), Unknown Name ("Pantera"), Jan Szpakiewicz ("Pikolo), Zbigniew Piatek ("Grabina"), Kazimierz Stobinski ("Piorun"), Wladyslaw Unknown Last Name ("Ramzes"), Zbigniew Pawlikowski ("Mimi-Raptus"), Zdzislaw Krzeminski ("Skrzydlaty"), Kazimierz Jarzyna ("Sokol"), Jan Osemlak ("Straceniec"), Mieczyslaw Granek ("Szpak'), Kazimierz Winiarz ("Wilk"), Edward Goetzendorf-Grabowski ("Zbiswicz"), Eugeniusz Winiarz ("Zawada"), Jozef Brudek ("Zuch"), Unknown Name ("Zmija") and Edward Stanczak ("Zyrafa").[78]

Jozef Wiacek ("Sowa"), who served as a commanding officer of the Jedrus

Group, remained in charge of both units after the merger. His younger brother, Stanislaw Wiacek ("Inspector"), served as the next in command. Both of them grew up at their parents' large farm in the village of Tczcianka, received a primary and secondary education, and served in the Polish army before World War II. Their older brother, Father Jan Wiacek, was a priest of the diocese of Sandomierz. Just like their parents, the Wiacek brothers were well known and highly respected in the whole area. Also, they were related to numerous families in the region. Our next door neighbors, the Podsiadlys in Jeziory, were their relatives, the Kwiatkowskis from Niekrasow, the Bien family from Ossala, the Kasprzyckis from Gaj, and many others were their relatives and cousins.

I knew Jozef and Stanislaw Wiacek from the early part of the war when Wladyslaw Jasinski (Jedrus) was in charge of the *Odwet* and then of the Jedrus Group. At that time, I used to deliver copies of the clandestine newpaper *Odwet* (Revenge) to the Wiacek brothers at their farmhouse in Tczcianka. I also knew a number of other members of the Jedrus Group from those days. Therefore, after the merger of the two units I did not have any problem adjusting to the new reality. With the exception of Lieutenant Jozefowski ("Mis") and Chief Stefan Franaszczuk ("Orlicz"), all my friends and former members of the Flying Commando Unit were there plus the familiar members of the Jedrus Group. The unfamiliar members of the group did everything possible to be welcoming and friendly. What else could one expect?

Shortly after returning from Domoradzice manor to the forest near Lesisko, I became acquainted with Charles Roesch ("Jerzy") and Edmond Klenck ("Edmund"), who deserted from the German army in the village of Padew Narodowa on June 12, 1944, and joined the Jedrus Group. They brought with them one machine gun, MG42, with a support base, two German rifles, ammunition, hand grenades, binoculars and, literature for German military combat training. Charles came from Alsace and Edmond from Lorraine in France. Although their names sounded German, they claimed to be of French origin and their mother tongue was French. Jozefa Czaja, a very attractive lady who operated a general store in the village of Padew Narodowa, was instrumental in the desertion of the two German soldiers. She used to wrap up in newspapers some of the goods that she sold to the German soldiers. These underground German-language newspapers, such as *Der Kampfer, Ost Wache*, and a number of others were printed in order to promote a spirit of defeatism in the German army and to encourage desertion among its soldiers. After Charles and Edmond decided to desert, they approached Jozefa Czaja, who contacted them with Jan Mazur ("Stalowy"), a member of the Home Army. He in turn brought them to the Jedrus Group. Following their desertion, Jozefa Czaja was arrested by the German police and lodged at the

Montelupi Prison in Cracow. During interrogations she refused to incriminate anybody and she was murdered by the Nazis on June 23, 1944. Her brother, Jan Czaja ("Powsinoga"), who was arrested with her, was afraid that he might not endure the Nazi tortures; therefore, he swallowed a cyanide pill and died in the German prison. Mrs. Czaja, the mother of Jozefa and Jan, was tortured by the Nazis but did not give them any information concerning the defectors nor the local members of the Home Army.

My acquaintance with Charles Roesch and Edmond Klenck was extremely beneficial to me because, as highly trained machine gunners, they conducted training sessions for all who were interested in learning about the very modern and high-quality German machine gun, the MG42. During these training sessions, Zbigniew Kabata ("Bobo"), who spoke German, served as an interpreter. Since I was always interested in mechanical things, I took special interest in the construction of the German machine gun and its functioning. Therefore, I took it apart and put it together time after time and examined all its parts and their purpose. After learning all about the function and parts of the MG42, our instructors took us out into the local terrain for field exercises with the machine gun. They showed us how to choose firing positions, how to mount the machine gun on the support, how to aim and fire at ground targets and at aircraft, how to replace the overheated barrels with new ones, and many other things. One of the things that I will never forget was their demonstration of falling down and crawling under enemy fire. Their German method of falling down to the ground while under the fire was such that when one started to fall in one place, one ended falling in another place. The entire action of falling down occurred with the speed of lightening. Needless to say, we admired and attempted to imitate the German combat training. We knew that the German combat training was superior to ours. That is why we were anxious to learn as much as possible from our good instructors.

Besides the two machine gun instructors, we also had a very interesting teacher in the person of Sargent Stanislaw Klusek ("Fugas"), who attracted a great number of students. Before the war, he was a professional soldier in the Corps of Engineers and had a lot of experience in teaching recruits. His lectures were very practical and full of anecdotes and jokes that were very instructive and to the point. He became very popular not only with us, the former members of the Flying Commando Unit, but also with the old timers of the Jedrus Group. Already at that time, he had a vision that the wars of the future would be won not by the nations with the greatest number of soldiers but by the ones that produced the most up-to-date war technology and the most powerful explosives. In a sense, he predicted the production of the atomic bomb by the United States.

Our life in the forest quarters near Lesisko was well organized. We lived in very simple temporary shelters constructed of wood and tarpaper. There was enough water for drinking and washing. We ate our meals in the farmhouse that belonged to Mr. Marian Slawinski ("Mamloch") and his wife Mrs. Slawinski where food was abundant and well prepared. All of us rose early in the morning, about 5:00 A.M. After taking care of our morning hygiene we assembled for our morning prayers. At the end of the morning prayers we always sang a very beautiful hymn, "When the Morning Glows Arise" ("*Kiedy ranne wstaja zorze*"). The first stanza of the hymn reads as follows: "When the morning glows arise, to You sing the earth and the sea. To You sing all things that are alive. May You be praised Great God." (In Polish: "*Kiedy ranne wstaja zorze, Tobie ziemia, Tobie morze. Tobie spiewa zywot wszelki. Badz pochwalon Boze Wielki.*") When about two hundred of us sang this song, our young and powerful voices could be heard in nearby villages and we enjoyed the echo of our singing. Following morning prayers, we walked two by two or in small groups to the "Mamloch's" farmhouse for our breakfast. From the breakfast table we returned to our quarters for a variety of daily activities. Some of us had guard duties, others attended lectures, repaired guns at the gunsmith shop, fixed bicycles, or went to neighboring villages or towns to gather intelligence on German troop movements and to take care of urgent business. Our lunch was usually served at noon. It was not as well attended as the breakfast because many men were working outside of our forest camp. If on a given day we were not involved in an attack on the Germans, attendance at the dinner table was as large as during breakfast time. One of our men, who was Jewish, acquired a good German radio, which was good enough to receive news and music from the BBC in London.

The Jewish man's name was Jerzy Bette ("Papcio"). A member of our reserves, Marcin Kozlowski ("Lysy"), was instrumental in bringing him to the Jedrus Group in the summer of 1943. One day during that summer, Kozlowski walked from Sulislawice to Klimontow and on the road he encountered a suspicious looking stranger going in the opposite direction. Kozlowski pulled out his pistol and asked the stranger who he was. The stranger told him that his name was Jerzy Bette and, as a Jew, he was running from the Germans. He also confessed to Kozlowski that he escaped from the German prison in Sandomierz. After a short conversation with Kozlowski, Bette figured out that he was dealing with a member of a Polish underground organization. Therefore, he said to Kozlowski that he would like to join his organization and added that as a highly educated man, he had something to offer. Marcin Kozlowski put Bette in touch with the commanding officer of the Jedrus Group, Jozef Wiacek ("Sowa"), who, for humanitarian reasons, decided to admit Bette to the Jedrus Group. When Jerzy Bette joined the group, he

## 18. The Merger of Two Units

brought with him two German submachine guns. The type of the submachine guns (Bergman) he brought was used exclusively by the Nazi police force. When Sowa accepted Bette, he was not aware of the Nazi secret organization called Zagiew (Firebrand). The membership of this organization was composed of Jewish collaborators who were forced to serve the Gestapo. These Jewish collaborators were trained by the Gestapo and sent to infiltrate Polish underground military units as spies and provocateurs. Soon thereafter, Sowa learned of the existence of this organization and was ordered to keep a very close watch on Bette and his activities. Bette spoke a number of languages and was very helpful in receiving radio news from the BBC in London. He was also helpful in renewing publication of our underground newspaper *Odwet*. To my knowledge, he did not take an active part in any of our military activities. When the Soviet army approached our area in the summer of 1944, Jerzy Bette disappeared from our group and joined the Soviet troops. Following the war, he became one of the high-ranking officials of the Polish Communist Radio. He was also helpful to some of our men who were hiding from the Communist police. An examination of the Sandomierz prison records after the war did not confirm Bette's claim that he was a prisoner there.[79]

During the days or nights when we attacked the Germans, we had an irregular schedule and ate wherever we were and whatever we could get after the attack. The people in the villages and towns were very solicitous about our well-being and, many times they jeopardized their lives and safety, always provided food and shelter for us. From time to time, the Germans attacked us as well. In such cases, if the enemy's force was considerably larger that ours, we tried by all means to avoid a major confrontation. If the German force was equal to ours or smaller, we always tried to take advantage of surprise and attack the enemy when and where he was most vulnerable. The fact that we knew quite well the countryside and had a very friendly population around us was a great advantage to us. Wherever the Germans went, they faced an icy hostility from the patriotic population. In the early stages of the war, the Nazi authorities did not care what the population of Poland thought of their army and of the various branches of their police force because their armed forces were victorious wherever they went. Now, fortune had drastically changed for the German army, air force, and navy. They were no longer conquering new countries but, on the contrary, they had serious trouble in holding what they previously took by force. The Western Allies were systematically destroying their forces on the ground, at sea, and in the air, and the powerful Red Army was rapidly annihilating their once invincible Wehrmacht and pushing what was left of it toward the *Vaterland*. At the same time, the freedom fighters in every occupied country were cutting German communication lines and blowing up military trains and strategic bridges. No wonder that, at this time, the hostility of the Polish people annoyed the Nazi authorities and their troops but they did not know what to do. They used to have a radical solution to every problem but, now, they were helpless and hopeless. They began to sense that Hitler's evil empire was coming to an end. At the same time, they came to understand the reality behind the hostility of the Polish people. It meant that the Polish people knew about their forthcoming miserable end. They began to read in the eyes of the Polish people question marks: Why did you listen to your fanatical leaders and go to other countries to rob, to rape, and to murder innocent people who did not hurt you in any way? What are you doing here in our country so far away from Germany and your home? Most of the soldiers of the Wehrmacht and the members of the Nazi police could no longer hide their fear and their lack of self-confidence. They were no longer supermen as Adolf Hitler and his gang wanted them to be. They were human, all too human, consumed by uncertainty and fear.

During these days our comrade-in-arms, Stanislaw Duma ("Topola") and Janusz Szczerbatko ("Zygfryd"), disarmed two German soldiers who were in charge of delivering hot meals to their comrades who were guarding the bridges on the Vistula River near Sandomierz. In delivering hot meals the Germans used a horse and a two-wheeled carriage. One of the soldiers walked about thirty feet ahead of the carriage and the other rode the carriage. When our men surprised them from behind a large willow tree and ordered them to raise their hands, the Germans obeyed the order without hesitation. When Topola aimed his submachine at the soldiers, Zygfryd first disarmed the soldier who was walking and then asked the soldier in the carriage to step down, and the soldier did so. Then, Zygfryd reached for his holster but the holster was empty. Zygfryd then put his hand in the soldier's winter coat pocket and there was a fine Russian TT automatic pistol ready to fire. Both of the Germans were scared beyond measure, especially the one who walked ahead of the carriage. His hands up, he squatted and begged for his life. Zygfryd reported that, out of fear, the soldier's eyes became as big as his glasses. The other soldier, who was considerably older than the first one, was decorated with the Knight's Cross for bravery; nevertheless, he was not an *Ubermensch* (superman). When our men assured the soldiers that they were interested only in their guns and not in killing them, the Germans relaxed somewhat and the older one began to talk. He called our men "Polish soldiers" and told them that the TT pistol that they took from him belonged in the past to the Russian military commandant of Kiev.

A few days later, Zygfryd went to a store and, among the customers, there was the younger German soldier whom he disarmed. The soldier recognized

Zygfryd and squatted in the middle of the store and began to shake with fear. Zygfryd pretended that he did not recognize him, so the soldier took his grocery bags and left and did not cause any trouble. Again, a few days later, Zygfryd encountered the same soldier on the bridge. The German soldier at that time was on guard duty and recognized Zygfryd again. This time, Zygfryd was convinced that the soldier would aim his rifle at him and arrest him. But instead of that, the soldier squatted and trembled with fear. Zygfryd walked to the end of the bridge without any trouble, although there were two other German soldiers on the bridge, one in the middle of the bridge and the other one at its end.[80]

# 19. The Battle of Osiek

As I described in the above chapter, our life in the forest near Mamloch's farm in Lesisko was rather regular and even comfortable. The makeshift shelters, which we called villas, were very commodious, the weather was nice, and the air carried a light fragrance of pine trees, which were abundant in this part of the forest. Toward the end of June 1944, some of the lectures and classes in military art were coming to a close and all of us anticipated an unofficial graduation and celebration. Our commanding officer, Jozef Wiacek ("Sowa"), sensed our anticipation and decided to provide some extra food for the occasion. Therefore, early in the morning on July 1, 1944, he asked Marian Mieczyslaw Gaj ("Cap") to hitch two horses to a britzka and take him to Stefan Dobrowolski's grocery store in Osiek to order some special food. As his assistant, Sowa took with him Fryderyk Sielecki ("Lokietek"), a midget, who, during the early stages of the war, lived with his parents in a suburb of Tarnoberzeg.[81]

When they arrived at the marketplace in Osiek, on that warm and beautiful day, the town appeared to be quiet and very peaceful. Sowa entered the grocery store, Lokietek remained outside to keep watch, and, Cap turned the carriage around on Polaniecka Street in the direction from which they came and waited for Sowa and Lokietek to return. Before Sowa completed ordering the food, Lokietek entered the store in a hurry and reported that a number of German military trucks had arrived from Staszow and had parked in the middle of the marketplace. Immediately, Sowa left the store and stepped out onto the sidewalk at the western edge of the market. At that moment, he noticed a good number of excited uniformed Germans searching the marketplace. Then as he turned to the right and walked from one house to another, a small group of Germans ran toward him and asked, "Where are the bandits?" Sowa, who was dressed like a farmer, pointed out with his hand toward the fields behind the houses and said, "They ran away over there." The Germans went in that direction. Then Sowa continued walking toward the next yard and noticed that a small gate in the fence of that yard was wide open. He decided to walk through that gate and hide from the Germans behind the house that was there and eventually disappear in the fields of rye. Unfortunately, one of the Germans watched him and shouted, halt. At that moment, Sowa began to run to the gate and, when he reached it, in order to negotiate a quick turn into the gate, he caught with his hand the post of the gate. The German fired at him and the bullet hit Sowa in the arm. Sowa kept running and managed to escape into the fields. The Germans were frustrated. They caught in the marketplace a seventeen-year-old boy named Kotarski, brought him to the same yard through which Sowa escaped, ordered him to run, and shot him in the back.

Cap saw what was going on and while attempting to drive his carriage away from the market through a suburban orchard, the horses became entangled in the low growing fruit trees. The situation became hopeless; therefore, Cap decided to leave the horses and the carriage and run. The Germans noticed him and began to fire. One of the bullets hit him in the back of his head and tore out his eye. Cap lost one of his eyes in our previous battle with the Germans at the Szczucin Bridge and now he lost his second eye and soon his life in the struggle against the Nazi barbarians.

Lokietek realized that some of the Germans in the market were going to enter the grocery store where he was; therefore, he asked Mrs. Dobrowolski to help him hide his pistol. Then he took off his boots, cut himself a slice of bread, sat next to the Dobrowolskis' little son, and ate the bread. Soon, a couple of Germans entered the store and asked Mrs. Dobrowolski whether she saw any "Polish bandits." She replied that she never saw any Polish bandits. They looked around the store and, of course, they saw Lokietek and the Dobrowolskis' son, but obviously they took Lokietek for a little boy so they left the store.

When the Germans arrived at the marketplace in Osiek, Ryszard Skorupski, a member of the Home Army, hid somewhere and observed what they were doing. When he saw the Germans shoot at our chief, Sowa, he thought that they seriously wounded him. Therefore, he left his hiding place under the fire of German guns and ran into the fields. There, he saw a farmer hoeing his potato field with a horse. So he took the horse out of his harness and galloped to our quarters in the forest. As he was riding through the village of Ossala, Skorupski shouted at the top of his voice: "Jozef Wiacek was wounded and captured by the Germans in Osiek!" Men in the village of Ossala, whose farm wagons were ready for hauling hay from the fields into the barns, hitched their horses to the wagons and waited for us to respond to the tragic news.

As soon as Ryszard Skorupski arrived at our quarters, Stanislaw Wiacek

("Inspektor") ordered an instant alert and soon we were on the way to Osiek in order to rescue our commanding officer from the German hands. After reaching Ossala, we took advantage of the farm wagons and the drivers who were ready for us. The drivers stood in their wagons and urged the horses to run as fast as they could. As we rode, Inspektor shouted orders, which were communicated from wagon to wagon. Soon, we were near Osiek. We left the wagons on the side of the road, formed an extended line, and began to approach the town of Osiek very cautiously in combat readiness. At the same time, Inspektor sent two units with machine guns to secure the roads to Osiek from the direction of Sandomierz and Staszow. These two units rushed to their assigned positions. They were to halt the Germans' withdrawal from Osiek and to prevent any German relief coming from these cities.

As our extended line, which was formed on both sides of the road, came very close to the town and its left flank approached the town from the northern side, the Germans noticed us and opened fire. We responded with our fire and accelerated our forward pace. I happened to be in the extended line on the right side of the Polaniec-Osiek road. As we ran toward Osiek and fired at the county building from which the German fire was coming, the bullets whistled by our ears. One of them hit Stanislaw Kuras ("Szkot"), who was running a few paces to my right. He fell to the ground and could not get up. The bullet damaged one of his hips and his pelvic area. Several of our medics carried him back to the wagons. We kept on moving but more cautiously. During that time, Stanislaw Wiacek ("Inspektor") was slightly wounded. Our attack was checked for the moment. However, soon we concentrated our fire on the county building, and we ignited it from our tracer ammunition and hand grenades. Most of the Germans left the burning building in a hurry and ran to their trucks, which were parked at the market. However, some of them were trapped in the county building and burned with it. Those Germans who reached their trucks attempted to escape in the direction of Sandomierz, but our unit of men with a machine gun manned by Czeslaw Gawronski ("Wojek") and Marian Wiktorowski ("Maniek Polikier") stopped them near St. Stanislaus Church with machine gun fire. The Germans were trapped on Koscielna Street. Nevertheless, they defended themselves in a desperate house-to-house fight until they found protection behind the stone wall of the churchyard. Protected by the stone wall and the two-story stone belfry, which was situated above the main entrance to the churchyard, they fired their guns and threw hand grenades both at the machine gun crew and at us who were attacking them from the direction of the marketplace. Our machine gun, which was operated by Charles Roesch and Edmond Klenck, discouraged the Germans from poking their heads above the wall. At one time, when Charles and Edmond carried on a loud conversation with each other in the German language, one of the Germans behind the wall overheard them and shouted: "Are you the German soldiers who were left outside the wall?" Charles and Edmond responded with machine gun fire and hand grenades. The Germans had no more questions but I am sure they were still puzzled.

As we kept on attacking the Germans behind the stone wall, I had the impression that their defense was getting weaker and weaker moment by moment. They must have been running out of ammunition and hand grenades. On the other hand, our firepower was increasing continuously because most of our men concentrated their attack on one single objective: to neutralize the German fire and take the churchyard from the enemy. We needed about half an hour to accomplish this task but unfortunately we were ordered by our commanding officer, Stanislaw Wiacek ("Inspektor"), to slowly disengage from the action and pull out to our wagons, which we left on the road. We were ordered to do so because the small unit of our men who secured the highway from the direction of Sandomierz opened up with machine gun fire on a large column of German military trucks. The trucks were transporting men to Osiek to rescue their comrades who defended themselves behind the stone wall at the churchyard. On the way back to our quarters, we took with us Cap's body, which was distorted not only by the German bullets but also by his having been kicked by some of the "supermen's" boots after he was already dead. We also took with us mortally wounded Szkot, whom our men transported to the city hospital in Tarnobrzeg. After two weeks of severe suffering, he died there. His family took charge of the funeral. We buried the body of Cap temporarily near our quarters in Lesisko. We later moved it for permanent burial in the parochial cemetery in Sulislawice. There is a special section of the burial grounds set aside for members of the Jedrus Group who died in the struggle against the Nazi military forces.

Toward the end of the same day on July 1, 1944, a new German military unit arrived again in Osiek. The inhabitants of the town expected a severe reprisal at the hands of the Nazi troops for our attack on their comrades earlier in the day. Most of the young persons left the town and found safety in the fields and wooded areas. One of the young men who took part in the field exercises of his squad away from the town needlessly returned to Osiek. As soon as the Germans patrolling the streets noticed him, they shot and killed him without warning. His name was Stanislaw Slodkowski. He was a member of the local Home Army squad commanded by Stanislaw Miernowski.

Our chief, Jozef Wiacek ("Sowa"), and his brother, Stanislaw Wiacek ("Inspektor"), were very aware of the Germans who arrived recently in Osiek because they were receiving continuous intelligence about their activities and their possible intentions. Our leaders and the rest of us were convinced that the Germans would do everything to retaliate for our attack on them in Osiek. However, we were not sure whether they would strike at the people of the town only or at both the town's population and us as well. In any case, we were ready to fight the brutal enemy. For this reason, our chief ordered our unit to spend the evening and the night on total alert and in constant readiness. All roads leading to our quarters were secured with manned machine guns. Intelligence from Osiek was received in a continuous stream by our leadership. Since we expected the Germans to make their move early in the morning of the following day, there was no time to move our many valuable possessions, including our military equipment, weapons, ammunition, clothing and, food, which were stored at our quarters in Lesisko, to a safe place. However, we managed to hide and camouflage in the forest some of the most valuable things. The only thing that remained for us to do was to wait for the morning to see what the Germans were up to.

# 20. German Raid on Our Quarters

Our expectation of the German attack on us proved to be quite realistic. In the early morning on July 2, 1944, German military units began to approach the forest in which were our quarters. We could hear at first the remote sound of motor vehicles on the roads leading to the forest. As far as I know, the German troops that stayed during the night in Osiek were coming toward the forest from the north. Other German units in 52 trucks were coming in our direction from the west by the road that led from Staszow and Rytwiany. I do not remember which of our units guarded the highway from Osiek but I do remember that I was assigned to the unit that guarded the road from the direction of Staszow and Rytwiany. Czeslaw Gawronski ("Wojek") was in charge of the machine gun, which was aimed along the road at the entrance to the forest. While facing west, both the machine gun and the rest of us with rifles were on the left side of the road so we would not have to cross the road during the exchange of fire. It was still dark in the forest when the head of the German motorized column approached the entrance to the forest. We did not open fire until we could clearly see the trucks entering the forest road. All of us who were armed with rifles and hand grenades waited for Wojek to open fire on our side with his machine gun. Wojek kept waiting until the Germans came closer. Obviously the Germans did not expect us at that section of the forest because they were riding comfortably in the trucks instead of entering the forest in an extended line.

When the German trucks came close enough for us to fire effectively, Wojek aimed at the first vehicle and commenced firing. The rest of us joined him in opening fire at the Germans. Immediately, the trucks came to a stop and the troopers jumped from their vehicles and took cover behind the trees on both sides of the road. They, too, began firing in our direction. While we

**Four members of the Jedrus Group in battle readiness to protect our forest home from the Germans. Courtesy of Dr. Piotr Sierant.**

were holding the Germans on the road near the entrance to the forest, one of our men ran to our quarters to report back to Jozef Wiacek ("Sowa"). The same man returned to us with Jozef's order to hold the German convoy for a short while and then to join the main body of the group in its withdrawal into the eastern part of the forest. As we kept firing at the German troopers we became aware that they were forming an extended line in order to encircle us. It was time for us to pull out from our firing positions and follow the group. While some of us kept firing, other men were pulling out and soon the rest of us withdrew. By the time the Germans became aware that we were gone, all of us joined the main body of our group and followed our leader, who, on account of his wound, rode his horse. He led us very cautiously toward the village of Tursko Male, which was near the Vistula River. Soon, we crossed the dirt road that linked Osiek with Polaniec. Obviously the Germans did not yet control this road. Now we were in the eastern part of the forest. Our chief suspected that the Germans were not only in the western part of the forest but also in its northern part. Therefore, he decided to lead us in a southeastern direction toward the Vistula. This road was very marshy and inaccessible not only to the German vehicles but also to the heavily armed German troopers. Our chief's horse proved to be a blessing in choosing the

## 20. GERMAN RAID ON OUR QUARTERS

passage through the marshes. The chief let his horse follow its instinct and we followed the horse. In such a way our passage through the marshes was quite successful. Soon we were again on solid ground, and we hastened our march through a mature pine forest. Fortunately, there were no German troops in this section of the forest. After we crossed the forest, the chief led us through fields of grain toward the Vistula. Near the river we were able to hide in the willow bushes that grew very abundantly there. As soon as we disappeared into the thick bushes, a German airplane appeared in the sky. It flew around and around searching for us in vain. We were quite safe under the cover of the thick green bushes. After the German aircraft flew away, we kept walking along the river until we came to the area where the Czarna River flows into the Vistula. There we felt secure and waited until the Germans withdrew from the entire forest.

During the night we returned to our quarters and were very surprised to find that the Germans had not ransacked our shanties. Everything there remained the way we had left it in the morning and our storerooms were intact. The German troopers evidently limited their penetration of the forest to the roads that went through it. They did not venture into the thickly wooded sections. Although they noticed the path that led from our quarters to the farmhouse where we ate our meals, the troopers did not follow this hard-beaten and wide path. I must add that this path was visible on both sides of the road by which the Germans traveled with their trucks. They probably suspected us of mining the approach to our quarters and were also probably convinced that we would put up a stiff defense. What confirms my thinking along these lines is the fact that when the troopers were passing near the houses that were part of our quarters, the farmers in the field saw them pointing toward these houses and overheard them warning one another by saying, "*Polnische Banditen*" (Polish bandits). They did not enter these houses and discouraged others from attempting to enter them.

We were not destined to rest during the night when we returned to our quarters in the forest. Needless to say, we anticipated the return of the Germans. Therefore, we had to move all of our supplies from the present quarters in Lesisko to the new quarters in Opalina and Smerdyna. When we began to load our supplies, including weapons, ammunition, explosives, food, and personal belongings, we became aware that we had more possessions than we realized. Twenty farm wagons came to move our supplies and all of them were overloaded. For obvious reasons we had to rush in order to move everything during the night. As the wagons were rolling along the country road, we escorted them by walking on both sides of the road. We were going through the villages of Strzegom and Czajkow. The crossing of the highway between Osiek and Staszow was the most dangerous part of the route. On this highway, even during the night, there was considerable traffic. Many of the trucks on the highway were loaded with German troops and supplies heading east toward the Russian front. Other trucks carried wounded soldiers from the eastern front and some those of the German administrators, their families and belongings from the areas of the Soviet Union once occupied by the German forces and now again in the hands of the Red Army. When we watched the traffic from the edge of the forest, we were able to sense in its movement a feeling of urgency. The troops were rushing eastward to patch up the line of the front that was broken again and again by the swift and powerful Soviet tanks. The wounded soldiers and the administrators were in a hurry to seek medical help and safety in the Fatherland. Both of these groups of people had more than enough of Hitler's Russian adventure. Under their breaths, they surely cursed the Führer and his Nazi associates for sending them to Russia.

In spite of the heavy traffic on the highway, our wagons crossed it without a major problem. What appeared to be a problem was a small creek near the village of Opalina, which swelled as the result of a heavy rain. At first we were afraid that our wagons would not be able to cross the water on the road but after a while the drivers discovered that the water that covered the road was rather shallow and as such did not constitute any obstacle. Soon we made ourselves very comfortable in our new quarters; nevertheless, we posted very strong patrols on every road that led to Opalina. Our chief, Jozef Wiacek ("Sowa"), did not come with us to the new quarters but remained with Tadeusz Mittelstaedt ("Budiet") in the area of our old quarters. He wanted to see whether the Germans intended to take some retaliatory action against the local population. When the two of them were patrolling the area between the villages of Ossala and Trzczianka, some German troopers who took their positions on willow trees near the road opened fire at them. Sowa managed to escape from the line of their fire but Budiet was wounded in one of his feet and could not run. Soon other German troopers who were hidden on the ground sent their police dogs to attack the wounded man. Budiet pretended to be dead and let the dogs attack his body. When some German troopers approached him, he began to fire at them with his pistol. The troopers responded with their submachine guns and killed him instantly. The following night, a number of our men brought his body to Opalina. At the same time, the body of Cap, which was temporarily buried near our quarters in Lesiko, was also transported to our new quarters. The bodies of our dear friends were placed in caskets that were decorated with flowers and greenery. An honor guard stood for hours near the caskets while all of the members of our group and our friends prayerfully passed by to pay their respect and say good-bye to the young heroes who gave their lives for the freedom of Poland.

## 20. GERMAN RAID ON OUR QUARTERS

The official interment took place at the special section reserved for our men at the parochial cemetery in Sulislawice.

During our stay in Opalina a number of new members joined our unit. Among them were three German soldiers who were stationed at the military base in Sandomierz from which they defected during the night of June 12, 1944. Captain Leon Torlinski ("Kret"), a regional chief of the Home Army, was instrumental in bringing them to us. One of these men was Manfred Zanker who was born in Bautzen in Saxony. He made himself more known to us than his comrade-in-arms who came with him. He also appeared to be the leader of the group.[82]

The second German soldier who defected with Manfred from the Wehrmacht was Jerzy Karol Pyka from Katowice. He served in our unit until the demobilization and then returned to his city, where he died some years following World War II. The third German soldier who joined our group with Manfred Zanker and Jerzy Karol Pyka was Robert Thuman, who was born in Strasbourg (Lorraine). We called him Robert the Frenchman because he preferred to speak French rather than German. Robert was a good cook and tended to prepare his own meals rather than receive them from the common pot. His clothing was always clean and pressed and his shoes had always a proper shine. During the Action Storm (Burza), whenever we had our quarters in villages, we slept on straw or hay in farmers' barns. Robert's bedding was always in perfect order. If somebody accidentally disturbed the arrangement of his bedding, he was very unhappy and rearranged it from the beginning. After our

Lieutenant Zbigniew Kabata ("Bobo") on his way from guard duty received a rose from a young lady. The rose was delivered to him by a comrade-in-arms who took this picture as proof that he delivered the rose to the proper person. Courtesy of Dr. Zbigniew Kabata.

general demobilization, he stayed with a small group of men who, under the leadership of Captain Tadeusz Strus ("Kaktus"), attempted to cross the front to the areas under the control of the Red Army. Shortly before Kaktus decided to disband his small group on account of very great difficulties in crossing the German front line, a patrol of a Soviet guerrilla unit commanded by Major Hory accepted about ten of Captain Kaktus's men who were Soviet citizens, a small group of Jewish men (8 to 10), and Robert Thuman. Major Hory also intended to cross the German frontline so as to reunite with the Soviet troops.

During the time in which we had our quarters in Opanina and Serdyna, the number of young men who wanted to join our group increased from day to day. Therefore the need arose to organize our group into a full-fledged military company. Our chief, Lieutenant Jozef Wiacek, became the Jedrus Company commanding officer. The newly formed company had three platoons and each platoon had four squads. There were about 60 men in every platoon. With this reorganization came a great need for weapons to arm all the young men who were joining us at that time. Needless to say, all the weapons that we had received from the airdrops were welcome additions.

In the second part of July 1944, our company took quarters in the areas of Strzegom Granicznik, Wiazownica, and Rybnica. These areas were not easily accessible to the Germans; therefore, we used them continuously for training and military drill. After several weeks in these areas, some smaller German units that were stationed in the neighboring towns became very uncomfortable and moved away.[83] During the transformation of our group into a military company, we became aware that a small group of the National Armed Forces (NSZ) was stationed in the proximity of our quarters in the area of Rybnica. The leader of the group was Lieutenant Wladyslaw Zwirek ("Mirecki") with whom I was acquainted in the early stage of my underground activities. Some time before the merger of our Sandomierz Flying Commando Unit with the Jedrus Group, two members of the "Mirecki" group, Zbigniew Rolski ("Boruta") and Wlodzimierz Milbert ("Pat") joined our unit. Now the group was rather small and poorly armed. The leader of the group did not want to join our company. Therefore, our commanding officer, Lieutenant Jozef Wiacek sent a few of us from our company under the leadership of Zbigniew Fialkowski to disarm the group and invite its members to join us. When we went to their quarters at the residence of Mr. Jop, who was a local forester, we met a very friendly group of men who received us with open arms. They knew that their existence as an independent group in the middle of our company and regiment was no longer feasible due to the approach of the Russian armies. They gave us their weapons without resentment and also received our invitation to join our company with great joy. Soon, all of them assembled with their weapons and belongings

## 20. German Raid on Our Quarters

under the leadership of one of their men and were ready to march with us to the Jedrus Company. At the last moment Lieutenant Zwirek appeared on the scene and, when he became aware of what was taking place, he began to upbraid his men, plead with them to reconsider their decision, and stay with him as a separate group. Although he was a very persuasive speaker, only a few of his men, who were ready to join us, changed their minds and remained with him. The lieutenant was very disappointed, hurt, and angry and, the following day, he filed an official complaint with our commanding officer, Lieutenant Jozef Wiacek.[84]

In the evening of July 24, 1944, Lieutenant Wiacek received information that a large wagon train, which carried movable property from the central offices of the district of Bilgoraj and the property of its chief executive, was on the way to Germany. According to the information, the wagon train stopped for the night in the village of Osieczko, which is an extension of the town of Osiek. The wagon train was escorted by a group of uniformed Germans and by a larger unit of former Russian soldiers in German service.[85]

One time, my comrade-in-arms and I carried sacks of ammunition on our bicycles and rode into a large village in which a unit of Vlasov's army was stationed. It was early in the morning and it was somewhat dark so at first we did not notice that in every house in the village the soldiers were quartered. Only when we were in the middle of the village did we notice the soldiers watering and grooming their horses. At that time, we stepped down from our bicycles, loaded our rifles, and began to walk beside the bicycles. We decided not to walk back in the direction from which we came but rather to walk forward until we passed the village. The soldiers observed us and exchanged comments about us, but they did not attempt to stop us or to attack us. We remained calm and passed through the village without any incident. Only after we reached the other end of the village did we jump on our bicycles and pedal as fast as we could. The soldiers did not pursue us.

On another occasion, our unit traveled at night. We had a number of farm wagons with us to carry our ammunition, military equipment, and personal belongings. Men walked on both sides of the wagons. We had some men securing the end of the wagon train and four of us were assigned to walk some distance ahead of the unit in order to provide front reconnaissance. The sky was clear and the moon shone brightly so we were able to see the road ahead of us quite well. At one point, we noticed a group of soldiers walking on the same road in the opposite direction to ours. One of our men rushed to the wagon train and reported the presence of the unknown group of men on the road. In the meantime, the three of us walked very cautiously toward the group coming toward us. Then, we stopped on both sides of the road and waited for the unknown men to come close to us. As they came near us we halted them and asked them who they were. The answer came in Russian. Then, one of them asked us who we were. Since I spoke some Russian, I explained to them that we were a group of Polish partisans engaged in fighting the Nazis and that we were their Slavic brothers and therefore there was no need for us to shed fraternal blood. Obviously, their leader liked what I said and ordered his men not to shoot. He and two of his men walked toward us and we came out from our secure positions and walked toward them. We met, greeted each other, and shook hands. Before the idea of disarming us crossed the Russian leader's mind, I told him that our large unit was right behind us and all our men were well armed. Soon, we could hear some of our men approaching and our wagon train became visible on the horizon. When a strong patrol of our men approached, they joined us in our conversation with the soldiers. Since our conversation with the Russians was rather friendly, I asked one of them to show me some unusual weapon he carried. He pulled back from me and refused my request. I am sure he was convinced that I intended to take his weapon away. I assured him that I did not intend to take his weapon because we had enough weapons of our own but I was merely interested in its construction. So, he came back toward me and showed me the weapon but never let it out of his hands. Our wagon train came up and passed by the Russians, who looked at it with amazement and admiration. Before we said good-bye to them, I asked the leader of the Russian unit not to report to the Germans about their encounter with us. He solemnly assured us that the Germans would not know anything about the whole thing. The following day, all of us knew that he did not keep his word. Numerous German SS units were searching for us in the whole area. Fortunately, we were already beyond their reach.

 The German escort of the wagon train took up quarters in Osieczko to protect the lives of the staff and the valuable property of the central offices of the district of Bilgoraj. The unit of Vlasov's army found quarters in the Loniow Forest between the villages of Gaj and Zawidza. The distance between Osieczko and the Loniow Forest was less than two miles. When our men, under the leadership of Lieutenant Jozef Wiacek, attacked the wagon train in Osieczko, the Germans who protected it opened fire but soon they were overpowered and forced to surrender. Lieutenant Wiacek ordered his men to disarm the Germans and let them go wherever they wished. The chief executive of the district of Bilgoraj disappeared during the short exchange of fire and his subordinates did not know what happened to him. Everybody took for granted that he managed to escape under the cover of darkness. The unit of Vlasov's army did not bother to leave the comforts of its forest quarters and did nothing to protect the wagon train. Our men took twenty German wagons loaded with weapons, ammunition, and very valuable goods and rode away

## 20. German Raid on Our Quarters

into the darkness of the night. The horses of the German wagon train were rather small but very durable and as such became a great asset to our unit.

The following day, we learned that the chief executive of the district of Bilgoraj indeed escaped from the wagon train under the cover of night but did not have good luck in reaching the town of Staszow in which German units were stationed. Instead he went into the area of our former quarters in Lesisko and entered Mamloch's farmhouse. It happened that one of our men, Stefan Malinowski ("Masnyciu"), was there and when he saw the stranger enter the house, he aimed his pistol at him and terrorized him. Then Masnyciu searched the stranger and found a submachine gun under his topcoat and a fine pistol in a holster. Of course, Masnyciu lost no time in disarming the stranger. A short interrogation revealed the identity of the uninvited visitor. At the same time, Masnyciu knew that he could not let the German chief executive of the district of Bilgoraj go free without endangering the Mamloch's family and the neighborhood. Therefore, he took the German to the forest, shot him, and buried him near Cap's temporary grave.[86] Both Masnyciu and all the others who learned about the misfortunate end of the chief executive wondered why he came to the center of our former quarters in Lesisko to find directions about the best way to Staszow. Soon we learned that, after escaping from the wagon train in Osieczko, he walked all night through the countryside in the direction of Polaniec until he came to the village of Struzki, which was annihilated by the Nazis on June 3, 1943. In the morning, he went to the county offices there and inquired about directions to Staszow. One of the county officials sent him to Mamloch's farmhouse to get more comprehensive directions or perhaps to get a horse and buggy ride to Staszow. There is no doubt in my mind that the county official who sent the German to the farmhouse anticipated his falling into our hands there.

Shortly after our seizure of the German wagon train in Osieczko, our unit moved to the village of Rybnica on July 28, 1944, because we intended to attack a detachment of German soldiers who had taken quarters in a very solidly built two-story school building in Koprzywnica. The attack on the Germans that took place in the evening of the same day was very well prepared and very well executed. However, our leadership underestimated the military virtues of the frontline soldiers of the Wehrmacht, who wielded fantastic firepower and who were protected from our fire by the thick masonry walls of the school and around the school as well. Shortly after midnight on July 29, 1944, Jozef Szelest ("Romek Uszaty"), who was in charge of the attack, ordered our men to pull out from the combat area and return to the farm wagons that were left on the western peripheries of the town. I remember two unusual occurrences from this attack. One of my comrades-in-arms who carried his crudely made English submachine gun, Sten, on his chest, was hit by a German submachine gun bullet that damaged the weapon but did not enter his body. His life was miraculously saved. The other comrade-in-arms lost a major part of his Sten submachine gun. He was in the front line of our men who were attacking the German soldiers in the school building. Just like others, he fired his submachine gun and moved forward. All of sudden, a German bullet hit his gun and shattered it. What was left in his hand was just the crude handle of the submachine gun.

# 21. Mobilization for the Operation "Storm" or "Tempest"

Following our attack on the unit of the Wehrmacht at the school building in Koprzywnica, Lieutenant Jozef Wiacek ("Sowa") ordered a full mobilization of our men. Within a few days our 4th Company had 280 soldiers.[87] We moved from our quarters in Opalina, Smerdyna i Rybnica, to higher ground in the village of Zyznow. There, we protected the General Staff, which took up quarters at Zyznow manor and was involved in the formation of the Second Division of Infantry. Our 4th Company, formed out of the Jedrus Group, was a part of the Second Battalion, which in turn was one of the battalions of the Second Regiment of Infantry of the Legionnaires. This regiment constituted a part of the Second Division. The Home Army was well accustomed to the plans for the formation of all these military units, whether small or large. They were developed by groups of Polish officers in secret during the early stage of the war, and they were continuously updated in accordance with major and decisive events. Plans covered every region of the country to mobilize underground military forces against the Nazi aggressor in a general uprising at an opportune moment. The supreme command of the Polish Home Army believed that with the approach of the German and the Soviet front line to the Vistula River, the opportune moment for our general uprising against the Germans was also coming. However, the supreme command of the Home Army had very serious doubts about the attitude of the Soviet government toward Poland. A group of officers, who drew up the plans for the organization of the Polish underground army and a general uprising against the enemy, took for granted that the leadership of the Soviet Union would act in accordance with international law and thus respect the sovereignty of Poland once the German forces left the country. But the behavior

The four members of the Jedrus Group at the farmyard of Andrzej Wieczorek ("Chebons") in Bukowa are (left to right) Jan Pawlak ("Sprezynka"), Mieczyslaw Korczak ("Dentysta"), Walenty Ponikowski ("Walek"), and an unknown member. The photograph was taken in 1944. Courtesy of Dr. Piotr Sierant.

of Stalin's government toward Poland during the war indicated nothing more but overt hostility. For instance, in the agreement between the Polish government-in-exile and the government of the Soviet Union signed on July 30, 1941, Stalin was unwilling to restore the eastern borders of Poland, which existed before the Soviet Union joined Nazi Germany in attacking Poland in September 1939. The Soviet Government demonstrated hostility toward Poland also when it broke diplomatic relations with the Polish government in London. This happened on April 25, 1943, when the government of Poland demanded Stalin's government reveal the truth about the mass murder of Polish officers in the Katyn Forest. Now, in the light of the Soviet hostility toward the Polish government in London, the supreme command of the Home Army no longer believed possible a general uprising in accordance with the early plans. Therefore, it developed a new modus operandi for its underground army that constituted a middle ground between the present limited attacks on the enemy and the general uprising. This new modus operandi was named the Action Storm or Action Tempest (Akcja Burza) or just the Storm (Burza). According to instructions issued by the national command, all the underground units of the Home Army were to be employed in disrupting the enemy's lines of communication by attacking and harassing the German administration and military units that were moving west under the pressure of the Red Army. All the soldiers of the Home Army were to be attired in such a way that no one would have any doubt that they were members of Polish units.[88] As far as the relationship between the Home Army units and the Soviet guerrilla units was concerned, the instructions did not advise any cooperation. At the same time, plans prohibited any kind of interference that would limit the Russians' abilities in fighting the Germans. Nevertheless, a limited cooperation, in isolated cases, was left to the discretion of individual leaders of the Home Army units. Toward the units of the Red Army who were entering the territory of Poland the Home Army was to function as a host, as a legitimate representative of the Polish government, and as an administrator of the country. Commanding officers of the individual units of the Home Army were prohibited from merging any of their units with the so-called Polish units that were organized in the Soviet Union and were a part of the Red Army.[89]

As we mobilized in accordance with plans for Action Storm in Zyznow, our commanding officer, Lieutenant Jozef Wiacek took every opportunity to attack the German units that were moving west on the highways through our area. On July 28, 1944, two of our platoons ambushed, on the highway between Osiek and Staszow, two German military vehicles in which the passengers were high-ranking officers. Sowa chose for the ambush the southern side of the highway not far from Osiek. We took up our positions in the underbrush about fifty meters from the highway and waited. It was a hot day and we were thirsty. We waited patiently for the German vehicles to appear on the road. For some time we did not see anything worthwhile to ambush so we continued to wait. Then two military limousines appeared on our limited horizon. Our machine gunners and the rest of us aimed our weapons at them and waited for the commanding officer to order fire. The vehicles were about 200 yards from us and then 150 yards but still we waited. When they came within 50 yards, Sowa shouted "Fire!" The fire lasted for just a few seconds and the vehicles came to a sudden stop. When some of our men approached the German vehicles, one of the high-ranking officers was hanging on the door of one of the vehicles and he cried, *"Meine Schwester!"* ("My sister!"). Another officer still holding his submachine gun in his hands moaned from mortal wounds as he lay dying on the ground. Others were dead in various positions on the side of the highway. In the second vehicle there was a dead colonel with a bundle of military papers near him. The papers appeared to be of some importance so one of our men took them to our quarters for a closer examination. Besides the bundle of military papers that our men seized in this ambush there were three submachine guns, eight beautiful German

Home Army soldiers from Pawel's Battalion in the Inspectorate of Sandomierz. Courtesy of Dr. Piotr Sierant.

pistols, and many personal possessions of the officers, which were in the trunks of the vehicles. Before our men finished taking the weapons and personal property from the dead officers and their damaged vehicles, our machine guns opened up an intensive fire. The machine gunners were firing at a column of German military trucks that was moving on the highway from the direction of Osiek toward the ambush area. Once the military column received our machine gun fire, it came to a stop, the German soldiers evacuated the trucks, began to form an extended line on both sides of the highway, and opened fire at us. When our machine gun fire kept the Germans pinned to the ground for a while, our men in the ambush area were completing their work. Since our commanding officer did not want us to get involved in a prolonged battle with an unknown number of German soldiers in the column, he ordered us to pull out under the cover of our machine guns. Soon we disengaged from the German soldiers and were in the safety of the Staszow Forest. After returning to our quarters, we examined and reexamined the weapons and the papers that we seized in the ambush and discovered that we eliminated the staff of one of the regiments, which was a part of the Fourth Panzer Army. The reg-

The concentration of the Second Infantry Regiment of the Home Army in the Klimontow Forest in July 1944. From left to right are Sgt Kowalski ("Golab"), Lt. Medrzycki ("Reder"), and Lt. Czosnek ("Polny"). Courtesy of Dr. Piotr Sierant.

iment moved along the highway a few miles behind their leaders. In the bundle of military papers there were German plans for fortifications on the Nida River near the town of Malogoszcz.[90] After some of the Red Army units crossed the Vistula River near Baranow, the German plans for the abovementioned fortifications were handed to Russian officer Colonel D. A. Dragunsky.

On July 30, 1944, we were ordered to move from the Zyznow area to Bogoria and Lagow. Before moving, we had to leave our unnecessary personal belongings in Zyznow manor. As we moved to the new quarters, our wagons, which carried our heavy military equipment such as heavy machine guns, ammunition, hand grenades, mortars and their ammunition, explosives and many other things, rode in the middle of the road and we marched on both its sides. Many people who lived along the road came out of their dwellings to greet us and wish us good luck in fighting the enemy. They did not see such numbers of Polish soldiers since September 1939. They admired our uniforms and weapons and they were telling us that all of us looked tall. They wanted to know in which part of the country we grew up. I am convinced that the uniforms that we wore (Polish and British) and the weapons that we carried made us appear tall.

We moved to our new quarters without seeing a single German soldier. The Germans concentrated their forces on the Vistula River whose east bank was already occupied by some units of the Red Army. The German forces were doing everything they could to repair an interruption in their front line and thus prevent the Russians from crossing the river. In spite of the best efforts of the Germans, small units of the Russian Third Army, aided by some members of the Home Army, crossed the Vistula during the night of July 30-31. They secured the beachhead in the area of the villages of Dorotka and Winiary and also near the town of Annopol. As the result of the German counterattack, the Russians lost the beachhead near Dorotka and Annopol but they managed to keep the one near Winiary. The units of the Thirteenth Army of Infantry had better luck. They moved through the forested areas south of Tarnobrzeg toward the three crossings on the Vistula: Sucharzow-Gagolin, Dymitrow-Katy, and Krzeminica-Szwagrow. In the evening of July 29, a Red Army unit, under the leadership of Lieutenant S. I. Awdoszkin and aided by the partisan group of Stanislaw Ordyk ("Czernik") reached the eastern bank of the river and explored the abovementioned crossings. Then, during the night of July 30-31, the main force of the 24th Corps of the Thirteenth Army of Infantry and the units of the Sixth Division of Infantry crossed the Vistula River and penetrated its western bank all the way to Staszow. In crossing the river the Soviet troops received a great deal of help from the partisan unit of Marian Lech ("Marian"). In the evening of July 31, the units of the

**Concentration of the 8th Company of the Second Infantry Regiment in Gorki Forest in July 1944. Courtesy of Dr. Piotr Sierant.**

Sixth Division expanded the beachhead by capturing the highway between Osiek and Polaniec.[91]

When the Red Army units were crossing the Vistula River, one of the newly organized battalions of our regiment under the leadership of Captain Ignacy Zarobkiewicz ("Swojak") was attacked by powerful units of the Wehrmacht near the village of Pielaszow. In spite of the great heroism of the officers and soldiers of the battalion, the Germans, with their superior numbers and fire power, killed 65 members of the battalion.[92] My first cousin, Lieutenant Antoni Mazgaj-Marglewski, who was the battalion's adjutant, was one of the 65 killed. Since there was a great concentration of the enemy in the area of Pielaszow, the Swojak Battalion was unable to force its way through the strong German units and our units that were stationed near Bogoria were also unable to rescue the battalion. After the battle the battalion ceased to exist and survivors joined other units.

In the evening of July 31, 1944, Colonel Antoni Zolkiewski ("Lin"), who was the commanding officer of the Second Division of Infantry, received good news from Major Antoni Wiktorowski ("Kruk"), the commanding officer of the Second Regiment of Infantry, that considerable Soviet forces crossed the Vistula River in the area of the Baranow beachhead. At the same time, intelligence informed the colonel that the Germans maintained a strong defense of Sandomierz against our regiment and the Russians. According to this intelligence, the positions of the Russians forces clearly indicated that they intended to enlarge the Baranow beachhead in a westerly direction. In such a case our forces could more quickly seize from the Germans the city of Kielce than they could the city of Sandomierz. In the light of this intelligence, Colonel Lin decided that the Second Regiment should concentrate its forces in the region between Bogoria and Rakow. The 3rd, 7th, and 8th companies moved to the villages of Malkowice, Niedzwiedz, and Niemirow. Our 4th Jendrus Company took up quarters in the neighboring villages of Ujazdek and Wierzbka. During our relocation, Colonel Lin ordered the partisan units of Captain Eugeniusz Kaszynski ("Nurt"), Lieutenant Kazimierz Olchowik ("Zawisza"), and the forces of the Home Army and the Peasants' Battalions from the western part of the district of Opatow to combine. The partisan units from the district of Opatow increased their attacks on the highways between the cities of Opatow and Kielce and also Opatow and Staszow. Of course they did not attack very large and formidable columns of the Wehrmacht but rather smaller units of the enemy. However, in the village of Niedzwiedz, our units smashed and dispersed one of the larger German columns.[93] Since our units were crisscrossing the whole area in search of small groups of the enemy, they soon discovered that many large units of the Wehrmacht were being unloaded at the Ostrowiec Railroad Station and moving toward the gap in the German front. The Germans also became aware of our presence in the Opatow District and, on September 2, 1944, their artillery began to shell our quarters. Most of the German artillery fire was directed on the villages of Ujazdek and Wierzbka where our 4th Company Jedrus was stationed. Both the shelling of the German artillery and the relocation of their troops endangered the safety of our regiment. Therefore, our commanding officer ordered our 4th Company to relocate to the village of Jastrzebska Wola in order to secure the road from Iwaniska and to move the 5th Company to the village of Lagowica in order to close the road from Lagow. These relocations offered our regiment more security.

On September 2, our regiment learned that the people of Warsaw rose up against the Germans. The Red Army had already reached the eastern bank of the Vistula River and the supreme command of the Home Army in Warsaw was under the impression that the Russian armored divisions would continue rolling west toward Germany. Therefore, it issued the order to all of the Home Army troops in the capital to commence the uprising. All of us were very happy about the uprising and were ready to join our comrades-in-arms in Warsaw in fighting the Germans. We were convinced that with the Red Army's presence in the eastern suburbs of the city and with our help, the

Warsaw insurgents would have no problem in overpowering the enemy's forces in the capital. We did not know, at that time, the full scope of Stalin's perfidy vis-à-vis Poland. No one could even imagine that Stalin would keep his Red Army generals on the leash until the Germans suppressed the Warsaw uprising. He was afraid that if the leaders of the uprising succeeded in liberating the capital, they would have restored Poland's sovereign government. At that time, Stalin had already assembled his own puppet government for Poland composed solely of Communists. They came from three ethnic backgrounds: Polish, Jewish, and Russian.

The members of the puppet government who were of Polish ethnic background were former citizens of Poland who either defected to the Soviet Union before World War II or found themselves in the Soviet Union as the result of the Soviet occupation of the eastern part of Poland in 1939. The Jewish members of that government were either former residents of Poland who as Communist agents defected to the Soviet Union before 1939 to avoid punishment for their subversive activities or who joined the Communist Party after the Soviet government's annexation of the eastern part of Poland in 1939. The members of the puppet government who were of Russian origin were basically some of the Soviet citizens who were either of Polish descent or had Polish-sounding names. Most of these persons did not speak Polish at all.

During the night of September 3-4, 1944, one of our units, about one hundred men strong, attacked and dispersed a unit of Wehrmacht in the village of Ceber. During the attack, the Germans lost 31 soldiers and 19 troopers surrendered. The following day 40 more soldiers were found hiding in the fields who also surrendered. As the result of this successful battle our regiment was enriched by 5 field-kitchens, 15 military wagons loaded with war material, 9 machine guns, a great deal of hand grenades, various kinds of ammunition, new uniforms, boots, blankets, and a great amount of food.[94]

On September 4, 1944, our regiment took up quarters in the villages of Zbielutka, Stobice, Stobiec Poreba, and Szumsko. As usual, the command of the regiment and also the command of the Second Division, which was in the process of formation, had their quarters protected by the Jedrus Company. The following day, a number of light Soviet tanks reached the village of Zbielutka and some units of the Russian infantry followed them. Cooperation between our officers and the Soviet officers was satisfactory. The Russian commanding officer allowed our regiment's commanding officer to man a section of the front against the Germans. On September 5, our units and the Soviet units launched a coordinated attack on the German front line. Our physicians and nurses helped to treat some of the wounded Russian soldiers. For the first time in our lives we had a chance to see Soviet troops and mingle with them. They appeared to be very friendly toward us and shared with us their war experiences. Some of the Russian soldiers traded their weapons with us. One of the soldiers carried two submachine guns: one Russian and one German. When he saw that I had a small caliber Belgian FN semi-automatic pistol, he offered me his German submachine gun (MP) for it. Needless to say, I accepted his offer without hesitation because my pistol had a lot of wear and tear on it and his weapon was in fantastic condition. One of my friends traded his English-made submachine gun, Sten, also for a German submachine gun. Another good deal because the poorly and crudely made Sten could never compare with the German *Maschinenpistole*. After the trade was completed, my friend showed the Russian soldier one of the shortcomings of the English submachine gun. He took the Sten gun in his right hand and, while keeping the barrel of the gun up and away from himself, he hit the ground with its butt and the gun fired. The soldier learned the lesson. This crudely made gun can fire when it falls to the ground on its butt.

While talking with the Russian soldiers, I noticed that they had a German prisoner with them. He appeared to be a German officer who was very recently apprehended and condemned to death. When the time for the execution came, the Russian soldier, who guarded the prisoner, called very gently to a young boy, about twelve years old who wore a Red Army uniform, and asked him whether he wanted to shoot the German. The boy responded "*da*" (yes) and soon the execution took place. A Russian soldier who stood next to me during the execution explained to me that since German soldiers killed the boy's entire family in the Soviet Union, his platoon adopted the boy and gave him a chance to kill in revenge as many of the German soldiers as he wanted. After the shooting, I observed the young soldier-boy for a while and was struck by the paternal love that the soldiers of the platoon had for him.

One of the Russian soldiers whom I encountered that day was a female physician. At that time, female physicians were rare and female soldiers were even more rare. I must admit that in the initial stage of our conversation I did not know that she was a woman. I took for granted that she was a male physician and our conversation was as if man-to-man talk. We talked mostly about the war and various weapons of war. She showed me her fine Tokarev (TT M1933) automatic pistol and I showed her my German submachine gun. Only when we began talking about our families, did I discover that the doctor in the Red Army uniform was a woman. I was embarrassed and apologized to her for my mistake. She was very kind and understanding.

On Sunday, September 6, 1944, our units and the Russian units continued a coordinated attack on the enemy in the region of Lagow. Our patrols aided the Soviet units in conducting a reconnaissance toward Nowa Slupia and Kielce. The Soviet officers were attempting to discover the weakest place in the German front through which they could launch their offensive in the direction of Ostrowiec Swietokrzyski.[95]

Sunday, September 6, 1944, was the last day of close cooperation between our regiment and the Soviet units. From this day on the relationship between our officers and the Russian officers began to progressively cool. This happened because some of the NKVD units arrived on the scene.[96] Many members of these units spoke Polish and were given authority by their superiors to investigate and disarm soldiers and officers of the Home Army. In the case of Home Army soldiers, they attempted to persuade them to join Polish units that were a part of the Red Army. As far as Home Army officers were concerned, the NKVD agents disarmed them and escorted them to the rear of the front for further interrogations. Eventually all of them ended up in Soviet prisons or concentration camps for so-called political reorientation.

As the relationship between our units and the Soviet units continued to cool, the Russian officers aggravated the situation by issuing orders to our troops without consultation with our officers. This tense situation called for a conference between our commanding officer and the Russian commanding officer. The Russians proposed such a conference. Colonel Adam Zolkiewski ("Lin"), commanding officer of the Second Division, who did not reveal his identity to the Russians, asked Major Antoni Wiktorowski ("Kruk") to represent our forces at the conference. In order to find out the intentions of the Soviet commanding officer, Major Kruk asked for a preliminary meeting to which he sent Captain Stefan Kepa ("Pochmurny"). The captain took with him to the meeting Lieutenant Dionizy Medrzycki ("Reder") and Lieutenant Witold Jozefowski ("Mis"). The three of them met with General W. A. Mitrofanov. During the meeting, Mitrofanov demanded the subordination of our forces to the Polish Committee of National Liberation (Polski Komitet Wyzwolenia Narodowego), which was Stalin's sponsored committee. He also insisted that our forces join the army of General Berling, which again was a part of Stalin's Red Army. After hearing the demands of General Mitrofanov, our three officers told him that they did not have their superiors' authorization to decide on these very important matters and they suggested that the meeting be postponed until they could obtain such authorization. The meeting was postponed but not for long. Soon, General Mitrofanov requested a meeting with the commanding officer of our regiment. In order to gain time, Major Wiktorowski took his time in attending the meeting. In the meantime, Colonel Zolkiewski considered the possibility of crossing the still fluctuating front and moving toward Warsaw. The numerical limitation of the Russian troops in the area favored such a possibility.

In anticipation of crossing the front, our forces moved from the previous quarters to the region of Nieskurzow, Wszachow, and Stobiec. The Russians were not alarmed by this move because the headquarters of their 7th Tank Corps were in Wszachow. When Major Wiktorowski and three of his fellow officers went to see General Mitrofanov at his headquarter in Wszachow, he repeated his previous demands in very strong terms. Major Wiktorowski refused to comply with the demands. Shortly after the meeting ended, Russian troops and tanks began to concentrate in the vicinity of our quarters. It was obvious to us that General Mitrofanov intended to use his troops and his tanks to force us to comply with his categorical demands.

In the morning of September 9, 1944, Colonel Zolkiewski sent two squads with orders to reconnoiter a possible passage through the German front line.

The first patrol went on foot under the leadership of Officer Cadet Zdzislaw Rachtan ("Halny"). Halny attached to his patrol two cavalry liaison officers who, in case of necessity, could carry an important intelligence to his superiors. One of his cavalrymen was Officer Cadet Jerzy Lubowicki ("Wiktor"). Both of these mounted men were members of the Scouting Detachment under the leadership of Officer Cadet Stanislaw Skotnicki. I do not have firsthand knowledge about the events that took place during this patrol with the exception of what I learned from Halny's short description of what happened during the patrol's penetration of the German front.

In his letter written to me on October 2, 2000, Halny writes as follows:

> I do not know what others wrote. However, I remember very well that during the night of August 8-9, 1944, my squad conducted a reconnaissance of the passage, from the south to the north, through the Jelenow Range of the Holy Cross Mountains. After 50 years, I remember well this experience because I still remain in the environment of my youth.... During the time when the Soviet Army established its Baranow-Sandomierz Bridgehead, the "Nurt" units began to gather together in the village of Wszachow. The Russian light artillery batteries were already there. They were well dug in behind the row of houses and their barrels were turned north toward the Jeleniow Range of the Holy Cross Mountains. All our troops received an order of instant readiness. We were not allowed to put our weapons away even for a short while. At the same time, we were told to be very careful in our contacts with the Russian soldiers. If I remember well, there were no incidents of disagreements between our soldiers and the Russians. We had a few drinks together and talked about our experiences in the war. This is what I remember. We knew that our command in chief was involved in official conversations with some Russian officers who represent the Soviet army in the Baranow-Sandomierz bridgehead. We were also aware that the Russian command of the bridgehead expected our units to attack and take over the city of Ostrowiec.
>
> On the second or the third day (after arrival in the village of Wszachow), I was ordered to report to our commanding officer Major Eugeniusz Gedymin Kaszczynski ("Nurt"). When I reported to his headquarters, I found there a

number of Russian officers who were involved in a conference with some of our officers, such as Leszek Popiel, the aide-de-camp of Major Nurt, Lieutenant Marianski, and my immediate superior "Szort." Major Nurt led me to the road and, while walking with him, he gave me an order and some relevant explanation. He said that the conferences with the Russian officers were becoming increasingly difficult. Therefore, he was waiting for a decision of Major Lin, the commanding officer of the division. In the meantime, he ordered me to conduct a reconnaissance in the direction of the front to find out how far away the Russian units were in our area. He also ordered me to cross the Jeleniow Range of the Holy Cross Mountains and make a reconnaissance on its northern side. He said that he counted on me very much. I remember very well that my heart was pounding with joy at being chosen for this mission. I remember being proud because of the nature and the form that my mission was to take. A commanding officer of our mounted scouting unit would give me two mounted men, who were to serve me as liaison officers and who would carry my reports to headquarters. My squad was to receive more hand grenades and seven anti-tank hand grenades. Nurt appeared to me to be very worried when he asked me to be very careful and not to say anything to anybody about my mission.

In the evening of the same day, I received the watchword. I was also told what to say to the Russian outposts, namely, "I am going with my squad to a nearby village to get some provisions." We left our quarters at 1:10 A.M. My squad was armed with three light machine guns, two MP submachine guns, one Pepesha (PPSh M1941) submachine gun, five rifles, seven anti-tank hand grenades, twelve hand grenades, fifteen extra magazines of ammunition for light machine guns, and one hundred cartridges of ammunition for each rifle. The Soviet outposts let us go after I gave them the watchword that I no longer remember. The mounted liaison officers followed us as if they needed feed for their horses.

We went through the villages of Nieskuzow Stary and Nieskuzow Nowy and reached the forest. As we were walking through these two villages, we had to take cover from time to time because some German airplanes were flying very low. As we moved forward, we took all possible precautions. Near the village of Nieskurzuw Podlesie and by the road in the direction of the village of Przelecz, I briefed my two mounted liaison officers. Soon all of us entered the forest to take a short rest and to have a cigarette. Then we resumed our walk and, after a few minutes of walking up the hill, we reached the mountain pass where we came face to face with a group of five to six Soviet soldiers who were involved in mining the road through the pass. They were surprised that we came so close to them and they did not hear us at all. At first, they took us for German soldiers but when they saw the Polish eagles on our field-caps, they began to rejoice and touched with their fingers the eagles on our caps to reassure themselves that we were not Germans. They showed us where they placed their anti-tank mines and where more mines would be placed. While we were smoking cigarettes together, I made a quick sketch of the area. Before we left the Russians, they gave us some of their own hand grenades. Around 11:00 A.M., we descended from the northern side of the Witoslaw Mountain. From the edge of the forest, we looked through our binoculars on the wide terrain all the way to the village of Wasniow. There was no traffic on the highway between Opatow and Nowia Slupia. Quiet. We rested for a moment and checked our equipment. We noticed that the people of the village of Witoslawice were in their fields making sheaves of wheat and putting fifteen of them into each shock. We were able to hear their laughter and songs. We moved in their direction and hoped to get some information from them. Soon they noticed us but, contrary to our expectations, they did not rejoice upon seeing us but ran away and hid behind the shocks of wheat. What can you do? Now, we were going to the closest manor, which happened to be Nagorzyce manor, situated very close to the highway between Opatow and Nowa Slupia. Our mounted men remained in the grove of trees near a meadow. I divided the squad into two halves in order to approach the manor buildings from the right and the left sides. We met in the manor. There was not a living soul in it; no sign of life. Everything was opened. We were in the orchard that lightly sloped toward the road and were trying to figure out how to get some information since no one was there. All of a sudden, we heard the powerful sound of motors. We hit the ground in the middle of gooseberry and currant bushes and fruit trees. We lived through a moment of real terror and fear. On the curve of the road, in front of us, appeared two German Tiger type tanks. They were going toward the city of Slupia. As we nestled on mother earth, two huge steel, two-story-high monsters rolled near us with a horrible sound of their motors. Divine Providence must have protected us because they did not notice us at a distance of fifty to sixty meters. Even today, I can still visualize these huge steel monsters with their frighteningly long and unusual barrels that were aiming forward. We were like the Davids or, better, the little Davids in front of the Goliaths. I constantly reexperience that moment. You, my dear friend, made me interrupt my writing of these disclosures to take a drink. Yes, yes. I am already calmer to conclude this writing. There was still another Tiger that was parked about one hundred meters from the manor of Nagorzyce. It was parked on the road in the direction of Opatow but, as Kipling would say, that is a different history.

From the village of Nagorzyce we went to the nearby village of Rostylice, which is near the forest. There we found a number of Home Army underground soldiers who belonged to the local outpost. They were fantastic informers who knew quite well what was going on in the whole area. I wrote a report that contained indispensable information about the movements of the enemy's units and a sketch of the area where the Russian soldiers placed their mines. Our mounted liaison officer took my report to our commanding officer, Nurt, who was in the village of Wszachow. In accordance with the order (of Major Nurt), we remained in the village of Rostylice. During the night of August 8-9, 1944, all the Nurt soldiers who gathered together and also other units that were a part of the mobilization of the Second Regiment of the Legionaires of the Home Army, and even the Second Division under the leadership of Colonel Lyn went the way of our reconnaissance…. After going through the German front lines, our combined units took up quarters in the villages of Skoczyn and Kunin. This is all that I remember."

The second patrol left its quarters on August 8, 1944. Until I received the above information from Lieutenant Zdzislaw Rachtan ("Halny") about the first patrol, I was under the impression that he was the leader of the second patrol. Unfortunately, no one seems to remember who was the leader of this patrol. There were about twenty of us in the second patrol. We were armed with light weapons such as rifles, submachine guns, one light machine gun, pistols, hand grenades, and some anti-tank hand grenades. We left our quarters early in the morning and walked in the direction of the German front line that appeared to be to the northwest of our own front. After walking for about fifteen minutes, we reached the positions of our heavy machine guns camouflaged in the field. We greeted the machine gunners and kept walking toward the enemy's front line. After we distanced ourselves about two kilometers from our own front line we reached a country manor situated in a large park. The manor house was near the southern edge of the park. As we entered the park and approached the mansion, we noticed three ladies on the patio who appeared to be a mother and two daughters. They were extremely agitated by our presence near their mansion. With tears in their eyes, they begged us to withdraw from the park immediately because a German patrol was there just a few minutes before. They said that our presence there seriously endangered their lives and the lives of the rest of their family. Before the ladies had a chance to finish pleading with us, German submachine guns opened up in our direction. Cut by the enemy's projectiles, some maple tree leaves and small branches fell down on us and on the ladies. With the speed of lightning, the ladies disappeared from the patio and found safety in their mansion. We found protection behind the large trees in the park and tried to determine the location of the Germans who fired at us. Soon we discovered that the fire came from the northwestern side of the park. Immediately, we responded with our fire in that direction and began to move from tree to tree toward the Germans to take better aim at them. As we moved forward, one by one, the Germans pulled back. When we pushed them toward the edge of the park, we noticed that the Germans were withdrawing toward their horses, which were kept in the field by some of their comrades-in-arms. Soon we reached the edge of the park. The Germans were already in the field shooting at us and running for their horses. We ran after them and also fired but did not kill any of them. We were very excited and did not aim well. The same must have happened to the enemy soldiers. As some of the Germans began to reach the horses, something very funny happened. Some of the "supermen" became so frightened that they acted like clowns in the circus. When they attempted to mount their horses, the fear gave them so much energy that they went clear over on the other side of their horses. Then they jumped on their horses from the other side and landed on the side from which they started to mount. Instead of aiming our guns and firing at the Germans, we watched their incredible act and laughed our heads off. In the meantime, all the Germans mounted their horses, dispersed, and rode beyond the effective range of our guns.

Our harmless encounter with the enemy's patrol encouraged us to penetrate deeper into the German front line. Therefore, we kept walking in the same direction as before. However, we became more careful and more circumspect. We did not want another German patrol to fire at us before we had a chance to see it. After walking for about three miles, we met a group of farmers who worked in their fields. At first, we frightened them because they took us for a German patrol. As we came closer to them and wished them God's help in their harvest, they came to us and shook our hands. Then they looked at our uniforms, weapons, and white-and-red armbands. Nevertheless, they were still afraid. When we asked them why they were so frightened, their answer was that they feared for our lives because we were in the midst of the German front, filled with the enemy's soldiers and tanks. When we explained to them that there were many strong Polish and Russian units behind us and that the Germans were losing the war, we saw in the farmers' faces obvious disbelief. Soon we left the farmers in the fields and kept walk-

The Second Infantry Regiment hears mass in the fall of 1944. In the middle of the picture, behind the priest, left to right, are N.N. acolyte, Major Antoni Wiktorowski (Kruk) and Lieutenant Stefan Franaszczuk ("Tarzan" vel "Orlicz"). Courtesy of Dr. Piotr Sierant.

ing closer to the front. After we walked about two miles and were crossing a field full of rye shocks, we noticed a German cavalry patrol riding toward us. To my best recollection there were about fifteen Germans in the patrol. They were riding in an extended line and approaching us very slowly. We hid behind the rye shocks and waited. Our commander asked us to hold our fire until they came closer to us. We watched the Germans approaching us cautiously and scouting the fields. When they came within the range of our submachine guns, the commander ordered, "Fire!" Needless to say, the Germans did not anticipate our presence so deep in their front line. Immediately, they turned their horses backward, dispersed and rode away as fast as their horses could carry them. As they rode away, we kept firing at them. One of our men to my left was firing a Finnish submachine gun (Suomi) that might have been the type on which the Russians patterned their submachine gun called Pepesha (PPSh M1941). For its magazine, it had a large drum somewhat larger than the Pepesha had and it had an extremely rapid fire. After I emptied my magazine, my comrade-in-arms, to my left, was still firing. When I looked at him, I could not see his face because of a cloud of casings that formed around his head. This phenomenon looked very funny to me and I burst out in laughter. A few others in our group noticed the same thing and also laughed. All of us were young and were able to see comedy in the most tragic situations.

After the enemy patrol rode out of our sight, we continued walking deeper into the area under German control. For a long time, we did not see any military activities on the part of the Germans in the fields and on the secondary roads. We had excellent visibility because the sky was clear and the temperature high. In the afternoon, we became thirsty and did not see any water around. After walking for a while and hoping to find some water, we noticed an isolated manor in the midst of large fields. As usual, the manor had a park around it. Our commander decided to take us to the manor so we could satisfy our thirst. We walked more quickly and soon reached a spacious yard around the mansion. From the farm workers whom we encountered in the yard we learned that the manor was a so-called *Liegenschaft* (manor) operated by a German administrator (*Landwirt*). He and his family had returned to Germany just the day before. The ladies who worked in the manor house invited us in and offered us cold milk to drink. Our commanding officer posted several men outside and the rest of us entered the mansion. Before we finished drinking our first glass of milk, one of our guards rushed in and shouted, "Germans are coming!" We rushed into the yard with our weapons ready to fire. Since we did not see any Germans, we were convinced that the soldiers entered the park and were coming toward the mansion from a northwestern direction. Therefore, the commander decided to lead us in the direction from which we came (southeast). He was convinced that our patrol penetrated the enemy's front deep enough without great obstacles, therefore, we should start on the way back to our own front line. We believed that the soldiers of the German patrol were also thirsty and they were going to the manor that we just left to get something to drink. Since we were not interested in getting involved in a long exchange of fire with the enemy, we did everything possible to avoid any unnecessary confrontation. Soon we discovered that our speculation as to what the German patrol would do proved to be totally wrong. The Germans did not enter the park and did not go to the manor house. They followed their leader in a long line like geese and kept walking on the western edge of the park while we were walking on its eastern edge. When we came to the southern end of the park, the Germans also came to the same end of the park. There was a great surprise on both sides. I am sure that the Germans were more surprised because they did not know anything about our presence there but we knew about theirs. When they noticed us, they stopped, turned toward us, and observed us very intently. The distance that separated us from them was about two hundred yards. As soon as the Germans stopped we also stopped and watched them. They must have been puzzled for two basic reasons: we were coming from the German side of the front and going in the same direction as they, that is, toward the Russian front, and we were wearing British army uniforms. As soon as the German patrol resumed its walk, we too resumed our walk. While walking we observed them and they in turn watched us. After a while, they stopped to take a better look at us and we also stopped and observed them. There were about sixteen of them and they were well armed. One of them carried a very fine machine gun MG42, which was perhaps the best machine gun used in World War II by both sides in the conflict. We had a great respect for this type of machine gun because we had some of them in the Jedrus Company. As the Germans resumed walking again, they veered somewhat to the west. At the same time, our patrol turned a bit toward the east so the distance between the patrols began to increase as time went on. After a while, we lost visual contact with the German patrol.

After walking toward our front line for a while, we encountered the enemy again. This time, two German tanks surprised us in the open field. They were coming toward us from the west. We were convinced that one of the last two German patrols reported our presence in their front line and they radioed their armor unit to liquidate us. As soon as we noticed the tanks rolling through the fields, we hit the ground. I noticed that there was a small trench in front of us, so I crawled into it and others followed suit. As we aimed our weapons toward the tanks and readied our hand grenades and English plastic explosives, I said, "Brothers, let's fight to the last bullet." I was convinced that, as the tanks were coming closer and closer, most of us faced our mortality. When the tanks came to about fifty yards north of us and began to pass by our positions, we began to realize that the crews in the tanks did not notice us at all. We began to breathe freely and started to speculate that the tanks were rushing to challenge a Russian tank patrol that might have penetrated the German front lines east of us.

As soon as the enemy tanks disappeared from our view, we got up and resumed our walk toward our lines. We hoped that we would not encounter more German patrols. As it happened, our hope was not quite realistic. After walking for about three miles southeast, we received fire from the rear. The enemy equestrian patrol purposely followed us and obviously attempted to wipe us out or at least to chase us out of the area under German control. We responded with fire and kept the Germans at a safe distance from us. Nevertheless, they followed us and annoyed us with their rifle fire. In order to slow the walk of the German patrol, our leader left two of our men with a light machine gun behind us and ordered them to wait until the Germans came within range of an effective fire and then to fire at them. Our two men found a well-protected and camouflaged position and waited. When the Germans came near, our men opened fire at them. The men of the enemy's patrol hit the ground and responded with their fire. Our men waited until the Germans attempted to continue to trail us, then they opened fire again. The Germans were forced to take cover on the ground again. At that time, our two men, unnoticed by the Germans, withdrew in a hurry and followed us.

As we were approaching our own front line, we hoped that the enemy's patrol would follow us within the range of our heavy machine guns. However, the Germans must have anticipated the proximity of our front and discontinued pursuing us any further.

After returning to our quarters on the northern edge of the forest, our commanding officer went immediately to headquarters to report our findings during the crossing of the German front lines. The rest of us shared our patrol experiences with our comrades-in-arms, washed ourselves, had something to eat, and got ready to cross the German front again during the night.

## 22: Crossing the German Front

During the night of August 9-10, 1944, our troops left, in utter secrecy, the village of Zbielutka, where we stayed next to the Soviet units, and crossed safely the German front through the pass in the Jeleniow Range of the Holy Cross Mountains. As soon as we left Zbielutka, we encountered some Russian troops who were returning from a major encounter with German soldiers. They walked on both sides of the road protecting many of their comrades-in-arms who were seriously wounded and who were riding in numerous farm wagons. Some Soviet medics and nurses were taking care of the wounded soldiers but obviously the wounded men were not given morphine because they were shouting at the top of their voices, "*Ubiy mienia! Ubiy mienia!*" (Finish me off! Finish me off!). We extended our hands to them and sympathized with them but could not do anything to help them. The Russian officer who was in charge of the wagon train was puzzled by our march toward the German front and wanted to speak to our commanding officer. In the meantime he was asking us who we were. Our answer was: "*Ubiyom Germantza!*" (We will kill the Germans!). When he insisted on seeing our commanding officer, some of our soldiers sent him to the front of our marching column and when he reached the front of our column, he was sent to the back of the column. Finally, he got frustrated and stopped bothering us.[97]

The Nurt units marched through the villages of Piorkow and Skoszyn Stary. The Second Regiment of Legionaires took the road through the villages of Nieskurzow Stary and Rostolice.[98] The Nurt units took the road that was reconnoitered by the Halny patrol and the Second Regiment followed the route that was determined by the second patrol, that is to say our patrol, to be safe.

## 22. Crossing the German Front

Early in the morning of August 10, 1944, the Second Regiment reached the northern slopes of the Jeleniow Range, made camp on the side of the Wesolowka and the Witoslawska Mountains, and took up defensive positions toward the German strongholds. Even though the area occupied by the Second Regiment was not in immediate proximity to fire exchange between the Russians and the Germans, nevertheless, the Luftwaffe attacked our camp from time to time. Fortunately we were covered by forest, therefore the enemy's aerial attacks were not very effective. In the evening of August 10, 1944, the units of the Second Regiment took up quarters in the villages of Rostylice, Witoslawice, and Milejowice. The presence of the regiment in its new quarters deprived the Germans of easy access to a very important highway between Opatow and Nowa Slupia.[99] The German detachments, which were stationed nearby in the region of the villages Nagorzyce and Janowice, did not try to stop our regiment from taking up its new quarters but rather withdrew toward the villages of Garbacz and Czerwona Gora. The new positions of the Second Regiment blocked the enemy's access to the roads in the area of the Jeleniow Range and enabled the Russians to get an upper hand in the area of Lagow and Opatow.

In order to reconnoiter the areas surrounding the regiment's positions and to protect the assembling of the Third Regiment, the commanding officer sent a number of platoons into the northern foreground on August 11, 1944. The patrols went toward the villages of Jeleniow, Stara Slupia, Stara Zwola, Wasniow, Garbacz, Czerwona Gora, and Michalow. These patrols reported a concentration of German forces along the highways that connected Opatow with Nowa Slupia and then the Nowa Slupia Pass with Lagow, Nowa Slupia, and Bieliny. They also reported that in the vicinity of the mountain called Kobyla Gora and in the villages of Debniak and Trzcianka there were German units that were equipped with tanks and artillery. They blocked the mountain passes through which the highways went from Lagow and Piorkow to Nowa Slupia. In a number of instances there was an exchange of fire between our patrols and the German patrols.[100]

During the night of August 11-12, 1944, the Second Regiment and the Third Regiment, which constituted an incomplete Second Division, went through the town of Nowa Slupia, which the Germans had abandoned. The people of the town welcomed us with great joy. There were flowers, patriotic songs, and kisses.[101] Then the two regiments marched to their new quarters in the villages of Debno, Jeziorko, and Wola Szczygielkowa. Our regiment took quarters in Debno. The people of Debno under the leadership of their priest received us with open arms. On Sunday, August 12, Father Andrzej Pyrek, pastor of Debno parish, celebrated mass and Father Jacek, a Franciscan priest from Niepokalanow, our chaplain, preached a patriotic sermon.

Toward the end of his sermon, which he preached to young soldiers who were ready to fight and to die for the freedom of Poland, Father Jacek was moved to tears.[102]

On August 15, about 1,200 soldiers concentrated under the command of Colonel Lin (Antoni Zolkiewski) celebrated the Soldier's Day. The celebration consisted, first of all, of two masses. One mass was held in the parish church of Debno. Father Andrzej Pyrek was the celebrant of the Mass and Father Jacek preached the sermon. The second mass was celebrated at the meadow by Father Jaskolski, chaplain of the First Battalion, Second Regiment. Father Jerzy Brodeecki ("Szkarlatny Kwiat"), chaplain of the Second Regiment, preached the sermon. During the services, we all thanked God for guiding us safely through the German and Russian fronts. At the same time we prayed for a successful outcome to the fight against the Nazi forces behind their front lines. We hoped that in the near future we might be able to force the Germans to leave our land and return to their own country.

# 23. Behind Enemy Lines

On August 17, we had to leave our hospitable quarters in the parish of Debno and move north toward Warsaw, where the supreme command of the Home Army ordered the total uprising against the German forces to be launched on August 1, 1944. The Polish supreme command ordered the Warsaw Uprising because the Red Army had reached already the Vistula River and had occupied the suburbs of Warsaw on the eastern side of the river. Contrary to the Soviet government's promises, the Red Army did not offer any help to the heroic soldiers of the Home Army fighting in Warsaw. On the contrary, the Soviets did everything possible to enable the German Wehrmacht units to destroy the Polish forces during the insurrection. When the American and British governments asked the Soviet Union to allow their transport aircraft with military supplies for the Polish fighters to land near Warsaw on territory already occupied by the Red Army, the answer was "*Niet*."

During the second week of the Warsaw Uprising, the German forces began to divide the Polish fighters and thus endanger their very existence. Therefore, the supreme commander of the Home Army, General Tadeusz Komorowski ("Bor"), issued the following order: "I am ordering all available and well-armed units to move by forced march toward Warsaw in order to fight the enemy on the peripheries of the city, in its suburbs and in the center of the city."[103] Our commanding officer, Colonel Antoni Zolkiewski, received this order on August 14, 1944. After a necessary reorganization, our troops moved through the town of Tarczek to Siekierno, where we found our new quarters. During our march to Siekierno, we noticed German troops were moving increasingly toward the front. Therefore, we had to double our alertness. On August 18, one of our outposts, which had been posted in the village of Wzdol Rzadowy, encountered a number of German trucks, which were going toward Siekierno. During a short exchange of fire, one German officer, three noncommissioned officers, and some privates were killed. One of the officers survived and was taken as a prisoner of war. Among the documents that he had with him was an order from the Commander of the Fourth Armored Army ordering its corps to liquidate all partisan units to the rear of the German front.[104]

In the evening of August 18, 1944, our regiment left Sikierno and marched through the forests south of Skarzysko and Starachowice. Between the villages of Mnichow and Ostrojow, we hurriedly crossed the railroad tracks, which were guarded by Germans. We marched all night and before noon on August 19, 1944, we halted our march in the forest south of the village of Sorbin. The rest of the day we rested. During the repose, we were ordered not to make fires because their smoke would have uncovered our presence to the Germans. In the evening of the same day, our troops resumed their march toward Warsaw. On August 20, 1944, we reached the point of concentration of our division. According to Piotr Sierant, at that point the Second Division had 3,075 men. Although we did not have enough heavy weapons to fight German tanks and aircraft, our esprit de corps was great. In the evening of the same day, we continued in the direction of the forests near the town of Przysucha. Then during the night of August 20-21, we reached the villages of Rusinow, Ruski Brod, and Kacprow. On August 23, 1944, the units of our division came together again in the forests south of Przysucha. We were now about 80 miles from Warsaw and began preparations for a crossing of the Pilica River.[105] During the final week of August, we were getting ready to join with the Seventh Infantry Division to cross the Pilica River in the most accessible and safe places. During this week our forces increased to 6,500 fighting men.[106] We were all excited about crossing the Pilica River and marching toward Warsaw. In the meantime, some of our patrols selected a number of places that appeared to be feasible points for a possible crossing. The access to these places was covered by forest. At the same time, when some of our patrols attempted to cross the river in the general area of Nowe Miasto, they clashed with German troops, who protected their fortifications on its northern side. Other patrols managed to cross the Pilica River and reconnoiter the area in the direction of Warsaw. The intelligence that they brought back with them to our commanding officers was not very encouraging. They reported that, in addition to the German troops who guarded the northern side of the river, there were strong enemy units, including panzer units, that were located in various places near the Pilica. In the light of this intelligence, very discouraging news from Warsaw, and lack of military airdrops from the West, Colonel Jan Zientarski ("Mieczyslaw") called the commanding officers of the divisions together for a briefing. During this briefing, the commanding officers decided that our further march to Warsaw was impossible. Colonel Zientarski notified General Tadeusz Komorowski ("Bor") about the officers' decision and obtained his approval.[107]

Since our march to Warsaw was impossible, Colonel Zientarski decided to attack and to take control of various cities in the region in which there were centers of German administration. The most important among these cities were Kielce and Radom. Soon he realized that in order to succeed in seizing one of these cities we needed light artillery. Since a unit of German artillery was stationed in the village of Dziebaltow, Colonel Zientarski ordered some of our most experienced units to attack the Germans there and take weapons. During the night of August 26-27, the chosen units of our forces attacked the Germans in Dziebaltow. The German soldiers proved to be experienced fighters and defended themselves quite well. Nevertheless, our men seized the village and the artillery pieces. Unfortunately, they were heavy artillery pieces that were useless to us. Therefore, our soldiers disabled them and left them behind in the village. Because our units did not have artillery, Colonel Zientarski abandoned his plans of taking by force Kielce, Radom, and other larger cities in our region.

Colonel Wojciech Borzobohaty ("Wojan"), chief of staff of the Corps of Kielce. Courtesy of Dr. Piotr Sierant.

From August 29, 1944, the German forces in our area began to endanger us wherever we took up quarters by sending out small patrols, which opened fire at our advanced guards. The leadership of the German forces in our area was quite aware of our existence and decided to do everything possible to liquidate our concentrated units. The proximity of the Soviet front made our strong units seriously endanger the German home front in our area. In the eyes of high-ranking German officers, our forces constituted a threat to the safety of their supplies and reserves. Therefore, from the end of August 1944 our forces gradually ceased attacking the Germans and switched, in most instances, to defensive activities.

On August 31, 1944, our regiment moved into the region of Radoszyce. At the same time, the Third Regiment took up quarters in the same general area. Both regiments arrived in the area to secure an airdrop that was expected

The soldiers from the 5th Company, Second Battalion of the Home Army. Courtesy of Dr. Piotr Sierant.

near the village of Gracuch during the night of September 1-2. For obvious reasons our forces did everything possible not to be discovered by the Germans. In spite of our utmost caution, some of our units were discovered and clashed with a German unit in Radoszyce and Grodzisko on September 2, 1944. In this clash, our patrol, which was getting provisions in Radoszyce, fired at two German military trucks that were coming to Radoszyce from Pijanow. During the exchange of fire, two German officers, two noncommissioned officers, and one enlisted man were killed. The second German truck managed to get away. Then, more German troopers arrived in two military trucks and a bus. Some of the Germans remained in Grodzisko and others went toward Radoszyce. Soon, the Germans began to burn some of the houses both in Grodzisko and in Radoszyce. Our units responded immediately to German atrocities in Grodzisko and Radoszyce.[108] Under the leadership of Lieutenant Zbigniew Kabata ("Bobo") our machine gun squad and a rifleman squad patrolled in the direction of Grodzisko. As we moved toward the road near the village, the German troopers greeted us with a heavy machine gun fire. They also attacked us with their mortars that were hidden in a wooded area. This was the first time in my life that I was under mortar fire. We responded with machine gun and rifle fire and began to move slowly toward the enemy, who appeared to be strong and well situated. We were not sure whether or not we could dislodge the Germans from their positions. All of a sudden, we received help from an unexpected quarter. An extended line under the leadership of Lieutenant Ludwik Wichula ("Jelen") appeared to the rear of us and began to fire at the German positions. Soon, we became a part of the extended line, caught its enthusiasm, and began shouting "Hurrah"! As we moved forward toward the enemy's line, I noticed some of the nurses in the line. They were enthusiastic and brave; they also shouted "Hurrah" at the top of their voices. Seeing our long extended line, the Germans began to abandon their firing positions and run as fast as they could. At that time, our riflemen put their bayonets on their rifles and all of us accelerated our pace in following the enemy. We no longer walked but rather ran in pursuing the supermen.

For one reason or another, we did not pursue the enemy far enough and thus failed to cut off his return route to Wloszczowa. The enemy troopers ran to their vehicles and disappeared from the battlefield. Under the leadership of Lieutenant Jelen we occupied the village of Grodzisko, which was vacated by the Germans. At that point in time, the lieutenant did not know whether the Germans who were in Radoszyce also abandoned that town. The best way to find the answer to this question was to move toward Radoszyce. As soon as we left Grodzisko on our way to Radoszyce, the Germans opened strong fire in our direction. We also responded with strong fire and pushed the Germans toward the hill near Radoszyce. The Germans wanted to use the hill as a cover in breaking off from us. Their stratagem did not work because one of our companies, which had been going from Radoszyce toward Grodzisko, closed the route of their escape. At that moment, the Germans were attacked from both sides and defended themselves to the very end. Twenty-two of them died in the battle and two were taken prisoner. Our losses were two dead and ones lightly wounded.[109] After this battle was over, our machine gun squad under the leadership of Lieutenant Kabata returned to our quarters in the village of Mularzow.

We had a peaceful night on September 2-3, 1944. Nevertheless, we were ready for German retaliation because of the losses and humiliation that they suffered at our hands the day before. The commanding officer of our division, Colonel Antoni Zolkiewski, was convinced that, in so short a time, the Germans would be unable to use great force against us. They needed more time to bring into our area a larger force. He speculated that they would rather limit themselves to a retaliatory action against the people of Grodzisko and Radoszyce. His speculation was correct.

On September 3, 1944, our advanced posts reported a strong concentration of German military trucks on the southern edge of Grodzisko and in

Medical services treating the wounded during fighting involving the Second Infantry Regiment of the Home Army. Courtesy of Dr. Piotr Sierant.

the center of Jakimowice. The troopers who arrived in these trucks were moving behind an armor-plated truck toward Radoszyce.[110] Soon they surrounded the town and began to burn its houses and round up the people.[111] When Colonel Antoni Wiktorowski learned about this, he ordered Captain Tadeusz Pytlakowski ("Tarnina"), who was the commanding officer of the Second Battalion, to attack the Germans in Radoszyce, push them out of the town, and destroy them as soon as possible. In ordering this urgent attack, Colonel Wiktorowski had in mind the safety of the town's population. As the Second Battalion moved toward Radoszyce, its left wing protected the Heavy Machine Gun Platoon that was a part of the Jedrus Company. In the early phase of the attack the battalion did not encounter any resistance. In the meantime, the Germans rounded up a great many people in the marketplace. Some of these people were brought from the parish church where they were attending mass. Some of them were locked by the German troopers in the fire hall and threatened with cremation. The people who were guarded in the marketplace were also told, by the German troopers, that they would be fried in the fire of their own homes.

As the battalion approached the outskirts of Radoszyce, it clashed with the German cavalry patrol. Our fire made the twenty-horse patrol abandon its horses and take up defensive positions in a building. As a result of our fire, the building in which the cavalrymen took cover exploded in flames. The troopers, who were forced to abandon the building, were killed by our fire one by one. A unit from the Jedrus Company pushed toward the road that went in the direction of Momocicha, but when it reached the top of the elevation that divided it from the enemy, the German machine gun fire, from a nearby windmill, forced it to hit the ground. I will never forget that heavy German machine gun fire that almost cost me my life. When the Germans fired at our unit from the windmill as well as from its vicinity, we responded with our fire. I happened to fire a German-made machine gun MG42 from a fine position. At the same time, I was doing everything possible to discover the German position from which the enemy was firing at us with the same kind of machine guns, MG42s. According to my humble estimation, model MG42 was the best machine gun used in World War II. While I was totally engaged in the exchange of fire with the enemy, one of our soldiers crawled to my position and asked me for help. He told me that his MG42 machine gun fired only single shots and refused to fire a series of shots. I decided to help, left my machine gun in the hands of one of the machine gun crew who was more than eager to fire the gun, and crawled to the neighboring position where the defective MG42 was. After fixing the defect, I fired the gun and it worked perfectly. I was very proud of my accomplishment and very happy. Instead of crawling back to my machine gun, I wanted to show off how well I was able to fire the MG42 at the Germans. Instead of using the same position that my fellow machine gunners used, I pulled the gun onto a little dirt hill (probably made to mark the borderline of two neighboring farms). Then I placed the gun on the dirt hill, aimed at the enemy's machine gun position in the windmill, and fired a series of shots. A great amount of dirt in my face and in my eyes interrupted my series of shots. I pulled the machine gun down, took cover behind the dirt hill, and thanked God for saving my life. Obviously, the German machine gunner in the windmill aimed at me at the same time I was aiming at him. When he fired, his bullets hit the dirt hill under my machine gun without harming me. If he had aimed about one foot higher, these words would never have been written.

After I returned to the position where my own machine gun was, I continued to fire at the German machine gunners who were in the windmill and around it. Some of the Germans who advanced toward our positions were separated a bit from the Germans in the windmill and its vicinity. They fired their rifles at us but their fire was rather sporadic and ineffective; nevertheless, it was annoying to us. Therefore our commanding officer sent some of his riflemen to neutralize their fire. While our MG42s kept the German fire down, a small group of our riflemen crawled toward the German riflemen

Personnel of the Second Infantry Regiment of the Home Army. Major Eugeniusz Kaczynski ("Nurt") stands between the two nurses. On the left, Anna Mirecka ("Hanka") and Janina Bratkowska ("Janka"). Sitting on the ground is Liaison Officer Ewa Ostrachowska. Courtesy of Dr. Piotr Sierant.

and silenced them. When all our riflemen returned to our line, they brought with them German rifles, submachine guns, pistols, and hand grenades. They also described their experiences in close combat. One of our riflemen said that when he was exchanging fire with one of the Germans at very close range, the German attempted to throw a hand grenade at him. At that very moment another of our men fired at the German and hit him in the raised arm that was holding the hand grenade. Needless to say, the hand grenade fell to the ground and exploded in the face of the enemy soldier.

When we were engaging the enemy from the southern side of the windmill hill, our other units attacked the hill from the northwestern side. One of these units — the Second Battalion of the Second Regiment — shocked the Germans with its vigorous attack. The enemy's resistance gave in. The Germans were forced to withdraw to Radoszyce. Soon our units reached the suburban areas of Radoszyce and were on the way to its center where the Germans were burning residential dwellings and were about to shoot the innocent victims whom they kept in the marketplace and in the fire hall. As our troops were rushing toward the center of Radoszyce, some local boys were showing them the best shortcuts to the back of the German positions and the marketplace. As the Germans in the marketplace noticed our troops pushing toward the center of Radoszyce, they abandoned their work of burning homes and guarding the captives and immediately took defensive positions. The exchange of fire between our troops and the enemy did not last long. As soon as the Germans became aware that some of our troops were encircling them, they decided to save themselves by pulling out. Their superior officer, Colonel Klaus, urged his men to abandon their defensive posts and run.[112] The German troopers ran to their military trucks and managed to escape encirclement by our units. They withdrew in the direction of the village of Ruda. The battlefield that they left in a hurry looked horrible. Flames rose from three-fourths of the town, and a number of charred human bodies lay on the deserted streets amid the loud crackle of fire.[113]

Before returning to our quarters in Mularzowo, the commanding officer of the Second Battalion sent a number of patrols in the direction in which the German forces withdrew. He wanted to be sure that the enemy did not remain in the area of our quarters. For obvious reasons, during the night of September 3-4, 1944, our regiment moved to new quarters in the area of Adamow, Przylogi, Kawenczyn, and Cisownik. Other units of our division took up quarters in the neighboring villages of Straznica, Kawenczyn, and Zborowice. We stayed there from September 4 to 12, 1944, and there we created an independent republic in the middle of the German occupied country. Some of our men named this area "The Partisans' Republic" (Partyzantcka Republika).[114] The staff of our division took up headquarters in Adamow and the staff of our regiment was in Przylogi. The elementary school building in Przylogi became our temporary hospital where three of our military physicians — "Lepszy," "Andrzej," and "Mieta" — took care of our wounded and sick soldiers. In Przylogi, Stanislaw Szwarc ("Roman") began to publish a regimental newspaper. Divisional military police, under the leadership of Lieutenant "Reder," kept order in the area occupied by our division. Our military authority approved or appointed village administrators. To protect our territory from intrusion by enemy forces, a squad of our engineers blew up some of the bridges that provided the Germans with easy access to the area that we occupied.

On September 10, 1944, we expected an airdrop from the Western Allies to be made in the region of Klucko. The Jedrus Company was ordered to secure the immediate area of the airdrop. Early in the evening, our company began its march through Piaski Krolewieckie, Krolewiec, Smykov, and Kozlow. During our march, we walked on both sides of the road and a number of farm wagons were driven along the middle of the road. These wagons carried some heavy weapons and extra ammunition. It was rather dark when we reached

A photograph of our few, dedicated, and overworked medics at the front in the forest. On the right is Dr. Wladyslaw Chaciej ("Dr. Andrzej"), and on the wagon is Nurse Edyta Nawratil ("Baska"). Courtesy of Dr. Piotr Sierant.

the village of Kozlow. Some people whom we met on the road in the village told us that three German military trucks full of soldiers had driven in the same direction we were going (northwest) just moments before. Therefore, they asked us to be careful. We thanked the people for the information and kept going. A number of us were in the front of the marching column and kept our weapons at the ready to fire. As soon as we passed the village of Kozow, farm fields lay on both sides of the road. Suddenly, we noticed pairs of small rectangular lights on the road ahead of us. We stopped our wagons and moved forward to take a better look at the lights. Once our wagons stopped, we saw not only numerous lights but also we could hear the motors of trucks. Therefore, we passed the word to our men behind us that German military vehicles were moving in our direction. The enemy drivers did not notice us at all and kept moving toward us. Those of us who were in the front of the marching column had to stop them by all means. I placed my MG-42 in the middle of the road, aimed at the first German truck, and fired a short series of shots. The truck kept moving. I fired again a longer series of shots but the truck continued moving toward me. I kept firing at it until it came dangerously close to my firing position and forced me to pick up my machine gun and move to the right side of the road. While I was picking up my MG42, the middle finger of my left hand accidentally touched the barrel of the gun. The barrel was very hot and the tip of my finger was severely burned. The truck finally stopped. In the meantime, my comrades-in-arms attacked the second German truck and brought it to a stop. Some of the German soldiers jumped from the first and the second truck and took cover in the fields. Our men surrounded them. One of the German soldiers shouted in perfect Polish: "Brothers, don't shoot! I am a Pole from Silesia. I did not want the war. The son of a bitch Hitler wanted the war" ("*Bracia nie strzelajcie! Ja jestem polakiem ze Slaska. Ja nie chcialem wojny, Skurwysyn Hitler chcial wojny*").

While we were preoccupied with the first and the second truck, the driver of the third German truck managed to turn around and disappear into the darkness of the rainy night. We had enough to do with the enemy soldiers who rode in the two trucks that we halted. Needless to say, most of the Germans died from our bullets, some were wounded, and a few of them tried to escape, but we apprehended them later on. As soon as our fire ceased, a good number of people came from the village to see the battlefield. Men, women, and youngsters helped us to collect the enemy's weapons and ammunition. In order to bury the dead, men returned to their homes to bring shovels. Women procured buckets full of water and brooms. While the men were burying the German corpses in the nearby forest, women washed blood from the surface of the road so that there would be no visible trace of the battle. We used strong farm horses to pull away the German trucks that were damaged by our bullets. Before the morning came, all traces of the battle disappeared. Some of our men took the trucks and prisoners to our quarters in Przylogi. They stored the trucks in the forest and delivered the prisoners to our superior officers for interrogation. The rest of the Jedrus Company went to the area of Klucko to protect the airdrop basket. The following day, the company remained in the vicinity of Kozlow to protect its population from possible German retaliation. Since the Germans were preparing a comprehensive attack on our division, there was no retaliation against the people in Kozlow.[115]

In preparation for their attack on our division in the "Partisan Republic," the German forces sent spies into the villages that we used as our quarters. It appeared that the enemy's military authorities did not have enough spies among the local population because they were sending SS men who spoke Polish. Shortly after we returned from Kozlow to our quarters in Przylogi, we learned that some of the German spies were apprehended by our military police in various villages in which we had our quarters.[116] I witnessed the execution of one of them. He was a German policeman from the city of Konskie. He spoke Polish and was dressed like a farmer, but he did not speak like a farmer and act like a farmer. The local people recognized him as a pretender and pointed him out to one of our officers. During the interrogation, he confessed who he really was and was sentenced to die by our military tribunal. The execution took place in a young pine forest near our quarters in Przylogi. Two of our soldiers with submachine guns walked behind the spy on the road through the young forest. After walking about one hundred feet into the forest, the spy attempted to run away. He jumped to the left of the road into little pines and tried to run. At that point in time, our men fired their submachine guns and the spy fell to the ground dead. He appeared to be about thirty-five years old.

On September 13, 1944, German forces attacked our concentrated units. The Germans mobilized a few thousand troops for this attack. Some of them came from the 318 Security Division (318 Sicherungsdivision). The first attack took place at 2:00 P.M. in Miedzierza. A German military truck entered the town, where it clashed with our post. In the encounter all the enemy troops were killed. The second German truck, which followed the first one, escaped. The second German attack occurred along the road between the villages of Smykow and Przylogi. The third German attack took place in the direction of the villages of Kawenczyn and Cisownik. Then, about 4:00 P.M., a large German unit equipped with light artillery and seven armored vehicles entered the village of Miedzierza. There the men of the 8th Company of the 2nd Regiment attacked them with plastic explosives and set afire some of the armored vehicles. The German column of artillery and armored vehicles was halted. The fire from the burning armored vehicles spread to some of the houses and barns in the village. This skirmish delayed the German attack until 5:00 P.M. At that time, the enemy attacked the village of Kawenczyn without success. Although the enemy did not succeed at Kawenczyn, he kept attacking time after time and was thrown back by the 8th Company under the leadership of Lieutenant Witold.[117]

The commanding officer of the Second Division, Colonel Lin was convinced that the enemy's lack of success during his attacks on September 13, 1944, would prompt him to mobilize a larger force of infantry, artillery, armored vehicles, and also to bring in some airplanes. Therefore, he decided that all our units should abandon the present quarters and move south, where there was no concentration of German armed forces. The colonel ordered that each regiment should breach German lines in different places of the encirclement. I will never forget the early night when our regiments began their march south because there were conflagrations wherever the regiments marched. The fires were caused by exchange of machine gun fire and other weapons in villages through which the troops proceeded.

I remember that our Jedrus Company marched south through a meadow toward a small creek. As soon as we reached the creek, we discovered that the bridge on the creek was destroyed. The water was shallow, so we walked through the creek to the other side. I was under the impression that our squad of machine guns under the leadership of Lieutenant Zbigniew Kabata ("Bobo") was in the very front of the Jedrus Company. At the same time, I am convinced that as soon as we crossed the creek, several of our scouts went to the right of us and proceeded south toward a higher elevation in the terrain. A few minutes later after they left our unit, somebody fired a gun in the direction of our scouts. One of our men made a remark that one of our scouts accidentally fired his gun. As soon as he finished saying this, a German flare went into the air and German machine guns started to fire at the crossing of the creek. We all hit the ground. Obviously, the Germans fixed the sights of their machine guns on the location of the bridge. They fired tracer bullets that scared some of our horses. After the first series of German tracer bullets went above our heads, Lieutenant Bobo was the first one on his feet and ordered us to follow him toward the elevated terrain. Even though the bullets were still coming as before, we followed him. Bobo was a fine leader and, as such, he walked in front of us. Soon we formed an extended line and kept moving south. The German machine guns continued to fire in our direction but somehow their tracer bullets were missing us. Through the grace of God, no one near me was killed or wounded.

We did not fire our machine guns at the enemy because we did not want to disclose our positions. Our intention was to get behind the German machine gun positions and neutralize them with our submachine guns or hand grenades. According to my best recollection, there were two German machine gun positions: one to our right and another to our left. I recall that the position to our right was the more active and we avoided it as much as possible by going to our left side. When our unit reached the highway that connected the city of Kielce with the city of Konskie, we reached the line on which the blazing German machine guns were located. At that time, we hoped that soon we would be to the rear of the German machine gun positions. As we were rushing across the highway, I caught a German telephone cable with my foot. I pulled the cable to the southern side of the highway to examine it. After examining it, I had no doubt that it was indeed a working military cable. I attempted to cut it with my pocketknife but could not. Then I looked around for a couple of stones and soon found one. When I was looking for another stone, I came across a granite mile-marker on the southern side of the highway. So I drew the cable to it, put it on the upper sharp edge of the marker, and hit the cable with the stone until it severed. At the same time, the German machine guns became silent. I was convinced that my cutting of the German telephone cable had something to do with it. It is quite possible that when the Germans discovered that their telephones went silent, they were convinced that we already overran one of their machine gun positions. Therefore, they pulled out from the second machine gun position. Our passage through the highway was totally free of any German interference. In fact, most of our men from the Jedrus Company had already crossed the highway, when a messenger arrived from our rear with an order from Captain Tadeusz Pytlakowski ("Tarnina") that we should pull back because another unit, east of us, found a better passage through the German lines.[118] We were disappointed but followed the order immediately.

After rejoining our regiment, we moved with it across the same highway again in the direction of the village of Salata. Then, we went through the villages of Gliniany, Stanowiska, and Klucko to arrive in the vicinity of Falegi and Filipy and then in the forest near Jozdzwikow. The Germans became aware of our presence in our new quarters; therefore, we left during the night of September 14-15, 1944, and moved into the forest near the village of Snochowice.[119] During the day on September 15, 1944, the Germans learned of our presence in the forest near Snochowice and our patrols exchanged fire with the enemy's patrols. At the same time, the Germans began to move some of their Wehrmacht units into our area. Obviously, they intended to attack us with a larger force. Therefore, our regiment moved again, this time south into the vicinity of the villages of Fanislawice and Fanislawiczki during the night of September 15-16. Soon the Germans discovered us. Our patrols clashed with the enemy's patrols on September 17. We had to move again and so early in the morning on September 18 our regiment and the Third Regiment took up quarters in the forest in the general area of the historic town of Checiny. After fifteen hours of strenuous marching, the enemy did not let us rest. Before 9:00 A.M., a platoon of Wehrmacht moved from the direction of the village of Szewce toward the quarters of the Third Regiment, where it encountered the company of Lieutenant Ludwik Wichula ("Jelen"). The company permitted the Germans to come to within a distance of about 25 meters and then they completely destroyed them.[120]

On September 18, 1944, the German units in our area began a well-organized attack. The attack started about noon and lasted until 1:50 P.M., when it was stopped by our strong defense. During their attack, the Germans used mortars, light artillery, and heavy artillery. The next attack began at 3:00 P.M. and failed. It was resumed at 3:30 P.M. and lasted until 8:00 P.M. This attack also ended with the enemy's complete defeat. Seventy-seven German soldiers died in the attacks. We lost three of our soldiers and eleven were wounded.[121]

During the night of September 18-19, 1944, our regiment left its present quarters in the forest near Szewce and moved into the vicinity of the village of Mlyn-Wyspa. The following night our entire division moved into the forest north of the city of Jedrzejow. Early in the morning our regiment made its camp in the forest near the village of Kanice and Mniszek. Soon German artillery and airplanes began to attack us. We were forced to move on. At the end of the day on September 20, 1944, we began to march west. Our regiment marched through Kanice, Wegleszyn, Lopata, Zakrzow, Ogarka, and Rogienice. We pitched our tents in the forest near the villages of Radkow and Kossow.[122] In this new location we tried to avoid any encounters with the enemy. Our soldiers needed rest after marching long distances from one battle to another.

During the night of September 21-22, 1944, our division received a very substantial airdrop. In the containers we found weapons, ammunition, some British uniforms, medicine, and money. The same airplane that dropped the containers full of goods also dropped four officers and two noncommissioned officers in British uniforms. The noncommissioned officers were communications specialists. I have no doubt that the German units that were stationed in the general area of our new quarters were aware of our presence there and also knew about the airdrop. Nevertheless, they did not bother us at first, being preoccupied with protecting their lines of transportation and communication. However, in the morning of September 26, 1944, our headquarters received reports from Radkow about a suspicious movement of German forces there. Needless to say, these reports put our forces on alert.

In the afternoon, over 800 German troops began to move in the direction of our camp. The Germans had with them six tanks and four panzer trucks. At first, they fired a barrage of artillery fire along the edge of the forest and then the enemy troops attacked us along the roads from Radkow to Sulikow and from Radkow to Krasow. The road toward the village of Sulikow was rather good, therefore the main German attack with panzer vehicles went in that direction. Another attack of the enemy in the direction of the villages of Krasow and Podlazie did not amount to anything considerable. The enemy troopers fired their machine guns at the peripheries of the forest on its western and southern sides and did not advance toward the forest. The Second Battalion and the Third Battalion of our regiment (the Second Regiment) that were assigned to defend the southern and western sections of the forest did not exchange fire with the enemy at a great distance.

It is quite possible that these two battalions did not take very seriously such a long distance attack. It is also quite possible that the Third Battalion was posted on the edges of the forest while the Second Battalion was deeper in the forest, serving as a reserve force. The observations of Zbigniew Piatek ("Grabina") may confirm this possibility.

> The battle began with a sound of fire and the appearance of the airplane that fired aimlessly. There was a short confusion at the command post where I saw Colonel Kruk (Antoni Wiktorowski) and his constant companion Colonel Kruk

II (Czeslaw Nakoniecznikoff-Kluckowski, who parachuted during the last airdrop). I was there when Colonel Kruk sent a messenger to the Second Battalion. He ordered the Second Battalion to move to the edge of the forest, to establish contact to the right with a company of the Third Battalion (the 7th or 8th Company — I do not remember) and to the left with the 9th Company of the Third Battalion, and to fight to the point of collapsing. (As a messenger, I listened, with a great excitement, to all these feverish consultations and orders.) Kruk sent me to the Third Battalion with the following order. "The 9th Company should take its positions on the edge of the forest, establish contact to the right with the Second Battalion, and fight to the point of collapsing." He issued the same orders to the 7th and the 8th Companies, which were to go in a different direction. After a few minutes, I returned to headquarters and continued to observe our commanding officers. At the same time, Pochmurny (Captain Stefan Kepa) and Nurt (Captain Eugeniusz Kaszynski) joined the main body of our commanding officers. A good friend of mine, Jerzy Szczerba was with me at headquarters. He was a messenger of the First Battalion under the leadership of Nurt and Ponury (Major Jan Piwnik). After a moment, the drama began that is the main theme of this letter.

An out-of-breath messenger who was sent to the Second Battalion returned and reported that he was unable to find the Second Battalion. Kruk was furious. He gave the messenger a good dressing-down and sent him back to find the Second Battalion. A moment later, Kruk caught a horse rider (Gontek, whom I knew from Zdanow) and sent him also to the Second Battalion with the same order: "Rush to the line, contact the 7th Company to the right, the 9th Company to the left, and fight to the point of collapsing!" A minute later Kruk, who was very nervous, sent somebody else. Each time Kruk issued the order, it sounded louder than the previous one. Gontek returned and the other messenger also returned and both of them reported that they could not find the Second Battalion. The passing moments appeared to be like an eternity and one could feel an atmosphere of desperation.

During their heated discussion, Kruk I and Kruk II began to exchange sharp words. I asked Captain Pochmurny for his permission to join the 9th Company, where my group was under the leadership of Walter. Then, on the way to the 9th Company, many feverish thoughts were running through my head. After all, during our extended camp near Radkow, I visited my friends who were formally in the Jedrus Group and in the Zawisza Group and were now part of the Second Battalion. They certainly must be somewhere between where I am and Radkow. Impulsively, I began to run through the forest in the direction of Radkow. After a few minutes, I ran into a group of fully armed soldiers waiting in full readiness. "Is this the Second Battalion?" I asked. "Yes" was the answer. "Where is the Commanding Officer?" I asked again. A number of hands pointed in the direction in which I should go. As I began to run, somebody shouted behind me, "Don't be afraid, kid!" I got used to being called kid or pup on account of my young age.

Soon, I stood in front of the commanding officer of the Second Battalion. When he asked what order I brought him, I said, "Sir, I brought you an order of the Regiment's Commanding Officer. According to this order, the Second Battalion must move to the edge of the forest and establish contact to the left with the 9th Company and to the right with the 7th Company and to fight to the point of collapsing!"

When, a minute later, I was watching the ranks of soldiers in orderly formations going toward the battlefield, I was frightened because I gave this order on my own initiative. Scared out of my wits, I ran back to Colonel Kruk. When I appeared at the clearing, Kruk I, Kruk II, a number other officers, and also some messengers at headquarters pierced me with their eyes. As I stood in front of Colonel Kruk, I reported, "I have found the Second Battalion." He said, "Go back with my order: Move the lines and so on." I interrupted him and said: "I report that I have already conveyed this order and the Second Battalion is on the way to the edge of the forest."

You cannot imagine, Sir, how the stern, bearded face of Colonel Kruk changed. He did not smile but his eyes became soft and he softly said, "Thank you, but go there once more and repeat my order."[123]

The German unit that attacked our regiment in the forest in the vicinity of the villages of Kwilina and Kossowo, also attacked the positions of our division in the area of the brick-kiln in Radkow and also along the forest road that went from Radkow to Podlazie. In this attack, the enemy lost one tank and a good number of soldiers.[124]

At one point in the battle near Radkow, our forces began to encircle the German units in the midst of meadows, marshes, and small lakes. The enemy called in his airplanes. Four Luftwaffe airplanes flew over us, dropped various sizes of bombs, and fired their heavy machine guns at us, but they did not cause us much damage. However, the enemy pilots' flying over the tops of the forest trees, shooting at us, dropping bombs, and hand grenades on us was a rather terrifying experience. I will never forget it. Our Jedrus Company, which was the vital part of the Second Battalion, was at that time on the southern periphery of the forest. When the German airplanes began to bomb and machine gun us, we hit the ground and attempted to fire at the enemy's airplanes. As soon as the first bomb craters were blown in the ground, we took our positions in them and felt more secure than on the flat ground. The airplanes followed a merry-go-round pattern, so when they flew over another section of the forest, we were able to change our firing positions and fire at them when they returned.

After awhile, the German airplanes ran out of their bombs and ammunition and returned to their airport. At that time, the enemy troopers, supported by tanks and armored vehicles, began to approach the outskirts of the forest. We took defensive positions on the edge of the forest and greeted the enemy with fire at selective targets. My machine gun position happened to be next to the machine gun position of Charles Roesch ("Jerzy") whose ammunition man was Edmund Klenck ("Edmund"). Both of them were the finest machine gunners we had in our battalion. As far as their military training is concerned, Jerzy and Edmund received it from the Wehrmacht. They served as field instructors for a number of us in Jedrus Company in the use of the German machine guns (MG42s). In the midst of the German fire Jerzy crawled toward my position and helped me to identify the targets. As he was pointing out some targets to me, a German sharpshooter was firing at us time after time and missing. I asked him, "Jerzy, are you afraid?" His answer was: "Frenchmen are never afraid." His courage was exemplary and contagious. I began to ignore the sharpshooter and fired my machine gun at any German target that I was able to identify. At the same time, I did everything possible to avoid German fire. I knew that the enemy's sharpshooters and machine gunners used scopes attached to their weapons. We seldom had such things, therefore, they had an advantage over us. While I was doing my best aiming at the German soldiers, I wished my machine gun had been equipped with a good Zeiss scope.

In spite of the German superiority in weapons, the enemy troopers were not eager to charge at our positions. They were shooting at us from a great distance until the evening. Obviously, the enemy's purpose was not so much to liquidate our division as to force it to abandon its quarters in the forest of Radkow. With the Russian front coming closer and closer, the Germans were quite uneasy with us at the rear of their front lines.

The battalions of our regiment kept their positions on the edge of the forest until 9:00 P.M. and then moved deeper into the forest. According to the reports from various units of our division, the enemy lost 82 soldiers. Our side lost four men and 18 of our soldiers were wounded. During the night of September 26-27, 1944, our regiment left its campgrounds in the forest near Radkow and marched through the towns of Radkow, Sulikow, Bebelno, Rogienice, and Ogarek and then stopped in the forest north of the village of Podgradow. We were extremely tired following the battle near Radkow and the all-night march and hoped to rest at our new camp. In order to protect ourselves from German airplanes, we did not make fires in the new camp. Nevertheless, at about 11:00 A.M., the enemy aircraft discovered us. To avoid a new bombardment, our regiment moved deeper into the forest north of the village of Lipno. In the evening of the same day, we took up our quarters in the villages of Lipno and Zalesie. Very early in the morning of September 28, we continued our march through Zakrzow, Wegleszyn, and Kanice until we arrived in the forest near Mniszek and Kanice Nowe.[125] All of us were extremely tired, cold, and hungry. At the same time, we began to realize the hopelessness of our situation. Without heavy weapons, we were unable to fight against the enemy's tanks and airplanes. Our food supplies grew limited. At times we were short of bread. Due to chilly rains and cold nights of autumn, many of our men were ill.

## 24. Demobilization

The operation and even the very existence of our units became increasingly difficult in the final months of 1944. The Soviet summer offensive halted on the Vistula River and the intensity of the military operations across the river decreased to a bare minimum. The Russians were gathering their strength for a new offensive. The Germans did all they could to strengthen their defenses. The relative tranquility at the front gave the Germans a chance, if not to eradicate then at least to diminish the threat of our troops in the rear of their defenses. In order to accomplish this, the Nazis utilized their SS units and infantry reserves. They also used their Luftwaffe for both reconnaissance and bombing.

At times, our division[126] was surrounded by the enemy and only the cover of the forest saved it from total annihilation.

The enemy's coordinated efforts, the cold weather, and a great difficulty in obtaining provisions for men and horses made our military leadership decide to begin a gradual demobilization of the troops. As we moved from one area to another, we left hundreds of men in villages and small towns. The Home Army operatives in each area took care of placing demobilized men with families that were members of the organization. Each demobilized man was given civilian clothing and some money for initial expenses. Weapons were stored in the forest.

A group of my friends and I were demobilized in the forests of the forest district administration of Jedrzejow at either the end of October or the beginning of November 1944. The commandant of the local post placed us in neighboring towns and villages. I was placed with a farm family that lived near the town of Zlotniki. I do not remember the name of the family I lived with. It was a small family: an elderly mother and her middle-aged unmarried son. The mother and son treated me very well, but since my friends were placed in a large village about ten miles away, I felt lonely. So after several weeks I asked the post commander to transfer me to the village where my friends were. He approved my request and placed me with the Joseph Knap family in the village of Zarczyce Duze. I was extremely happy with my transfer. The Knap family took me in as if I was their dearest friend. They showed me not only great hospitality but also love. Soon Mr. and Mrs. Knap treated me like their own son, and their children treated me like a brother. I loved them dearly, just like my own family. The oldest daughter must have been about eighteen years old and the youngest about seven. The couple had also two sons: Stefan and Wladyslaw. The oldest daughter, Teofila, dated a young man who was a member of the local post of the Home Army.

The love and hospitality of the Knap family and the proximity of my friends made me very happy. I was lonely no more. My friends often visited me and I visited them. From time to time we got together for a small celebration at which a bottle of whiskey — most often moonshine — kielbasa, and ham were served. At such gatherings we talked about the progress of the war and our hopes and dreams for the future. Sometimes we planned a group action against the Nazi administration in our area.

The Nazi administration closed all the grade schools in the area. Educational opportunities for Polish children and youth were completely restricted. After the Nazis occupied Poland in September 1939, they closed all the universities, colleges, and high schools, but they permitted the early grades of elementary school to remain open for instruction. They believed that the peoples of the countries under their occupation were to serve Nazi Germany as manual laborers and as such did not need much education. In the final years of the war, the Nazi administration closed even the grade schools.

Already in May 1940, Heinrich Himmler issued an educational policy for Poland that stated: "There must not be a more advanced education for the non–German population of the east than four years of primary school. This primary education had the following objective only: doing simple arithmetic to 500, writing one's name, learning that it was God's command that Germans must be obeyed, and that one had to be honest, diligent, and obedient. I don't consider reading skills necessary. Except for this school no other kind of school must be allowed in the east."[127] Martin Bormann, the head of the Nazi Party Chancellery, agreed with Himmler when he wrote: "The Slaves are to work for us. In so far as we do not need them, they may die.... Education is dangerous. It is enough if they can count up to 100.... Every educated person is a future enemy...."[128]

As soon as I began living with the Knaps, I took an interest in their younger children and volunteered to instruct them. With a little effort we found proper textbooks for each grade, and a daily instruction began in the family's large kitchen.

At first, the Knap children were my only students. But after a few days of instruction, the number of students began to increase. Relatives, friends, and neighbors of the Knap family started to come and ask me to teach their children. I refused no one. I was delighted to be able to pay my debt to the wonderful Knap family for their love and generosity toward me.

In order to accommodate more students, Mr. Knap and his friends secured some school desks from the local school. The family's kitchen became a makeshift classroom. Every two hours my students changed. Various grades came and left at different hours. Everything went very smoothly. I experienced much personal satisfaction and even some financial rewards from the parents of my students. They were very generous. Every time a group of Nazi soldiers or policemen approached the village, the people notified me, and I dismissed my students in a hurry. The presence of the school desks worried me. The Knaps and I took a calculated risk. Fortunately our school operated successfully without being discovered by the Nazi authorities.

Soon after initiating my "kitchen school," I discovered that I was not the only teacher in the village who operated a clandestine school. There was another newcomer to the village, a seminarian who came from the area of Czestochowa. His name was Miszczyk and he lived with the Petniak family.[129] Obviously he felt insecure in his hometown, so he hid in the village. Unlike myself, he was a high school and college graduate. After graduation from college, he entered the major seminary in Cracow operated by the diocese of Czestochowa. As a seminarian he attended classes in the Department of Theology at the University of Cracow. When the Nazi authorities closed the university and prohibited the operation of the seminary, he must have returned to his hometown and then gone into hiding. In order to support himself, he taught students at the high school level. Unlike myself, he instructed students one at a time; sometimes, he taught two students at the same time.

When I became aware of his teaching work, I decided to become his student. I must confess it was very difficult for me, at the age of twenty, to become a high school freshman. Besides, I had my own school and everybody in the village considered me an educated man. In spite of this psychological obstacle, I was determined to begin my high school instruction. The Knaps gave me directions to the high school teacher's apartment, and I went to see him. He received me in a very friendly way and told me that he had heard good things about my teaching work. I was gratified. At the same time, I felt awkward about asking him to instruct me on the high school freshman level. Once the preliminary conversation ended, I asked whether he could instruct me. At that point, I saw surprise in his face. He took me for a high school graduate. When I explained that I was interested in instruction on the freshman level, he was totally amazed. His amazement at my educational level embarrassed me considerably, but I thought it was a small price to pay to begin formal high school education, which I desired for such a long time. At the end of our conversation, my new teacher gave me the name of one of his students who was willing to sell the books I needed for my studies, and he told me the time for our afternoon meetings. I left the teacher's apartment with a great excitement and went to the house of the student who had the books I needed. After obtaining the books, I rushed home to page through them. While looking through the books, I learned that they were published before the war for use in the first year of state high schools.

The Polish language textbook contained excerpts from the works of outstanding writers. It appealed to me very much. I felt comfortable with the German language handbook. I had studied German on my own a few years before. I felt quite uneasy with the textbooks for Latin and math. The textbooks in history, geography, biology, physics, chemistry, and religion did not appear difficult to study.

I met with my teacher six days a week for about two hours each time. Soon he discovered that in some areas of studies, such as Polish literature and history, I was well versed and he did not have to give me much attention. Latin and algebra were my weak points, so we spent more time on these subjects. Since we only met for two hours a day, my homework was always very extensive. This necessitated my staying up until midnight and studying night after night. My youthfulness and good health enabled me to do so without a problem. There was no electricity in the village and naphtha was not available on the market, so I used a homemade carbide lamp.

After a week of taking instruction from my teacher, I lost two students in my home school. They were the children of the Sklaczynski family who were relatively wealthy and operated a local sawmill. One of the family's older children received instruction on the high school level from the same teacher I did. One day he met with the teacher just before my meeting. I must have come too early and waited about ten minutes until the instruction ended. Then the instructor introduced us to each other as fellow students. The boy went home and told his parents that I was a high school student. The following day, the parents did not send their children to my classes. They obviously felt that I was not educated enough to teach their children. This did not bother me much because I had more students than I could take care of. I am sure the parents of my other students were aware of my high school studies, but as long as they saw educational results in their children, they did not care about the level of my education.

In order to improve my knowledge of Latin, I was given a chance to receive additional instruction in this language. One of my friends introduced me to a young lady who was a college student before 1939. The Latin language was one of her favorite subjects. Her name was Maria Kuzelowna, a daughter of a pharmacy owner in the eastern part of Poland. The Soviet invasion in that part of the country separated her from her parents. In the village she was one of the displaced persons put there by the Nazi authorities. She had a heart of gold and offered me as much instruction in Latin as I needed. She refused to take any remuneration. During our evening meetings, Maria introduced me to Latin grammar. Her instruction was always very clear and understandable, and her patience with my limitation admirable. As we met more and more, we became very good friends. Our friendship flourished beyond the time of our residence in the same village.

On the outskirts of the neighboring village of Wegleszyn there was a group of our demobilized men who lived in a safe house situated in a small forest. Under the leadership of Zdzislaw Fialkowski ("Tarzan II"), the members of the group were assigned to protect Major Antoni Wiktorowski ("Kruk") who was hiding in Lipno manor. (He was the commanding officer of the Second Regiment of the Infantry of the Home Army). I knew all of them but, at the time of this writing, I remember only some names. They include Andrzej Fialkowski ("Tarzan I") who was Zdzislaw's twin brother; Henryk Kuksz ("Selim"); Jerry Rolski ("Babinicz"); Tadeusz Robakiewicz ("Grom"); Andrzej Lukasiewicz ("Kmita"); and a nurse whose pseudonym was "Basia." The most impressive of the group were the "Tarzan" brothers, the gigantic twins who came to the Jedrus Group from Buda Starowolska, a village southeast of Tarnobrzeg. They were identical twins, very tall, well built, and handsome. I knew them from the time our Flying Commando Unit united with the Jedrus Group in the spring of 1944.

There was another group of demobilized men in a small hamlet near our village of Zarczyce. Two of them were brothers; the older brother was Henryk Kedzierski ("Jaskolka") and the younger brother was Adolf Kedzierski ("Wilczur"), both of them from Olbierzowice.

Others in that group might have come from the same area. My friend, Piorun, and I became acquainted with them and visited them a few times. I remember that during one of these visits, we had a drinking party, and I drank more moonshine than I should have and became half drunk. In such a state, I was showing off my limited knowledge of Latin. Piorun was the only one at the party who could understand what I was saying.

The younger of the two brothers, Adolf Kedzierski — Wilczur — fell in love with the oldest daughter of the farmer in whose home he stayed. He intended to marry her as soon as possible. Unfortunately, merciless fate shattered his intentions and plans. To my best recollection this is what happened. The village of Wegleszyn, surrounded by forests, was located a few miles away from the hamlet there. A group of Russian guerrillas, under the leadership of Andrzej Lukasiewicz ("Kmita"), was stationed in the forest near the village. From time to time, two members of the group came to the village to get food. It is quite possible that they used force to obtain food from the villagers. One day, as two of them came to get their supplies, a number of armed men ambushed and killed them. Who were the killers? I really do not know. They might have been members of the National Armed Forces (NSZ), a Polish nationalistic organization, strongly anticommunist, which at that time collaborated with the Nazi authorities in opposing communism. It is almost certain that the killers were strangers in the village. It seems to me that the killing took place late in the afternoon.

Early in the morning of the following day, Wilczur, who was unaware of the killing, went to the village of Wegleszyn to buy some blankets. He was accompanied by one of his friends. As he and his friend entered the village they noticed a number of Kmita's armed men who were investigating the death of their friends. The Kmita men noticed Wilczur and his companion and rushed toward them with weapons ready to fire. Since Wilczur was a stranger in the village and had a pistol in his pocket, the Russians took for granted that he and his companion were the killers of their friends. So they took them away from the village into the nearby forest, interrogated them, tortured them, and, in spite of their innocence, executed them. Before the execution, the Communists tied up their hands behind their backs with wire and shot them with a hand gun in the back of their heads and covered up their bodies with branches of trees.[130]

When we went to the forest to get the body of Wilczur, some members of the family of his companion were also there to retrieve the body of their dear one.

We brought the body of Wilczur to the farmhouse where he and his older brother stayed. His girlfriend and the older brother, Jaskolka, prepared the body for the funeral.

For reasons of security, we held the funeral at night at the local cemetery near Wegleszyn. As the casket of our dear friend was lowered into the grave, some of our men got ready to fire their guns in his honor; others were against an unnecessary provocation of the local Nazi units. At that moment, his girlfriend, who was overwhelmed by grief, spoke and said, "Boys, do not hesitate to fire your guns to honor your friend. If the Germans come and kill one of you, it will be pleasing to Wilczur to have a companion in death." After hearing her emotional plea, we fired our guns and left the cemetery as soon as possible.

Wilczur was our second friend who was buried at the Wegleszyn Cemetery. Antoni Janicki "Grot" from Gorki near Klimontow, who was mortally

## 24. Demobilization

The funeral of Antoni Janicki ("Grot"), who was mortally wounded in the Battle of Radkow. He was buried at the Wegleszyn Cemetery. From right to left are Henryk Kuksz ("Selim"), Henryk Kedzierski ("Jaskolka"), and, behind the young women, Adolf Kedzierski ("Wilczur"), who was murdered by the "Kmita's" men in the winter of 1944. Author's photograph.

wounded near Radkow, was buried there before Wilczur. As a matter of fact, Wilczur attended Grot's funeral. The tragic death of Wilczur was very painful to all of us, especially to his older brother, his girlfriend, and her family. His death would have been more bearable to all of us if he had died fighting the Nazis. A death that resulted from mistaken identify was extremely hard to accept.

A few weeks after the tragic death of our friend, about ten Communist guerrillas came to the Knaps' home where I was staying. It was in early evening. We had just finished our dinner. Mr. Knap and I sat at the kitchen table talking. The kitchen door was not locked. The guerrillas entered the kitchen without knocking. They were armed with Russian submachine guns. Most of them were Russians whose Polish was very poor. Others were natives of Poland. They looked us over and asked whether there was somebody else in the house. Mr. Knap answered in the negative. I must have looked suspicious to them, because they began to ask me such questions as who I was, what was I doing, and so forth. Then they asked me to show them my ID. When I opened my wallet, one of them grabbed it from my hands and began examining its contents. In addition to my false ID card, I had in it some cash and photographs. As he viewed the photographs, one of them caught his attention. It was a group picture of a number of us, demobilized Home Army soldiers, who resided in the immediate area. The young man killed by the Communist guerrillas and his older brother appeared in the picture. The man who had my wallet called some of the guerrillas over to look at the picture. As they did so, they whispered to each other and exchanged meaningful glances. The man looked at the picture and then at me. I started to think that these men were the ones who killed our friend Wilczur. I began to fear for my life. Then all of a sudden, the man who took my wallet returned it, looked at me with a degree of sympathy, and said to his companions, "Let's go." They left as abruptly as they came. All of us in the house, especially myself, felt a great relief after their departure.

I believe that Kmita's men had identified Wilczur in the photograph, whom they had killed two weeks before their uninvited visit to the Knaps' home. During these two weeks it must have become apparent to them and to their leader Kmita that they had killed an innocent man.[131] Also they must have realized that I had been a friend of Wilczur. That is why they had left me alone.

My painful experience with Kmita's men taught me a lesson as to how providential it was for me to have the group picture in my wallet. At the same time, I became aware of the possible danger to myself and others if I would have been caught by the Nazis with the same picture in my wallet. I shared my experience and reflections with my friends and advised them not to carry any pictures or addresses on them.

Soon after my encounter with Kmita's band, I was arrested by Nazi SS-men and taken to the labor camp in the city of Malogoszcz.

It happened early in the morning before my students arrived for the eight o'clock class. We were in the process of eating our breakfast when one of our neighbors told us that the Germans had surrounded the village. Mr. Knap advised me to hide in the stable, which was not too far away from the house. I put my winter coat on and began to walk toward the stable as if nothing had happened. I hoped to reach the stable without being noticed by the SS-men. But when I had gone about three-fourths of the way, I heard somebody shout to my right, "Halt!" I turned my head and there was an SS-man in our neighbor's yard pointing a submachine gun at me and commanding, "*Hände hoch!*" ("Hands up!"). I obeyed his command and raised my hands. He came over and searched me. Then he ordered me to walk toward the village street. As I walked, he walked behind me, pointing the gun at me. On the street, the SS-men guarded a few dozen young men whom they had arrested in other households of the village. The SS-man who arrested me made me join the

## 24. Demobilization

group. After a while, more young men were rounded up and brought to our group.

At about 9:00 A.M., the Nazis commanded us to march toward the city of Malogoszcz. As we marched, the SS-men surrounded us from every side so no one could escape. Some of them walked in front of us and some in back of us. The others proceeded, at a certain distance, on each side of the road. By about noontime, we reached Malogoszcz. The labor camp was on the outskirts of the city. It was surrounded with barbed wire fences and guarded by SS-men. We were herded through the main gate guarded by two SS-men and taken to the administration barrack. There we were registered and lined up for a physical examination. A young lady, no more than twenty years old, did the registration. When my turn came to be registered she showed me a great degree of sympathy. After writing down my personal data, the young lady explained to me that the inmates in the camp were used by the Nazis for digging defensive trenches and bunkers. She said that the labor was hard, living conditions very poor, and that we were arrested by the Nazis for slave labor. She suggested to me, in a whisper, that I should claim some health problem to be released from the camp. I asked if a heart problem would be a good excuse. She smiled and wrote on my chart, "heart illness" and then talked to the physician who examined the new prisoners. When I stepped into the physician's office, he gave me a brief examination, smiled at me, and said, "You will be home today." Then he wrote something on my chart and asked me to give it to the young lady. She wrote me a certificate, in German, and went to the office of the commandant to have the document signed. Soon she returned to her desk, handed me the paper, and said, *"Auf Wiedersehen!"* ("Goodbye!") She attempted to control a happy smile. I thanked her and left. My eyes said more than my words.

As I walked toward the gate of the camp, I felt a tremendous lightness in my legs and joy in my heart. An SS-man examined my certificate at the gate and let me go. Once outside the camp, I found the road to the village of Zarczyce Duze and began to walk home. At times I was running rather than walking and did not feel tired at all.

When I reached the village of Zarczyce Duze, it was already dark. The lights were lit in the farmhouses. At the Knaps' home no one expected me to return so soon. When Mrs. Knap and her oldest daughter, Teofila, who were cooking dinner, heard my familiar, noisy steps in the hallway, they could not believe their ears. As I opened the kitchen door, their faces expressed great surprise and joy. Soon the other members of the family surrounded me and looked at me with amazement and love. I had tears in my eyes feeling their love and joy. It was a wonderful reunion.

After dinner, I went to see my friend Piorun who lived near the Knaps with the Musial family. He knew about my arrest and worried about his own safety. He was happy to see me safe and sound. After describing to him the experiences of the day, I showed him the certificate signed by the commandant of the labor camp, which set me free. He read it and smiled to himself. Then he asked if I would mind if he made a copy of this certificate and inserted his own name. I did not object at all.

After finding a proper paper and ink, Piorun began to copy the certificate. I could not believe what I saw before my eyes. Piorun imitated the handwriting of the document. His imitation was excellent. He also forged the signature of the commandant. From that day on, Piorun and I carried the German certificates in our wallets to protect ourselves from being arrested and put in the labor camp. Later, Piorun forged more certificates for other demobilized men. Fortunately we never had to use them.

After my arrest and safe return from the Malogoszcz labor camp, my life at Zarczyce Duze returned to its regular pattern. I taught children, took instructions from my high school teacher and from Miss Maria Kuzelowna, visited my friends, and studied late at night. One night when all the members of the Knap family were already in bed, a group of armed guerrillas entered the yard and knocked on the window near where I was studying. At first, I thought they were German policemen or Russian guerrillas. When I opened the kitchen door, the leader of the group introduced himself as a friend of the Knap family and told me that he and his group represented the National Armed Forces organization (Narodowe Sily Zbrojne). As I mentioned above, this organization was radically nationalistic and, at that time, collaborated with Nazi authorities in fighting Communists.

The knocking on the window and subsequent conversation between the group leader and myself awakened the Knaps. One by one they joined us in the kitchen. Mrs. Knap prepared some cold cuts and tea for the visitors. Since the leader's sister had visited the Knaps on several occasions and I had been acquainted with her, he was aware of my background.[132] Even though I was the Knaps' friend, he made a few cutting remarks about the Home Army. He praised the National Armed Forces for their efforts in fighting communism. He bragged about his organization's cooperation with the Germans and quoted instances in which Nazi armed forces permitted his group to cross their trenches in pursuit of Communist guerrillas.[133] All of his men were well armed and warmly dressed. One of the guerrillas had a blue and lacerated face. When I asked what had happened to him, he replied that a mine placed by Communists exploded near him and almost killed him.

The guerrillas who visited the Knaps' home that night and thousands of their comrades-in-arms in various parts of Poland eventually withdrew to Germany, together with the Nazi forces. In the final months of the war, they were incorporated into various formations of the German army.[134]

In the beginning of December 1944, when the Nazi armed forces were totally absorbed in preparing defenses for the Russian offensive, they began to lose their administrative control over the area of Malogoszcz. Some farmers in villages near Zarczyce Duze, such as Wisnicz and Gory Lasochowskie, took advantage of this and began to fell trees in the state forest of the forest district administration of Snochowice. They did it indiscriminately, cutting all the trees in the forest regardless of their age. More educated farmers shook their heads in disbelief at the vandalism of their neighbors. Something had to be done to stop it. To notify the Nazi authorities was not patriotic. The farmers in Zarczyce Duze, who did not participate in the vandalism, applied some moral pressure on us, demobilized soldiers, to discourage the destruction of the forest. Piorun and I went to the forest to plead with the greedy farmers. When our appeal to their patriotism produced no effort, I unbuttoned my winter coat and pulled out a pistol. The farmers became frightened and immediately ceased felling trees. I told them to take with them the trees that were on their wagons and go home. They left immediately. Piorun and I walked the forest for most of the day and wherever we found farmers cutting trees, we ordered them out of the forest. The following day the vandalism in the forest stopped altogether.

Toward the end of December, just before Christmas, rumors about an imminent Russian offensive began to circulate in Zarczyce Duze. Because of these rumors, the villagers started to dig holes in their back yard to bury valuables and provisions. I helped Mr. Knap to dig a sizeable hole near the stables. After it was finished, the whole family became involved in storing their most precious things and some grain. I was invited to store some of my belongings there. Since I did not have much of anything, I did not take advantage of the invitation.

We celebrated Christmas of 1944 in the spirit of anticipation of new events to take place. On Christmas Eve, we broke the traditional *opatek* (wafer) before the dinner and wished each other the best of things, but in particular the collapse of Nazi Germany and the independence of Poland. During this celebration, I thought about my own family who were celebrating Christmas in that part of Poland that was already "liberated" by the Russian army. My home village, Jeziory, and dozens of neighboring villages constituted the Baranow bridgehead, which the Russians seized from the Germans during the 1944 summer offensive.

After the traditional dinner, most of the Knaps went to the parish church in Zlotniki for midnight mass, called in Polish *pasterka*—the Mass of the Shepherds. I stayed home with the younger children. I did not have to stay home that night, but at that time in my life, I did not care much for the church. For one reason or another, my religious life reached its lowest ebb. I do not remember attending church even once during my stay with the Knaps. My friends did not practice religion either. We were a group of young atheists. I personally remember discussing my youthful atheism with the Knaps' oldest daughter and being proud of my disbelief. It seems to me that I also discouraged her from attending church.

On New Year's Eve all of us demobilized soldiers in the area, gathered together for a little celebration during which our spirits were high. We sang patriotic songs and felt that the day of liberation was near. After having a few drinks of the local moonshine, we began predicting when and how the war was going to end and what was to happen after its end. At midnight our spirits dampened when we saw the German fireworks over the city of Malogoszcz. The Nazis greeted the new year with great exuberance, as if they anticipated the course of events in 1945 would turn in their favor.

The first week of January 1945 passed quietly. Most of the people in Zarczyce Duze felt disappointed because the Russian offensive did not materialize as predicted for the very beginning of 1945. Farmers in the village returned to threshing grain in their barns. The weather was cold and dry. There was no snow on the ground. The fields were frozen solid. After a short Christmas break, I resumed teaching the children in the Knaps' kitchen and studying under the direction of my high school teacher.

When many of us in the village began to lose hope in the possibility of the Russian winter offensive, Marshal Koniev's divisions launched their attack on the German lines from the Baranow bridgehead on January 12th. This attack marked the beginning of the new Russian offensive. The news of the offensive was received in our village with great relief and joy. However, some of the older farmers who had taken a part in the Bolshevik war of 1920 were somewhat apprehensive about the coming of the Red Army. My demobilized friends and I, who had spent a couple of weeks with the Russian troops when they first secured the Baranow bridgehead at the end of the summer in 1944, tried to assure them that the Red Army was easy to get along with. The skeptical farmers listened to our reassurances but they remained uneasy about the Soviets.

A few days after the Russian offensive began, German military units appeared on the road near our village. They were marching west. Obviously, they were retreating from the front. The soldiers were tired and dirty; their faces expressed discouragement. When they marched on the Soviet Union, they sang victorious songs; now they marched in silence. They no longer caused fear in the villagers who watched them — they evoked pity. Five years of suffering and fear under the Nazi occupation made the people of the village very sensitive to human misery including the misery, of the enemy soldiers.

## 24. Demobilization

As the Nazi troops moved westward, the Russian and German artillery fire was heard, at first in the distance, and then it became louder every day. The front line was approaching our area. The excitement in the village increased when the German troops no longer marched in formation but rushed away from the front in disorganized groups leaving behind their equipment. Some German soldiers separated themselves from their units, abandoned their weapons, changed uniforms for civilian clothing, and tried to save their lives pretending to be Polish citizens. They were no longer supermen.

One week after the beginning of the Soviet offensive, a unit of Red Army tanks appeared in Zarczyce Duze. The Russian tanks rolled into the village in the evening. The gunners in the tanks fired a few machine gun rounds in the air; the Germans, who were supposed to halt the Russians, scattered into the fields like a bunch of rabbits without firing a single shot. One of the Russian tanks rolled into the Knaps' yard and, after turning its cannon westward, the crew came into the house for a late dinner. Mrs. Knap offered them hot tea, boiled eggs, and bread. The soldiers brought with them some American canned meat and Russian vodka. They insisted that the Knaps and I eat their meat and drink vodka with them. Shortly after dinner started, several officers came in and joined us at the table. A few drinks of vodka made everybody happy and warm from within. We drank to victory over the Nazi criminals, to peace, and to prosperity. At the end of the dinner, the Russians sang some popular military songs. The atmosphere in the dining room was very jovial and friendly. We talked and talked for several hours. One of the officers asked whether I took part in fighting the Nazis. I told him about my membership in the Home Army and my activities as a soldier. The officer began to quiz me about political matters. The first question he fired at me was, "Who is the leader of your new Polish government?" He meant the new Polish government formed by Stalin in Lublin during the summer of 1944. In order not to appear ignorant, I lied to him and said, "I knew the name of the leader but I forgot." By saying this I got myself into an embarrassing situation. The officer said, "I will help you by giving you the first letter of the leader's name." When I agreed to play his game, he began pronouncing the letter "O," but the Russian pronunciation of "O" sounds to the Polish ear more like an "A" so, in the midst of my confusion, I said Anders. When he heard the name of General Anders, he became extremely agitated and angry because General Anders was an anti–Soviet Polish general in the west. I knew then that I had made a terrible mistake and felt extremely humiliated. The officer at the table did not give me another chance and shouted, "Osobka-Marawski is your government's new leader!" My ego was totally crushed. In order to salvage at least part of my reputation, I lied more and said, "Oh yes, yes Osobka-Marawski, now I remember his name." This was my first Communist political indoctrination. The officer did not pay much attention to my embarrassment and was proud of his performance. After a while we drank more vodka, but the joyful atmosphere of the first part of our social encounter did not return. As we were getting up from the table, the officer said something in a low voice to one of the soldiers that sounded to me like, "Kill him." At that point I became frightened. I regretted telling the officer about my membership in the Home Army, which was under the command of the Polish government-in-exile in London, England. Obviously I did not hear well enough what the officer said to the soldier because I did not suffer any harm from our "guests." However, the experience taught me to be very careful in conversations with officers of the Red Army.

After the Russians left the Knaps' house to attend to their duties, no one was able to go to bed. There was so much activity and excitement around the house. Tanks and military vehicles moved along the village street, officers shouted commands, and the roaring of diesel engines dominated the village of Zarczyce Duze. In the midst of this I decided to visit the adjacent village of Zarczyce Male, where a few of my friends lived. The night was not very dark and the Russians did not prevent me from walking there. On the contrary, they were friendly and assured me that my short walk to that village was safe. I told the Knaps where I was going and I left. As long as I was walking through our village everything was fine. But once I left the village behind and began walking through fields that were unoccupied by the Russian soldiers, I realized that if I encountered a group of Russians, they might take me for a German and fire at me. As soon as I approached Zarczyce Male, I heard a tank rolling near the first houses of the village and a machine gun opened up. Its tracer bullets went high above me and I knew that the Russians were attempting to flush out German soldiers who might have been there. As I approached the village in the light of the moon, a group of Russians halted me at a distance of two hundred feet from the village and asked me who I was. Speaking Russian, I identified myself. They asked me to come to them. We exchanged greetings and shook hands. The soldiers were very cordial and let me visit my friends. My friends were packing their belongings with the hope of going home as soon as possible. They advised me to do the same and be ready for the trip. After talking for awhile, we decided that as soon as the front passed by we might begin our journey home. We were full of joy at the thought of returning to our homes. The Nazis, whom we fought and hated with a passion, were gone from our area. They had begun the cruel war and now they were perishing by it.

It must have been after midnight when I returned to Zarczyce Duze. The Knap children went to bed finally but the adults were up watching the property and helping soldiers in various tasks. In spite of freezing temperatures,

## 24. Demobilization

soldiers slept outside on the bare ground. They looked like bears sleeping in their quilted uniforms. The guards watched tanks, trucks, and supplies. I spent the rest of the night talking with the soldiers and the Knaps. I was too excited to fall asleep.

As soon as morning came, the soldiers began to wake and wash themselves outside with cold water. Many of them took off their shirts before they washed their bodies in freezing temperatures. Cold weather did not bother them at all. In the meantime, the field kitchens prepared breakfast for the soldiers. The behavior of the soldiers interested me very much, so I started my new day of "liberation" by mingling with them. Soon they discovered that I could read Russian and asked me to read their newspaper aloud. As I read, a dozen or more soldiers gathered around me to listen to the news from home. It did not take me long to figure out that most of the soldiers were illiterate and that was why they appreciated my reading. Mingling with the soldiers took me to the main road on the edge of the village. There I saw a horrible scene. The body of a German soldier was in the middle of the road. It was totally flattened by the tanks and other vehicles that were passing by. Near the road, in a meadow, I saw lots of German military hardware, which was abandoned there. Among the hardware I remember seeing small missile launchers and cannons. All other weapons such as rifles, machine guns, or submachine guns were promptly taken by the Russians.

My mingling with the soldiers in Zarczyce Duze made me aware of the modern military equipment they were using. The most impressive were their tanks, T-34s. The crew of the tank, which was parked near the Knaps' barn, invited me to enter the vehicle and examine its controls, cannons, and machine guns. I was duly impressed by everything I saw in it. The military trucks that carried ammunition and pulled cannons were heavy and well built. Most of them were of American origin. On some of the trucks parked away from the village, I could see batteries of yoked rails fixed at a certain angle. When I attempted to come closer to these trucks, I was stopped by the guards and told angrily to keep out of there. Later, one of the soldiers explained to me that those trucks were rigged with the famous Stalin's Harmonicas. These weapons, which caused so much fear and panic among the German troops, were also called *katiushas*. They were rocket launchers capable of firing a dozen or so rockets at the same time. The sound of the rockets flying in the air terrorized and demoralized the German soldiers. It seems to me that the kind of sound the rockets made earned the weapon its name, Stalin's Harmonica.

On the second or third day of our "liberation" by the Red Army, I saw units of infantry marching west. The soldiers of these units had insufficient provisions. Their uniforms and shoes were in very poor condition. Some of the soldiers had rags wrapped around their feet. They pulled heavy machine guns behind them. From time to time, individual soldiers separated themselves from marching units and rushed to the houses of the village asking for bread or moonshine. They were disciplined and well behaved. In the afternoon of the second day of the Russians' presence in the village, a high-ranking officer entered the Knaps' kitchen. A number of soldiers were already there drinking tea and coffee. They all got up to salute the officer. The officer inquired about the location of some unit and was about to leave when he noticed me in the corner of the kitchen. I was happy and smiling. For some reason my smile disturbed him. Immediately he asked the soldiers, "Who is this young man? What is he doing here?" The soldiers replied, "He is a farmer, he is all right." He looked at me again with his serious eyes and left. He might have suspected me of being a German soldier or spy. I was amazed at his perceptiveness. I did not appear to him as being a member of the Knap family, and he was correct in his perception. I am sure his experience in fighting the Nazis taught him to distinguish between various kinds of people.

As Russian infantry marched through the village, I observed their units with a great curiosity. Most of the people in the village did the same. All the farm work was suspended for the time being. Feeding the animals was the only work the farmers did at that time. My home school was terminated. One day as I watched the units go by, I noticed the most unusual unit, an orchestra unit. The musicians rode on farm wagons pulled by huge Russian cows similar to Texas longhorns. Another interesting spectacle was a machine gun unit in which husky dogs were used to pull heavy machine guns and small carts of ammunition. One of the machine gunners explained to me that the dogs, pulling machine guns at the front, proved to be very helpful in approaching the enemy lines without being noticed. Under battle conditions, the dogs lay on the ground to avoid the enemy's fire.

The unit of Russian tanks stayed in the village for two days and then proceeded west to pursue the enemy. The infantry, combat engineers, and work battalions continued to move through our village for about a week. At the end of this week, the front line had moved so far away from us that we could no longer hear artillery fire. Life in the village began to return to normal. For us, demobilized soldiers of the Home Army, the time had come to return to our families.

# 25. Our Secret Quarters

My feeling of profound gratitude to the patriotic people who invited the Sandomierz Flying Commando Unit to their homes for days, weeks, and months during the Nazi occupation of Poland compels me to acknowledge their contribution to the struggle against the demonic empire of Adolf Hitler. My gratitude toward these noble people increased as I grew older and as I realized the immense sacrifice that they had made on the altar of Polish patriotism. These patriotic and heroic people were always ready to sacrifice not only their own lives but also the lives of their children and others among their dear ones. In writing about our secret quarters and the persons who provided them, I regret that I fully comprehended the immensity of their sacrifice only later, after many years of life. I always remembered their sacrifice but I never fully realized how great it was until I grew older. It is still growing in its intensity. Unfortunately, at this time of my life, I no longer remember the names of all our benefactors who generously provided us our secret quarters. Therefore, I will write only about those families whose names I retain in my memory.

## *The Kosterski Family*

The ancient manor house that belonged to Mr. and Mrs. Mieczyslaw and Michalina Kosterski opened its hospitable door to our small unit when it was still just forming in the early summer of 1943. The official name of our group was the Sandomierz Flying Commando Unit and it was organized by the Sandomierz District of the Home Army. Since our first commanding officer was Stefan Franaszczuk, whose pseudonym was "Tarzan," our unit was called the Tarzan Group.

The Kosterskis lived at Skwirzowa manor. Formally, Skwirzowa manor had a considerable acreage but before World War II some of the land was sold to the local farmers and the rest was divided among the family members. At the time we were invited to take our quarters at the manor it was one of the smallest manors in the parish of Sulislawice. The land that belonged to the manor was not the sole source of income for the family. Support for the family came also from the salary that Mrs. Kosterski received as a teacher in the public school in Sulislawice.

The Kosterskis were not a wealthy family but they were hospitable and generous. At the same time they were very patriotic, friendly, and loving. Mrs. Kosterski, who was one of my teachers, did everything possible to implant in her students the love of God, the love of neighbor, the love of country, and the love of learning. She was an excellent teacher who taught not only by word but also by example. I will never forget the class during which she spoke about the idealism of the Polish youth who took part in the uprising against Russia that took place in a large part of the country after the eighteenth-century partitions of Poland. As matter of fact I learned the term "idealism" from her in that class.

During the times our unit stayed at Skwirzowa manor we used the large living room in the manor house as our bedroom and classroom. We received our meals with the host family in the dining room, which was rather spacious. Our hosts did everything they could to make us comfortable and well fed in their home. With the exception of our commanding officer, all of us were assigned to stand guard outside of the manor house during the day and at night. Every two hours our guards changed.

Following World War II, the Kosterskis continued living at their manor house. Their land was not nationalized and distributed to the landless because it was not larger than 50 hectares. Mr. Kosterski supervised the work on the land and his wife resumed teaching in the public school in Sulislawice. They attended my ordination to the priesthood at the Cathedral Church in Sandomierz on May 25, 1952, and my first solemn mass at the Parish church in Sulislawice. At the time of this writing (October 29, 2001), Mr. Kosterski is deceased but Mrs. Kosterski is still living and, as always, she is young in spirit. During the solemn dedication of the memorial plaque commemorating the birth of our unit at the Parish church in Loniow (St. Nicholas Church) she was there with us, or more correctly with those who were left of us, as our teacher and a spiritual mother.

## *The Zarzycki Family*

Mr. and Mrs. Stanislaw and Zofia Zarzycki and their family lived in Beszyce Dolne manor. The German authorities resettled them by force from the city of Katowice to the Sandomierz District. Mr. Zarzycki was a mining engineer and worked as such in Katowice before the war. In order to support his family, he rented the manor of Beszyce Dolne from the Nazi government and became a gentleman farmer. Mr. and Mrs. Zarzycki had two teenage children: son Stanislaw and daughter Barbara. A single cousin Domicela (Dosia) was also a member of the Zarzycki family. Mr. Zarzycki was an excellent administrator of the manor. He hired good workers to cultivate the land that was more fertile than the land at Skwirzowa manor. Cultivation of the manorial fields appeared to provide a sufficient income for the family.

The Zarzyckis were very patriotic, cultured, and hospitable. During the times we stayed with them, they made us feel that we were an extended part of their family. After our meals in the family dining room, we had long conversations about the war and other current events. Sometimes we told jokes and entertaining stories. We kept two guards on duty day and night. One of our men stood guard in front of the manor house and the other on the main road near the village of Beszyce Gorne. During our stay with the Zarzycki family, the membership of our unit increased considerably. After the war, I had a chance to see them once or twice at their residence and then they left for Katowice.

## *The Bak Family*

Mrs. Maria Bak was a widow. To my best recollection she had one son about twelve years old. She lived in the very small village of Granicznik near Wiazownica. The village was on the edge of the Bukowa Forest. With the help of a hired hand, Mrs. Bak operated a small farm. She appeared to be a very industrious person. At the same time she was a very patriotic and maternal lady. She treated all of us, young men, as if we were her older sons. She provided very comfortable quarters for us, cooked our meals, and did our laundry. Even though the Bak farmhouse was rather large it could not accommodate all the members of our unit. Therefore, a number of our men were given quarters in the neighboring farmhouse located south of the Baks' house, which was also near the forest. During the times we maintained our quarters in Granicznik, we always posted three guards: one around the two farmhouses, one at the crossroads of the road that went from the village of Bukowa toward the city of Staszow, and one on the road toward the city of Osiek. Due to the proximity of the Bukowa Forest to our quarters in Granicznik, all the members of our unit felt very safe there. Therefore we did a great deal of military training in Granicznik.

During one of my visits to Poland, a number of years ago, I attempted to see our old quarters in the village of Granicznik, but unfortunately I could not find the Bak family farmhouse. The old country roads that I knew so well no longer existed. They were replaced with new modern highways that went in different directions and bypassed many villages and towns. The old houses in the village of Granicznik were replaced with new ones that changed the appearance of the village. After looking for the Baks' home for a long time, I became discouraged and gave up the search.

## *The Bielecki Family*

Mr. and Mrs. Bielecki lived in the small manor of Bystrojowice. Needless to say, they were very hospitable and patriotic and they never stopped inviting us to take quarters in their bright and large home. They had two beautiful daughters our age. No wonder that our unit quite often took advantage of the Bieleckis hospitality. The manorial land provided an abundant support for the family. We launched many attacks on Germans while staying at Bystrojowice manor. I did not keep in touch with the Bieleckis following the war; therefore, I do not know much about their family background.

**Our secret quarters were not always in country manors or farm houses — quite often we slept in dense forests. Our mattresses were made of soft pine branches and our pillows from sacks of hand grenades. Clean ground covered with pine needles served as a dining room table. Courtesy of Dr. Zbigniew Kabata.**

One thing I know is that they were one of the finest and the most loving among the families our unit encountered during the war.

## *The Ropelewski Family*

Mr. and Mrs. Ropelewski lived in Byszow manor near Klimontow. There were four members of the family. Mr. and Mrs. Ropelewski; the adult daughter from Mr. Ropelewski's first marriage, Wanda Ropelewski; and Mrs. Ropelewski's grown-up brother, Andrzej Lukasiewicz. All of them showed us much kindness and hospitality during our stay at the manor. A large park that was adjacent to the manor house provided a modicum of security for our quarters and an opportunity for a relaxing walk.

## *The Bernatowicz Family*

The Bernatowicz family resided in Krzysin manor near Loniow. To my best recollection there were four members of the family. Mr. and Mrs. Bernatowicz, their teenage daughter Tekla (Tecia), and a cousin who was a single, middle-aged lady. There was also a younger lady who was Tekla's tutor. Mr. and Mrs. Bernatowicz had also three other children who were older than Tekla and lived on their own. Mrs. Irena Bernatowicz Kudyk lived with her husband in Loniow. Professor Stanislaw Bernatowicz lived after the war in Gizycko, and the younger son, Witold Bernatowicz, who was an engineer, lived in Poznań. Mr. and Mrs. Bernatowicz did not own Krzysin manor. It was owned by Mr. Malkiewicz, who owned other manors. Mr. Bernatowicz was its administrator. Mr. and Mrs. Bernatowicz had a very large manor in the eastern part of Poland that became part of the Soviet Union after World War II.

Mr. and Mrs. Bernatowicz invited our unit many times to take quarters in their hospitable manor house. They were very patriotic and loving toward us. I will never forget all the good and abundant meals that Mrs. Bernatowicz and her cooks prepared for us. Whenever we left Krzysin manor, Mrs. Bernatowicz always offered us sandwiches to take with us on our way. I visited the Bernatowicz family a number of times shortly after the war and was always welcomed with great kindness. When I attended John Tarnowski High School in Tarnobrzeg and was in dire need of high school textbooks that were out of print, Miss Tekla Bernatowicz offered me her own textbooks that she no longer needed. Miss Tekla Bernatowicz studed argiculture in graduate school and then became the wife of Mr. Marian Drewenko, an auto mechanic. The young couple left Poland for Canada to join his brother who was there for some time. Eventually the Drewenkos invited Tekla's sister, Irena, to join them in Canada. Irena's marriage to Kudyk ended in divorce. In Canada she married a gentleman named Boston. Her husband died in Canada in 2001. Tekla's husband died at a young age and she became a widow. There were no children from their marriage. Shortly after the death of her husband, Mrs. Drewenko returned to Poland and presently lives in Starachowice. Mr. Bernatowicz died at the age of 77 and Mrs. Bernatowicz lived to be 86. Both of them are buried in Gizycko.

## *The Mierzwinski Family*

Mr. and Mrs. Mierzwinski of Suliszow manor opened the hospitable doors of their home to our unit a good number of times. They also offered us their horses and wagons for various raids against the Germans. I remember that some of our wounded men found shelter in their manor. Mr. and Mrs. Mierzwinski were very patriotic and loving toward us. Toward the end of our war activities, their young son Janusz Mierzwinski joined the Second Regiment of Legionnaires and fought the Nazis to the end of the war. After the war, when the Communist government expropriated the Mierzwinskis property, they moved to Sandomierz. As a college student, I took some French language classes from Mrs. Mierzwinski's sister and then, as a deacon, I often took Holy Communion to Mrs. Mierzwinski when she was ill. She was always a great lady, very gracious and appreciative.

## *The Targowski Family*

Mr. and Mrs. Targowski lived at Dmosice manor near Klimontow. They had two teenage children: a daughter and a son. I will never forget their hospitality. They were not very rich but very generous toward our unit. They gave us the impression that it was a privilege and an honor to offer us shelter and food during those perilous days of the Nazi terror. When the Communists took away their manor, the Targowskis moved to the village of Skwirzowa and lived there in a small house. I visited them a number of times during my vacation. Their nobility, piety, and gentleness always inspired me.

## *The Kuksz Family*

The Kuksz family resided at Jurkowice manor near Klimontow. Mr. Wilhelm Konstanty and Mrs. Antonina Lubieniecki Kuksz had two unmarried children: Henryk Kuksz and Maria "Muszka" Kuksz. Mrs. Kuksz very capably administered the manor while Mr. Kuksz spent most of his time in Warsaw where he operated his large engineering firm. Therefore Mr. and Mrs. Kuksz kept two homes for their family: one in Jurkowice and another in Warsaw. The Kuksz family was not only very patriotic but hospitable as well. Our unit was not the only group of freedom fighters who were invited to hide from the Nazis in Jurkowice manor. There were other units of various political orientations that enjoyed the hospitality of the manor. To my best recollection, Mrs. Kuksz and the children belonged to and were active in an anti–Nazi conspiracy and in the underground Home Army. As a member of the Home Army, Henryk Kuksz ("Selim") joined the Jedrus Company of the Second Regiment of Legionnaires toward the end of the war and fought bravely against the Germans and was wounded in the Battle of Radoszyce. After the demobilization of our forces in the late fall of 1944, Henryk Kuksz and I had our secret quarters in the same general area; therefore, we were able to see each other from time to time. After the war when the Communist government took over Jurkowice manor, the Kuksz family moved to Warsaw. Having completed her university studies, "Muszka" married a physician and Henryk became a forester. Soon after the end of the war Communist police arrested Henryk, kept him in prison for a long time, and tortured him for being a member of the Home Army. After the political situation changed somewhat in Communist Poland, Henryk was released from prison, married, and continued to work as a forester. Eventually, he became an administrator of a state fox farm, where he raised silver foxes. In 1991, Henryk Kuksz published his book *Jedrusiowa Dola* (The Jedrus Lot) in which he describes his experiences during the war. After he retired, Henryk operated his own fox farm near Warsaw until very recently when he was forced to give up its operation because of poor health. During my visit to Poland I visited Henryk at his fox farm and stayed in his hospitable home for many days. I also visited Maria (Muszka) and her husband in Warsaw. Henryk lost his wife a number of years ago and his children are grown up and married. I am in touch with Henryk through our mutual correspondence. In spite of his poor health, Henryk is involved in Home Army veterans affairs in Warsaw.

## *The Bronikowski Family*

Mr. and Mrs. Bronislaw Bronikowski resided at Jachimowice manor. The Bronikowskis inherited the manor from his parents, Stefan and Stefania (Woynarowski) Bronikowski who, on account of his poor health, were forced to lease their manor and live in Cracow. Their only son, Bronislaw Bronikowski, attended high school and college in Cracow and intended to do his graduate studies in the field of agriculture but World War I forced him to change his plans. At the end of the war, Mr. Bronikowski enrolled in the School of Agriculture at the Jagiellonian University in Cracow but was unable to complete his studies because the lease on Jachimowice manor expired and

The hospitable manor house of Mr. and Mrs. Bronislaw and Zofia Bronikowski in Jachimowice, where the Flying Commando Unit took quarters quite often. Following the war, the Communist administration exiled the Bronikowski family and destroyed the manor house. Author's photograph.

he had to take over the administration of the manor. Having taken over the administration of his patrimony, the young heir had to cope with many difficulties. Some of the farm buildings, which had been constructed of wood, had been burned to the ground by the artillery duels between the Russians and the Austrians and the neglected soil had to be cultivated again.

In order to make the manor functional again, Mr. Bronikowski took out a loan from a bank to construct housing for farm workers and their families and farm buildings and to buy tractor, horses, cattle, and other animals. To augment his income from the fields of the manor, he cultivated a large garden and orchard. Finally, he had a two-story, modern residence constructed with running water and other conveniences. After accomplishing all these things, he began to think seriously about marriage.

Bronislaw Bronikowski married Zofia Mieszkowski, the daughter of Jozef and Anna (Lekczynski) Mieszkowski from Rachwalowice manor, in 1921. She completed her secondary education at the high school run by the Sisters of the Immaculate Conception of the Virgin Mary in Nowy Sacz and then attended the School of Business Administration in Chyliczki. With this kind of educational background, she was quite able to assist her husband in the administration of the manor. In addition to her work at the manor, Mrs.

## 25. OUR SECRET QUARTERS

Bronikowski reached out to the community at large. She helped to organize the local housewives club and invited speakers who gave talks on hygiene, horticulture, cooking, needlework, tailoring, and so on. At the same time, her husband was involved in social activities at the community, county, and district of Sandomierz levels. He was also a cofounder of the cooperative bank in Sandomierz and a member of its board, cofounder of the dairy cooperative in Gorzyczany, and a member of the committee that established the Liberal Arts College in Chobrzany at the end of World War II. Mr. and Mrs. Bronikowski had three children. The oldest of the children was Krystyna Bronikowski, who was born in 1922. Following the war, Krystyna became the wife of Mr. Jerzy Radlinski, a professional forester. Next to Krystyna was Stefan Bronikowski, born in 1924, who died at the age of seventeen on July 6, 1941. His death was a great tragedy to his parents and relatives. The youngest child was Maria Bronikowski, who was born in 1928. She became the wife of Mr. Stefan Konopka after World War II.

During the Nazi occupation of Poland, Mr. and Mrs. Bronikowski and their two daughters were deeply involved in Home Army activities. They provided shelter, food, and hospitality for a number of combat units; they also opened the hospitable doors of their manor house to many homeless people who were hiding from the Nazi police. In the second half of 1943 and in the early part of 1944, our commando unit enjoyed the warm hospitality of the Bronikowski Family on numerous occasions.

In the final months of the war, Jachimowice manor opened its doors to many persons who were displaced by the constantly moving front. Some of these persons were relatives and friends and some were perfect strangers. The Bronikowskis accommodated everyone who had no place to stay. The great majority of these people expressed sincere gratitude to the Bronikowskis at the end of the war, but some individuals were not so grateful. One of these persons, a professional poet, wrote and published a satirical poem about the Bronikowskis' hospitality. It appeared in the Communist publication after the war. With the royalty that he received for his poem, the writer paid off his loan that he obtained from Mr. Bronikowski when he was hiding at Jachimowice manor.

After twenty-three years of hard work and many personal sacrifices, Mr. and Mrs. Bronikowski had made Jachimowice manor into one of the finest manors in the area. At that time the Communist regime of Poland issued the decree of September 6, 1944, which deprived the Bronikowskis and other manor owners of their patrimonies. Under the draconian law they were allowed to retain neither a small section of their land nor the manor house. At the same time, they were not permitted to take residence in the county in which their property was located. In the beginning of November 1944, the Bronikowskis were forced to move out of their manor house to provide housing for a group of Russian army officers. The family did not have any prearranged place to go. The Zych family from the village of Gorzyczany, who lived in the neighboring county of Samborzec, offered the Bronikowskis the largest room in their farmhouse. They accepted the offer and moved into the large room at the farmhouse. However, Mr. Bronikowski could not get any employment at that time. In the beginning of 1945, he was employed as a manager of a factory named Eternit in the city of Lublin. When the Russian front moved westward toward Germany, Mr. Bronikowski obtained a job as an administrator of Bzinica manor, near Lubliniec, and then became an administrator of the large manor of Obrowiec on the Oder River. There the Bronikowski family regained some stability and normalcy in their lives. On the land of the new manor, Mr. Bronikowski planted a large orchard. Under his talented supervision and creative administration, the manor prospered beyond anybody's expectation. The people of the area respected the Bronikowskis for their professional hard work and for sharing what they had with others who were less fortunate. Imaginative hard work and sharing with others what they had were always the distinctive characteristics of the Bronikowskis throughout their entire married life.

Before the first Communist elections in January 1947, Mr. Bronikowski was arrested and lodged in prison for two weeks. This was the beginning of his persecution by Communist police agents. The unjust persecution of Mr. Bronikowski led eventually to his dismissal from work. The Communist agents dismissed him from work without giving him any reasons for his dismissal. At the same time they prohibited him from applying for a job in other state farms. The Bronikowskis found themselves again in a critical situation. They did not know what to do and how to earn their living. When Mr. Hernhut, who found refuge in the Bronikowskis' manor during the war, learned about the Bronikowskis' economic predicament, he interceded with the government on behalf of his benefactors. As the result of this intercession, Mr. Bronikowski was offered a position of an administrator of two landed estates, Wola Krzystoporska and Niechcice, that belonged to the yeast industry. He accepted the position and worked there, but cooperation with the Communist committees was next to impossible. Therefore after a few years Mr. Bronikowski resigned his position and moved his family to Cracow in 1950, where he obtained work in the firm Herbapol. He worked mainly as a supervisor in planting and producing various medicinal herbs. This type of work entailed much travel. Due to a reorganization of the firm, Mr. Bronikowski lost his work in 1950. At that time he was already sixty. His new job was with an insurance company, which also required extensive travel. His health did not allow him to keep this job for long. Therefore, Mr. Bronikowski got himself an office job in a lending institution. This was his last employment, during

## 25. OUR SECRET QUARTERS

which Mr. Bronikowski became ill and died on February 13, 1962. As he was all his life, Mr. Bronikowski remained cheerful to the very end. He was buried in the family crypt at the Rakowiecki Cemetery in Cracow. I will never forget his friendly and happy face when he walked the hallways of his manor house and called us to the dining room in Jachimowice.

Mrs. Bronikowski survived her husband by eleven years. After Mr. Bronikowski's death and after the marriage of their older daughter Krystyna, she moved in with her daughter and her husband in Huta Gawrolinska, near Warsaw, where she worked and took care of the grandchildren until her death of heart failure on July 21, 1973. Every time I think or write about her, I always visualize her loving maternal face in which there was always a trace of pain left after the death of her son, Stefan. Since a number of us in our unit were of the same age as Stefan, she treated us as if we were her spiritual sons.

I visited Krystyna and her husband Jerzy Radlinski two times during my visits to Poland and obtained from Mrs. Radlinski most of the information

This picture was taken during my visit at the residence of Mr. and Mrs. Jerzy and Krystyna Bronikowska Radlinski on April 4, 1997. On the left is Henryk Kuksz ("Selim") and on the right, the couple's daughter Miss Teresa Radlinski. Mrs. Radlinski's parents, Mr. and Mrs. Bronislaw and Zofia Bronikowski, provided excellent quarters at their manor for our Flying Commando Unit during the war. Author's photograph.

about her family. At the time of this writing, Krystyna's husband and their only daughter are deceased. She lives by herself at Ruda Gawrolinska.

In addition to the quarters described above, we found accommodations in Skotniki manor, where we stayed a number of times and were received with opened arms. Mr. and Mrs. Kurzanski invited us many times to their manor in Doly Michalowskie. Mr. and Mrs. Adamczyk offered us their residence in Slabuszawice–Wesolowka. Mr. and Mrs. Abramczyk opened the doors of their home to us at Jachomowice, and Mr. and Mrs. Zwierzyk asked us to stay in their farmhouse in Postronna. The two families, who operated a mill on the river in Opalina, were known to us for their hospitality. I wrote about our quarters in the farmhouse of Mr. and Mrs. Marian Slawinski ("Mamloch") in one of the previous chapters. We also took quarters, though only once, in Niedzwice manor. However, the lady of the manor was not too happy with our presence there because her husband was in a German POW camp, and she maintained friendly relations with the Nazi authorities in order to gain an early release for him. Nevertheless, her young daughters were very hospitable and quite delighted to see us in the manor, and they entertained us by playing patriotic songs on the piano.

# 26. Returning Home

After a short meeting, my friends and I decided to leave the area of Zarczyce Duze the following day. Since there was no bus service, we were determined to walk all the way if necessary. Our bags had been packed for several days. On the day of our departure, we rose early in the morning, ate breakfast, and said goodbye to the families we had stayed with. Then we were on the road toward the city of Jedrzejow. There we hoped to catch a train to Bogoria and Staszow. Six of us began the journey from Zarczyce Duze to Jedrzejow. On the road we saw Russian troops moving west as fast as they could. Russian fighters controlled the sky. No trucks moved in the direction of Jedrzejow, so we had no hope of getting a lift. Our bags proved to be heavier than we had thought when we packed them. From time to time we stopped to rest and eat our sandwiches. We were young and healthy; therefore, walking long distances did not bother us too much. Toward the end of the day, we reached the railroad station in Jedrzejow. Fortunately the train had not departed yet for Bogoria and Staszow. We were jubilant. We boarded the train and waited for its departure. In spite of cold weather, the cars were warm. Soon the train began to roll. Its speed was slow, and it had to stop several times to pick up firewood for the locomotive. Therefore it took us all night to reach Bogoria.

We arrived in Bogoria early in the morning. There our group split. Two from the group continued to travel on the train to Staszow, the other two walked toward Klimowtow, and Piorun and I went to visit my first cousin Franciszek Mazgaj-Marglewski, who lived in Bogoria. He was the principal of the grade school there and lived in a part of the school buildings as was customary in Polish schools at that time. My cousin and his wife received us with open arms but cautioned us about a group of Russian officers who made their headquarters in the school building and were using their kitchen. They did not want us to say a word that would give away our membership in the

Home Army because the new Polish government, supported by the Soviets, had already begun arresting those who were members of the Home Army. We promised to be very cautious. As my cousin's wife prepared a meal for us, several officers entered the kitchen. She introduced us as her relatives visiting for a while. The Russians were satisfied and left us alone. During our conversation at the table, my cousin told me that my father and my stepmother would be very surprised to see me alive. On the basis of various reports, they were convinced that I had been killed by the Nazis in one of the battles with them. After the meal, we rested for a while and then continued our journey home on foot.

After we left Bogoria, Piorun and I walked east through Jurkowice, Samotnia, Rybnica, and Krolewice. We knew the road well and all the shortcuts. When we reached my home village of Jeziory it must have been 9:00 P.M. We entered our farmyard from the back so we would not have to walk through the village. Knowing about my parents' conviction that I was dead, I did not want them to experience a shock at my appearance, so I asked Piorun to go to the house first, inquire about me, and slowly break the news to them that I was alive and well. This worked very well.

After conversing with my parents for about fifteen minutes, Piorun opened the kitchen door and called my name. As I entered the kitchen, I could hear my stepmother's and my sisters' loud cries of joy. My father, stepmother, sisters, and brothers rushed toward me to hug and kiss me. I myself could not stop my tears. It was indeed a very emotional reunion with my family, much more so than the one in 1939 when I returned home after taking refuge from the Nazis after trying to join the Polish army. This reunion remains one of the most memorable experiences of my life and I hope no amount of time will ever erase it from my mind.

As Piorun and I described the experiences of our journey home, my stepmother and my sisters prepared something to eat. Soon we were sitting at the table and enjoying our meal in the midst of a loving family. During the meal, my parents briefed us about their experiences with the Red Army units, which had been stationed in Jeziory for about six months. When our meal was over, we talked and talked until midnight. Piorun stayed with us for the night and left for his home in Loniow during the morning of the following day. I stayed home for a few days to catch up on all the developments that had taken place in the family and in the village of Jeziory during my long absence. I discovered that both my sisters, Henryka and Danuta, were enrolled in the upper grades of the local grade school, which was closed during the final years of the war. My brothers, Klemens and Eugeniusz, were attending lower grades of the same school. While visiting my relatives, I learned that my first cousin Jan, a son of Uncle Franek, deserted from the Polish Communist army, was arrested, and had been imprisoned by the new government. In order to comfort him, I wrote him a letter. His older brother, Jozef, who was terribly wounded by the SS-man named "Bloody Eddie," survived the war quite well and was ready to return to his professional work in Rembertow near Warsaw. Uncle Wladyslaw's son Jan, who was arrested by the Gestapo at the Adamczak's farmyard, returned safely from the Nazi death camp in Auschwitz. He miraculously survived it. However his two brothers, Jozef and Antoni, died in the war against Nazism. The first one, who was a pilot, lost his life in a dogfight with a Luftwaffe fighter over London, and the second one was killed in a battle with the Nazi units near Sandomierz. My best friend's older brother, Henryk Kos, was killed by the agents of the new Polish government's Public Security Police for possession of firearms. There was no trial. He was arrested, taken away from his home, shot, and buried in the woods nearby. The new Polish Communist government adopted its philosophy of justice from its Kremlin sponsors.

While visiting my fellow Home Army members, who did not go with us into the Holy Cross Mountains and eventually toward Warsaw, I learned that most of them had been arrested, imprisoned, and interrogated by the government's Public Security Police in Sandomierz. The imprisonment and interrogations were brutal and, at times, sadistic. Torturing of prisoners was a daily occurrence. One of the questions asked over and over again during the interrogations was: "Who are the other members of the Home Army?" The prisoners seldom revealed any names besides those names that were already known to the interrogators. I was told that one of our men imprisoned in Sandomierz was tortured beyond his endurance to reveal the names of his fellow soldiers. In order to experience some relief from pain, he told the interrogators: "All right, I will give you the names of my friends." The officers stopped beating him and helped him to a chair. The chief interrogator said: "I am happy you decided to cooperate with us. The names please." The prisoner began to list a dozen names. There was a joy in the faces of the police officers. Their torture had paid off, they thought. The recording officer wrote each name with great precision on his writing pad and waited for the next one to be uttered by the prisoner and then repeated loudly by the chief interrogator. When the prisoner concluded the litany of names, the chief interrogator said, "Are these all the names you remember? Couldn't you think of anybody else?" The prisoner replied, "These are all the names I remember." The chief officer was very pleased with his achievement and gently said, "Now, take your time, think, and tell us where we can find each of these men." The prisoner looked at him and said, "I don't have to take much time to tell you that. They are all in the same place." The officer was somewhat surprised and asked, "Where are they? Where can we find them? What's their address?" The excitement and curiosity of the Communist agents reached its peak and then came the prisoner's answer, "You can find them at our parochial cemetery." On hearing this, the agents rose up in fury and began to beat the prisoner again. The chief interrogator shouted: "I asked you for the names of living enemies of our state and you gave me the names of dead ones!"

After several months of imprisonment and interrogation, the prisoner failed to admit any wrongdoing against communism and revealed no names of his Home Army friends. He was released from the prison, returned to his family, and gave an account of the above episode. According to my information, the imprisonment and interrogation of the young men took place in Sandomierz at the Diocesan Seminary College building, which the State Public Security Police seized from the church.

My contacts with local Home Army friends made me more and more aware of the hostile attitude the new Polish government had toward the Home Army and its members. Even though the first wave of hatred and persecution of the Home Army had passed, its members were still being arrested here and there. I felt insecure at home and decided to leave Jeziory as soon as possible. What I wanted most of all was to continue my high school education. To do so, I had to go away from home. By doing so, I thought, I had a chance both to hide from the inquisitive eyes of the local secret police and to pursue my education.

I learned from my friends that the new government of Poland had opened a new high school in the village of Struzki. I went there to inquire about the possibility of my enrollment. The new high school occupied a relatively small building, which was formerly used for a local grade school. The government opened this school for the benefit of students in the Baranow bridgehead, who could not attend high school in Sandomierz, Staszow, or Opatow because they were still in German hands.

The principal of the school received me very cordially and tried to help me as much as he could. After learning of my background, he was inclined to think that I should not enroll in his school, but go to a large city high school in Tarnobrzeg, which was on the other (east) side of the Vistula River. When I agreed to go there, he wrote a letter of recommendation to the principal there, whom he knew, and wished me the best. The following day I crossed the Vistula and went to Tarnobrzeg.

## 27. In School Again

My journey to Tarnobrzeg was very pleasant. From Jeziory I walked through Sulistawice, Skwirzowa, Beszyce, and Cegielnia to Koprzywnica and then through Blonie and Ciszyca. Near Lukowiec I boarded a ferry, which took me across the Vistula to a suburb of the city of Tarnobrzeg. It was my very first visit to this city. I was impressed by its modern buildings and friendly people who gave me directions to the Jan Tarnowski High School and Lycée (college). Although the war was still going on in western Poland and Germany both of these schools were in session. They occupied a magnificent building in the center of the city.

Once in the building, I found my way to the principal's office. After presenting my case to the principal, I was referred by him to the vice principal, who happened to be a priest. His name was Father Tomasz Gunia. The vice principal was a kind and soft-spoken man. He took care of my formal admission and scheduled my examination, which covered the material of the first year of high school that I had studied in Zarczyce Duze under the direction of my teacher there. I was admitted to the second year of high school, which began its session in the beginning of January 1945. I had missed the first three weeks of classes and had to catch up with my fellow classmates.

After taking leave of the vice principal, I met a student, Edward Sliwinski, to whom I delivered typed stencils for our secret newspaper, *Odwet*. At that time, he had lived with his parents around the village of Sosniczany. Now he was completing his college (Lycée) and lived with other students in a nearby apartment. He gave me his address and invited me to stay with him overnight if I needed a place to sleep. I accepted his offer because I wanted to look for a place of my own and had to inquire about a number of possibilities. So after leaving the school building, I went to various parts of Tarnobrzeg in search of a room. It was a difficult task. Wherever I went there was no vacancy. Disappointed to the highest extent, I went to my former underground coworker's apartment. He and the other students who lived there had returned from school already and were doing their homework. They were all friendly and hospitable, and they had an extra bed for me. I was delighted and grateful.

The following day, I kept looking for board and room. Then it occurred to me that my father's first cousin, Alexander Mazgaj, lived in Tarnobrzeg; so I decided to look him up and ask whether he could accommodate me. Soon I discovered his address and walked to 24 Koscielna Street, where he lived.

It was one thing to find his home and another thing to enter the yard. A high fence and gate protected the yard and the orchard. My futile attempt to open the gate brought out a watchdog, which barked ferociously at a stranger. Soon my father's first cousin appeared at the gate. I introduced myself, and he opened the gate very promptly. After looking me over he said, "You are a Mazgaj indeed. You resemble our family." Then we shook hands and he asked me to follow him to a large multistory building. As we walked across the yard, his wife appeared on the porch to see who the stranger was that her husband was bringing to their home. Uncle Alexander, as I began to call him, introduced me to his wife and then we walked into their spacious living quarters. As we sat down at the kitchen table to have a cup of tea, I felt that they appreciated my visit very much. They told me that I reminded them of their only son who was my age when he drowned while swimming in the Vistula River toward the end of the war. They were still mourning his death and lived in self-imposed seclusion. They carried on a prolonged mourning partly because their son's body was never found in the river. There was no funeral.

After we became acquainted with each other, I explained the main reason for my visit. My uncle and aunt looked at each other and smiled with love. Then they both turned their eyes toward me and nodded approvingly. I was delighted. My search for a room was over. Soon my uncle and aunt showed me a large vacant bedroom, which I could use. I liked it very much. As soon as we walked out of the room I was anxious to move in as soon as possible. Therefore I brought my pleasant visit to a close and started on my way home.

My parents, who were somewhat skeptical about my high school enrollment in Tarnobrzeg, could not believe their ears when I described to them my experience there. They were very grateful to Uncle Alexander and his wife for offering me a room in their home and decided to take them a present of our farm products. Since I did not want to miss any more classes, I asked my father to move my bedding, clothes, books, and other things to Tarnobrzeg the next day. He agreed and I began packing my things. My stepmother busied herself preparing my food supplies such as fresh homemade bread, cereals,

## 27. In School Again

homemade white cheese, melted butter, eggs, smoked bacon, kielbasa, flour, homemade oil, and potatoes. Some of the flour and potatoes were destined for my Uncle Alexander and his wife as payment for my room and board. In addition to all these supplies, my Uncle Franciszek's wife, Aunt Julia, gave me several dozen eggs and some money. She was always sensitive to my needs.

Before sunrise of the following day, my father and I were on the way to Tarnobrzeg. We rode in our farm wagon and reached the city before noon. After unloading the provisions and other things, I said good-bye to my father and went to school. As I walked to school for the first day of formal high school instruction, I was extremely excited. I could not believe that I was actually enrolled in one of the finest high schools in the whole region. I had thought that my chance to go to high school would never come. The financial difficulties and other obstacles that had barred my admission to the same high school in the summer of 1938 were still fresh in my memory. Now my dreams were coming true after five years of delay. My happiness on account of my admission was great, but nevertheless, it was marred by the uncertainty of my future performance in the school. I did not know what to expect there. While visiting the high school in Struzki, I had noticed that the students there were very young. I did not see anybody my age among the students. This made me think that I might be in a class in which I would be the oldest of the students.

Once I was in the school building, I reported my arrival to the vice principal, Father Gunia. He promptly took me to my assigned class. I will never forget the experience of my first class in the Jan Tarnowski High School. It was a history class taught by a middle-aged lady teacher. As Father Gunia and I entered the classroom, the teacher interrupted her teaching and received us very courteously. Father Gunia introduced me to her and she, in turn, introduced me to the class. Then Father Gunia left and the teacher asked me to take a seat. I squeezed myself into one of the front seats, which was positively too small for me. It was the type of seat in which the seat and the desk are yoked. As I listened to the teacher's exposition of one of the Crusades, I felt the eyes of my new classmates on the back of my head. Toward the end of the class, the teacher asked me a question about something. I got up to answer her question, and my small desk hung on my hips. It was a funny scene. The teacher and the students laughed. I was extremely embarrassed but laughed with the whole class.

During the break, which followed our history class, I became personally acquainted with some of the students who sat in the back of the classroom. They were older than those who sat in the front seats. Some of them were of my age and older. This was a great consolation to me. The older students invited me to sit with them in the back where the desks were larger. I accepted the invitation and opted for a seat in the last row of desks near a window. It was a seat in the corner and very comfortable. Soon I discovered that the older girls sat in the last seats on the other side of the classroom.

My first day in school went fast. At the end of classes, I realized that I had to deal with two major problems. One of the problems stemmed from the fact that when I studied the material of the first grade of high school in Zarczyce Duze, I took German; but now I was placed in a class for study of the French language. Therefore, I had to study, on my own, the first year of French while participating in the current classes during which the second level of the language was taught. Unlike German, French was totally unfamiliar to me. Algebra was my second problem. I did not finish my first book of algebra under the direction of my high school teacher, and I had missed three weeks of the second book, which my classmates had already behind them. In order to solve both of my problems, I decided to take private instruction. My French teacher agreed to help me after school hours, and a young Jewish instructor, who taught college students, gave me private lessons in algebra.

After two months of accelerated private instruction, I caught up with my classmates both in French and in algebra. It took long hours of study and discipline. I studied late at night and got up early in the morning seven days a week. Soon this vigorous work began to pay off. My grades climbed higher and higher from week to week. I became popular in my class to such an extent that when our class president transferred to another school, the class unanimously elected me to the vacant position. I felt deeply touched by their trust in bestowing this honor on me.

Before I managed to get accustomed to my new office as class president, a new distinction came my way. The school administration appointed me to the post of commandant of military training for both high school and junior college. This training resembles somewhat the activities of the Reserved Officer Training Corps on the campuses of American colleges and universities. My military duties claimed some of my time and energy, but gave me a great deal of personal satisfaction. The school curriculum provided certain hours for theoretical and practical instruction. My military education and combat experiences in fighting the Nazis were still fresh in my mind; therefore, I did not have to spend long hours to prepare my lectures. However, the field training was time consuming because it was done after classes.

My election to the class presidency and appointment to the military post increased my social activities. I began to receive invitations to name day celebrations, student parties, dances, and offers of dates. At first, I enjoyed this new popularity and accepted all invitations, but soon I discovered that my studies began to suffer. I became selective in accepting invitations to parties and other social encounters. The students, teachers, and administrators put trust in me, and I did not want to disappoint them by lowering my grades. Therefore, I studied more than ever before. In Polish literature and history, I was always several lessons ahead of my instructors. In addition to textbook lessons, I read other things, which amplified them. I had no trouble in receiving A's in those subjects. In order to keep my A's in chemistry, physics, biology, and anatomy, I had to work very hard day after day. In algebra and French, I was able to maintain only B's. The study of Latin proved to be the most difficult area for me. My grades fluctuated from C to B to C again. Most of the time my performance in Latin was on a C level. In religious studies, an A was a customary grade unless a student got in trouble with Father Geneja.

After a few days of living under the same roof with Uncle Alexander and his wife, I began to discover their rich background. They were both musicians. He played a number of instruments, but violin and flute were his favorites. She played the piano. At times they played together. It was a pleasure to listen to them. They conversed in three languages — Polish, German, and Hungarian. He understood Russian and other Slavic languages. She knew some French. They were married in Budapest, Hungary, and spent the early part of their lives there. As a matter of fact, she was a native of Budapest. My Uncle Alexander was born in either Polaniec or Jeziory. What puzzled me was how in the world they met each other. Our conversations after dinner provided, little by little, an answer to my question.

Uncle Alexander, a son of Jan Mazgaj, grew up in the village of Jeziory. As a teenager, he helped his father in construction and carpentry work. My grandfather, Antoni, his brother, Jan, and Uncle Alexander were responsible, among other things, for creating all the woodwork in the new parish church in Sulistawice. Alexander showed a talent in designing and carving. At the same time, he was attracted to music. It happened that the parish church had its own orchestra, and the pastor of the church was a great promoter of music. Alexander joined the orchestra and began to study music. Soon he discovered that music interested him more than anything else. By the time he was drafted by the Russian army, he had become not only a valuable member of the church orchestra but also its conductor. In the military service, he was assigned to the orchestra. This assignment enabled him to improve his musical skills and was promoted to the rank of conductor. When World War I began in 1914, young Alexander took part in it and was taken a prisoner by the Austrians. Before the war ended, he managed to leave the Austrian POW camp and went to Vienna. He enrolled in the conservatory there and continued to study music.

From Vienna, Uncle Alexander moved to Budapest. There he met a young conservatory student who eventually became his wife. Obviously his musical career did not provide him with good financial security, because he decided to go into furniture making. Uncle Alexander either inherited from his father-in-law or bought a small furniture factory and began producing custom-made furniture. The business venture was a great success and the young couple lived very comfortably. However, when the war ended in 1918, Hungary became an independent nation, and Michael Karalyi, with the strong support of the Communists, became its first president. The economy of the country deteriorated rapidly. In March 1919, a radical form of Communist government was established and the citizens lived in continuous fear for their safety and lives. Life in Budapest was never the same. Communist rule destroyed its former charm and wealth. The hope for a better future was rather dim. At the same time, the Polish ambassador in Budapest began encouraging all persons of Polish origin to return to Poland and take an active part in rebuilding the now free, independent country. Uncle Alexander and his wife responded to the ambassador's appeal and decided to move their furniture factory to the city of Tarnów in Poland, where they bought some property.

Once the factory equipment, furniture, and other belongings were loaded onto a train, Uncle Alexander and his wife began their journey to Poland. The beginning of their travel was uneventful. The young couple anticipated pleasant experiences in the newly reestablished country. They were full of hopes and dreams for the future. Everything was going their way until they reached the Polish border. At the border, Polish officials examined their factory machines and other belongings, imposed an exorbitant duty on them, and treated them disrespectfully. The young couple experienced a great shock and terrible disappointment. The behavior of the border officials was totally out of line with the sugar-coated promises of the Polish ambassador in Budapest. Uncle Alexander and his wife felt that if the treatment they received from the custom officials was any indication as to what they were to expect from other government officials in Poland, their decision to go to Poland was a terrible mistake. They became apprehensive about continuing their trip and began inquiring about the possibility of returning to Budapest; they were told that to return was out of the question. They had to continue their journey to Tarnów.

In Tarnów, the young immigrants were faced with an incredible amount of government red tape and were treated as foreigners. In spite of all the obstacles, they established their factory and began producing a very fine line of furniture. After a number of years in successful production, they sold their factory and moved to Tarnobrzeg, where they bought land in two different sections of the city. On one piece of land, Uncle Alexander built both a large and very modern mill for grinding grain into flour and a house. On another parcel of land, he constructed a furniture factory, a warehouse, and a very spacious residence. The parcel was large enough to provide ample space for an orchard and garden. Shortly before the outbreak of World War II, Uncle Alexander sold his mill to a group of Jewish businessmen and concentrated his efforts on the development of the furniture factory. As in Budapest so in Tarnobrzeg, he opted to produce a line of furniture, which enabled him to utilize his talent for designing and carving. By doing so, he limited his market only to very exclusive furniture stores and wealthy customers.

The son of Uncle Alexander was born in the city of Tarnów, where he spent his early childhood. He went to grade school in Tarnobrzeg. When the Nazis attacked Poland in 1939, he must have been fourteen years old. During the war, as a teenager he helped his father at work. Toward the end of the war, he drowned in the Vistula River. He went swimming in the company of two young ladies who were sisters. He was dating one of them. While swimming across the Vistula, he was caught by a rapid current and went under water. No one was near him to save his life.

During my early stay in Uncle Alexander's residence, the house near the furniture factory was occupied by a high-ranking Russian officer and his family. The officer did not pay my uncle for living there. Also a group of soldiers used the warehouse as their quarters. Cleanliness was not one of their virtues. Uncle Alexander used to say his dog had more care for personal hygiene than some of the Russian soldiers. Fortunately the officers and the soldiers were not on the premises during the day. They left early in the morning and returned late in the afternoon. Sundays were something else. Since Uncle Alexander's furniture factory was the largest building on Koscielna Street, the Russians occupied it as their headquarters for many months. By the time I arrived in Tarnobrzeg and took up residence with my uncle and aunt, most of the soldiers were on their way to Germany. So the factory building was no longer occupied. But every Sunday, soldiers and officers who still remained in Tarnobrzeg used to come to the factory for their political meetings. These meetings resembled church services. In a large hall, which accommodated about six hundred persons, the soldiers placed three huge pictures — perhaps sixteen by ten feet each. The pictures were painted on canvas and had large frames made of two by fours. The pictures created a background for the top ranking political officers' main table, which looked like an altar. The picture of Karl Marx always had a central position. On its right side was the picture of Lenin and on its left the image of Stalin. During the Sunday meetings, Communist hymns were sung, doctrine explained, and exhortations given. Also the participants were encouraged to make public confession concerning any deviations from the Communist Party line. After such "confessions," political sins were forgiven, advice offered, restitutions imposed, and penances given to the sinners. A hymn or two usually concluded their Sunday meetings. Such meetings lasted about two hours each time. Since sometimes Uncle Alexander used the hall during the weekdays, the soldiers carried the images outside after each meeting and put them against the wall of the building. There they were exposed to rain and snow. No one cared about them. When another Sunday came, the pictures were brought into the hall again. This went on Sunday after Sunday.

During the early months of 1945 when the weather was still cold, I did not have much of a chance to converse with the Russian soldiers who occupied Uncle Alexander's premises. But when the early spring came and I began to study in the orchard, I encountered them quite often. As I talked to them, my conversational Russian improved from day to day. Also my knowledge of their way of life in Russia increased. The soldiers were very cautious in our conversations about the real life in their country when they were in a group. But my conversations with individual soldiers revealed many ugly features of the Communist paradise. They spoke to me about shortages of food, clothing, housing, and most of the basic tools of farming. They told me about labor camps and prisons. One of the soldiers who was inclined toward philosophy told me that the people in the Soviet Union were divided into three classes: the first class of people were the ones who were imprisoned, the second class were the people who are imprisoned, and finally those who will be imprisoned. According to him, the Soviet government felt most comfortable with those citizens who were imprisoned and returned to society. Their will had been broken and they promptly obeyed every directive of the government.

Uncle Alexander very seldom engaged in a conversation with the Russians. He hated the sight of them because of the damage they caused to his buildings, furniture, and other property. The officers seized some of his most valuable furniture and shipped it to Kiev. They let their garbage rot in the barrels and their latrines overflow in the orchard, they walked over his newly planted vegetable plants in the garden, and they broke the orchard fences. No wonder that he hated them and felt nothing but contempt for them as persons, for their uniform, and their form of government. His painful experiences with Communists in Budapest following the end of World War I contributed greatly to his hatred and contempt. In most instances he controlled himself and kept his feelings to himself and those he trusted. One time, however, he was provoked by two soldiers to such an extent that he lost his temper and got into a fight with them.

Uncle Alexander's fight with the soldiers took place on Sunday around 11:30 A.M. As I returned from mass, which I attended with the student body in the Church of the Dominicans, I heard a loud exchange of angry words in

Russian coming from Uncle Alexander's orchard. I walked into the orchard to see what was going on there. I discovered that one of the angry voices belonged to Uncle Alexander. He was arguing across the wooden fence with two Russian soldiers. One of them was a lieutenant and the other a private. Uncle's wife was there too. She was in tears pleading with her husband to come home. He refused to listen to her. The bone of contention in the argument was the soldiers' insistence on their right to walk across my uncle's orchard and garden whenever they pleased. Uncle Alexander, who tolerated their passage during the winter, denied it after he cultivated the garden and planted vegetables there. The opening in the board fence, which the soldiers made in the winter to go through, was now closed with new boards. The lieutenant who carried a submachine gun tried to remove the new boards by pounding at them with his shoes. Uncle Alexander attempted to keep him away from the fence by taking a swing at him with his steel rake. The officer shouted, "I will kill you for trying to stop me from going through!" Uncle Alexander shouted back, "This is my property and you have no right to walk across it and destroy my plants. If you put your foot on it, I will kill you!" Soon the lieutenant unfastened one of the boards in the fence, and then he began to kick off another one. Uncle Alexander stood nearby with the rake raised up ready to strike and kept repeating in Russian, "I will kill you!" When the lieutenant began to enter through the opening, Uncle Alexander waited until his whole body was on his side of the fence and then he hit the intruder right in his face with the side of the rake. Blood appeared on the face of the lieutenant. He lost his balance and almost fell to the ground, but then recovered and began to lift his submachine gun into a firing position. Before he managed to do so, Uncle Alexander grabbed the submachine gun and tried to pull it out of the Russian's hands. The officer did not let it go. He was recovering from the shock of being hit and, being young, his strength was returning. I felt that at any moment he would wrestle the submachine gun out of my uncle's hands and fire at him. I reached under the submachine gun, removed the magazine, and handed it to the officer's companion, who was still on the other side of the fence. In the meantime, a group of Russian soldiers arrived on the scene. Some of them were officers. They forcefully persuaded the wounded officer to cease the fight and take care of his wound. Cursing and threatening Uncle Alexander, the lieutenant was taken away by his fellow officers. Uncle Alexander had won the battle. Shaking with anger, he brought a hammer and nails and nailed the boards in the fence again. From that moment on, no Russian soldier ever attempted to break the fence and walk across the garden. Uncle Alexander was convinced that he had taught the Communist soldiers a good lesson in respect for private property. He expressed his gratitude to me for removing the magazine from the officer's submachine gun. His wife thought that both of us would be punished by the military authorities for attempting to disarm a Russian officer. When a few days passed without any trouble from the military, we took it for granted that the case had been dropped. What struck me about the whole thing was the difference between the Nazi and the Communist soldiers. Anybody who would strike or attempt to disarm a Nazi soldier would have been sentenced to death and executed without any questions asked. Communist military authorities showed a great degree of leniency toward misunderstandings and fights between soldiers and civilians.

In the first part of April 1945, the Russian soldiers left the city of Tarnobrzeg. The house in which the high-ranking officer and his family had lived became vacant. The soldiers who stayed in the warehouse left for the front in Germany. We were all relieved at their departure. After we removed the garbage left by the officer in the house he and his family occupied, Uncle Alexander asked me whether I would like to move to it. I accepted the offer and moved there. The walls were dilapidated and full of Communist propaganda posters, but I liked the house and the privacy it offered me. I only used one room. It was spacious enough to serve me both as a bedroom and as a study. With that room I associate the period of my life when I studied most intensely. I slept short hours and worked very hard. In order to keep myself from falling asleep, I paced the floor or a path in the orchard. Long hours of study in my new quarters began to unlock my intellectual potential and gave me a great degree of self-confidence in the world of intellectual achievement. At the same time, I experienced a great uncertainty about my future education. When everything was going my way in school and I experienced success in everything I did at that time, Communist public security began to arrest teachers and students for their previous membership in the Home Army.

One of the first teachers arrested by the Public Security Police was Mr. Stanislaw Sadrakula. He was very well liked and respected by the faculty and the student body. Everybody sympathized with him and his family. During his arrest and interrogation, he was locked up at police headquarters. After a week of detention, Mr. Sadrakula was released. He returned to his teaching post but did not utter a word about his experiences at police headquarters. Shortly after the release of Mr. Sadrakula, other members of the faculty were arrested, interrogated, and released. The arrests of the faculty members created a considerable degree of fear and uncertainty among both the teachers and the students. It was obvious to all of us that our school was unable to function without the key members of the faculty, especially prewar teachers, who symbolized to us the educational values of a free and independent Poland. For one reason or another, every teacher arrested by the police was a prewar teacher.

A number of older students were also arrested and imprisoned. Most of the students arrested were former members of the Home Army. I do not remember any students who returned to school after their arrests except for Eugeniusz Dabrowski, who was in charge of the school's scouting. He was detained for at least a month and then released.

I lived in continuous fear of arrest and imprisonment. I began to sleep with a Walther pistol under my pillow. Each time there was some commotion on the street or a dog barked I got up, grabbed my loaded pistol, and ran into the orchard. I was determined to fight for my personal freedom. My freedom and education became, at that time, as valuable to me as my life. I was very relieved when the arrests of faculty and students came to an end. Since I had no need for my pistol anymore, I took it home and asked my father to hide it well. He split in two a block of wood for cutting meat, cut a small hole in it, put the pistol in the hole, and nailed the block together. After a few months during which people were imprisoned and even killed for possessing weapons, my father removed the beautiful Walther from the block and put it in a full can of grease and threw it into our pond. I hope that somebody will find it well preserved. It is a fine weapon seized from a Nazi officer.

One of my fellow students who was also a former member of the Home Army shared with me his fear of arrest and an unusual premonition that saved him from it. He rented a room in the southern suburb of Tarnobrzeg. One night when he went to bed, he had a dream that the Public Security Police unit was coming to arrest him. He was awakened by the dream, got up from his bed, and looked through the window toward the street. There was no one there. He fell asleep again only to have the same disturbing dream. Again he got up and looked through the window. Everything was quiet. So he fell asleep again to be awakened by the reoccurring dream. This time he heard the sound of a slowly moving vehicle. He rushed to the window and saw a police truck stop on the side of the street and armed policemen jumping from it. He opened the back door and dashed into the orchard, hid behind a shed, and watched what was happening. After the police agents came out of their truck, they took up positions around the house and began pounding on the door. The landlord opened the door, and the agents invaded his home. At that point, the student managed to climb the fence and disappear into the night. According to the landlord's report, the police agents could not accept the fact that the student they had come to arrest was not in the house. They found the suit he was wearing, his shoes, and other articles of clothing; they discovered his bed was still warm, but they could not find him anywhere. They left the house angry and disappointed.

The student was given a safe place to hide by his friends until the wave of student arrests ceased. Then he continued attending classes without any trouble. The agents of the Public Security Police were given a new task—supervision of preparations for the national referendum. The new Polish regime was imposed on the nation by Stalin. It had no legitimacy in the eyes of the free world. The purpose of the national referendum was to provide a legal basis for the Communist regime. All the organs of the regime did everything in their power to make people vote for the new regime. Most of the people refused to be swayed by these efforts. Because of the pressure imposed on them, a great majority of the people went into voting centers and declared themselves against communism. Whenever they had a chance, they wrote derogatory comments about Stalin and his puppet regime in Poland. The tabulation of votes was not done at the voting centers but in Warsaw where the Public Security Police agents under the directive of their Soviet bosses falsified the votes of the nation.

I had the opportunity to witness the shipment of ballots from Tarnobrzeg to, most probably, Rzeszow. A Russian air force reconnaissance plane circled a number of times over the section of the city where the offices of the Public Security Police were and then landed in a meadow near Tarnowski Castle. A group of us students went to see the airplane. The Soviet pilot gave the impression of waiting impatiently for somebody for awhile. Then he took off, flew toward the city, and circled again and again over the tops of the buildings. Moments later he returned to the meadow. He was visibly agitated and kept his motor running to buzz the police headquarters again if necessary. Before he took off again, a group of Public Security Police agents emerged from the castle's park and were seen walking with accelerated speed toward the aircraft. All of them carried bags of referendum votes. As they came close to the airplane, the pilot scolded them in Russian with a mouthful of abusive words. The police agents took the scolding in silence and with reverential fear. Then the pilot ordered them to load the bags into the airplane, and one of them to get in as a passenger. A few minutes later, the referendum ballots from the Tarnobrzeg area were on their way to the city of Rzeszow. Soon the Communist news media announced that an overwhelming majority of Polish voters approved and supported the new Polish Communist regime. This was one of the most brazen Communist lies.

At the end of June 1945, school was over. My report card was excellent. Many of my instructors congratulated me and said that I was one of the best students in the school. I was very happy and wished my parents had been there to hear my teachers praise my academic achievements. It was too far for my father and stepmother to come to attend the parents' and teachers' conference and to pick up my report card. I went to the conference by myself.

When I was getting ready to go home for two months of vacation, Uncle Alexander asked me to stay with him for the summer and help him produce school supplies, such as rulers, protractors, set squares, drawing compasses, and so forth for the school district. He had received an order for such things and had to produce them during the summer vacation. I was torn between two staying or leaving. On the one hand, I wanted to go home and rest for awhile; on the other hand, I felt obliged to help Uncle Alexander. After discussing my feelings with him, we both compromised. I offered my services to him for the first month of my vacation, and I proposed to spend my second month at home. He agreed to such an arrangement. Therefore during the month of July, I worked with Uncle Alexander in his factory. The work was not hard but demanded a great degree of accuracy and precision. Uncle Alexander was pleased with my performance. After dinner each day, Uncle Alexander and his wife played the violin and piano. I enjoyed their music very much. On Sundays, I attended church in the morning and dated a young lady in the afternoon. She was very intelligent and pretty and sought my company. I did not dislike her but was not in love with her. Nevertheless, our dates were always pleasant and joyful.

When my work in the factory was over, I returned home to Jeziory. Since the harvest was not yet finished, I helped my father on the farm. It was a pleasure to be in the fields again and enjoy the sun and the smell of the grain being harvested. My stepmother's good farm cooking and the abundance of fruit in our orchard restored the energy that I had lost in the last five months.

After visiting all my relatives and friends in Jeziory during the evening hours, I took a day off from farm work to visit Krzysin manor, where my dear friends and benefactors, the Bernatowicz family, lived. The manor was about five miles away from Jeziory. I walked there. As I came close to the manor house, I noticed that two Russian soldiers stood guard at the entrance to the house. I felt apprehensive at their presence, but decided to walk boldly by them. It worked. They saluted me when I walked between them and asked me no questions.

Mr. and Mrs. Bernatowicz and their daughter, Tekla, were home. They were happy to see me and wondered whether I had any trouble passing the guards at the door. They explained to me that a part of their manor was being used as headquarters of a Russian military unit. We spoke in subdued voices.

Mr. and Mrs. Bernatowicz appeared to be intimidated and worried because of the Soviet presence in their home, and also because there was hovering over them the possibility of being evicted from their home and land by the new Polish regime. The couple knew what to expect from communism. As a young couple, they were deprived of their country estate and personal property by the Bolsheviks after the end of World War I. Their manor, then, happened to be on the eastern side of the Polish-Russian border. After crossing the border to Poland, they had to start from scratch, and now when they needed more security in their lives than ever before, the "blessings" of communism were being forced on them again. Their daughter, Tekla, whom they lovingly called Tecia, did not fully realize all the implications of the Soviet presence in Poland and therefore managed to keep herself cheerful. As our conversation went on, Mr. and Mrs. Bernatowicz seemed to forget their worries and became interested in recent news about the members of our commando unit they had known during the war. They also inquired about my experiences during the last year of war and my education in the Jan Tarnowski High School in Tarnobrzeg.

When I told them about my pleasant and rewarding experiences in high school, Tecia asked me whether I needed textbooks for the third and fourth years of studies. After I answered in the affirmative, she told me that she had all these books and offered to give them to me. Her offer made me extremely happy because prewar textbooks were getting scarce at that time. Soon she excused herself and went to her room to gather the books. After a while she returned with a pile of textbooks.

After lunch, Tecia asked me to walk with her to Beszyce Dolne manor. The weather was beautiful, and we enjoyed the walk and each other's company. Even though the distance between Krzysin manor and Beszyce Dolne manor was about six miles, we traversed it with great ease. Pleasant company, conversation, and laughter made the time go fast. Tecia had an excellent sense of humor and enjoyed laughing.

The administrator of Beszyce Dolne manor, Mr. Stanislaw Zarzycki and his family, received us with open arms. During our visit the hosts told us about their worries for the future. They no longer displayed their usual verve and optimism, which even the Nazi occupation was unable to quench. The Communist form of government has a distinct ability of enervating even the most optimistic and enthusiastic people. Our visit gave them a chance to share their worries and fears with somebody they knew and trusted. When Tecia and I said good-bye to our hosts, we did not know whether it was our last good-bye or not. At that time, each day brought new uncertainties.

From Beszyce Dolne we walked about one mile to Skwirzowa manor. We visited Mr. and Mrs. Kosterski and their children. They were as hospitable as always. After a short and pleasant visit with the Kosterskis, we walked back to Krzysin manor. Mr. and Mrs. Bernatowicz were happy to see us return safely. After dinner, it was time for me to return home. Before I left the manor, Tecia handed me the package of textbooks that I needed so much for my future studies. I was delighted with the books. I felt a great gratitude to Tecia and her parents. They were indeed my benefactors.

As soon as I returned home, I told my parents about Tecia's generosity and began examining the textbooks one after another. I was filled with antic-

## 27. IN SCHOOL AGAIN

ipation, looking forward to the intellectual enrichment to be found in these books. Among the books Tecia gave me, there was one I did not expect to find. It was a pocket-size copy of the New Testament in red cloth binding. At first I was puzzled by its presence among the books I brought home; but after giving some thought to it, I came to the conclusion that a priest who taught religion in Tecia's high school must have used the New Testament as a part of his course.

After reading a few pages of thes scriptures, I was deeply moved by the text. I kept reading and reading page after page. The more I read the more deeply I felt the words of the New Testament. These words attracted me and, at the same time, penetrated my very being. All of a sudden, I realized that this was the first time in my life I had held in my hands and read the Holy Scripture. I had heard priests and older people talk about the Holy Bible, but no one had ever showed me a copy of it. To my best knowledge, no one in our village and no one I knew in other villages had a copy of the Holy Scripture. Of course, I heard my pastor read the gospel on Sundays and holy days of obligation, but his readings were just excerpts from the teachings of Christ. What I held in my hands and read were not just excerpts of Christ's teachings, but the entire account of his words and deeds as recorded by the evangelists.

The following day after my discovery of the New Testament, I continued reading it chapter after chapter. As I read it, my youthful atheism that I had brought home with me from the war began to melt in a great warmth of Christ's message of love. During the remaining weeks of my summer vacation, I kept reading a number of chapters of the New Testament every day. Sometimes, I took long walks in the fields or woods to read and meditate on the teachings of Christ. Day after day, my life was changing from within. Christ was reclaiming my heart.

Toward the end of my summer vacation, I learned that our high school administration decided to open a limited boarding facility in a section of the magnificent Tarnowski Castle in the suburb of Tarnobrzeg called Dzikow. I decided to explore the possibility of moving from Uncle Alexander's home to the new facility. Therefore, I went to Tarnobrzeg to see what was happening. In the school office I was told that Father Gunia, as an assistant principal, was in charge of establishing the boarding facility. I went to see Father Gunia who gave me the necessary information and encouraged me to enroll in the new facility. I followed his advice and signed up. Uncle Alexander and his wife were somewhat disappointed with my decision. They liked me and felt secure with me during these uncertain postwar days. I promised to visit them as much as possible and moved my things to the castle.

The major part of Tarnowski Castle was occupied by the School of Agriculture, which had just been organized. Several rooms were taken by a lady and her four children. The lady's husband was a Polish officer who had been a POW in Germany, who was now residing temporarily in England. In the administration building near the castle, a group of men were learning vehicular mechanics and receiving instruction in driving of motorcycles, cars, and trucks. Both the castle and the administration building showed the wear and tear of the Russian troops' occupancy. Windows were broken, doors missing, toilets clogged, bathtubs full of human excrement, and all kinds of garbage everywhere. The administration building was not occupied at all with the exception of one large room, which was used for drivers' training. The Russians left it in an uninhabitable state — a state of devastation.

I moved my bedding and books to a room on the second floor of the castle and returned home to spend the final days of my vacation. I was excited about boarding with a group of young men of my own age and shared my excitement with my father and stepmother. My experiences as a member of a partisan group during the war made me appreciate communal living. Therefore, I could hardly wait for the beginning of the 1945-46 school year.

I returned to Tarnobrzeg several days before classes started. I was excited not only about living at the new boarding facility but also about pursuing my education, which I always desired so much. The new textbooks, which Tekla Bernatowicz gave me, interested me and offered me a glance into various areas of anticipated studies. I treated them respectfully because they were very rare and precious.

Upon my return to Tarnobrzeg for the beginning of the school year, I learned that Father Gunia had appointed me as his assistant in supervision of the boarding facility. I was to assist him in assigning students to various rooms, see to it that the students kept their rooms clean and neat, and ensure that they followed the rules established by the school administration. In addition to that, I was to be a liaison between Father Gunia and the agricultural school with whom we shared the building. A middle-aged gentleman whom everybody in the School of Agriculture called "Captain" was the dean of the agriculture students. He took a liking to me and was extremely helpful in establishing and maintaining a very good relationship between the boarding students of our school and the students of the School of Agriculture. Together, we soon organized a students' cooperative, which enabled all students to get three meals a day at a very reasonable price. Again I was elected president of the cooperative by the students from both schools. According to the cooperative's by-laws, every student was to contribute so much foodstuff every month. The amount of victuals members of the cooperative were requested to contribute was supposed to provide for them and for partial remuneration of the cooks. Since the dining room area was rather limited, we had to take turns eating. Since our school's number of student was smaller than the number of the agriculture school we usually ate first.

As the days went by, I grew accustomed to the new quarters, new duties, and new friends. My new friends included a young lady whose name was Danusia Danilewicz. She lived with her family on the first floor of the castle. She was a student in our school and so were her older brother and younger sister. Her youngest sister was still in primary school. Even though Danusia was a little bit younger than I was, she was one year ahead of me in school. She must have studied in an underground school when I was fighting the Germans.

Danusia's family was very cultured. Her mother worked hard to support and educate her children. It was not an easy task, but the children were bright and well behaved. Danusia's older brother, Mirek, was under my command in our school's military training. In the absence of his father, Mirek was the man of the house and helped his mother as much as possible. Danusia, also, was helpful in taking care of the apartment, cooking, and raising her two younger sisters.

After a number of visits to the family's apartment, Danusia and I became good friends. I liked her very much and dated her frequently. Soon I discovered that our affection was mutual. I was happy. I was successful not only in scholastic pursuits but also in social life. However, as I dated Danusia, I spent less and less time on my homework. My teachers began to notice my shortcomings, but, in most instances, they gave me the benefit of the doubt. I sensed it and felt guilty and remorseful. Since my reputation as a good student was at stake, I decided to limit my dates to a minimum and turned to books with a renewed vigor. The discipline of life I acquired during the war helped me to curtail my desire to be with Danusia in favor of my education, which I wanted to obtain for such a long time. Danusia knew of my passionate dedication to learning and accepted our separation. She, too, needed more time to study and help her mother at home.

As soon as I took up my new residence at Tarnowski Castle and began the new school year of 1945, I carried a copy of the New Testament in my coat pocket and read it a number of times each day. As the result of this daily scriptural reading, I went to confession, began to attend mass on Sunday regularly, and started to visit the church for a short prayer and meditation every day. I also joined a student organization directed by Father Gunia, which aimed to enrich and deepen the Christian spirituality of the students. At the meetings of this organization (Sodality), I met a student from Koprzywnica whose name was Stanislaw Kalinowski. He was one year ahead of me in his studies and very active in the students' Sodality. Soon Stanislaw and I became close friends and we spent our free moments discussing religion, education, and our future. In one of our conversations, he revealed to me his desire to become a priest. He intended to seek admission to the major seminary in Sandomierz as soon as he completed his studies in Tarnobrzeg and received a bachelor's degree. Father Gunia was aware of his intentions and was encouraging. I shared with Stanislaw the latest spiritual developments in my life and indicated to him that I too had thoughts of serving the church as a priest. Our mutual interest in the priesthood brought us even closer as friends. Many a time Stanislaw and I visited our homes on the same weekends and walked together from Tarnobrzeg to Koprzywnica. Most of the time, he invited me to stop in his home and rest for a while and then continue my journey to Jeziory. Stanislaw's mother was very hospitable and always offered me snacks during these visits.

The lack of running water and clogged toilets in Tarnowski Castle became an acute problem as the month of September passed and the weather began to deteriorate. I decided to organize a team of "plumbers" to unclog the toilets on our floor. Several students volunteered to join me in the "dirty" work. With very primitive tools and buckets of water brought from the outdoor spring, we succeeded in our work. At the same time we managed to restore electric lighting in our bathrooms. Since the water pipes were broken by freezing weather and the heating system was not yet fixed, we carried water in buckets for our personal use. This was a great improvement over the primitive outhouse built by the Russians.

After unclogging the toilets and cleaning the bathrooms, I spent some time and energy cleaning and fixing a room under the tower of the castle. It was circular in shape and had a balcony and many windows. I loved the room and decided to make it my study. Later on I moved my bed and clothing there. This room offered me privacy and an excellent atmosphere for study. I needed a good atmosphere for study because at the end of the school year I expected to take a comprehensive examination in the main subjects studied in our school.

Having organized my life at the new residence, I applied myself to studies again. Since I had a private room, I was able to study late at night without disturbing anybody. In Polish literature and history I managed to study chapters in the textbook before they were discussed in the class. Most of the time, I was not satisfied with the insights offered by the textbooks and searched in the school library for more extensive treatment of various subjects. My efforts came to the attention of my teachers who gave me a chance to add something to their lectures. Our history teacher, Mr. Stanislaw Sadrakula, had a weak voice and from time to time asked me to give lectures to the class. I always enjoyed this privilege. In our social encounters, he treated me as if I was his colleague rather than a student. His personal friend, Mr. Paz, who taught Polish literature, treated me with a great degree of courtesy and respect in the classroom. Even though he never asked me to take on his class, he always asked me to add my comments at the end of his lectures.

When our school observed the anniversary of Tadeusz Kosciuszko's victory over the Russians at Raclawice in 1794, Mr. Sadrakula and Mr. Paz asked me to give a lecture on the hero's contribution to freedom. I felt very honored. I wrote the lecture and delivered it before the school's entire student body and faculty. It was very well received, but there was some apprehension among the school administrators that the Communist authorities might apply some of my statements to the contemporary Russians who occupied the country.

Among my classmates, there were two brothers who had shared with me the last year of the war. They were Eugeniusz Winiarz ("Zawada") and his younger brother, Kazimierz Winiarz ("Wilk"). Both of them joined the Orlicz Group before it was united with the Jedrus Group and remained with the latter until the end of 1944. Their father, a former Polish policeman, was wanted by the Communist authorities for his work against communism in prewar Poland. He was hiding in the villages near Tarnobrzeg but from time to time came to visit his wife and children. On such occasions, he hid in the attic of the small building that stood in the back of the house. He constructed a double wall in the front of the attic, which concealed his bedding and food and storage space. This hiding space saved him from the Communist Public Security agents who from time to time raided the Winiarz home.

At times when the Public Security agents arrested a number of students for their former service in the Home Army, I myself used the Winiarz hiding place. It was a very fine place to hide but too cold in the winter and too hot in the summer.

The Winiarz brothers and their next door friends, the Busz brothers, formed a learning team. They studied together after classes. All four of them excelled in mathematics. As a matter of fact, they usually solved all the mathematical problems in the math textbook in the first two weeks of the school year. However, they experienced difficulties in analyzing short stories or poetry. Since I was never too strong in mathematics, I sought their help in moments of need. At times, they asked me to help them in Polish literature. On such occasions I visited their home; and after a session of learning, I had a chance to share in their family life and ate snacks their mother prepared for all of us.

There was another student who gravitated toward the Winiarz brothers. He was older in age and several years ahead of us in school and participated in military training under my command. He lived with his family not far away from the Winiarz family. My friends found him somewhat interesting because he read some of the works of Sigmund Freud and took on himself an effort to propagate some of his teachings. When I met him for the first time on a more personal basis, he impressed me as a Freudian fanatic. He had with him a text of Freud's *General Introduction to Psychoanalysis* from which he read certain passages and made comments. He refused to talk about anything else but Freud and his writings. He admitted to me that, as a student of Freudian psychology and philosophy, he no longer believed in God and Christian sexual ethics.

I had never met anybody like him before so I was amazed but did not take him too seriously. He reminded me, to some extent, of the Russian political officers who indoctrinated soldiers in communism. During my consecutive visits to the Winiarz home, I encountered him over and over again and had some discussions with him about religion and Christian morals. Our discussions convinced me that he was a practicing atheist. One time, however, as I entered the Dominicans' Church to pray for awhile, I noticed him sitting in one of the pews. I was happy to see him there and began to doubt his atheism. When we met again at the Winiarz home, I expressed to him my happiness at seeing him in the church. He began to laugh and said, "Please do not misunderstand me. I went to the church that day because it was so hot outdoors and the church was the coolest place around. I didn't go to the church to pray but to cool off." The Winiarz brothers burst out laughing at this reply. I didn't know what to think about it and gave up the hope of figuring out the motives of the young Freudian atheist. In spite of that, I was always friendly toward him and respected his personal convictions. One time, however, we had a very serious disagreement. It happened during one of our military training exercises. For that particular exercise, I borrowed some rifles from the local police station. After a group of students brought the weapons to the schoolyard, I distributed them to the students. One of the students there happened to be the young Freudian atheist. As soon as I handed him a rifle, I noticed that he took something from his pocket and began inserting it into the weapon. I was puzzled by his action and approached him to see what he was doing. I could not believe my eyes. He was inserting live ammunition into the rifle's magazine. In a flash, I grabbed the rifle and pulled it out of his hands. He was shocked and disappointed. When I shouted, "Why did you do such a foolish thing?" at him, he replied, "I didn't mean to do anything wrong. I just wanted to fire a couple of shots in the air." The students looked at him with scolding eyes as if he were a little boy. I did not return the rifle to him and asked him to use a stick for training. He felt humiliated and angry.

After I reported the incident to my superiors, they decided to expel the culprit from the school. I felt sorry for him and pleaded with the administrators. They were receptive to my pleading and changed their decision. The young Freudian student learned about my pleading on his behalf and showed me respect and gratitude from that time on. During our consecutive exercises, he was one of the most cooperative students.

Several weeks after the incident with the live ammunition, I led the male students from our school on field exercises near the suburbs of Tarnobrzeg along the highway that went to Sandomierz. As we developed our formations and began to approach the farm buildings of the former estate of the Tarnowskis, a number of police trucks appeared on the highway from the direction of Tarnobrzeg and armed policemen jumped from the trucks. They took defensive positions against us. One of the policemen fired his rifle in our direction. I realized immediately that the Communist policemen took us for some anticommunist guerrilla group and began shouting: "Stop firing! Stop firing! We are local high school students!" Then I approached the commanding officer and explained what we were doing there. We were lucky that there was only one trigger-happy policeman and perhaps he was not the best shot. Otherwise our field exercises would have ended tragically. After this incident, I always reported to the city police and the State Public Security Police about our intended field exercises.

Toward the end of 1945, one of our teachers invited our class to her house for a dance. She was single and lived with her younger sister, who was unmarried also. The ladies prepared cookies and other snacks for about thirty-five of us students. We had a wonderful time dancing and socializing. Our teacher's sister danced with all of us boys and paid us compliments on our ability to dance.

When I danced with her, she told me that I was the best dancer she had ever danced with. I did not know what to say. I was flabbergasted. I always had thought of myself as a poor dancer but accepted the lady's compliment with humility. When we were returning home after the dance, one of the boys told us that the lady said to him that he was the best dancer she had ever danced with. He obviously took the compliment very seriously. Soon we all discovered that she paid the same compliment to every one of us.

In the beginning of January 1946, I began the fourth grade of high school, which was the final year of high school. Since at the end of the semester I was to take a comprehensive examination, I applied myself to studies with all my strength. I seldom dated or went to movies. I took the comprehensive examination very seriously and was afraid of failure. I had come too close to completing my high school education and did not want to jeopardize it. I worked systematically day after day denying myself, at the same time, legitimate joys of life such as dating and entertainment.

In the early spring, our school experienced a terrible shock. A number of our teachers were arrested again by the Public Security Police agents. Our history teacher, Stanislaw Sadrakula, was among them. They took him during the break between classes. I saw him led away between two agents of the Public Security Police. He just smiled and went away. There was fear in the student body, especially in those classes that were getting ready for the comprehensive examinations, that school activities might be interrupted and our exams postponed.

After three or four days of interrogations at the Public Security building, our teachers were released and returned to their classrooms. There was jubilation in the student body. When Mr. Sadrakula was on the way to school after his release from imprisonment, our whole class met him half-way between his home in the country and our school and led him with flowers to our school for his history class. From that day on, our classes were uninterrupted by arrests of the faculty members. We continued our classes until a few days before the comprehensive examination, which lasted for about a week. First we took written exams in major subjects, and, after completing and passing them, we were subjected to oral examinations.

I did very well in all my comprehensive examinations so I was admitted to the Lycée with a major in physics without entrance examinations. But since I wanted to major in humanities, I had to take an entrance exam because of my grade of C in Latin. After taking the examination, I went home for a well-earned vacation. During the summer vacation, I decided to go to the diocesan seminary in Sandomierz. By that time, my friend, Stanislaw Kalinowski, was already accepted as a first-year student at the same seminary. He completed the Lycée and passed the comprehensive exams at the same time I completed my high school.

When I told my father and stepmother about my decision to enter the seminary, they took it calmly and were supportive of my decision. Then I went to see my pastor, Father Jan Budzinski. First of all he was surprised at my decision and, second, he discouraged me by saying that seminary studies were extremely hard and only very capable students could succeed. I replied that I was one of the best students in my graduating class and I had no fear of any studies. He was taken aback by my strongly expressed self-confidence and he changed his tune. The strong terms in which I expressed my self-confidence were most probably inspired by the fact that Father Budzinski dissuaded my father from sending me to high school in the summer of 1938. The memory of that was still very fresh in my mind. It was a painful memory to me. Anyhow, by the end of our conversation, Father Budzinski treated me more seriously and promised to write a character reference and recommendation to the rector of the diocesan seminary in Sandomierz.

Several days later, Father Budzinski handed me a letter addressed to the

Very Reverend Dr. Adam Szymanski, rector of the Diocesan Major Seminary in Sandomierz, and wished me the best of luck. His attitude toward my desire to enter the seminary had changed within a few days. Now he was friendly, cheerful, and well disposed. Father Budzinski's attitude toward me indicated that he had given me a positive character reference and recommendation. I was delighted. My official road toward the priesthood began.

After obtaining certificates of Baptism, Confirmation, health, transcripts of high school grades, and so forth, I went to Sandomierz to see the rector of the seminary. He lived in the seminary building, which was located at No. 2 Zeromski Street. Since the seminary building was not far from the city's marketplace, I had no trouble finding it. As I approached the main door of the building, my heart trembled. I did not know what kind of reception to expect. I pushed the doorbell button and waited. Soon the door opened and a small man of an advanced age appeared, looked me over, and said, "Do you want to see the rector?" I replied, "Yes, I do." He opened the door wider and said routinely, "Please come in and follow me to the parlor." I followed him to a large arched room with a pillar in its center. There were only two small windows in the room. An electric light hanging from the ceiling was not much help in dispelling the darkness of the parlor. The furniture of the parlor was rather heavy and solidly built. The porter asked me to sit down and wait. Obviously he went to announce my arrival to the rector. After awhile, the rector walked into the parlor. I stood up and greeted him with the traditional Polish greeting, "Praise be Jesus Christ!" He responded, "Forever and ever. Amen!" Then I walked to him, shook his extended hand, and kissed it. He seemed to like my manners and smiled approvingly. I introduced myself and handed him Father Budzinski's letter, an application for admission to the minor seminary, and various documents that accompanied it. As soon as we sat down, the rector began to reminisce about his experiences in our parish. He told me that he had spent some time in Sulislawice as a young seminarian. He stayed at the rectory with one of our former pastors and helped him in the parish work. What struck him about the people of the parish, he said, was the fact that many of them were dark complexioned and had somewhat Mongolian features. He speculated that their ancestors must have been taken prisoners by the local noblemen during the Cossack Wars in the seventeenth century. He had many pleasant memories of his short stay in Sulislawice. After finishing his reminiscences about our parish, the rector asked me about my family and schooling. Then he took me to the apartment of Father Lagocki, which was just across the hallway from the parlor. Father Lagocki, who was the vice rector of the seminary, was very pleasant and hospitable. The rector introduced me to him and told him that I was from the parish of Sulislawice and had just applied for admission to the minor seminary. Father

Lagocki explained to me that if I was admitted, I would see more of him because, as a vice rector, he would have immediate charge of the minor seminarians. At the end of our short visit to Father Lagocki's apartment, the rector told me that I should hear from him within several weeks. My interview was over.

From the seminary, I walked to the neighboring institution, the State High School and Lycée of Sandomierz. There I inquired about the possibility of being admitted into the first year of the Lycée with a major in humanities. I explained in the admission office that I had applied for admission to the seminary and since the seminary did not have its own Lycée, I would like to attend the state Lycée. The director of admissions looked over my high school transcripts and told me that I should have no problem in being admitted into the first year of the Lycée. With this assurance, I returned home in good spirits and shared my experiences in Sandomierz with my father and stepmother.

About a week after I handed my application to Monsignor Szymanski, I received his letter that brought me good news; I was accepted to the minor seminary. I felt blessed but at the same time unworthy. I thought about a number of young men who had gone to school with me in Tarnobrzeg who could have been much better candidates for the priesthood than I was. Why did the seminary accept me?

As soon as I had a chance to see Father Budzinski, I showed him the rector's letter. He was genuinely happy for me and expressed his congratulations. I told him that he was responsible in part for my admission.

In spite of my personal desire to keep a lid on the news about my admission to the minor seminary, some people in the village learned about it and came to congratulate me. I did not want any publicity about it because I was not sure whether I could stay in the seminary beyond the first year.

Shortly after I was accepted to the minor seminary and first year of Lycée in Sandomierz, I went to visit my friend Stanislaw Kalinowski in Koprzywnica. During my visit with him, we both decided that we should take our vacation together at the Baltic Sea. Neither of us had been to the Baltic. We were excited about our trip and the vacation at the beach. After several days of preparation, we boarded a bus in Koprzywnica and traveled to the Nadbrzezie railroad station near Sandomierz. There we bought our tickets to Gdynia, a port city on the Baltic Sea. On the way to Gdynia, we wanted to stop in Bydgoszcz to visit a mutual friend who worked there. He invited us to visit him and promised to feed us and provide a room for us in his spacious dwelling.

Our train came on time and we boarded it as soon as possible. In the early afternoon, we began our journey north. We expected nothing but joyful experiences. On the train we became acquainted with several university students who traveled with us to Skarzysko. They advised us to go to Bydgoszcz through Warsaw instead of through Łódź. In such a way, we could see the capital city. When I brought up a question of an additional fee for such a route they said that there should be no additional fee. We trusted them and did not bother to ask the train conductor. So in Skarzysko we took a train to Warsaw instead of Łódź. It was already dark and we fell asleep. After traveling for a few hours toward the capital, a conductor came and woke us up to check our tickets. When we produced the tickets he looked at them and said, "Young men, you are on the wrong train and must get out of this train at the next station, return to Skarzysko, and board the train which goes to Łódź." When we explained to him why we decided to go through Warsaw and pleaded with him to let us continue our journey, he laughed at us and said that there was nothing he could do for us.

Needless to say, we were greatly disappointed and distressed. We regretted that we did not ask a conductor about the possibility of changing our route of travel. At the next station, we left the train and waited for the train to Skarzysko.

Fortunately, the train came soon and we returned to Skarzysko without any trouble. There we had to wait for several hours for the train bound for Łódź. Once we were on the right train again, we decided never to deviate from our route. However we stopped in Łódź for a day to visit with my first cousin Maria Mazgaj, who worked there and also attended the University of Łódź. The city of Łódź did not impress us very much.

From Łódź, we traveled through Wloclawek and Toruń to Bydgoszcz. Again we stopped in Toruń for a day to visit the city of Michael Copernicus (Michael Kopernik), the famous Polish astronomer, who brought about a revolution in the science of astronomy. We liked Toruń very much and enjoyed visiting ancient churches and other historical buildings.

We left Toruń late in the afternoon and arrived in Bydgoszcz about 10:00 P.M. It was too late to look for our friend's residence. Therefore, we decided to find some accommodations near the railroad station. At the railroad information desk, we were directed to a nearby shelter for travelers. When we walked there we found ourselves in front of a building that looked like a hotel. Unfortunately, the door was locked. After a few knocks on the door, a first floor window opened and one of the guests explained that the manager of the hospice had locked the door and left for the night. Since the door could not be opened from the inside of the building, the friendly guest suggested that we enter through his window. He extended his hand to pull us up. Stanislaw climbed through the window first. Then I handed him our suitcases and I followed my friend through the window. Fortunately there were a few vacant rooms in the hospice. The rooms, the beds, and the bathrooms were very clean. We were lucky to find this place.

After a very restful night, we were on our feet at about 8:00 A.M. After having some coffee and rolls, I went to the office to pay for the accommodations and breakfast. A clerk in the office told me that there was no charge for anything. He looked at the registration book and said, "It's too bad that you two did not register last night because we would have given some money for your further journey." I could not believe the words that I heard.

After expressing our gratitude to the clerk, we left the hospice and began to look for the street on which our friend lived. Soon we located it and had no trouble finding his apartment, which was near a large dairy. Our friend was a general manager of the dairy. He was still at home when we knocked on his door and greeted us very warmly. His sister, who kept house for him, came out from the kitchen to greet us. Stanislaw and I liked her very much for her kindness and her excellent culinary skills, which she had demonstrated so well at our boarding cooperative in Tarnobrzeg.

Following a large breakfast, our friend took us with him to his office, gave us a tour of the dairy, and introduced us to some of the people engaged in very sophisticated production of various kinds of dairy products. Since Stanislaw and I had lived in small towns, we had never seen such a modern, large dairy. Having completed the tour of the dairy, we left our friend in his office and spent most of the day in the city of Bydgoszcz exploring its historical buildings.

During the dinner time in our friend's apartment, we exchanged news about ourselves and our mutual acquaintances. We discovered that our host had a very prestigious position in the state-operated dairy industry. A fine German car was part of his fringe benefits. He was quite happy with his job and at that time did not have to join the Communist Party. In order to show us his official car, our friend proposed a ride to various important parts of the city. Stanislaw and I embraced his proposition very enthusiastically because we wanted to visit remote parts of the city. During the day we had a chance to explore the downtown of Bydgoszcz and now an opportunity presented itself to see the suburbs.

Our excursion was very pleasant. The weather was beautiful and the company of our good friend and his lovely sister very agreeable. By the end of the day, Stanislaw and I had a fairly good image of the city of Bydgoszcz.

Having spent a restful night in our friend's apartment, we continued our journey toward the Baltic Sea. Before we left the apartment of our hospitable friends, we were given a great amount of food for our journey. A large package of victuals contained pounds of Swiss cheese, dry kielbasa, ham, bread, and fruit. We were grateful for the hospitality and generosity of our friends.

On the final leg of our journey to the sea we traveled through the part of Poland that is called Pomerania. Some of the names of the towns and cities on our way reminded us of our nation's painful experiences with the Teutonic Knights who for centuries controlled this area and endangered the security of Poland and Lithuania.

The Teutonic Knights were a German religious order founded in the Holy Land in 1090-91. The order was modeled on the orders of Knights Templars and Knights Hospitalers. The main goal of the order was to protect the Holy Land from Mohammedan Turks and thus allow Christian pilgrims to visit holy places. After the Holy Land returned into Mohammedan hands, the king of Hungary permitted the Teutonic Knights to settle in his kingdom. Then the Polish prince of Pomerania invited them to his principality and commissioned them as missionaries to the pagan Prussians. The knights, however, were more interested in conquering the Prussians than in converting them to Christianity. After exterminating most of the Prussians, the knights brought in German colonists to resettle the area. When the Teutonic Knights attempted to subjugate Lithuania and to threaten the security of Poland, these two countries became unofficially united through the marriage of the Polish queen Jadwiga with the Duke of Lithuania, Ladislaus Jagiello. At the same time, Lithuania received Christianity from Poland. In order to break the unity of Poland and Lithuania, the Teutonic Knights declared war on Poland. In spite of the military superiority of the Teutonic Knights, the Polish and Lithuanian armies, united under the leadership of Ladislaus Jagiello, defeated them at the historic battle of Grunwald in 1410. Following the battle, Poland regained all the lands controlled by the knights with the exception of the eastern provinces. From that time on, the Teutonic Knights never recovered their former power.

In 1515, the grand master of the Teutonic Knights, Albert of Brandenburg, and most of his followers converted to Protestantism and organized the area that was left of their former domain into a hereditary duchy under Polish control. Most of the knights married, thus giving rise to the new Prussian nobility.

The dukes of Prussia were obligated to pay homage to the kings of Poland. The first homage of the Prussians, which took place in Cracow, the old capital of Poland, in 1525, is depicted by the famous painting of Jan Matejko called "The Prussian Homage." Tradition has it that schoolboys were whipped by their teachers on the day of the Prussian Homage so they would always remember the historic event.

While reflecting on the early history of Poland and her struggle with the Teutonic Knights, we arrived to the city of Gdańsk (Danzig), which for some time was also in the hands of the knights. As the train stopped at the main railroad station in downtown, a great desolation appeared before us. Most of the buildings were reduced to heaps of rubble during the war. Small groups of German children, who looked like little skeletons, came to our train and begged for food and money. It was a pity to see the city and its inhabitants in such a miserable condition. What a tragic state of affairs Hitler brought on his own people. The Soviet army subjected the proud and beautiful city of Danzig to such a crushing humiliation.

Someone who was on the train with us explained that the Russian troops did not have to destroy the city to any great extent because German resistance was very minimal. The Russians looted the city, raped the women, murdered many innocent civilians, and then destroyed the city to cover up their crimes. Among many architectural jewels of the city's antiquity that were destroyed by the Russian artillery was St. Mary's Church.

During our short stop in Gdańsk, we were unable to explore the ruins of the city but promised ourselves to return to it at a later date. In the meantime, our train headed toward Gdynia. Soon we reached Sopot with its beautiful beaches, modern houses, and public buildings. After awhile, the train entered the city of Gdynia, which was a totally modern city. It was built between the end of World War I and the beginning of World War II. Since at the end of World War I, Gdańsk became a free city controlled to a great extent by the Germans, the government of Poland, with the overwhelming support of the entire nation, built its own modern port.

From the train station in Gdynia, we went to visit our friends who lived in a very beautiful residential section of the city. Our friends anticipated our visit and received us very cordially. The parents of our friends built their house sometime before 1939. It was a large and beautiful villa. After the Nazis occupied Poland in September 1939, they ousted Polish people from their homes in Gdynia and replaced them with Germans. Our friends and many others were exiled to Tarnobrzeg, where they spent the war years. That is how Stanislaw and I met them in Jan Tarnowski High School and Lycée.

As soon as the Soviet army pushed the Nazis out of Gdynia, our friends and other families left Tarnobrzeg and went to Gdynia to recover their property. Fortunately, our friends' house and other houses in the area were left by the German families in excellent condition. I must say that as a rule Germans did not destroy the houses and furniture that they used during the war. I could not say the same thing about the Russians.

Since our friends had a number of rooms that were unoccupied, we did not have to worry about accommodations during our vacation at the sea. We were invited to stay as long as we wanted and take meals with them. However, we did not want to take advantage of our friends; therefore, we used the rooms but ate our meals wherever we happened to be during the day in our excursions on the coast.

Our exploration of the coast was quite exciting. At first, we explored the city of Gdynia and the port. We had never been to any seaport before and had never seen the Baltic Sea or any other sea. In the port there were a number of foreign ships. There was also an American ship, and we noticed some black sailors onboard. We watched them with a great degree of curiosity because we had never seen black people before. They appeared very handsome and it never occurred to us that some people might have a racial prejudice against them. As we kept exploring the port we encountered black sailors on the street and were able to take a closer look at them.

Having explored the city of Gdynia and its port in a couple of days, we boarded a ship and sailed to the Hel Peninsula, which provided an excellent harbor for the ships in the port of Gdynia. I had a great time onboard the ship, but my friend Stanislaw became seasick and spent most of the voyage in the middle of the ship. He was very happy when we reached the port of Hel. Once we were on solid ground again he recovered very fast and we were able to start exploring the peninsula.

After visiting the port and the city of Hel, we went to the beach, which was littered with Nazi military hardware. As we walked along the seashore we saw large and small cannons, mortars, heavy and light machine guns, all sorts of ammunition, hand grenades, and explosives. There were also hundreds of helmets emblazoned with the Nazi and SS insignia that we had seen so many times worn proudly by the Nazis who enslaved our country and attempted to exterminate our people. While looking at all these symbols of Hitler's empire, anger filled our young hearts. As soon as we made a little camp on the beach, we decided to vent our anger by desecrating the Nazi symbols. We went around and collected as many Nazi helmets as we could and threw them into the latrine used then by the Nazi soldiers and now by occasional visitors. We thought that the latrine was the best place for the hateful insignia of the evil and criminal Nazi empire.

The desecration of the helmets at the Hel Peninsula reminded me of the days during the war when my friends and I, as members of the Home Army, used Nazi helmets for our pistol target practice. At that time, I discovered that these helmets were not as strong as they appeared. They were no match for our 9mm pistols.

Having desecrated the Nazi helmets, we spent the rest of the day exploring the peninsula and swimming. There were very few people on the beach and we had an impression that the place was deserted. We came to the conclusion that the abundance of weapons and ammunition left there by the Nazis kept most of the people away. Toward the evening, we boarded the same ship and returned to Gdynia. My friend took the sea voyage much better this time.

Several days later, Stanislaw and I went to the resort town of Sopot and then took a train to the old town of Oliwa. The main point of our interest in Oliwa was a medieval church, which was built by a group of Cistercian monks. It was one of the largest churches I ever saw. Its organ had two parts: the part over the vestibule of the church where the keyboard and controls were and the other part placed high on the wall on each side of the main altar.

A Cistercian monk, who conducted a tour of the church, gave us an account of the very dramatic history of this unusual organ, which is considered one of the finest in Europe. He told us that when the Cistercians constructed the church at the end of the thirteenth century, they were looking for a good organ maker. After some time, they found a highly recommended young man who agreed to build a proper organ for the new church.

Since his work was to run for many years, the monks invited the young man to stay with them in the monastery. He accepted their invitation gratefully and began his task. After a number of years, the organ builder took a liking of the monastic life and decided to become a Cistercian monk. He was received into the order and kept building the organ day in and day out. At the same time, he took part in the prayers and services of the religious community. While thinking about the organ or working on it, the organ builder seemed to hear sounds and melodies that were totally new to him. They were all pleasant and joyful as if coming out of the various pipes of the organ, which he was building.

By the time the organ maker completed his labor of love to the glory of God, the abbot set aside a Sunday for the blessing and dedication of the new organ. Many guests were invited to attend the dedication and the organ recital that was to follow it.

On the day of dedication, thousands of people filled the large church. As soon as the ceremonies of dedication were over, the organ maker began his recital on the new organ. He played the well-known hymns and songs as they were listed in the program. The organ sounded great and the skill of the performer matched its quality. The organ maker and performer was very pleased with both his instrument and his music. The people in the audience were jubilant. It was a rare experience for them to hear such beautiful music.

When the performer was playing the last piece of the recital, all of a sudden he recalled the joyful melodies that came to his mind when he was building the organ. So when he completed the last scheduled song of the recital, he did not stop but kept on playing these inspired melodies that he remembered. He did not realize how beautiful these melodies were until he heard himself playing them. As he continued playing these, as it were, divine melodies, the people in the audience were convinced that the melodies unknown to them were the central part of the recital and all the music that preceded them was just a prelude.

The performing organ maker was more and more affected by his inspired music. With each new melody that came to him, his elation increased to such a high degree that his heart was unable to endure it. The musical genius collapsed on the keyboard and died of excessive joy.

The following day after having visiting Oliwa and its historic church, my friend and I took a train to Gdańsk. The ruins of the city were very depressing to us. However, we discovered some beautiful sections of the city that were not destroyed during the war. These sections exemplified to us the architectural beauty of Gdańsk before its destruction.

After exploring the old city of Gdańsk, we spent the rest of our vacation on the beach in Sopot. Swimming and walking on the beach for miles helped us to relax and regenerate our energies for our new academic year, which was to start again in September.

At the end of our vacation at the seashore, Stanislaw and I expressed deep gratitude to our friends for their great hospitality toward us and we left Gdynia by train. On the way home, my friend and I recollected our experiences at the Baltic Sea and felt greatly enriched by them.

Toward the end of August 1946, my father took me to Tarnobrzeg, where I left my books and personal things. I stayed there for a day or two to say good-bye to my friends, to obtain a letter of recommendation from Father Gunia, and to get more transcripts of my grades for admission to the State Lycée in Sandomierz. My transportation from Tarnobrzeg to Sandomierz was arranged by my friend Zygmunt Komorowski, who at the last moment decided to go to the seminary. His family ran a large farm near Sandomierz. One of the farm workers brought a wagon to take us and our belongings to the seminary. We loaded our things on the wagon and rode to Sandomierz to start a new chapter in our lives.

# Part Three: After World War II

## 28. Sequel

My enrollment in the minor seminary in Sandomierz was very pleasant. I found myself in a large group of young men of my age, who arrived from various parts of the diocese. At that time, the diocese of Sandomierz had over one million baptized members organized in 275 parishes. The day following my arrival at the seminary, I enrolled at the State Lyceum (Collegium Gostomianum), whose campus was adjacent to the seminary campus. Even though my major was in humanities, my curriculum included Polish, French, and Latin literature; philosophy; history; sociology; political science; astronomy; physics; geometry; mathematics; biology; and religion. My positive scholastic experiences that I brought with me from high school, organized manner of life, and academic atmosphere at the seminary gave me a great degree of hope that I would be able me to cope with the study topics contained in the college curriculum.

When college classes began in the first week of September, I discovered that most of my classmates were fellow minor seminarians. Our professors treated us respectfully and at the same time expected us to excel in the subjects that they taught. I also became aware that Father Jozef Stepien, who resided in the seminary, was one of the professors in our college. He taught German, mathematics, physics, and religion. With the exception of the professors of history and philosophy, all of our professors were very talented and highly respected prewar scholars. However, a young professor of philosophy became the most popular among her students. She was not only beautiful but also a knowledgeable and most enthusiastic instructor.

Following the end of the first semester, some of my fellow minor seminarians were advised to leave on account of low grades. Needless to say, they were very disappointed. I sympathized with them and at the same time, I studied hard to receive high grades in all my classes because just passing grades was not good enough for the seminary administration. We were expected to receive high grades in all classes. Since I did not have enough command of conversational French in my French literature classes, I made a private arrangement with a lady who spoke French from her early childhood to give me some lessons. She was a sister of Mrs. Mierzwinski from Suliszow manor, which was near my hometown. My private teacher refused to speak Polish with me and thus forced me to converse in French one hour a day. Soon, my conversational French improved and I began to memorize a number of French poems by La Fontaine.

The academic atmosphere of the seminary and my desire to become a priest were conducive to my prayers and study to such an extent that when I had to take comprehensive examinations for my B.A. degree, I passed them with high marks and was selected by the seminary administration for the first year of theology. However, some of my fellow seminarians, who passed their B.A. examinations with low grades were not admitted to the major seminary. Even though there was a shortage of priests in the diocese, the seminary faculty was very selective in choosing their students.

I spent my summer vacation at home with my family. Our pastor, Father Jan Budzinski, asked me to instruct a large group of children in preparation for their First Holy Communion. The children were coming day after day from all the villages of the parish to our historic church, which was beautifully restored but no longer used for Sunday worship. A main section of this church was constructed in the twelfth century. I had many joyful experiences teaching about fifty lovely and enthusiastic children. They anticipated making their solemn First Holy Communion in the middle of August.

One day during recess, I ran into my grade school classmate who was learning to play the organ. We did not see each other since the early part of World War II. He told me about his desire to become a church organist and I let him know about my intentions to become a priest. Then, when I mentioned to him that I just graduated from college, he attempted to correct me and said, "You mean, you just graduated from high school." I responded, "No, I meant what I said, I graduated from college and presently, I am enrolled in the first year of theology." When I looked at him, I could see that he remained skeptical. Then, he said, "You are so thin, you must have tuberculosis." I explained to him that to the best of my knowledge, I had no tuberculosis but I had lost weight due to a number of years of hard academic work. When he was leaving, he still looked doubtfully at me.

At the end of September 1947, I began the first year of theology in a class of thirty-five young students. With the exception of two members of my class, who were much older, all of us were recent college graduates in our early twenties. It did not take us long to form a congenial and homogenous group of men, who desired more than anything else to become priests. Our professors were saintly priests with an excellent academic background and much experience in teaching in various fields of knowledge. The five-year curriculum was quite extensive. It entailed the following areas of learning: philosophy, psychology, sociology, epistemology, apologetics, education, homiletics, ecclesiastical history, sacred art and its conservation, biblical Hebrew, biblical Greek and Latin, introduction to the Bible, exegesis of the Old Testament and the New Testament, introduction to theology, dogmatic theology, moral theology, pastoral medicine, canon law, chant, and liturgy. In addition to the above subjects, all of the seminarians were obliged to attend seminars in the history of Christian art and its conservation. These seminars were conducted in various ancient churches of the historic city of Sandomierz. We also had practicum in preaching in our refectory and in the seminary church, which was opened to the public. During our Christmas, Easter, and summer vacations, which we spent in our home parishes, most of us preached at the request of our pastors. Our daily classes, which were conducted Monday through Saturday, together with Sunday services at the cathedral and semester examinations made the time pass quickly.

The picture was taken on the occasion of my graduation from the State College (Collegium Gostymianum) in Sandomierz, Poland. Author's photograph.

On the feast of St. Stanislaw Kostka, November 13, 1947, my class was officially vested, in black cassocks and white surplices, by our dear Bishop Jan Kanty Lorek. When he vested us individually in cassocks, we repeated after him a Latin prayer, *"Dominus pars hereditatis mae...."*—"The Lord is a part of my inheritance"; and when the bishop helped us to put on our white surplices, we were saying, *"Indue me Domine hominem novum...."*—"Vest me, oh Lord, a new man." From that time on, our external appearance was similar to that of older seminarians and the diocesan priests, who wore their cassocks not only in the church but also on the street. Following our first semester examinations, we went to our homes for Christmas vacation. During Christmas break, my family and the parishioners saw me for the first time wearing a clerical outfit. Many of them told me that I looked much taller in my long clerical garb. Father Budzinski congratulated me on account of my new cassock and asked me to assist him at the altar during Christmas masses.

In the second week of January 1948, with the blessings of my parents and Father Budzinski, I returned to the seminary to continue my studies for a second semester. Again, I was absorbed in my daily classes and prayers. The time flew very fast. Soon, we began to observe the season of Lent and Holy Week before Easter. Toward the end of Lent, our spiritual director, Father Jan Sinka, conducted a three-day retreat for the benefit of all seminarians. On Saturday before Palm Sunday, most of the students left the seminary for our Easter vacation. However, a number of us remained in the seminary in order to assist in the services conducted by Bishop Jan Kanty Lorek during Holy Week, on Easter Sunday, and on Easter Monday. It was a pure spiritual joy to take part in these liturgical celebrations at the altar of God. In the afternoon of Easter Monday, I joined my family for what remained of Easter. Some of the food from the traditional Polish Easter basket, blessed on Holy Saturday, was still stored in the kitchen. I wished my parents, brothers, and sisters happy Easter and they shared with me an Easter egg. The following day, I went to the church to see my pastor, who asked me to assist him in Sunday services. During my short vacation, I enjoyed visiting with my family, Father Budzinski, my relatives and friends.

Shortly after Easter, I returned to the seminary to continue the second semester of theological studies. My hard work paid off when the second semester of examinations came at the end of May; I received good grades in all subjects, which we studied in the first year of theology. Another reward for my hard academic work came in the form of a summer vacation in the Sudeten Mountains.

My first cousin Jozef Mazgaj and his wife Maria, who lived in Kowary, invited me to spend three months of my summer vacation in their home. Their city was located in the most beautiful section of the Sudeten Mountains. This western part of the country belonged to Germany before World War II. It took me about twenty-four hours, by train, to reach my destination. My hosts lived in a very spacious residence, which had two guestrooms. Two of my other first cousins also had their residences in Kowary. Soon I discovered that one of my comrades-in-arms, Jan Szpakiewicz ("Pikolo"), lived in this city as well. As soon as I arrived in Kowary, I asked my cousin's wife to take me to their parish church and to introduce me to their pastor, who happened to be a Franciscan priest. The pastor and I established a good rapport and I began to attend daily masses in his church.

After a few days on my vacation in Kowary, my first cousin, Stanislaw,

The Josef Aleksander Mazgaj family in the Mazgaj family orchard in the summer of 1948. Standing, left to right are Eugeniusz, Danuta, Marian, Henryka, and Klemens. Sitting, left to right are Mother Anna holding Zbigniew and Father Joseph Alexander holding Zdzislawa. Sitting on the ground are Aleksander (Olek) and Robert (Robek). The youngest child Anna was not born yet. Author's photograph.

and his wife invited all the Mazgaj relatives in the city to their home for dinner. My cousin, Jan, came to dinner with his wife, and he also brought with him a very personable and cultured German gentleman. The dinner turned out to be a small family reunion. During this reunion of sorts, we were able to catch up on the latest news in the family and in our individual lives.

As soon as I could, I visited my friend, Jan Szpakiewicz, in his office. We spoke about our lives following demobilization. He told me about his arrest by the Communist security agents, his imprisonment, and his torture, during which he lost some teeth and suffered broken ribs. He underwent all this due to his membership in the Home Army and in the Flying Commando Unit. I acquainted him with my studies and told him of my desire to become a priest. Before I left his office, we made plans to visit the city of Wroclaw (Breslau), which was partially destroyed by Soviet and German artilleries during the war. Soon we traveled to the ancient Polish city and spent several days there visiting mediaeval churches and other ancient buildings. Our time together gave us the chance to recollect our wartime experiences and to speak about our dreams for the future. A few days later, I joined a group of Franciscan priests in an excursion to the highest mountain in the area of Kowary. The border between Poland and Czechoslovakia ran along the top of the mountain. We met there with a congenial group of Slovak tourists and shared our sandwiches with them. Border guards let us cross the frontier into their country. This was the very first time I crossed a border of another country.

Since Josef and Maria were unable to have children of their own, they decided to adopt a little child from an orphanage, which was being operated by a group of Catholic nuns in a neighboring town. Because of his work, Jozef was unable to accompany Maria to the orphanage in order to select a child. Therefore, he asked me to go with her. The orphanage was in a very large modern building. One of the nuns gave us a tour of the building. We walked from one room to another and saw various groups of children of different ages. Finally, we came to a room in which the children were of ages three to four. All of them were on the floor playing with their toys. As we entered their room, all the children got up and transfixed Maria and me with their little eyes, because they were told, by the sisters, that their parents were looking for them. All of a sudden, one of the little girls ran toward Maria with open arms, embraced her leg, and shouted, "She is my mommy!" Soon, a little boy went to Maria and said to the little girl, "She is not your mommy, she is my mommy." In a moment, all the children surrounded Maria, and claimed that she was their mother. However, the smallest little girl, who was unable to compete with the others, stood at a distance from Maria; therefore, Maria went to her and picked her up and held her in her arms. Needless to say, at that very moment Maria decided to adopt the smallest child. On that day, the process of adoption began.

## 28. Sequel

My pleasant and eventful vacation came to an end the third week of September and it was time to return to the seminary for the second academic year of theology. On the way back to Sandomierz, I read a number of books on the ancient history of Greek and Roman art, which Jozef and Maria gave me.

Our classes began at the end of September. At the same time, myself and another student in our class enrolled in the master's degree program at the Jagiellonian University in Cracow. The Reverend Dr. Wincenty Granat, professor of systematic theology, who had doctorates both in philosophy and theology, was our adviser. The master's degree program entailed extra study and research. After submitting to my adviser a topic and an outline of my dissertation, I began to spend much time in our extensive library.

Following a silent retreat for three days, all members of my class received clerical tonsure and two minor orders from Bishop Lorek on November 18, 1948. In the middle of December, we began to study for our semester examination. After the exams, we began Christmas vacation. During the second part of the vacation, Father Budzinski asked me to teach his religion classes in public schools in Sulislawice and Gieraszowice. The students were very receptive so I greatly enjoyed instructing them. At the same time, I had the privilege of associating with my former teachers.

At the end of January, I went back to the seminary. I was happy to return to the academic atmosphere of the seminary, to complete the second semester and continue working on my dissertation. Before Easter, the rector of the seminary, Father Szymanski, sent two of us to Holy Family Church, in the diocese of Przemyśl, to assist its pastor in his services during Holy Week and Easter. The pastor received us with open arms and treated us as if we were his younger brothers. He provided us with the most enriching pastoral experiences and his personal friendship. On Easter Monday, we returned to the seminary, gave our dear rector an account of our experiences, and thanked him for the assignment. On May 22, nine deacons completed their fifth year of theology and were ordained to the priesthood. This was the first class ordained to the priesthood since the end of World War II. Therefore there was a great joy not only in the seminary but also in the whole diocese. Since many priests died at the hands of the Nazis, there was a great need for young priests in many parishes. One of the newly ordained priests was Father Marian Lucima, who during my time in the seminary, served as *Magister Ordinis*— Master of Order. His responsibility was to see to it that physical aspects of the seminary functioned in an orderly fashion. Two days before Father Lucima's ordination, the seminary's faculty appointed me to his vacant position. Following our semester examinations toward the end of May, our summer vacation began. I spent my vacation in my home parish preparing children for their First Holy Communion.

My class at our seminary campus at the end of my first year of theology in 1948. Out of 35 in the class at the beginning of the academic year only 26 of us remained. Out of 26 only 21 of us were ordained priests four years later. Author's photograph.

I returned to the seminary at the end of September 1949 in order to begin my third year of theology. In addition to regular theological subjects, our third year class began to attend seminars in the field of church architecture and conservation of ancient sacred art in which our city and the diocese abounded. Our seminars began at the Romanesque St. James Church, which was constructed in the thirteenth century. We then moved to the Nativity of the Blessed Virgin Mary Cathedral Church, build in the Gothic style around 1360. From there, we went to the Baroque St. Joseph's Church constructed by the Reformed Franciscans in 1672. Finally, we studied St. Michael's Church constructed in the Baroque style for the benefit of Benedictine Sisters from 1686 to 1692. The church is situated on the seminary campus.

In the last week before Christmas, I took my semester examinations and left the seminary for a well-deserved winter vacation. During this vacation, Father Budzinski asked me to take his place at the pulpit several times. I felt honored to preach in my home parish.

After returning to the seminary at the end of January 1950, I continued my studies. At the same time I worked on my dissertation. In the early spring I completed my work and submitted my dissertation to the Reverend Dr.

## 28. Sequel

Ignacy Rozycki at the Jagiellonian University in Cracow. Toward the end of the second semester, I received a letter from the dean of the School of Theology in which he advised me that my dissertation had been accepted and that I should prepare myself for the comprehensive examinations in the early fall of 1950. The dean's letter made me excited and happy. As soon as my final examinations at the end of the third year of theology were over, I began to study for my master's comprehensive examinations in philosophy and theology.

Again at the end of September, I was back in the seminary to start my fourth year of theology and to complete my master's degree. When all the seminarians returned from summer vacation, I discovered that the number of my classmates decreased to twenty-one. Unless something unexpected happens, I imagined all twenty-one of us would become priests. We all felt a calling to the priesthood, had good motivation, and a desire to go on. In the second part of October, I took my comprehensive examination for my master's degree at the Jagiellonian University. Dr. Rozycki was very strict and demanding. I passed the exam in theology but failed in philosophy. He rescheduled my philosophy examination for January 1951. Shortly before Christmas, my seminary class received the order of Subdeacon, which was considered, at that time, the first major order in the Catholic Church.

I spent my Christmas vacation helping a priest who suffered from poor health. He celebrated all the masses and I preached all the sermons. During the week days, I studied the philosophy of Plato and Aristotle in preparation for my examination with Dr. Rozycki. Before Christmas vacation ended, I met with him and pasted the examination. This time, he was very friendly and kind and congratulated me on my successful answers to his questions. I was elated and thanked God for my achievements. I was eager to return to the seminary to share my experiences with my superiors and classmates.

The second semester of my fourth year of theology began promptly. The time was going fast. At the end of the season of Lent, our class had a weeklong retreat before receiving the Order of Diaconate. When Easter came, two of us from my class were assigned to a large parish to preach and assist in Holy Week ceremonies. This assignment forced us to prepare sermons in a short time. After we returned to the seminary, we began to prepare ourselves for the final exams for the fourth year. My exams went very well. At the end of May, I returned to my home parish where I spent some time with my family and considerable time working in the parish under the gentle guidance of Father Budzinski.

At the end of my vacation, I returned to the seminary for the fifth and the final year of my theological studies there. The official opening of the academic year 1951-52 took place in one of the lecture halls where all the semi-

**With Polish Mountaineers, the "Gorale." The regional outfits are men's Sunday best suits. The picture was taken at Nowe Bystre during Archbishop Baziak's visitation of the local parish in August 1951. Author's photograph.**

narians and the faculty members gathered together. Due to increased persecution of the church in the final two years of Stalin's life, a cloud of uncertainty marred our inauguration. A number of theological seminaries were already closed by the Communist authorities and we did not know which seminary would be closed next.

When Bishop Jan Kanty Lorek entered the lecture hall, all of us stood to express our respect for his office and his person. He was accompanied by our rector, Father Adam Szymanski, and Father Antoni Kasprzycki, formally a professor of music and also an apostolic administrator of our diocese. All three of them were in a serious frame of mind. Bishop Lorek led us in an opening prayer and in his short speech warned us against a spirit of discouragement and apathy and encouraged us to go on with our studies and to put our future in the hands of God. I do not remember what else the bishop said. What I remember most were the words of Father Kasprzycki, who was the oldest priest in the diocese. In his short speech, he asked his audience to pray often with three prayers in Latin: "*Domine, adauge nobis fidem*" (Lord, increase our faith), "*Domine, salva nos, perimus!*" (Lord, save us, we are perishing!) and "*Salvator mundi, salva Russiam!*" (Savior of the world, save Russia!). Father Kasprzycki knew of the faith of the Russian people before the revolution and

Members of the fifth year theology class on the seminary campus in Sandomierz, Poland. From left to right are Fathers Waclaw Krzysztofik, Jerzy Smerda, Mieczyslaw Krajewski, Marian S. Mazgaj, and Stanislaw Wroclawski in May 1952. Author's photograph.

earnestly sought their salvation. In spite of Stalin's persecution, our classes began the following day and continued without interruption.

During Christmas vacation, I served as a deacon at Holy Trinity Church, a large parish in Starachowice. I returned from there to the seminary in the middle of January 1952 for the second and the final semester of my studies before my priestly ordination. The ordination to the priesthood for members of our class was scheduled for Sunday, May 25, 1952.

Since Father Budzinski opted for a larger parish, Father Tadeusz Switek became our new pastor in Sulislawice. After meeting with him we scheduled my first solemn mass in my home parish for the second day of the feast of Pentecost on June 2.

During the final exams, I did very well. Once the exams were over, I kept practicing the ritual of the celebration of mass with my classmate, Henryk Michalek. Both of us had a good memory and had no trouble memorizing the Latin texts for certain sections of the mass.

One week before ordination to the priesthood, our class began a silent retreat. At the end of the retreat, we all went to confession and asked God that we might receive Holy Orders with pure and holy intentions. I felt good about becoming a priest. My scruples about being unworthy and unfit for the priesthood on account of my military activities during the war ceased to a large extent. I felt that by serving Christ and the Catholic Church, I would have a chance to expiate for my sins, especially for killing Nazis during the war. I spent much time in the chapel reflecting on my life. My prayer life was good and I had a very warm relationship with my Maker.

Our weeklong retreat ended on Saturday afternoon. On the same afternoon, all of the deacons had to go to the rector's suite to take the profession of faith prescribed by canon law. I spent the evening in prayer and concentration and then packed my suitcase for my trip to Czestochowa. All of us in our class decided to go to Czestochowa to offer our very first masses at the chapel of Our Lady.

On the day of ordination, all of the seminarians — numbering, at that time, 150 men — marched two by two to the Cathedral Church for the ordination ceremonies and mass. Since Bishop Lorek was ill, his assistant, Bishop Franciszek Jop, was asked to take his place in performing the rite of ordination and in celebrating mass. As we entered the cathedral by the side door and walked to the sacristy, we became aware that the church was packed with our families and friends. After we were vested we joined a procession to the altar, and I noticed, in the crowd of people, my parents, brothers and sisters, relatives and friends. They were all happy and smiling when they noticed me in the procession.

As soon as we arrived in the sanctuary, the ordination mass began. Following some preliminary prayers, the rite of ordination started to unfold. Before the All Saints Litany began, all of us to be ordained prostrated ourselves on the floor of the sanctuary and remained there during the chanting of the litany. When the chanting of the litany ended, Bishop Jop robed us in our priestly vestments, anointed the palms of our hands, handed us chalice, paten, wine, and water for celebration of the mass, baptismal water, and the book of the Gospels. Then he laid his hands on our heads individually and pronounced the sacred words of priestly ordination: *"Accipe Spiritum Sanctum, quorum remiseris peccata, remittuntur eis; et quorum retinueris, retenta sunt"* (Receive the Holy Spirit, whose sins you shall forgive, shall be forgiven; and whose sins you shall retain shall be retained). From the Offertory on, we joined Bishop Jop at the altar as concelebrants of the mass. At the end of the mass, all twenty-one of us newly-ordained priests blessed the clergy and the people in the church. After the ordination mass, all of us and our visitors went to the seminary, where we spent the rest of the day with our dear ones. After our guests left, Father Stanislaw Legiec, our scripture professor, asked me to be the celebrant of the evening May Service at St. Michael's Church, which was well attended on Sundays. After the service, Father Legiec came to the sacristy, where I was taking off my vestments, and told me hat he was very happy because I conducted the service according to the ritual. In the evening of our ordination Sunday, all of us new priests took a train to Czestochowa.

We traveled all night and arrived in Czestochowa early in the morning of the following day. We had reservations in the monastery for one day and night and also in the chapel of Our Lady to offer twenty-one masses. At that time, concelebrated masses were not in style with the exception of priestly ordination masses. We said our masses in alphabetical order: Father Eugeniusz Cieslik was the first and Father Stanislaw Wroclawski was the last. Those of us in the middle heard pilgrims' confessions until our time came to say the mass. My celebration of mass in the chapel dedicated to the Mother of Christ, the Blessed Virgin Mary, made a very profound impression on me. The eyes of her image were on me when I asked her to pray to her Son that I might be a good and holy priest all my life.

For most of us, our visit to the national shrine at the Bright Mountain in Czestochowa was our first. We read about the shrine and its miraculous defense against the Swedish attack, in the middle of seventeenth century, in the Polish classic *The Flood*, written by Nobel Prize writer Henryk Sienkiewicz. At that time, the whole country was occupied by the Swedish army and the Pauline Monastery on the Bright Mountain (Jasna Gora) was like an island, which the Swedes were unable to conquer. The miraculous defense of the monastery by its heroic prior, Stefan Kordecki, and a handful of brave knights inspired the nation to take up arms against the enemy and liberate the country. On account of this miracle, Polish king Jan Kazimierz declared the Blessed Virgin Mary to be the Queen of the Polish Crown.

After spending a restful night at the monastery, we returned to the seminary to retrieve our books and clothing and return to our families in order to get ready for our first solemn masses in our home parishes the following Sunday.

On the second day of Pentecost, June 2, 1952, every one in our home was up early to prepare for the celebration of my first solemn mass. Shortly after breakfast, Monsignor Tomasz Gunia and Father Eugeniusz Cieslik arrived. Monsignor Gunia was my prefect at the Jan Tarnowski Gymnasium in Tarnobrzeg and Father Cieslik my seminary classmate. Soon a group of children and adults came into our farmyard. Little girls and young ladies were dressed in white gowns with wreaths of white flowers on their heads and flower petals in their baskets. A group of twenty-five young men rode in on their horses under the leadership of my first cousin, Jan Mazgaj. I was amazed at this gathering because I did not expect such an expression of love and respect, and I began to realize that Father Switek and some of the parishioners

Relatives, friends, and neighbors pose with me after my first solemn mass on June 2, 1952. The picture was taken at our orchard in Jeziory. Author's photograph.

organized the entire celebration. Before a procession started on the way to the church, the visiting priests and I put on our surplices and stoles. Then a group of young ladies with a long wreath of flowers surrounded us, so we were encircled both by the wreath and the young ladies. As the procession started, the little girls went before us and from time to time turned toward us to put flower petals on our path. The young men on horses led the procession. I felt so humble and so unworthy. I prayed to God that He might forgive me all my sins and make me worthy of my priestly calling. As the procession reached the gate of the churchyard, it was halted by a large group of people under the leadership of Father Switek, who was vested in his liturgical garments and surrounded by altar boys. As we stopped there, the priest gave a short speech in which he invited me to the church for the celebration of my first solemn mass. The church organist also spoke and, in the name of the parishioners, he too asked me to enter the church. As we entered our large Gothic church, I noticed that it was overcrowded. Near the altar there were priests from our deanery and Father Julian Jarzyna, who was my Latin professor in the seminary and the preacher for the solemn mass. My parents, brothers, and sisters were also near the altar. After getting vested in the sacristy, I went to the altar with Monsignor Gunia, who was to assist and guide me in the proper celebration of mass in Latin. I felt inspired and relaxed at the altar while reciting and chanting Latin prayers. My voice was clear and resounded throughout the church. This gave me a great degree of confidence in celebrating my first high mass. Soon, Father Jarzyna ascended the pulpit and delivered a fine sermon. After the sermon and the Apostles' Creed, the celebration proceeded through the Offertory, the Canon, and the Holy Communion to its conclusion. After the mass was over, I blessed the people by laying my hands on their heads: first the priests, the members of my family and my relatives, and then everybody in the church. At the same time, my brother Klemens distributed small holy pictures as a memento of my ordination and the first solemn mass. Secret agents of the State Security Police were among the people observing everything that I did and said. However, they were intimidated by a spontaneous love of the people for a newly ordained priest. As soon as I finished blessing the people, I went to the rectory where all the priests who attended the mass were gathered together in the dining room. Father Switek asked me to sit at the head of the table and to give a speech. While standing, I spoke off the cuff. I thanked the priests for honoring my priesthood with their presence and told them that their good example helped me on the way to the altar of God and asked them to pray that I might make a good priest. I also expressed my gratitude to my parents, to Bishop Lorek and Bishop Jop, to the rector and the faculty of the seminary, in particular to Father Jarzyna, to Monsignor Gunia, and to Father Cieslik for making this celebration possible. At the end of my short speech, I thanked Father Switek for organizing so well my first solemn mass. As a token of my gratitude to him and to the parish, I offered, in honor of Our Lady of Sulislawice, a set of my priestly vestments, which I wore during my first solemn mass and which my aunt Antonina Mazgaj from Lackawanna, New York, gave me as a present for my ordination. Then I invited all the priests present there to an abundant dinner served under the fruit trees in our orchard.

The priests were given places of honor at the dinner tables. In addition to the priests, our relatives and the people of our village came to the dinner. All of them brought food and presents. I did not realize until that moment how sensitive and loving toward our family were our relatives, friends, and neighbors.

Toward the end of the week, I traveled to Julianow to preach at Father Cieslik's first solemn mass at his home parish church in Tarlow. I had the privilege of meeting his pastor and many members of his family. Then I returned home to wait for my priestly assignment. In the meantime, Father Jan Madejski from Osiek invited me to offer solemn mass in St. Stanislaus Church for the benefit of his parishioners who were unable to attend my mass in Sulislawice. Since I was born in the parish of Osiek, baptized in its church, and received my First Holy Communion there, I accepted the invitation and celebrated my second solemn mass, which was very well attended. I offered the mass for all the living and deceased members of my immediate family, relatives, friends, and especially for the soul of my mother, who was buried at the local cemetery.

After returning home in Jeziory, I received Bishop Lorek's temporary assignment at the parish of Wisniowa where the pastor, Father Stanislaw Dylo, became seriously ill and was hospitalized. Needless to say, I enjoyed this short ministry because the parishioners were very kind and loving toward me and supplied the rectory with a variety of food. During this short ministry, one of the parishioners took me to the nearby Sataszow Forest and showed me a mass grave in which the Nazis buried an entire wedding party. He told me that he happened to be in the forest when a group of uniformed Nazis and their victims arrived at a clearing and witnessed the execution of the newly wedded couple, their relatives, and the wedding guests.

At the end of June, Father Dylo returned from the hospital and was able

**This picture was taken in the early spring of 1952 during our assignment to All Saints Parish in Starachowice. From left to right are Fathers Ludwik Skrok, Henryk Kiemona, Stefan Rola (Pastor), Zygmunt Lewinski, and myself. Author's photograph.**

to continue his work in the parish. At the same time, Bishop Lorek assigned me to the parish of Krynki, near the city of Starachowice, as an assistant pastor and instructor of religion in the local schools. Our neighbor, Walenty Stefaniak, hurried to finish constructing a large bookcase so I could take it to my new assignment. After kissing everyone in my family good-bye, my father took me to the railroad station in Nadbrzezie, near Sandomierz. Before boarding the train, I kissed my father's hand and received his customary blessing and we hugged and kissed each other on both cheeks. Both of us had tears in our eyes as we parted. Soon I was on the way to my new assignment. On the way, I recited my breviary in Latin and prayed for God's blessing in my new experiences as a parish priest and instructor.

I arrived at the railroad station in Krynki about 9:00 P.M. and left my heavy luggage for safekeeping at the station and walked to the rectory with a light suitcase. Father Wladyslaw Dzubek invited me to the rectory and offered me a guest room for the night. In the morning after we offered our masses in the church and had breakfast, Father Dzubek asked a sexton to transport my belongings from the station to my apartment, which was in a parish house near the church. I felt quite comfortable in my new residence, which had a kitchen, a living room, and a bedroom. After a brief conference with my pastor, I became aware that the people of the parish were in a state of rebellion against the pastor and the bishop for the removal of my predecessor, Father Jozef Janicki, whom everybody loved. The parishioners wanted the bishop to remove Father Dzubek and make Father Janicki their pastor. Bishop Lorek refused to do so and transferred Father Janicki to another parish as an assistant pastor.

In order to gauge the sentiments of the people in the town of Krinki, I took a long walk through the town and became acquainted with scores of children who were playing on the street and in their yards. Soon many children followed me in my walk and introduced me to their parents and grandparents. One of the grandparents I was introduced to was Antoni Galka, who happened to be my father's friend and comrade-in-arms in World War I. At that time, both of them were soldiers in the Russian Imperial Army. When I was returning to my apartment, many children followed me. I showed them my residence, and then took them to the church for a short prayer and an explanation of sacred symbols and holy images. This walk through the town and meeting children and adults was extremely fruitful in my public relations. The following Sunday, which was the sixth Sunday after Pentecost, instead of boycotting my appointment by not attending the services, a great number of parishioners attended the masses.

Following Father Dzubek's resignation in September 1952, Father Michal Koziol, who formally served as an instructor of religion in Radom, became my new pastor. From the very beginning of his ministry in Krynki, he and I worked harmoniously and became good friends. When public schools reopened in the beginning of September, I rose at 5:00 A.M., said the early mass, ate early breakfast at the rectory, and was on the way to a different school every day. There were eight grade schools in various villages of the parish. Therefore, two days of every week I was teaching in one school in the morning and at another in the afternoon. Since the children, under the Communist regime, were hungry for Christ's teachings, it was such a joy to teach them. Not only did they never tire me, they energized me. After returning to my apartment late in the afternoon, I still had enough energy to work on my dissertation for a doctorate in theology at the Jagiellonian University in Cracow.

On Sundays, before and after the high mass, groups of young people visited me at my apartment to ask questions and to borrow books from my library. In one of the groups there was a young lady who had survived mass execution by Nazi SS-men when most of the people in her village had been buried in a mass grave. After the Nazi executioners left, some of those who arrived at the scene of the mass murder noticed that dirt in one section of the

With some of my seventh grade students in one of the public schools in the parish of Krynki near Starachowice, where I served as a religion instructor. Author's photograph.

grave was moving. They immediately removed the dirt with their hands and uncovered the young lady, who was wounded on the side of her chest but still alive. When I met her for the first time, she was engaged to be married. She was attractive and humble, and her eyes seemed to look beyond this visible world.

Although I enjoyed my assignment as a parish priest and expected to stay there for a number of years, Bishop Lorek transferred me, in the beginning of June, to the diocesan seminary in Sandomierz, which I left as a newly ordained priest only one year before. This happened because Father Stefan Siedlecki, who was one of the professors of philosophy and an administrator of the seminary, was arrested by the Communist Secret Security Police and imprisoned. At the recommendation of the rector of the seminary, the bishop appointed me pro tempore to Father Siedlecki's administrative position. I gladly accepted my new assignment because the intellectual atmosphere of the seminary was conducive to my doctoral studies at the Jagiellonian University. I had the use of the seminary's library and an opportunity to associate with my former professors, who were very intelligent and highly educated priests.

From the first day of my work in the seminary, I developed a daily schedule. My alarm clock rang at 5:00 A.M. At 5:30 A.M. I was at St. Michael's Church (the seminary church) to recite morning prayers and to meditate on the scriptures for a given day. At 6:00 A.M. I opened the church so some people from the street could enter to pray or go to confession. At that time, I was already in the confessional, near the main door of the church, to make it easy on the penitents. Many students from the dormitories of the neighboring State Teachers' College, who were indoctrinated with the philosophy of dialectical materialism, used to come to pray and go to confession very early. They performed their religious practices as an antidote to Communist indoctrination. At 7:00 A.M., I celebrated mass for the early risers. Shortly after mass, I had breakfast in the faculty dinning room. After breakfast, I gave instructions to my secretary and other seminary workers. Most of the hours before lunch I spent in the office. After lunch, I joined the seminary priests for a long walk outside the city. In the afternoon, I studied moral theology in preparation for my comprehensive doctoral examination. In order not to loose touch with pastoral ministry, I visited the patients at Holy Ghost Hospital for an hour before dinner. After dinner on Saturdays, Father Wojcik, professor of canon law, used to come to my apartment in order to prepare our Sunday sermons. After reading the scriptures assigned for a given Sunday, we paced the apartment floor and brainstormed the best possible ideas. Usually, it took us about one hour to come up with a solid outline of a sermon. This method worked quite well for us. We celebrated Sunday masses and preached in different churches in Sandomierz. At the end of each day, I was accustomed to go to the seminary church and, in its contemplative atmosphere, review my activities for that given day and plan my activities for the following day. I also thanked God for the day just ended and asked for His blessings for the day to come.

Although, I was attracted more to teaching than to administration, I worked effectively in administration, with the hope that Father Siedlecki would be released from prison so I could dedicate my life to teaching. During the early months of my work in the seminary, I completed my doctoral dissertation and submitted copies to the dean of the School of Theology at the Jagiellonian University. After my dissertation was accepted by the university, I began preparing myself for the comprehensive exams. During three years of my administrative work in the seminary, agents of the Communist regime attempted to undermine the institution on numerous occasions. First of all, they attempted to control our finances. They seized by force a very modern seminary's college building, then they imposed on the seminary exorbitant and illegal taxes; they also prohibited the seminary to buy food and gasoline. Finally, they attempted to infiltrate the seminary with their informers and secret agents. At the same time, they terrorized the faculty with arrests and interrogations. I was personally interrogated for hours and threatened with punishment for being a soldier of the Home Army during World War II. In spite of all these difficulties and personal threats, I was determined to keep the seminary open as long as possible. At times, I felt that I would follow Father Siedlecki to a Communist prison.

In the summer of 1954, the university notified me that my doctoral comprehensive examination was scheduled for September 29. I kept studying every day in preparation for that date. The more I studied the more confidence I had that I would successfully pass my exams. On September 28, I arrived in Cracow and found accommodations at the Franciscan Monastery near the university. My exams were scheduled for 8:00 A.M., the following day. I was up early that day, celebrated mass at the Franciscan Church, had a light breakfast, and walked to the university. As I entered the building where my exams were to take place, I met a small group of priests and a layman near the office of the dean of the School of Theology. All of them were doctoral candidates whose examinations were scheduled on the same day as mine. One of the priests was a Jesuit. He was a superior of the Jesuit House in Radom. The priests were middle aged and older. I was the youngest in the group. The Jesuit superior and I worked in the same diocese but never met before. Our examinations began and lasted until noon. In the beginning I was rather tense but eventually I relaxed and felt confident. Professors, who were my examiners, congratulated me on my successful answers and wished me well. I was elated and humbled at the same time and thanked God for His help. After our graduation at 4:00 P.M. on the same day, I thanked the rector (president) of the Jagiellonian University, Dr. Mieczyslaw Klimaszewski, the dean of the School of Theology, Dr. Tadeusz Kruszynski, and Dr. Wladyslaw Wicher, the professor of moral theology under whose supervision I wrote my doctoral dissertation. Finally, I thanked my examiners and then returned to the Franciscan Monastery. The following morning after celebrating an early morning mass, I had breakfast with Bishop Franciszek Jop at his official residence, and then took the first train to Sandomierz to share my good news and joy with Bishop Lorek, Father Szymanski, Father Granat, my family, and friends.

After returning to the seminary, I visited the rector and told him about my experiences at the university. Then I showed him the certificate of my graduation. He read it, looked at me, and said: "Son, your doctorate in theology is just the beginning of your deeper studies. Be humble and you will be learning all your life." He congratulated me and encouraged me to continue my theological studies. From the rector's apartment I went to see Bishop Lorek. He was very pleased with my graduation and glad to hear of my visit with his former assistant, Bishop Jop. After reading my graduation certificate, Bishop Lorek smiled, congratulated me, and expressed hope that I would use my degree well. Father Granat, who encouraged me to begin my graduate studies in theology and assisted me in its initial stages, advised me to prepare myself by writing a special dissertation in moral theology, which would enable me to obtain a teaching position at the newly created Academy of Theology in Laski, near Warsaw. Father Piotr Golebiowski asked me to assist him in the examination of his students in moral theology.

A few days before Christmas of 1955, Bishop Lorek suggested that I take a Christmas vacation in Zakopane, which was located in the heart of the Carpathian Mountains. On account of abundant of snowfall, skiing flourishes there. He arranged my accommodations and gave me spending money. I was surprised and extremely moved by his paternal attitude. The following day, I packed my suitcase, waxed my skis, and took a train to Zakopane. In the villa, where I had a room, I met a priest, Professor Swiezawski and his family from Cracow. We became friends and spent much time together. Dr. Swiezawski, a professor of philosophy, was employed by the Catholic University of Lublin. From time to time I listened to his explanations of philosophical problems and asked him questions. He recognized my interest in philosophy and encouraged me to enroll in his Graduate School of Philosophy. At the same time, he told me that a priest from Cracow, who taught Christian ethics in his school, would be glad to meet with me to explain how graduate study of philosophy would buttress my theology. He offered to make me an appointment with the priest, whose name was Father Karol Wojtyla. I gladly accepted the offer and met with Father Wojtyla in his university office. We had a very lovely conversation and exchange of ideas about Christian ethics and moral theology. I explained to him my intention to enroll in the Graduate School of Canon Law and eventually to study philosophy on the graduate level. At that time, neither I nor anybody else could have imagined that Father Wojtyla would become Pope John Paul II.

Another guest at our villa was Jerzy Zawiejski, a well-known playwright from Warsaw, with whom I also spent much time visiting various points of interest in the area of Zakopane. He and the other guests attended daily mass, which I offered at the local convent's chapel. During our meals, which we received in the convent's dining room, we always had long intellectual conversations about religion, literature, philosophy, and art. During one of our long walks, Mr. Zawiejski and I visited a historic house in which the founder of Russian communism, Vladimir Ilich Lenin (1870–1924), hid from the Russian police after the unsuccessful Russian Revolution of 1905. In this historic home a series of meetings took place between Lenin and Brother Albert, whose real name was Adam Hilary Bernard Chmielowski (1846–1916). Both of them were social reformers. Lenin was a Communist reformer and Brother Albert a Christian reformer in the spirit of St. Francis of Assisi. And both of them tried to convert one another to their modus operandi. In the final discussion, Lenin lost his temper and shouted on the top of his voice: "The world will belong to us, Communists! But if we fail, it will belong to your Franciscan Christianity."

When my winter vacation ended in January 1956, I returned to the seminary refreshed not only physically but also intellectually and spiritually. I was ready to meet the challenges of 1956. Soon, our seminarians returned from Christmas vacation and I resumed my regular activities: working in the office, teaching a few classes in the Minor Seminary, and preaching on Sundays. As we entered 1956, we could feel an air of change and hope all around us. The Communist authorities appeared to be less hostile toward the Catholic Church. The people, in general, became more outspoken in their criticism of communism as a philosophical and economic system. The agents of the Public Security Police pretended that they did not hear such criticism. They began to take the side of their own people against Soviet communism. Certainly Nikita Khrushchev's famous speech to the Twentieth Party Congress, delivered on February 16, 1956, in which he condemned Stalin and his crimes against humanity, had something to do with these changes.

A few weeks before Easter, Father Siedlecki was released from prison. As soon as he visited Bishop Lorek, he was asked to resign his position and my position was upgraded from interim to permanent administrator. I was disappointed because I hoped that Father Siedlecki would resume his duties and I could continue my postdoctoral studies in moral theology. I prayerfully decided to resign my position and to ask the bishop to allow me to begin my postdoctoral studies at the Catholic University of Lublin. When I asked the bishop to let me resign, he was not happy about it and said that he needed time to consider my request. After I left the bishop's residence, I ran into Father Granat and asked him to speak to the bishop in support of my resignation and my postdoctoral studies. He did so and during my next visit to the bishop's residence, he accepted my resignation and let me continue my studies. Soon I went to Lublin and made arrangement for my studies. In the meantime, I went to Gdynia, found accommodations at the Franciscan Monastery, helped somewhat in the parish ministry, and spent most of the summer on the Baltic Sea shore.

In the early part of September, I went to Lublin to begin my studies. Since there were no provisions for postdoctoral studies at the Catholic University, I decided to enroll in the graduate school of canon law. Moral theology and canon law had a considerable affinity at that time. All the students of canon law were priests from various parts of Poland. Our professors were experts in various fields such as the history of ancient Roman jurisprudence and its sources and institutions, Polish law and its codifications, the history of canon law and various parts of the Code of Canon Law (*Codex Juris Canonici*). All of us had to study the German language from a very personable professor, who was born in Germany. I also had to take English, taught by a very competent professor. I lived at the dormitory for priests near the university library and had fantastic conditions for academic work. I hoped that in three years I would be able to earn my second doctorate.

My studies were interrupted briefly by the Polish October Revolution, which began on October 19, 1956, and ended the following day. During this time, Polish Communists replaced Russian Communists in the Polish government in Warsaw. Due to this transition, Cardinal Stefan Wyszynski, the primate of the church of Poland, and a number of bishops and priests were released from Communist prisons. During this time I joined a group of young priests who applied for passports to the United States. We were pleasantly surprised when our applications were approved and we received our passports. As soon as I received my passport, I wrote to my uncle Anthony Mazgaj in Lackawanna, New York, who had sponsored my visit to the United States of America. Soon I received my visa from the American embassy in Warsaw. After completing my first semester of canon law studies with good results, I began the second semester in January 1957. At the same time I taught classes in religion in the Teachers' College in Radom. I was working hard and the time went fast. At the end of the second semester, I took my final examinations and received good grades in all my courses. The professors in each field of my studies entered my grades in my university student book, which

**With children at their first Holy Communion breakfast at St. John the Baptist Church in Radom, Poland, in May 1957. Author's photograph.**

I always carried on me. Then I traveled to Sandomierz to visit with Bishop Lorek and to obtain his blessing and recommendations to the bishops in the United Sates. Finally, I went to Jeziory to visit with my dear family and to receive my parents' blessing. However, for security reasons, only Bishop Lorek and my parents knew about my trip to the United States. While saying goodbye to my dear parents, all three of us had tears in our eyes. As usual I kissed my parents' hands and cheeks and we hugged. I also kissed and hugged my brothers and sisters. Then I returned to Sandomierz.

On June 20, 1957, I took a bus to the railroad station in Nadbrzezie where I boarded a train for Warsaw. After reaching Warsaw, I took a taxi to the Clergy Hotel, where I spent my last night before going to the United States. On June 21, I got up early in the morning. The weather in Warsaw was beautiful. In spite of communism in Poland, the city of Warsaw was preparing to celebrate the traditional feast of Corpus Christi *(Swieto Bozego Ciala)*. Soon, the church bells began to peal in every section of the city. At the same time, colorful processions began to emerge from all the churches. The individual processions moved to the main avenue, where one mighty procession was being formed under the leadership of the primate, Cardinal Stefan Wyszynski. The large procession marked not only an expression of deep Christian faith but also a manifestation of Polish patriotism directed against the Russian rulers at the Kremlin, who still interfered in Polish affairs.

At first, I observed the great procession but when it came close to where I stood, I became a part of it and walked with my fellow Christians and sang processional hymns. While walking and singing with thousands of people, I experienced a great spiritual victory of Christ and His Church over communism and its slavery.

Late in the afternoon, I boarded a Polish LOT airliner and flew to Poznań, where I boarded a KLM turbojet en route to New York City. Only after the turbojet took off and crossed the Polish border, did I no longer fear the Communist Secret Security agents. In the morning of June 22, the KLM liner landed at the main airport in New York from which I traveled to La Guardia Airport in order to catch a flight to Buffalo, New York. As soon as the airliner landed at Buffalo, I walked to the airport building to claim my luggage and I noticed my uncle Anthony Mazgaj, waving to me from a distance. We recognized each other even though we had never met before. We warmly greeted each other and, after I claimed my suitcases, we were on the way to my uncle's home in Lackawanna, where I was offered a large guest room. At the same time, Uncle Anthony's sons, who operated Mazgaj's Supermarket, came to greet me. In the afternoon of the same day, my first cousin Max took me to the rectory of St. Michael's Church and introduced me to the pastor, Father Jankowski and his assistant Father Czechowicz. The following day, Father Jankowski took me to the

My uncle, Anthony Mazgaj, from Lackawanna, New York, who sponsored my immigration to the United States in 1957 and enabled me to continue my graduate studies at the Catholic University of America in Washington, D.C. Author's photograph.

bishop's office and introduced me to the bishop of Buffalo, who in turn granted me priestly jurisdiction in his diocese, which authorized me to celebrate masses, preach, hear confessions, and administer other sacraments. The pastor asked me to celebrate daily and Sunday masses at St. Michael's Church. All of these experiences made me feel that I was in my home environment again. Soon, I visited my Uncle Adam, who also lived in Lackawanna, a small city bordering Buffalo, and other relatives who lived in Buffalo and in Hamburg and other small towns near Buffalo. Most of them greeted me by saying, "You came just in time for the Fourth of July." At that time, I did not understand what they meant by the Fourth of July, but I soon discovered the meaning when Uncle Anthony and I were invited, by one of my cousins, to a Fourth of July picnic.

On the Fourth of July, the picnic was held at the spacious yard of Walter Kaminski's beach house on Lake Erie in Angola, New York. There were about sixty persons at the picnic. At that picnic, I became acquainted not only with most of my American relatives and their friends but also with the uniquely American food, hot dogs, hamburgers, ketchup, 7-Up, Coca-Cola, and Pepsi-Cola. When the meats had been cooked on the grill and all the other food ready, I was asked to bless the food, thank God for its abundance, but most of all for America's freedom and independence. The food and drinks were delicious and when everybody had enough to eat, ladies organized some games for children, men played horseshoes, and teenagers went swimming and boating. At the end of the day, men sat down and talked about things present and past. As they talked about their experiences in World War II, politics, work, life, and their hopes, I began to understand the meaning of the American celebration of the Fourth of July. Its meaning goes beyond the flying of the flag, having a day off from work, and enjoying a picnic with relatives and friends. It is a celebration of life by free, independent, self-reliant, industrious people who are ready to pay any price for their way of life. I was fortunate that I came to the United States just in time for the celebration of the Fourth of July, the Independence Day of 1957, during which some of its true meaning became obvious to me.

Following two months of vacation with my relatives in Lackawanna, my academic experiences followed one another in quick succession: Americanization school in Washington, D.C., where I studied the English language; Catonsville Community College in Maryland, where I learned English literature and American history; the Catholic University of America in Washington, D.C., where I earned my licentiate and doctorate in canon law and began graduate studies in philosophy; Duquesne University in Pittsburgh, Pennsylvania, where I continued my studies and earned a master's in philosophy and completed doctoral course work in the same field; St. John Vianney Major

Seminary in Bloomingdale, Ohio, where I taught moral theology and canon law for ten years; McKeesport and Fayette campuses of Pennsylvania State University, where I taught philosophy and humanities for nine years; and West Virginia Diocesan Studies where I taught theology for a number of years.

# 29. Epilogue

As I already mentioned, in chapter 26, my survival during World War II was a great and pleasant surprise to me, my family, and my friends. In the final months of fighting against various units of the Nazi evil empire, it was very difficult to survive from day to day. Each time I smelled the burning powder of my German MG42 machine gun, it smelled to me like death. In such moments, I cursed the war; not only World War II, but also any and all war and at any time in the history of humanity. I was convinced that a war with all its miserable consequences, especially the lost of human lives, was the most irrational way of solving disagreements between nations and between their leaders. In my teenaged mind, I attempted, many a time, to figure out why individuals and nations disagreed with each other and what was the ultimate basis for their disagreements. In spite of my numerous attempts, I was unable to come up with any plausible answer at that time in my life.

It took long years of formal studies in languages, philosophy, law, and theology and much deep reflection to secure a little gleam into the possible answer. It seems to me that one of the reasons why leaders of nations disagree with one another can be found, in most instances, in a linguistic perspective. By linguistic perspective, I mean the quality of various languages to name various objects, both concrete and abstract, and various experiences, from certain and unique perspectives that are usually different from the perspectives in other languages. For example, let us take an object, at which we sit to have our meals and which we call a "table." In the Greek language a table was named *trapeza,* which literally means four-footed bench. Therefore, the individual who named the table this way looked at it from the perspective of its four legs. The same object in the Latin language was named *mensa,* which has a very interesting perspective. As we know, the Romans did not eat at tables — they ate while lying on couches. However, their table was used for *measuring (mensura)* and cutting portions of food to be served in the dining

# 29. Epilogue

These photographs were taken during the blessing and dedication of a commemorative plaque of the Sandomierz Flying Commando Unit at St. Nicolaus Church in Loniow on September 26, 1999. The men in uniforms are veterans of the underground struggle with Nazism. Author's photograph.

room. The English word "table" is derived from the Latin term, *tabula*, which means a board; hence, the term boarding. In Polish and Russian, table has been named *stol* because it stands up (*stoji*); does not lay down and is not being moved from place to place. In the Latin and Slavic languages, table is seen from the perspective of measuring and standing upright in a permanent place. Let us take a "book" as another example. In Greek, book is called *biblos*, which means the inner bark of the papyrus. In the Latin language, *liber* means the inner bark of a tree. In the Anglo-Saxon languages, the word "book" comes from *booka*, which means beechwood tablets on which the preliterate ancestors recorded their history in pictures. In Polish, a "book" is called *ksiazka*. It appears that this name is derived from *ksiadz*— priest — or *ksiaze*— prince — because in the early times, a book was almost always the exclusive possession of a priest or a prince.

I must say, at this point, that not only individual words in various languages express different perspectives but also entire individual languages see things from radically different points of view. It appears to me that the initial and fundamental perspectives were influenced, if not created, by the geographical environments of various primordial linguistic groups. The presence or absence of mountains, rivers, lakes, seas, forests, meadows, and animals had a definite impact on the original perspectives of every language. Some of the sounds in nature and those made by animals gave rise to onomatopoeic words. The climate with its changing seasons also had something to do with linguistic perspectives. All these environmental factors are so rich in meaning that no single language can escape their impact in forming a special single perspective. If there were a divine language, such a language would be able to name things from all perspectives. Each language is limited to a single perspective.

Languages, with their unique perspectives, are the foundations of various cultures and civilizations. That is why cultures and civilization differ from one another. However, they complement each other because no particular culture and civilization has a monopoly on all phenomena of human inventiveness and creativity, both material and spiritual.

Various cultures and civilizations, which are based on the perspectives of their different languages, also gave rise to their unique religions. Therefore religions too have their own perspective from which they perceived, in their primitive stage of development, their polytheistic gods or, in their developed state, their monotheistic God. From the same perspectives, they see their encounter with the divine Being(s) and the fruits of this encounter.

The monument placed at the burial lot of the fallen members of the Jedrus Group at the parish cemetery in Sulislawice. Author's photograph.

# 29. Epilogue

In the early history of the human race and many centuries thereafter, various cultures and religions, which sprung from them, were separated from others by deserts, mountains, lakes, rivers, and seas. Therefore, in such isolation, they began to think of themselves as the only cultures, civilizations, and religions. At the same time, they became convinced that their way of life and worship and their answers to various questions were the most proper and correct ones.

Then, when they discovered other centers of culture, civilization, and religion, they considered them strange, improper, and barbarian. Of course, they were not sophisticated enough to realize that this new people, which they discovered, perceived the world from a different perspective and developed their culture, civilization, and religion accordingly. When the representatives of these two centers met, they tried to convince each other that their respective languages were the easiest to learn and their cultures and religions were the best. At that point, they disagreed with each other and began to argue about their respective differences. The arguing did not eliminate their disagreements. After a number of initial encounters, the leaders of both cultural centers began to fear that their way of life might be radically altered by the strangers. Therefore, the stronger of these two centers waited for a chance to neutralize or to eliminate the other by war.

In reviewing the history of humanity, we can easily discover that most of the wars, which took place in antiquity and in mediaeval, early modern, and our own times occurred mostly because of serious disagreements. These disagreements in turn occurred because the parties to the disagreement perceived things from different linguistic and cultural perspectives. Their biggest problem was that they did not know anything about the existence of such things. At the same time, both of the parties firmly believed that their own perspectives were the universal ones, while, in reality, they were partial, fragmentary, and one-sided because their other parts were in hundreds of different languages.

Something similar can be said about the existence of truth, which both of these parties of disagreements claimed. In most instances, truth is also based on their languages' perspectives. Unfortunately, the parties to the disagreements were ignorant of these facts and instead of learning, which is time-consuming, they preferred to solve their disagreements in the most primitive way, namely, by an irrational war.

I am led to believe that what I have written above applies partially to most of the leaders, the governments, and the peoples, that took part in World War II, because they were not quite aware as to why their disagreements occurred. Although two of the Western leaders were formally educated at great universities, it is possible that they did not know anything about the linguistic perspectives from which arise various cultures, civilizations, religions, philosophies, and political systems. The reason as to why they may not have known of these matters was because at that time the philosophers of language did not deal with these linguistic phenomena. Three of these leaders and some of their followers were fanatics, who had very little formal education and they would not even have granted a modicum of importance to such things as linguistic perspectives. They believed only in brute power. These three uneducated but street-wise and shrewd international criminals make me believe in Plato's advice, which he gave to his contemporaries in the *Republic*. He stated very emphatically that only true philosophers should be made kings and that those who are already kings ought to study philosophy.

If humanity is to avoid some of the serious misunderstandings that lead to international wars, the educational systems in every country should familiarize their students, on every level of instruction, with linguistic and cultural perspectives. It would also be very beneficial, in limiting misunderstandings, if the leaders of various nations and their advisers would become aware not only of the linguistic and cultural perspectives but also to learn the languages of their neighboring countries.

The popularization of the phenomenon of linguistic and cultural perspectives would lead humanity to the discovery that every nation's perspective, both linguistic and cultural, is unique, important, and as valuable as any other. This means that in the human family there are no supermen, super nations, and dominant languages. Each language, no matter how extensive it might be, has only one linguistic perspective. Some national and linguistic groups might be larger and culturally older than others but the importance of their perspectives are of equal value in the search for universal knowledge and truth. By a universal knowledge and truth I understand the knowledge and the truth obtained on the basis of all the linguistic perspectives known to humanity at a given time. I am not speaking here about mathematical truth but rather of the truth that continuously discloses itself in the light of education and new experiences and discoveries. It appears to me that as in the past history of humanity, so in the future, new languages will be born and their original perspectives will enrich the universal knowledge and truth of things, with which humanity has to deal continuously.

Present-day globalization, with its telephones, television, computers with the Internet and e-mail as well as air travel enable most of the nations of the world to discover, enrich, and appreciate linguistic and cultural perspectives of many other countries. These discoveries should enhance mutual understanding and friendship among various nations.

Another idea that may help to diminish international misunderstandings and wars is the realization that as is life in general (biosphere), so also human life, in particular, is closely interconnected. Therefore, as the partial destruction of the biosphere affects adversely the rest of life in general, so a partial destruction of the life of humanity impacts critically the entire human race. In other words, a partial destruction of the life of humanity brings about, in a way, an annihilation of a small part of every individual human being. Hence, when the soldiers of two opposing armies are killing each other, they are killing not only a part of humanity but also a part of themselves. In order to obscure realization of this truth, the propaganda of each army dehumanizes the soldiers of the opposing side by calling them enemies and other pejorative names. In the Civil War, for example, the soldiers of the Confederacy were dehumanized by Union propaganda in being called "Rebels." It was easier for the Union soldiers to kill the "Rebels" than to kill their fellow Americans and thus part of themselves. It was much easier for the American soldiers during World War II to kill the demonized "Nazis" than the German soldiers whose relatives inhabited parts of Pennsylvania and many other states of our country.

It seems to me that with the death, especially violent death, of every human being, a part of all of us human beings dies. At the same time, it appears to me that soldiers who kill others in war, those who consent to and those who bring about death of unborn infants, and those who kill others on their own authority impart into human nature a disregard for the sacredness of human life and an insensibility toward human suffering. Speaking about insensitivity toward human suffering reminds me of the training given to Hitler's SS troops. In preparation for the liquidation of the Jews during World War II, the Nazis established numerous educational centers, at which some of the SS troopers received insensitivity training by performing vivisection on rabbits. I am familiar with one of these centers, which was located in the former school of agriculture in Mokoszyn near the city of Sandomierz, Poland.

At the same time, no human being is insensitive and strong enough not to be adversely affected by killing others regardless of what they are branded by war propaganda. All war veterans who had returned from World War II, Korea, Vietnam, and Iraq needed extensive healing. One wonders whether the offspring of these veterans, conceived before their fathers and mothers had psychologically recovered, did not genetically inherit disorders stemming from combat experiences. After sixty years, I still dream of my combat activities and feel guilty at having killed uniformed enemies who attempted to kill our men. With the exception of pathological cases, normal men are not insensitive and strong enough to kill others. In creating us, the Creator did not mean for us to kill others. By killing others, we seem to usurp a prerogative that belongs exclusively to God, the giver of life.

If the killing of human beings brings about such horrible and disastrous

The western wing of the major Seminary of Sandomierz complex and the courtyard and the statue of the Good Shepherd; here the author spent five years studying theology and three years working in administration. Author's photograph.

consequences for humanity, educators in all nations should find space in their schools' curricula to discuss these issues. At the same time, the curricula should include a discussion of the lives and achievements of peacemakers throughout history as well the work of important teachers, defenders of human freedom, healers (physicians), discoverers, inventors and scientists, who by their work enhanced the progress and welfare of mankind everywhere. Furthermore, in discussions in world history, educators must avoid imparting misplaced admiration and glorification for warlords, who became more or less remembered and praised in proportion to the numbers of human lives they had extinguished in war. At the same time, educators should never fail to encourage their students to honor and respect national leaders and heroes who were instrumental in bringing freedom, peace, and prosperity to their peoples.

In spite of our painful experiences with wars, at the beginning of the twenty-first century, I strongly believe that humanity is at the threshold of a peaceful era in its history. I base my optimism on the fact that due to today's state-of-the-art communications technology, the educational level of all nations is rising. A broadminded education promotes democracy and helps to put an end to pathologically fanatical dictatorships. Democratically chosen and well-educated leaders of nations are aware of linguistic, cultural, and religious perspectives of other nations and they will be able to rationally, justly, and peacefully resolve their differences. However, as in the recent past, so too in the future it may happen that pathologically fanatical leaders of certain countries will appear on the international scene and disregard the use of reason and ignore truth and justice. In such cases, the old Roman proverb, *Si vis pacem, para bellum* (If you want peace, prepare for war), should be applicable. In this kind of a predicament, all democratically governed nations should have enough economic and military power to be able to neutralize the bellicose powers among them. As it is hoped that democratic forms of government will eventually be established all over the world, so too occasions will arise for the appearance of dictatorships.

In my lifetime, a number of very intelligent, capable and wise women have been elected to very important governmental positions and as leaders of nations. To my best knowledge, they all performed their duties with honor and distinction. As women and as mothers, they received from God the gift of the maternal instinct in giving, preserving, and saving human life. Their growing numbers in the leadership of various countries is for me a sign of a well-founded hope that they, as women and mothers, will become God's instruments of peace and will act as peacemakers in our times.

The example set by the countries of Europe that are now uniting, countries that used to wage wars against each other every few decades and that are now opening their borders to neighboring nations and are using a common market and a common currency, is another reason for my optimism that humankind can achieve universal peace and make wars obsolete in this new century. The Spanish people support, confirm, and express this optimism, which now exists strongly in contemporary Europe, in their proverbial saying, "*No queremos la guerra, queremos vivir en paz*" (We do not want war, we want to live in peace). In this phrase, the Spanish people give expression to the desire, hope, and aspirations not only of the nations of Europe but also of the nations of the world.

# NOTES

1. The other part of the Second Regiment of Infantry was stationed in the city of Staszow.

2. Piotr M. Sierant in his manuscript of "2 Pulk Piechoty Legianow Armi Krajowej," writes as follows: "A German reconnaissance unit consisting of four or five tanks managed to force its way from Staszow through Osiek and Swiniary to the vicinity of the bridge near Baranow. The members of the Polish unit which guarded the bridge noticed the tanks racing toward the bridge and blew up prematurely one of its piers and two spans collapsed into the river. Following the exchange of fire by both sides, the German tanks returned to Staszow," p. 41.

3. Some of the young men who did not go east with us but stayed home managed to salvage some rifles and even machine guns. My classmate and friend, Piotr Marian Sierant, was lucky to find an excellent machine gun.

4. It came to my attention that during one of the meetings of the village heads, in our county of Loniow, the SS-men whipped all of them and only then instructed those at the meeting how to "motivate" the farmers in their villages in discharging their duties toward the new rulers.

5. "There should be one master only for the Poles, the German. Two masters, side by side, cannot and must not exist. Therefore, all representatives of the Polish intelligentsia are to be exterminated. This sounds cruel, but such is the law of life," stated Martin Bormann in his memorandum on the projects of Adolf Hitler. Cf. *Trial of the Major War Criminals before the International Military Tribunal*, 15 vols. (Washington, D.C.: U.S. Department of State, 1957), vol. 7, pp. 224-26. "Poland can only be administered by utilizing the country through means of ruthless exploitation..., closing all educational institutions, especially technical schools and colleges in order to prevent the growth of the new Polish intelligentsia," stated Hans Frank. See *Nazi Conspiracy and Aggression*, 10 vols. (Washington, D.C.: U.S. Government Printing Office, 1946), vol. 7, pp. 420-21.

6. Piotr M. Sierant, "2 Pulk Piechoty Legianow Arni Krajowej," Manuscript, p. 48.

7. Piotr M. Sierant, "2 Pulk Piechoty," p. 49.

8. Cf. Piotr Matusak, *Ruch Oporu Na Ziemi Sandomiersko-Opatowskiej w Latach 1939-1945* (Warsaw: Wydawnictwo Ministerstwa Obrony Narodowej, 1976), p. 22.

9. The colorful Judge Pietrow and his wife Aleksandra Lisiecka Pietrow had a son who became their heir. His name was also Basili, who was born in 1878. He married Olga Jefremienko, whose mother, Maria Bronislawa Borowska, was Polish and a Roman Catholic. Olga Jefremienko was a school teacher. In the early part of World War I when the Austrian army crossed the Vistula River and was about to occupy the Pietrow estate, Basili and Olga Pietrow were forced to take refuge in Tambow, Russia. There, two of their children were born: Eugeniusz in 1917 and Aleksander in 1918. Following the revolution in Russia, the Pietrows returned to Poland where their daughter, Natalia, was born in 1923. During their absence from Poland, the new Polish government nationalized their

residence and all other property that belonged to them. Wasili Pietrow was forced to look for a job to support his family. He was employed as a supervisor in the work of loading and shipping coal at the Ignacy Coal Mine in Zagorze. This employment enabled him and his wife to raise and educate their children.

To conclude this very condensed family history, it is necessary to say that in 1998, Aleksander Pietrow, a bank president from Tarnobrzeg, managed to buy from the present Polish government the ancestral residence in Dzieki and intends to restore the dilapidated palace. He is one of the grandsons of Wasili and Olga Pietrow. Other grandchildren who work as members of various professions are also positively engaged in rebuilding post–Communist Poland. The information about the Pogodin and Pietrow families was given to me by Wasili Pietrow from Tarnobrzeg, Poland.

10. "Tamten Smigly-Rydz
Nie nauczyl nas roboty nic
A ten Hitler Zloty,
Uczy nas roboty!"

11. They were also convinced that a man from Sulislawice by the name Kamysz, a member of the Communist Party, was instrumental in organizing this sacrilegious crime. I was told by a very reputable person who lived in Sulislawice at the time the crime was committed that all perpetrators of this crime were members of the Communist Party and resided near the city of Ostrowiec.

12. Roman Dmowski was a Polish nationalist writer in pre–World War II Poland.

13. For instance, the beginning of British strategic air raids on Germany on May 10–11, 1940.

14. For example, Hubal and his unit. Cf. Henryk Kuksz, *Jedrusiowa Dola* (Warsaw: P.Z. Polmark, 1992), pp. 30–32.

15. The Nazi troops began to be deployed in Poland against the Soviet Union on April 3, 1941, but three days later, on April 6, 1941, the supreme command of the Nazi forces had to divert some of its divisions to launch an attack against Yugoslavia and Greece.

16. Actually, the German navy was ordered to engage in annihilating Soviet submarines and their crews without any trace as early as June 15, 1941.

17. "Army Group Center intends to apprehend forty to fifty thousand youths from the age of 10 to 14 ... and transport them to the Reich ... it is intended to allot these juveniles primarily to the German trades as apprentices.... This action is being greatly welcomed by the German trade since it represents a decisive measure for the alleviation of the shortage of apprentices." Rosenberg's memorandum taken from his files. Cf. *Nazi Conspiracy and Aggression*, Vol. 3, pp. 71–73.

18. The news of Waclaw's execution reached the Jedrus Group on November 23, 1942. Cf. Eugeniusz Dabrowski, *Salakiem Jedrusiow* (Warsaw: Pax 1966), p. 130.

19. The Nowrocki sisters returned home at the end of World War II.

20. Cf. Heinz Guderian, *Panzer Leader* (New York: Dutton, 1952), pp. 193–94.

21. There were about 2,500 Jews in Klimontow. In Sandomierz there were about 7,000 Jews. In Koprzywnica, Zawichost, and Bogoria, there were over 1,000 Jews. Piotr M. Sierant, "2 Pulk Piechoty Legionow Armi Krajowej," p. 67.

22. The concentration camp in Auschwitz was already in existence by an order of Himmler issued on April 27, 1940.

23. Mr. and Mrs. Kozlowski (Jan and Antonina), from Domoradzice manor, were one of the families who offered to shelter Dr. Kaplan and his family.

24. Cf. Marian S. Mazgaj, *Visiting Home In Poland after 33 Years* (Parsons, W.V.: McClain, 1996), pp.130–39.

25. Piotr Sierant, *Pacyfikacja Wsi Struzki w 1943 r.* (Staszow: Staszowskie Towarzystwo Kulturalne, 1998), pp. 8–9.

26. Piotr Sierant, *Pacifikacja Wsi*, p. 9.

27. In addition to the trucks, there were also a number of smaller motor vehicles.

28. According to Piotr (Marian) Sierant, the core of the German force constituted the 3rd Company of 1st Motorized Battalion, which was a part of the 17th Regiment of the SS. "Historia Drugiego Pulku Legionow Sandomierskich" (Manuscript).

29. Piotr Sierant, *Hitlerowska Pacyfikacja Wsi Struzki* (London: Wybor Prac Na Konkurs Imienia Jozefa Wyrwy, 1977), pp. 84–85.

30. Piotr Sierant, *Hitlerowska Pacyfikacja Wsi Struzki, loc.cit.*

31. The survivors reported that a soldier of the Wehrmacht, Heinrich Hesler, who was home on furlough in one of the German villages of the area, committed the most atro-

cious acts of barbarism in Struzki on that tragic day. See Piotr Sierant, *loc. cit.*

32. He was placed in a cell with a number of other political prisoners. Following interrogations, Jan was sentenced to serve his term in the death camp of Auschwitz. While waiting for shipment to Auschwitz, one of the prisoners in Jan's cell received a loaf of bread from a friend. In it there was a small hacksaw, which the Nazi prison guards did not detect. Using the hacksaw, the inmates managed to cut the iron grill in the cell's window. When they finished cutting the grill and were about to escape, the Nazi police came and shipped them to Auschwitz. Jan survived the death camp and returned home at the end of World War II. Instead of returning to his school as a teacher, Jan enrolled in the school of dentistry and became a very successful dentist.

33. The people in Poland do not celebrate birthdays but name days.

34. I had a chance to see these photographs that "Bloody Eddy" had in his possession. His real name was Edward Vau.

35. Piotr Matusak, *Ruch oporu na ziemi opatowsko-sandomierskiej 1939–1945* (Warsaw: Wydawnictwo Ministerstwa Obrony Narodowe, 1976), p. 278.

36. Wlodzimierz Gruszczynski, *Lotna Sandomierska* (Warszawa: Milla, 1991), p. 61.

37. Wlodzimierz Gruszczynski, *Lotna*, p. 63. Cf. Piotr Matusak, *Ruch oporu*, pp. 278–79.

38. Following World War II, we learned that Captain Kaktus was born Tadeusz Strus in Marianka, parish of Kruszczyna, district of Radomsko, on September 17, 1908. At the age of eighteen, he entered the Military Academy and majored in engineering. He graduated from the academy in August 1930 and received his commission as an officer. Soon he was assigned to the Seventh Battalion of Engineers in Poznan as a frontline officer. In October 1935, he was transferred to Warsaw and promoted to the rank of captain on March 19, 1939.

When the Nazis attacked Poland on September 1, 1939, Captain Strus was ordered to the front on September 4, 1939, as a commander of a company that belonged to the Fourth Regiment of Engineers in Przemyśl. In Rudnik, on the San River, the German Luftwaffe attacked the Fourth Regiment and many soldiers and officers lost their lives. At the same time, a number of Nazi divisions, which were concentrated in Slovakia, also attacked the Fourth Regiment from the south. Under the leadership of General Sosenkowski, the Poles fought bravely in an uneven battle near Grodek Jagiellonski. Then, after the battle the Polish units were ordered to march east to protect the city of Lwów. On the way to that city they were intercepted by a number of Soviet motorized divisions and disarmed.

In 1940, Captain Strus arrived in Rakow near Staszow and began to teach in an underground secondary school. He taught there for two years. In the fall of 1942, Colonel Antoni Zolkiewski ("Lin") ordered him to move to Sandomierz and to assume duties of the commanding officer of sappers and the chief of diversion in the districts of Sandomierz and Opatow. He remained in these positions until the end of the summer of 1944. Then, within the framework of the Action "Storm" ("Burza"), he continued to lead our troops in many battles against the Nazis until the very end of our struggle.

After the Communist takeover in Poland, Major Strus resided in Gliwice and worked as an instructor in the local trade school for eight years. Then he worked as an assistant chief mechanic in a furniture factory until his retirement at the end of October 1974. After his retirement, he took care of his blind mother. who died in April 1980 at the age of 92. Major Strus, a heroic officer and a great Christian, completed his earthly journey on June 17, 1991, in Wyszkowice, leaving us an example of godly and virtuous life.

The above information is based on the letter that Major Strus had written to Wlodzimierz Gruszczynski ("Jach") on March 3, 1985.

39. The shotgun was produced by the Fabrique Nationale (F.N.).

40. Cf. Marian S. Mazgaj, *Visiting Home*, pp. 108–16.

41. "Quiet! Hands up!"

42. "Good evening, gentlemen"

43. Cf. Marian Mazgaj, *Visiting Home*, pp. 117–30.

44. During the Nazi occupation and the uprooting of Poles from the territories of Poland annexed to the Reich, someone had conceived the idea of portraying the Blessed

Virgin Mary as Our Lady of Exiles. The artist's painting was reproduced as a small holy picture and distributed primarily among those persons who were dispossessed and exiled. Such a picture gave strength and perseverance to the Polish exiles who came to believe that the Blessed Virgin Mary, Mother of Christ, was present among them in their misery as their mother and protectress.

45. Wlodzimerz Gruszczynski, *Lotna Sandomierska*, p. 109.

46. After receiving necessary medical help from Dr. Aleksander Dobkiewicz at the Holy Ghost Hospital in Sandomierz, Blyskawica was recovering, at that time, in the hospitable manor of Mr. and Mrs. Bronislaw Bronikowski in Jachimowice.

47. He was hiding under the assumed name of Franciszek Wilczynski as an accountant in Jan Misiuda's Mill.

48. Walter, who at that time was about twenty years old, had been exiled by the Nazis from the western part of Poland and lived with his aunt in Usarzow manor. He was an extremely brave and dedicated member of the Home Army. As such, he carried out many death sentences on the Nazi criminals who were difficult to reach.

49. In ordering quiet and bloodless disarming Mis had in mind a strong unit of SS-men in Samborzec and also Nazi reprisals against the local population for wounding or killing of one of their own.

50. SD (Sicherheistsdienst) was the Nazi security police.

51. Gestapo (Geheime Staates Polizei) was the state secret police.

52. Cf. Woldzimierz Gruszczynski, *Lotna Sandomierska*, p. 218.

53. The attack on von Paul in Skrzypaczowice manor was not feasible for two basic reasons: (1) the presence of many well-armed Germans and (2) the makeshift fortifications built around the manor house.

54. The above quotation is taken from the letter written to me by Lieutenant Jozefowski on April 4, 1997.

55. Besides Lieutenant Jozefowski the following members of our unit took part in the ambush on von Paul: Arkadiusz Swierszcz ("Iskra"), Jan Osemlak ("Straceniec"), Wlodzimierz Gruszczynski("Jach"), Jan Szpakiewicz ("Piccolo"), Edward Stawiarz ("Sep"), and I, Marian Mazgaj ("Kozak"). According to Lieutenant Jozefowski, Mieczyslaw Bokwa ("Huragan") also took part in the ambush. The lieutenant is uncertain about the participation of Kazimierz Jarzyna ("Sokol") who, as far as I can remember, did not take part in this action. Had he been with us, he and not Edward Stawiarz ("Sep") would have carried the light machine gun.

56. Jan Osemlak's letter written to me on August 30, 1997, confirmed my recollection of the above-mentioned fact.

57. In his recollection of the initial part of our attack on von Paul, Lieutenant Jozefowski wrote to me as follows: "In accordance with the plan, as soon as the lady who stood near the sharp turn of the road raised her hand in which she held her handkerchief (she was about 500 meters from me), I began to walk toward Koprzywnica. After a while, I noticed the approaching britzka in which there were three SS-men, a driver, and von Paul. One of the SS-men sat on the driver's seat and the two others sat inside of the britzka on each side of von Paul. When I found myself about 15 to 20 meters from the britzka, I pulled out of the violin case my submachine gun and shouted, *"Halt und hände hoch!"* The britzka stopped one and half meters from me and the SS-man, who sat next to the driver, fired his submachine gun in my direction, missed me (the bullets damaged only my hat) but the frightened horses pulled the britzka toward me. I fired my submachine gun at the side of the left horse all the way from his front to his rear but, unfortunately, the horses took off with great speed. At the moment when the horses began to run forward, I noticed that the SS-man, who fired at me, dropped his MP but Sep's light machine gun, which was so much needed now, failed to fire. Now I was waiting for Sep to fire his light machine gun at the horses. Unfortunately, the machine gun jammed without firing a single shot! Therefore, our attempt to abduct von Paul ended unsuccessfully. I was sorry that I had failed and my sorrow became even more painful when I saw, in the britzka which was running away from us, the three disciplined Germans obediently holding up their hands. But I was unable to fire at them without violating the order of my superior officer." — This excerpt is taken from the above quoted letter.

58. Some writers who describe our en-

counter with the German troopers, following the attack on von Paul, claim that we were involved in a battle that lasted until the evening. Their reports are totally exaggerated.

59. Cf. Jerzy Slaski, *Polska Walczaca*, 2nd ed. (Warsaw: Institut Wydawniczy Pax, 1990), p. 735.

60. As a matter of fact, one of von Paul's horses, which pulled the britzka during our attack, was seriously wounded but did not collapse until it ran about one mile.

61. The reason our superiors wanted him alive was to interrogate him about the network of spies that von Paul maintained in various towns and villages of the area.

62. Zbigniew Piatek ("Grabina") lived with his mother, a school teacher, and two of his sisters in the annex of Uzarzow manor house. The Piatek family was expelled by the Nazi authorities from Zdunskawola and resettled at Uzarzow manor. Hence the association of Zbigniew Piatek with Jozef Bojanowski.

63. Jozef Bojanowski, personal letter to the author, written on April 8, 1998.

64. Left side was the northern side of the road.

65. Besidse Kret (Capitain Leon Torlinski) there were in the farm wagonette two other persons, namely, Major Jan Aleksandrowicz ("Szerszen"), chief of Medical Services in the district of Sandomierz and the unknown driver. This information came from the letter of Jozef Bojanowski to the author. Cr. Piotr Matusak, "Zamach Na von Paula" (Attack on von Paul) in *Wroclawski Tygodnik Katolicki*, no. 23/821 (April 8, 1969): pp.6–7.

66. According to the information that the author received in the Walter's letter quoted above, Kret suffered a broken collar bone and his topcoat had a bullet hole.

67. When Grabina caught up with von Paul, the Gestapo agent did not attempt to defend himself. He raised his right hand with which he was holding a beautifully engraved Colt 45 pistol, which was ready to fire. One may ask as to why von Paul did not raise both of his hands. The answer is very simple. He had bullet holes in his left hand. The author received this information from Grabina. Cf. Matusak, "Zamach Na von Paula," p. 7.

68. There were nine German patrols in the area. Cf. Matusak, "Zamach Na von Paula."

69. Jan Bojanowski, *Wspomnienia Dla Wnukow Z Lat Wojny 1939–1945* (Warsaw: JKG & Co., 1991), pp.21–23.

70. Cf. Wlodzimieriz Gruszczynski, *Lotna Sandomierska*, pp. 178–79.

71. Zbigniew Piatek described this to me in our personal conversation.

72. Jan Bojanowski, *Wspomnienia Dla Wnuków Z Lat Wojny 1939–1945*. Speaking about von Paul's last moments, Walter wrote to the author as follows: "Somebody came to inform us that Germans are going around from village to village searching for someone. Short interrogation which revealed nothing new. He gave some names of the people who were already liquidated. He went into his grave without blinking his eye. He was a very tough man. According to Kret, his wife was a sister of Hans Frank...." Letter to the author of April 8, 1997. According to Piotr Marian Sierant, whose home at that time was in the village of Rybnica, von Paul was executed and buried in a shallow grave in a small forest called Kolaska near Rybnica.

73. In the author's conversation with Mrs. Krystyna Bronikowska Radlinska on April 17, 1997, she stated that after the Germans left, she went to the orchard, unearthed the black, bulky notebook and gave it to Tarnina at his orders. Tarnina and Kruk are deceased. The only person who may know something about it is Leon Torlinski ("Kret") who lives in Sopot, Poland. In order to find out what was in the notebook I wrote to Kret but he did not respond to my letter. My further inquiries through the good offices of Walter were unsuccessful.

74. All the people who attended the Horodynski wedding in Zbydniow were murdered by the Nazis.

75. As quoted in the Polish language by Wlodzimierz Gruszczynski, *Lotna Sandomierska*, pp. 178–81.

76. Wlodzimierz Gruszczynski, *Odwet-Jedrusie* (Staszow: Staszowskie Towarzystwo Kulturalne, 1996), p. 195.

77. Wlodzimierz Gruszczynski, *Lotna Sandomierska*, p. 169.

78. Wlodzimierz Gruszczynski, *Odwet-Jedrusie*, pp. 182–83.

79. Cf. Wlodzimierz Gruszczynski, *Odwet-Jedrusie*, p. 162.

80. Cf. Wlodzimierz Gruszczynski, *Odwet-Jedrusie*, pp. 119–20.

81. When the Germans were massing their

troops for the surprise attack on the Soviet Union, some of the Wehrmacht units were stationed at that time in Tarnoberzeg and the officers were using private homes for their headquarters. Since Lokietek was still very young, perhaps about eighteen years old, the Germans considered him to be a child and did not mind him walking in and out of their headquarters. He took advantage of his small stature and began to take officers' pistols. For a long time he was very successful in doing this. One time, however, a German officer became aware that his pistol was missing before Lokietek managed to cross a large backyard full of fruit trees. The officer sounded alarm and a number of soldiers came to see what was happening. The officer ordered them to search the immediate area for somebody who stole his gun. When Lokietek saw the German soldiers searching the backyard arboretum, he took off his shoes and socks, put the stolen pistol on the ground, sat on it, and played with his toes. The soldiers were crisscrossing the wooded area of the backyard and ignoring Lokietek altogether. Before he came to the Flying Commando Unit, he took from the German officers' quarters a brand new submachine gun which was known to us as an MP (*Machinenpistole*). When he came to our unit, before the merger with the Jedrus Group, he was convinced that we were the Jedrus Group. Therefore, after staying with us for a number of weeks, he switched to the group that he intended to join in the first place.

82. Manfred Zanker was born on February 22, 1924. He was the only child of his parents. At the age of seven, he went to the grade school in his hometown. Although he disliked Hitler and his Nazi Party, at the age of fourteen he had to join the Hitler-Jugend organization. As a youthful pacifist Manfred totally disagreed with militaristic and bellicose Nazism and opposed it in every way he could. After completing his high school at the age of eighteen, he was called to a public work detachment in Hexengrund. While he was there, Manfred decided to escape to Switzerland. He managed to travel across Germany to the Swiss border without any problem but was apprehended on the border and lodged in prison in Feldkirch. During the court proceedings, Manfred testified that the reason for his attempt to cross the border to Switzerland was to join the Rommel's Afrika Korps. The judge took under consideration Manfred's youthful fantasy and sentenced him to only two-months imprisonment. After completing his prison term, Manfred rejoined his public work detachment. This time, however, he was stationed in Fraustein. From there, Manfred was transferred to the 24th Battalion of Engineers in the 154th Division of the Wehrmacht in Przemyśl, Poland. When the Red Army approached the eastern borders of Poland, his unit retreated to Sandomierz, where it constructed fortifications against the Russian army. Manfred took advantage of his military duties in Poland and began to study the Polish language. At the time, he and two of his associates defected from the Wehrmacht, Manfred could communicate in broken Polish. Manfred and the two others who defected with him in Sandomierz had guard duty at their base at the same time of the night. They brought with them not only the weapons assigned to them but also five Walther pistols, three machine guns model MG42, and a great deal of sensitive military papers from the office of the commanding officer of the Sandomierz base. I will never forget the day when Jozef Bojanowski ("Walter") brought to our quarters Manfred, Jerzy Karol Pyka, and Robert Thuman. All of us in our unit were jubilant to see the former German soldiers join us in fighting the Nazi demonic empire. The following day after their arrival in our group, I witnessed a fight between Manfred and Jerzy Karol that took place in the outhouse near our quarters. The bone of contention was the alleged fact that Jerzy Karol Pyka was nosing through the contents of Manfred's military knapsack and found in it an extra 9 mm Luger. Some of our friendly intervention brought a reconciliation between the two of them. Manfred was always very friendly and outgoing and soon made many friends in our group. He took an active part with all of us in the Action Storm ("Burza") not so much as a combatant but rather as a member of our intelligence service. His knowledge of the German language was very helpful to us. The Red Army offensive caught him in the vicinity of Radoszyce. Unfortunately, the Russian NKVD did not appreciate Manfred's anti–Nazi attitude and arrested him as a German soldier. After long interrogations, he was imprisoned in Siberia and

then in one of the concentration camps. Only after the death of Stalin (in virtue of an amnesty) Manfred and other German prisoners returned to Germany after nine years of imprisonment. Then he enrolled at the University of West Berlin where he studied for a number of years. After completing his studies, Manfred became an interpreter for three mayors of West Berlin: Klaus Schultz, Heinrich Albertz, and Willy Brandt. After his retirement, Manfred continues to live in Berlin and he spends much time in Bosko Zdroj Resort, Poland. He is the only German who received from the Polish government the Home Army Cross and the Partisan Cross. Piotr Sierant, "2 Pulk Piechoty Legionow Armii Krajowej," pp. 270–71.

83. For example, the Germans who were stationed in Skrzypaczowice manor left their well-defended quarters in a hurry, leaving behind one rifle, a case of hand grenades, a number of horses, and a great many groceries. Wlodzimietz Gruszczynski, *Odwet-Jedrusie*, p. 198.

84. Wlodzimierz Gruszczynski, *Odwet-Jedrusie*, p.198.

85. A Soviet general named Wlasov, a war prisoner in Germany, was persuaded by the German authorities to organize an army composed of Russian prisoners of war. This army was called the Russian Liberation Army and served Nazi Germany, in most instances under the command of German officers. In some instances, the units of this army committed atrocities against Polish civilians. In other instances, they gave the Germans only proverbial lip service.

86. Cf. Eugeniusz Dabrowski, *Szlakiem Jedrusiow* (Warsaw: Instytut Wydawniczy Pax, 1966), p. 374.

87. Eugeniusz Dabrowski, *Szlakiem*, p. 376.

88. Piotr Sierant, "2 Pulk Piechoty Legionow Armii Krajowej," p. 30.

89. Piotr Sierant, "2 Pulk Piechoty," pp. 30–31.

90. Eugeniusz Dabrowski, *Szlakiem Jedrusiow*, pp. 376–77. Cf. Wlodzimierz Gruszczynski, *Odwet-Jedrusie*, p.199.

91. Piotr Sierant, "2 Pulk Piechoty," pp. 36–38.

92. Wlodzimierz Gruszczynski, *Odwet-Jedrusie*, p. 201.

93. Piotr Sierant, "2 Pulk Piechoty," pp. 80–81.

94. Piotr Sierant, "2 Pulk Piechoty," pp. 82–84.

95. Piotr Sierant, "2 Pulk Piechoty," pp. 93–94.

96. NKVD stands for Narodnii Kommissariat Vnutrennikh Diel and means National Commissariat of Internal Affairs. In other words, the units of NKVD were formally units of the Soviet secret police.

97. Wlodzimierz Gruszczynski, *Lotna Sandomierska*, pp. 217–218.

98. Sierant, *op. cit.*, p.97.

99. Sierant, "2 Pulk Piechoty," p.101.

100. Sierant, "2 Pulk piechoty," p. 102.

101. Gruszczynski, *Odwet-Jedrusie*, p. 220.

102. Gruszczynski, *Odwet-Jedrusie*, p. 204.

103. Piotr Matusak, *Ruch oporu na ziemi Opatowsko-Sandomierskiej 1939–1944*, p. 396.

104. Piotr Sierant, "2 Pulk Piechoty," p. 115.

105. Sierant, "2 Pulk Piechoty," pp. 123–25.

106. Sierant, "2 Pulk Piechoty."

107. Sierant, "2 Pilk Piechoty," p. 128.

108. Sierant, "2 Pulk Piechoty," pp. 157–58.

109. Sierant, "2 Pulk Piechoty," pp. 160–61.

110. Eugeniusz Dabrowski in his work, *Szlakiem Jedrusiow*, writes (p. 390) that the Germans attacking Radoszyce used four armor-plated trucks.

111. Sierant, "2 Pulk Piechoty," pp. 163–64.

112. Sierant, "2 Pulk Piechoty," p. 392.

113. Dabrowski, *Szlakiem Jedrusiow*, p. 392.

114. Dabrowski, *Szlakiem Jedrusiow*, p. 392.

115. Dabrowski, *Szlakiem Jedrusiow*, p. 394.

116. Sierant, "2 Pulk Piechoty," p. 189.

117. Sierant, "2 Pulk Piechoty," pp. 190–93.

118. Gruszczynski, *Lotna Sandomierska*, pp. 277.

119. Sierant, "2 Pulk Piechoty," p. 202.

120. Sierant, "2 Pulk Piechoty."

121. Sierant, "2 Pulk Piechoty," p. 204.

122. Sierant, "2 Pulk Piechoty," pp. 206–07.

123. Copy of the letter written by Zbigniew Piatek ("Grabina") to Captain Leon Torlinski ("Kret") on September 15, 1988.

The correctness of the information that is contained in the above-quoted letter has been confirmed in the affirmation written by Tadeusz Luciak ("Bergson") on January 16, 1955. Bergson was also an eyewitness of the events described by Grabina.

124. Sierant, "2 Pulk Piechoty," pp. 215–16.

125. Sierant, "2 Pulk Piechoty," pp. 218–23.

126. The Second Division of Infantry of the Home Army.

127. Robert Goralski, *World War II Almanac 1931–1945* (New York: G. T. Putman's Sons, 1981), p.157.

128. Martin Bormann in a letter written to Rosenburg; see *Nazi Conspiracy and Aggression*, 10 vols. (Washington, D.C.: U.S. Government Printing Office, 1946), vol. 4, pp. 553–54.

129. Following World War II, Miszczyk returned to his seminary and, after the completion of his studies, was ordained a priest for the diocese of Czestochowa.

130. Cf. Henryk Kuksz, *Jedrusiowa Dola* (Warsaw: P.Z. Polmark, 1991), pp. 122–24.

131. Henryk Kuksz ("Selim") made Kmita aware that he condemned to death an innocent man. See Henryk Kuksz, *Jedrusiowa Dola*, pp. 122–24.

132. On one occasion, I visited her and her parents in Malogoszcz. During my visit, an SS officer came to visit the family. It was obvious to me that he was courting the young lady. His manner of speaking indicated to me that he was of Ukrainian origin. He might have been a member of the Galician Division of the Waffen SS.

133. The National Armed forces political creed, at that time, was expressed in the following words: "Temporally, we must abstain from any broader action against the Germans because it would facilitate the task of the Soviet Army; most of all we cannot permit an early uprising.... During the uprising, our goal will be to go to the western part of Poland and we will do the same work for Poland as we did before the uprising, namely, eliminating Communist guerrillas from the area." As quoted by Piotr Matusak, *Ruch Oporu Na Ziemi Opatowsko-Sandomierskiej 1939–1945*, pp. 431–32.

134. Piotr Matusak, *Ruch Oporu*, p. 434. Cf. Jerry Slaski, *Polska Walczaca* (Warsaw: Instytut Wydawniczy Pax, 1990), p. 696.

# BIBLIOGRAPHY

Bojanowski, Jan. *Wspomnienia Dla Wnukow Z Lat Wojny 1939–1945*. Warsaw: JKG & Co., 1991.
Dabrowski, Eugeniusz. *Szlakiem Jedrusiow*. Warsaw: Instytut Wydawniczy Pax, 1966.
Gruszczynski, Wlodzimierz. *Lotna Sandomierska*. Warszawa: Milla, 1991.
———. *Odwet-Jedrusie*. Staszow: Staszowskie Towarzystwo Kulturalne, 1996.
Guderian, Heinz. *Panzer Leader*. New York: Dutton, 1952.
Kuksz, Henryk. *Jedrusiowa Dola*. Warsaw: P.Z. Polmark, 1992.
Matusak, Piotr. *Ruch Oporu Ziemi Sandomiersko-Opatowskiej W Latach 1939–1945*. Warsaw: Wydawnictwo Obrony Narodowej, 1976.
———. "Zamach Na von Paula." *Wroclawski Tygodnik Katolicki,* no. 23/821. Kwiecien 8, 1967.
Mazgaj, Marian. *Visiting Home in Poland after 33 Years*. Parsons, W.V.: McClain, 1996.
*Nazi Conspiracy and Aggression*. 10 vols. Washington, D.C.: U.S. Government Printing Office, 1946.
*Rocznik Diecezji Sandomierskiej 1994*. Sandomierz: Wydawnictwo Diecezjalne, 1994.
Sierant, Piotr. "2 Pulk Piechoty Legionow Armii Krajowej" (Manuscript).
———. *Pacifikacja Wsi Struzki w 1943 Roku*. Staszow: Staszowskie Towarzystwo Kulturalne, 1998.
———. *2 Pulk Piechoty Legionow Armii Krajowej*. Warsaw: Wydawnictwo Bellona, 1996.
Slaski, Jerzy. *Polska Walczaca*. Warsaw: Instytut Wydawniczy Pax, 1990.
*Trial of the Major War Criminals before the International Military Tribunal*. Washington, D.C.: U.S. Department of State, 1957.

# INDEX

Action Storm (Burza) 177
Adamczak, Franciszek (Franek) 70, 71
Adamczyk, Col. Wladyslaw 28
Adomow 213
Akcja Burza 184
Aleksandrowicz, Dr. Jan 155
American supplies 235, 237
Americanization School 312
Anders, Gen. Wladyslaw 235
Andrzej, Dr. 213
Annopol 188
Anschluss 8
Atomic bomb 163
Auschwitz 36, 253
Austria 8
Awdoszkin, Lt. S.I. 188

Bak, Maria 87, 153
Bak farmhouse 87
Baltic Sea 280
Baranow 10, 21, 188, 189, 190, 194, 234
Barnow Bridge 21
Bari, Italy 149
"Basia" *see* Nawratil, Edyta
Battle of Radosyce 245
Bautzen, Saxony 177
Bebelno 222
Belgian FN pistol 192
Benedict XVI, Pope 5
Bergman machinegun 165
Berling, Gen. 193
Bernacki, Anna 6
Bernacki, Jan 29
Bernacki, Janka 29
Bernacki, Jozefa 29
Bernacki, Karol 29
Bernatowicz, Prof. Stanislaw 243, 244

Bernatowicz, Tekla (Tecia) 243, 244 267
Bernatowicz family 243, 246, 267, 268
Beszyce 255
Beszyce Dolne 85, 86
Beszyce Gorne 241
Beszyce manor 240
Bette, Jerzy ("Papcio") 154, 156
Bielawski, Panstwo 88
Bielecki family 242
Bielny 203
Bien family 162
Bilgoraj (district) 179, 180, 181
Blessed Virgin Mary of Exiles 326
Blessed Virgin Mary Queen of Poland 299
Blody Eddy Vau 77, 78, 79, 80
Blonie 255
Blyskawica (Boleslaw Szelag) 101, 102, 109, 161
Bobek, Wincenty 62
Bogoria 188, 189, 190, 251
Bojanowski, Jan ("Michal") 143, 144, 145, 327
Bojanowski, Jozef ("Walter") 142, 220
Bokwa, Mieczyslaw ("Huragan") 161
Borcycki 154
Bormann, Martin 224, 330
Borzobohaty, Col. Wojciech ("Wojan") 207
Boston, Irena 244
Bratkowska ("Janka") 212
Brindisi, Italy 149
British Airdrops 148, 150, 152, 219
British Broadcasting Company 41
Brodeecki, Father Jerzy 204
Bronikowski, Bronislaw 245, 246, 249
Bronikowski, Krystyna 247
Bronikowski, Maria 247
Bronikowski, Mr. & Mrs. 104, 140 145, 146

Bronikowski, Stefan 245, 247, 249
Bronikowski, Zofia 249
Brudek, Jozef ("Zuch") 161
Buda Starowolska 227
Budzinski, Father Jan 7, 74, 75, 276, 278, 288, 290, 293, 294
Bukowa 26, 29, 153, 184, 241
Bukowa Forest 241
Bystrojowice manor 88, 242
Byszow manor 88, 89
Bzinica Manor 248

Canada 242
"Cap" see Gaj, Marian Mieczyslaw
Catholic University of America in Washington, D.C. 312
Catholic University of Lublin 309
Catonsville Community College 312
Ceber 191
Cegielnia 255
Chaciej, Dr. Wladyslaw ("Dr. Andrzej") 213, 214
Checiny 218
Chmiel, Tadeusz ("Alfred") 143
Chmielowski, Adam Hilary Bernard (Brother Albert) 308
Church architecture 294
Chyliczki 246
Cieslik, Father Eugeniusz 299, 301
Cisownik 213, 216
Ciszyca 255
Code of Canon Law (Codes Juris Canonici) 309
Communists 191, 228, 244; elections 248; guerrillas 229
Corpus Christi Celebration (Swieto Bozeg Ciala) 310
Cossacks 122, 123, 131, 132, 134, 137
Cracow 163, 245, 249
Czaja, Jan ("Powsinoga") 163
Czaja, Jozefa 162
Czajkow 175
Czapow, Czeslaw ("Boleslaw") 161
Czarna River 175
Czerwona Gora 203
Czestochowa 225, 299
Czyzewski, Col. Ludwik ("Julian") 14

Dabrowski, Eugeniusz ("Pliszka") 265, 328, 329, 330
Danilewicz family 271
Danzig (Gdansk) 281, 282, 285
Debniak 203
Debno 203, 204, 205

Defectors 148, 177
Demobilized troops 223, 237
Deserters 162, 252
Deville, "Zdzïch" 41, 48
Diocesan Seminary in Sandomierz, Poland 305
Dmosice manor 158, 244
Dmowski, Roman 40
Dobkiewicz, Dr. 76, 78, 122
Dobrowolski, Stefan 168
Domoradzice manor 155, 156
Donath 120
Dragunsky, Col. D.A. 188
Drewenko, Irena 244
Drewnko, Marian 243
Drozd, Ludwik 62
Dudek, Henryk ("Smigly") 58, 81, 119
Duma, Stanislaw (Topola) 85
Duquesne University 312
Dyld, Father Stanislaw 302
Dymitrow 188
Dziebaltow 207
Dzubek, Father Wladyslaw 303

Ejmont, Dr. Jerzy 75
Eternit factory 248

Falegi 218
Fanislawiczki 218
Fialkowski, Andrej ("Tarsan I") 227
Fialkowski, Zbigniew 178
Fialkowski, Zdzislaw ("Tarsan II") 227
Filipy 218
Finnish gun 197
First Battalion Second Regiment 204, 220
Flohr vel Szymanski 120
Flying Commando Unit 161, 227, 246
Fourth Panzer Army 187
Franaszczuk, Henryk 83
Franaszczuk, Julian 58
Franaszczuk, Sgt. Stefan ("Oklicz") 58, 81, 83, 85, 86, 91, 96, 97, 104, 110, 118, 121, 129, 127, 198, 239
French literature 288
Freud, Sigmund 274

Gaj, Marian Mieczyslaw ("Cap") 5, 18, 87, 100, 109, 122, 124, 161, 168, 169, 171
Garbacz 203
Gawronski, Czeslaw ("Wojek") 170, 173
Gdynia 278, 283
Gerlachow 6, 37, 38
German Maschinenpistole 192
German Security Division 216, 318

# INDEX

Germany 6, 8
Gestapo 6, 8, 140, 143, 147, 253
Girzycko 243, 244
Gliniany 218
Gliszcynski, Father Steven 158
Glowinski, Captain Stanislaw ("Mirski") 138
Goethe 5
Golebiowski, Father Piotr 307
Gontek 220
Gorki Forest 189
Gory Lasochowskie 233
Gorzyczany 247, 248
Gozlice 158
"Grabina" *see* Paitek, Zbigniew
Grabowiec 28
Grabowski, Edward Goetzendorf ("Zbiswicz") 161
Gracuch 208
Graduate School of Canon Law 308
Granat, Father Wincenty 307, 309
Granek, Mieczyslaw ("Szpak") 161
Granicznik 153, 241, 242
Grodziska 208, 209"
"Gram" 161
"Grot" 161
Gruszczynski, Wlodzimierz ("Jach") 81, 99, 107, 108, 114, 115, 116, 117, 118, 129, 152, 161, 325, 326, 327, 328, 330
Gunia, Father Tomasz 255, 257, 269, 271, 299, 301
Gutowski, Ludwik 42

Hamerski, Lt. Adam ("Jastrzab") 58
Herbapol Firm 248
Hernhut 248
Himmler, Heinrich 224
Hitler, Adolf 148, 215, 239
Hitlerjugend 61
Holy Cross Mountains 253
Holy Ghost Hospital 115
Home Army 171, 185, 196, 205, 235, 239, 245, 247, 252, 254
Hory, Maj. 178
Hospodar, Richard 120
Huta Gawrolinska 249

Isbinski, Maria 64
Isbinski, Zofia 64
"Iskra" *see* Swiercz, Arkadiusz
Iwaniska 190

Jacek, Father 203, 204
"Jach" *see* Gruszczynski, Wlodzimierz
Jachimowice manor 104

Jachomowice 210, 250
Jagiellonian University in Cracow 23, 245, 295, 306, 307
Jajkiewicz, Mieczyslaw ("Jajos") 161
Janicki, Antoni ("Grot") 228, 229
Janicki, Father Jozef 303
Janow Lubelski 14, 16
Janowice 203
Jarzyna, Father Julian 300, 301
Jarzyna, Kazimierz ("Sokol") 161
Jasinski, Stanislaw 41
Jasinski, Wladyslaw ("Jendrus") 41, 42, 46
Jaskolski, Father 204
lastrzebska Wola 190
Jaworski, Jozef ("Jawor") 58
"Jedrus" Company 179, 183, 184, 190, 191, 210, 216, 220, 221, 227, 245, 316
"Jedrus" Group 46, 63
Jedrus Lot (Jedrusiowa Dola) 245
Jeleniow 203
Jeleniow Range 194, 195, 202
Jeziorko 203
Jeziory 6, 37, 252
Jodlowski, Pawel ("Okon") 161
John Paul II, Pope 5, 307, 308
Jop, Bishop Franciszek 298, 301, 307
Jop, Mr. 178
Jozdzwkow 218
Jozefowski, Lt. Witold ("Mis") 86, 97, 117, 118, 119, 138, 139, 140, 141, 152, 162, 193, 326
Julianow manor 150
Jurkowice manor 104, 156, 244, 245

Kabata, Zbigniew ("Bobo") 163, 177, 208, 209, 217, 241
Kaktus (Capt. Tadeusz Strus) 86, 97, 99, 100, 103, 109, 110, 114, 117, 127, 161
Kalina 61
Kalinowski, Stanislaw 27 I, 278
Der Kampfer Ost Wache 162
Kanice 219, 222
Kanice Nowe 222
Kaplan, Dr. 159
Kasprzycki, Father Antoni 296
Kaszynski, Capt. Eugeniusz ("Nurt") 190, 194, 195, 212, 220
Katiuszas 237
Katowice 177, 240, 241
Katyn Forest 184
Kawenczyn 213
Kedzierski, Adolf ("Wilczur") 227, 228, 229
Kedzierski, Henryk ("Jaskolka") 227, 228

Kepa, Capt. Stefan ("Pochmurny") 193, 220
Khrushchev, Nikita 308
Kielce 190, 192, 207, 217
Kiemona, Father Henryk 302
Klaus, Col. 213
Klenck, Edmond ("Edmund") 162, 163, 170, 221
Klimaszewsk Dr. Mierczyslaw 307
Klimontow Forest 187, 189
Klucko 213, 215, 218
Klusek, Stanislaw ("Jastrzab" vel "Fugas") 121, 161, 163
Knap, Joseph 224, 225, 226, 227, 228, 238
Knap, Stefan 224
Knap, Teofila 224
Knap, Wladyslaw 224
Knight's Cross 166
Kobyla Gora 203
Kolodziej, Tadek 155, 157
Kolonia Wojcieszyce 42
Komorowski, Tadeusz ("Bor") 205, 206
Koniev, Marshal 234
Konopka, Stefan 247
Konskie 215, 217
Koprzywnica 20, 24, 25, 181, 183, 255
Korbonski, Stefan 60
Korczak, Mieczyslaw ("Dentysta") 184
Kos, Henryk 253
Kos, Waclaw 13, 16, 75
Kosciuszko, Tadeusz 59
Kossow 219, 221
Kosterski, Michalina 81, 82, 95, 239, 240
Kosterski, Mieczyslaw 81, 95, 239
Kostka, St. Stanislaw 289
Kotarski, Walclaw 169
Kowalski, Sgt. ("Golab") 187
Kowary 80, 290
"Kozak" see Mazgaj, Father Marian
Koziol, Father Michal 303
Kozlow 213, 214, 215
Kozlowski, Antonina 155, 158
Kozlowski, Jan 155, 158
Kozlowski, Janusz 155, 157
Kozlowski, Marcin ("Lysy") 42, 43, 49, 164
Kozlowski, Zbigniew 155, 156, 157, 158, 159
Krajewski, Father Mieczyslaw 291
Krajewski, Stefan 156
Krajewski family 158
Krasnik 16, 17, 18, 19
Krasow 219
Krobath, Kazimierz ("Niedzwiedz") 85, 149
Krolewiec 213, 252

"Kruk I" see Col. Wiktorowski, Antoni
"Kruk" II see Niekoniecznikow-Kluckowski, Czestaw
Kruszczynski, Dr. Tadeusz 307
Krynki 303, 304
Krzeminica-Szwagrow 188
Krzeminski, Zdzislaw ("Skrzydlaty") 161
Krzysin manor 243, 267, 268
Krzysztofik, Father Waclaw 297
Kudyk, Irena Bematowicz 242, 244
Kuksz, Antonina Lubieniecki 245
Kuksz, Henryk ("Selim") 139, 227, 245, 249, 324, 330
Kuksz, Maria ("Muszka") 244
Kuksz family 244, 245
Kunin 196
Kuras, Stanislaw ("Szot") 170, 171, 195
Kurgan, Wladyslawa 62
Kurzanski family 250
Kuzelowna, Maria 227, 232
Kwiatkowski family 161

Labor camp 230 231
Lagocki, Father Michal 278
Lagow 188, 192, 203
Lagowica 190
Lake Erie 312
Latin 148
Lech, Marian ("Marian") 188
Legiec, Father Stanislaw 299
Legionnaires 183, 196, 202
Lekczynski, Anna 246
Lenin, Vladimir Ilich 308
Lesiko 161, 164, 171, 175, 176, 181
Lewinski, Father Zygmunt 302
Liberal Arts College 247
Liegenschaft manor 199
"Lin" see Col. Zolkiewski, Antoni
Lipno manor 227
"Lokietek" see Sielecki, Alfred
London 236, 253
London BBC 165
Loniow 25, 26, 243
Loniow Forest 154, 180
Lorek, Bishop Jan Kanty 290, 293, 296, 298, 301, 302, 305, 308
Lorraine 162
Lot Airline 311
Lublin 311
Lubliniec 248
Luftwaffe 221, 223, 253, 203
Lukasiewicz, Andrzei ("Kmita") 88, 143, 227, 228
Lukowiec Ferry 255

Lutheran Church 10
Lycee of Sandomierz (Collegium Gostomianum) 278

Machine gun (MG42) 200, 211, 214, 215, 222, 314
Machnicki, Mary Ann 44
Malinowski, Stefan ("Masnyciu") 181
Malkiewicz 190
Malogoszcz 88, 230, 231, 234
"Mamloch's" farmhouse 181
"Marianski" see Palac, Lt. Stanislaw
Matusak, Piotr 323, 325, 327, 330
Mazgaj, Adam 312
Mazgaj, Alexander 256, 257, 258, 259, 260, 261, 263, 267, 269
Mazgaj, Anthony 309, 311
Mazgaj, Antoni Aleksander 23, 37, 47, 81, 189, 251
Mazgaj, Franciszk 21, 70, 74, 251
Mazgaj, Jan 13, 16, 21, 22, 27, 45, 46, 73, 74, 75, 292, 299
Mazgaj, Jozef 22, 290
Mazgaj, Jozef Aleksander 5
Mazgaj, Marcin 90
Mazgaj, Maria 22
Mazgaj, Father Marian ("Kozak") 5, 81, 161, 195, 297, 325, 326
Mazgaj, Marianna Danida Bogdanski 5
Mazgaj, Mary 290
Mazgaj, Soja Jozefa 5
Mazgaj, Wladyslaw 31, 33, 70
Mazgaj-Marglewski, Stanislaw 291, 292
Mazgajski, Jacob 5
Medrzycki, Lt. ("Reder") 187, 193, 213
Michalek, Father Henryk 297
Michalow 203
Michalowskie, Doly 131, 250
Miedzierza 216
Mierzwinski, Janusz 244
Mierzwinski family 244, 288
Mieszkowski, Anna 246
Mieszkowski, Jozef 246
Mieszkowski, Zofia 246
Mikolajow 6, 8, 10
Milbert, Wlodzimierz ("Pat") 178
Milejowice 203
Military instruction 47
Military physicians 213
Mirecka, Anna 212
"Mis" see Jozefowski, Lt. Witold
Misiuda, Jan 118, 119, 326
Miszczyk 225
Mitrofanov W.A. 193 194 216

Mittelstaedt, Tadeusz ("Budiet") 176
Mlyn-Wyspa 218
Mnichow 206
Mniszek 222
Mokoszyn 6
Momocicha 211
Montelupi Prison 163
Moszczyski, Count 26
Mularzow 209 213
Musial family 231
Mussolini, Benito 148
Mydlow 156

Nagorzyce manor 196, 203
Naslawice 150
National Armed Forces (NSZ) 178, 228, 232
Nawratil, Edyta 214, 227
Nawrocki family 52, 53, 324
Nazi Administration 52, 165, 224, 232, 233, 235
New Testament 269, 271
Nida River 188
"Niedzwiedz" see Krobath, Kazimierz
Niekrasow 28
Niekurzak, Stanislaw 29, 30, 52
Niemirow 190
Niepokalanow 203
Nieskurzow 193
Nieskurzuw Podlesie 195
Nieskuzow Nowy 195
Nieskuzow Stary 195, 202
NKVD (Russian Secret Police) 193
Nowa Slupia 192 195 196 203
Nowakowski, Henryk ("Nalecz" vel "Doktorek") 161
Nowakowski, Romuald ("Msciciel") 85, 161
Nowy Sacz 246
"Nurt" see Capt. Kaszynski, Eugeniusz

Obrowiec 248
Oder River 248
Odwet 39, 41, 42, 54, 165
Ogarek 222
Ogarka 219, 250
Olbierzowice 227
Olchowik, Lt. Kazimierz ("Zawisza") 190
Oliva 284
Opalina 175, 176, 178, 183, 250
Opatow 156, 190, 195, 196, 203
Ordination 240 298
Ordyk, Stanislaw ("Czernik") 188
"Orlicz" see Franaszczuk, Stefan

"Orzel" see Siatrak, Leon
Osemlak, Jan ("Straceniec") 58, 81, 90, 118, 129, 131, 132, 134, 135, 140, 149
Osemlak, Jozef 140
Osemlak, Stanislaw 58
Osieczko 179, 180, 181
Osiek 6, 28, 29, 30, 153, 168, 170, 171, 172, 173, 174, 175, 185, 189, 241
Osobka-Marawski 235
Ossala 169, 176
Ostrojow 206
Ostroleka manor 86
Ostrowiec 157, 190, 193
Our Lady of Czestochowa 64, 69
Our Lady of Exiles 106

Padew Narodowa 161
Palac, Lt. Stanislaw 195
Panzer 206, 219
Partisans 180, 188, 190, 206, 213, 215
Pater, Jan 7
Pawel's Battalion 186
Pawlak, Jan ("Sprezynka") 184
Pawlicowski, Mieczyslaw ("Ghandi") 161
Peasant Battalions 150, 190
Pepesha (PPSH, 1941) 195, 199
Petniak family 225
Piaski Krolewieckie 213
Piatek, Zbigniew ("Grabina") 143, 144, 145, 161, 219, 327, 330
Piekniak, Teofilia 6
Pielaszow 189
Pietrow, Basili 31, 32, 33, 34, 91
"Pikolo" see Szpakiewicz, Jan
Pilica River 206
Piorkow 203
"Pioron" see Stobinski, Kazimierz
Piwnik, Maj. Jan ("Ponury") 220
Plato 318
Pliskowola 28
"Pochmurny" see Capt. Kepa, Stefan
Podgradow 222
Podlazie 219, 221
Podolecki, Stanislaw ("Rys") 85, 88
Podolski, Julia 7
Podsiadly, Waclaw ("Wacek") 20, 30, 38, 39, 40, 41, 42, 43, 44, 53
Podsiadly, Wojciech 10
Podsiadly family 162
Pogodin, Gen. Basili 31
Polaniec 174, 181, 189
Polanow 153
Polish Committee of National Liberation 193

Polish Communist Party 150, 151
Polish Mountaineers (Gorale) 296
Polish October Revolution 309
Polish units 175, 185
Ponikowski, Walenty ("Walek") 53, 184
Popiel ("Antoniewicz") 195
Postronna 250
Poznan 156, 243
Przemysl 16
Przylogi 213, 215, 216
Przysucha 206
Public Security Police 253, 264, 266
Pyka, Jerzy Karol 177
Pyrek, Father Andrzej 203, 204
Pytlakowski, Tadeusz ("Tarnina") 210, 218

Rachtan, Zdzislaw ("Halny") 194 196
Rachwalowice manor 246
Radkow 219, 220, 221, 222, 229
Radlinski, Jerzy 247
Radlinski, Krystna 145, 146, 247
Radlinski, Teresa 249
Radom 207
Radoszyce 207, 208, 209, 210, 211, 212
Rakow 190
Rakowiecki Cemetery 249
"Rarnzes" 161
Red Army 178, 185, 188, 190, 191, 192, 193, 205, 234, 235, 236
"Reder" see Medrzycki, Lt. Dionizy
Regimental newspaper 213
Rembertow 253
Robakiewicz ("Gram") 227
Rocket launchers 237
Roesch, Charles ("Jerzy") 162, 163, 170, 221
Rogienice 219
Rola, Father Stefan 302
Rolski, Jeerzy ("Babinicz") 227
Rolski, Zbigniew ("Boruta") 161, 178
Ropelewski, Wanda 89, 243
Ropelewski family 88, 243
Rostylice 196, 202, 203
Rozycki, Alicja 157
Rozycki, Mr. & Mrs. Czeslaw 157
Rozycki, Dr. Ignacy 295
Rozycki, Miss Janeczka 157
Ruda 213
Ruda Gawrolinska 250
Rusinow 206
Rusinowski, Dr. Ferdynand 75, 76
Ruski, Brod 206
Russian Third Army 188
Ruszcza 23
Rutkowski, Kazimierz ("Puszkarz") 42, 45

# INDEX

Rybnica 178, 181, 183, 252
Rytel, Barbara 155, 156
Rytel, Kazimierz 157
Rytwiany 60, 173

Sadlowice 149
Sadrakula, Stanislaw 254, 272, 273, 276
St. John Vianney Major Seminary 313
St. Michael's Church 312
St. Nicholas Church 240
St. Stanislaus Church 5, 170
Samborec 248
Samotnia 252
Sandomierz 252
Sandomierz Castle 53
Sandomierz Flying Commando Unit 132, 149, 178, 239
Schongarth, Karl Berhard 60
Schultz, Otto 120
Second Battalion 183, 208, 210, 213, 219, 221
Second Division 8, 191, 196, 206, 216
Second Infantry Regiment 187, 190, 202, 204, 212, 219, 227
Second Patrol 202
Secret quarters 242
Seminary of Sandomierz 320
"Sep" *see* Stawiarz, Edward
Siatrak, Leon (Orzel) 85, 107, 110
Siedlecki, Father Stefan 305, 308
Siekierno 205, 206
Sielecki, Fryderyk ("Lokietek") 168, 169, 328
Sierant, Piotr 184, 189, 198, 206, 214, 323, 325, 329, 330
Sisters of the Immaculate Conception 246
Skarzysko 206
Skorupski, Ryszard 169
Skotnicki, Stanislaw ("Bogoria") 194
Skotnicki manor 302
Skrok, Father Ludwik 302
Skrzypaczowice manor 142, 143
Skwirzowa 244, 255
Skwirzowa manor 81, 82, 230, 240, 241
Slawinski family 250
Slawinski, Marian ("Mamloch") 164
Sliwinski, Edward 43
Slodkowski, Stanislaw 171
Slupia 196, 203
Smerda, Father Jerzy 297
Smerdyna 175, 178
Smigly-Rydz, Gen. Edward 8, 35, 324
Smolinski, Zbigniew ("Korsarz") 161
Smrokowski 7

Smykow 216
Snochowice 218, 233
Sobieraj, Jan 44
Soja, Tekla Korzon 5
Soja, Tomasz 5
Sokol (Kazimierz Jarsyna) 149
Soldier's Day 204
Solemn Mass 299, 300, 301
Sorbin 206
Sosniczany 42
Soviet guerrillas 178, 185
Soviet Union 52
Stalin, Joseph 184, 191, 235
Stalin's Committee 193
Stalin's Harmonicas 237
Stalowa Wola 14
Stanczak, Edward ("Zyrafa") 161
Stanowiska 218
Stara Zwola 8, 203
Starachowice 206
Staszewski, Jerzy ("Murzyn") 7, 85, 161
Staszow 13, 153, 173, 175, 181, 185, 188, 190, 241, 251
Staszow Forest 302
State Teachers' College 305
Stawiarz, Edward ("Sep") 85, 110, 118, 122, 140, 141
Stawiarz Karolina 14
Sten gun 181, 192
Stepien, Father Jan 35
Stobice 191
Stobiec Poreba 191, 193
Stobinski, Kazimierz ("Pioron") 58, 81, 87, 88, 109, 117, 161, 231, 233, 251, 253
Straceniec (Jan Osemlak) 91, 92, 93, 102, 108, 119
Strasbourg 177
Straznica 213, 244
Strus, Capt. ("Katus") 86, 178, 225
Struzki 58, 59, 181, 254
Strzegom 175
Strzegom Granicznik 175
Strzelecki, Helena 62
Strzelecki, Jan 62
Strzesniak 26
Stylski, Zygmunt 45
Sucharzow-Gagolin 188
Suchowola 28
Sulikow 219, 222
Sulislawice 6, 20, 36, 74, 171, 177, 240, 255
Suliszow manor 244
Swiercz, Arkadiusz ("Iskra") 81, 98, 107, 118, 119, 161, 326

Swierk 50
Swierzawski, Dr. Stefan 307
Switek, Father Tadeusz 297, 301
Swojak Battalion 189
Szczeglice manor 156, 158
Szczerba, Jerzy 220
Szczerbatko, Janusz ("Zygfryd") 85, 129, 132, 166, 167
Szczesniak, Wanda 48
Szczesniak brothers 42
Szczucin Bridge 106, 107, 117, 169
Szelag, Boleslaw (Blyskawica) 86, 164
Szelest, Jozef ("Romek Uszaty") 181
Szewce 218
"Szkot" see Kuras, Stanislaw
Szpakiewicz, Jan ("Pikolo") 86, 107, 110, 127, 150, 151, 161, 326
Sztucinska, Helena 62
Sztucinska, Maria 62
Szumsko 191
Szwarc, Stanislaw ("Roman") 213
Szymanski, Father Adam 277, 278, 293

Tanks, T-34 237
Targowski, Antoni 158
Targowski, Irena 158
Targowski, Roman 157
Targowski, Wanda 158
Targowski family 244
Tarnobrzeg 7, 171, 188, 254, 255, 256
Tarnowski Castle 269
Tarnowski High School 162, 176, 203
Tczianka 162, 176, 203
Teutonic Knights 281
Third Battalion 220
Third Regiment 203, 207, 218, 219
Thirteenth Army of Infantry (Russian) 188
Thuman, Robert 177, 178
Tokarev pistol (TTM, 1933) 192
"Topola" (Stanislaw Duma) 129, 132
Torlinski, Capt. Leon ("Kret") 143, 177
Tursko Male 174
Tworek, Eleonora 62

Ubennensch 166
Ujazdek 190
University of Cracow 225, 245

Vaterland 165
Viasov Army 179, 180
Vistula River 19, 121, 138, 166, 174, 175, 183, 188, 189, 190, 205
Von Paul 138, 147, 326
Von Tutze 61

"Walter" see Bojanowski, Jozef
Warsaw 310
Wasniow 195, 203
Wegleszyn 219 227, 228
Wehnnacht 165, 177, 181, 183, 184, 190, 218, 222
Wiacek, Father Jan 162
Wiacek, Jozef ("Sowa") 161, 162, 164, 168, 169, 171, 176, 178, 179, 180
Wiacek, Stanislaw ("Inspector") 42, 162, 170, 171
Wiazownica 78, 153, 178, 241
Wicher, Dr. Wladyslaw 307
Wichula, Lt. Ludwik ("Jelen") 209, 218
Wieczorek, Andrzeg ("Chebons") 184
Wiktorowski, Maj. Antoni ("Kruk") 189, 193, 198, 210, 220, 221, 227
Wiktorowski, Marian ("Maniek Polikier") 170, 194
Winiary 188
Winiarz, Eugeniusz ("Zawada") 161, 273
Winiarz, Kazimierz ("Wilk") 161 274
Winiarz family 273, 274
Wisniowa Parish 302
Witoslaw Mountain 195
Witoslawice 196
Wloszczowa 209
Wnorow 39, 42
Wnuk, Jozefa 62
Wojcik, Father Walenty 395
Wojteczko, Karol 41
Wola Szczygielkowa 196, 203
Wolar Krzystoporska manor 248
World War II 13
Woynarowski, Stefania 245
Wroclaw (Breslaw) 292
Wroclawski, Father Stanislaw 297, 299
Wrona 49
Wryk, Feliks ("Dab") 161
Wszachow 193
Wzdol Rzadowy 205

Zagiew ("Firebrand") 165
Zajaczkowski, Longin 44
Zajezierze Manor 87
Zakrzow 222
Zalesie 222
Zamosc 16
Zanker, Manfred 177, 328, 329
Zarczyce 227
Zarczyce Duce 224, 231, 235, 236, 237, 251, 256, 258
Zarczyce manor 235, 236
Zareba, Mrs. 150

Zarzycki, Barbara  84, 241
Zarzycki, Henryk ("Grab")  85, 161
Zarzycki, Kazimierz ("Czarny")  85, 161
Zarzycki, Stanislaw  84, 240, 241
Zarzycki, Zofia  84, 240
Zawichost  19
Zawidza  180
Zawiejski, Jerzy  308
Zawisza Group  220
Zbielutka  191, 202
Zbofowice  213
Zeiss scope  222
Zientarski, Col. Jan ("Mieczyslaw")  206 207

Zlotniki  223
"Zmija"  *see* Stanczak, Edward
Zolkiewski, Col. A. ("Lin")  143, 190, 193, 194, 195, 196, 204, 205, 209, 216
Zulinski, Tadeusz ("Goral")  85
Zurawica  152
Zwierzyk family  90, 250
Zwirek, Wladyslaw ("Mirecki")  39, 40, 41, 47, 178, 179
Zych family  248
"Zygfryd"  *see* Szczerbatko, Janusz
Zyznow manor  188

www.ingramcontent.com/pod-product-compliance
Ingram Content Group UK Ltd.
Pitfield, Milton Keynes, MK11 3LW, UK
UKHW041922140426
5217IPUK00014B/275